THE VITAL SPARK

BOOKS BY LOWELL THOMAS

With Lawrence in Arabia
India—Land of the Black Pagoda
Beyond Khyber Pass
The First World Flight
European Skyways
Count Luckner, Sea Devil
The Sea Devil's Fo'c'sle
Raiders of the Deep
Woodfill of the Regulars
The Hero of Vincennes
Lauterbach of the China Sea
The Wreck of the Dumaru
Old Gimlet Eye
Rolling Stone
Tall Stories
Fan Mail
The Untold Story of Exploration
This Side of Hell
The Boy's Life of Colonel Lawrence
Adventures in Afghanistan for Boys
Spain—the American Traveler's Handbook
Kabluk of the Eskimo
Pageant of Adventure

Pageant of Romance
Pageant of Life
Born to Raise Hell
Men of Danger
Kipling Stories and a Life of Kipling
Adventures Among Immortals
Seeing Canada with Lowell Thomas
Seeing India with Lowell Thomas
Seeing Japan with Lowell Thomas
Seeing Mexico with Lowell Thomas
Hungry Waters
Wings Over Asia
Magic Dials
Great True Adventures
In New Brunswick You'll Find It
Softball
How to Keep Mentally Fit
Stand Fast for Freedom
These Men Shall Never Die
Back to Mandalay
Seven Wonders of the World
History as You Heard It
The Vital Spark: 101 Outstanding Lives

The Vital Spark

101 OUTSTANDING LIVES

by Lowell Thomas

Portraits by Louis Lupas

DOUBLEDAY & COMPANY, INC.

Garden City, New York, 1959

Library of Congress Catalog Card Number 59–12649
Copyright © 1959 by Lowell Thomas

CONTENTS

6   CONTENTS

INTRODUCTION

This book is one result of long years of newscasting and travel. Maybe the connection doesn't seem very obvious. Isn't news the opposite of history? News—contemporary, fast-breaking, about things happening *now*. History—over and done with, embalmed in the textbooks, belonging to the *past*. As a newscaster I have to keep my audience up to the moment, and nothing is more deadly in my trade than to repeat yesterday's headlines. I can't discuss the Suez crisis or the flight of the Dalai Lama from Tibet as if they were still news beats. My job is to stay abreast of day-to-day developments around the world.

Travel, too, appears different from history. When I'm abroad—north or south, east or west—I'm always struck by the changes on the map that have taken place in my time, changes that make me think about how geography marches with politics. I see the surface of the earth as it *is*, not as it *was*. When I first visited Egypt as a reporter in World War I, en route to cover the desert saga of Lawrence of Arabia, the Land of the Nile was governed by the British. The last time I found an independent Egypt, ruled by Nasser. In Palestine I saw Israel, the Jewish state resurgent after two thousand years. Its very possibility would have been considered out of the question only a few years before. Even our own country shifts before our eyes. In Alaska an American territory has disappeared and been replaced by our forty-ninth state. You can easily recall many other examples, like the division of Germany and exploration down around the South Pole. It's the *latest* redrawing of the map that impresses the traveler—the kind of thing I've tried to capture for Cinerama and my television series, "High Adventure."

So where do the men and women of the past fit into this picture of newscasting and travel? They're squarely in the middle of it.

Let's take the news angle first. Suppose I'm covering the day's events—one of which happens to be the discovery of Nero's garden in Rome. That's important news. But it's also history. I can't explain the story to my audience without some discussion of the Roman Emperor who persecuted the Christians, watched Rome burn (did he really fiddle at the time?—that question could be part of today's news too), and left a reputation that makes him the byword for the criminal tyrant. We had references to Nero all the time when Stalin was alive.

My broadcasts over thirty years are full of examples such as this one. Gandhi reminded us of Buddha, Churchill of Chatham, Foch of Napoleon.

History is old news. The news is future history. And they can't be kept in watertight compartments. The newscaster has to go to the experience of humanity if he is to unravel current events and make them comprehensible.

What about the traveler? Well, the places and people you find today are what they are because of influences reaching back over the centuries. Every visit to the Far East reminds me more forcibly that spiritually this part of the world belongs to Gautama Buddha, the Indian prince who became the Light of Asia. His effect remains dominant no matter how they may redraw the borders of Korea or Thailand. No one can understand Red China unless events in Mao Tse-tung's domain are interpreted as largely a clash between Buddha and Marx. Similarly, who can describe France under de Gaulle without going to the France of Foch and Louis XIV and Joan of Arc?

So my two main interests forced me to think about great historic personalities of the world. As a newscaster and a traveler I kept running into them, learning more and more about them, trying to imagine what they were like when they belonged, not to history, but to the news.

Fortunately this isn't all a matter of imagination. We have had the experience of earth-shakers in action—scientists like Einstein and Planck, artists like Picasso and Matisse, political figures like Roosevelt and Churchill, fiends like Hitler and Stalin. I've done full-length biographies of some of them. *Lawrence of Arabia* followed the exploits of the British scholar who turned guerrilla leader and led the Arabs of the desert to victory over their Turkish masters. *The Sea Devil* told the story of Count Felix von Luckner, German sea captain and scourge of the sea lanes in World War I. From time to time I turned my hand to the short biography with Kipling and others.

This time, a volume of short biographies. I've tried to bring to life a hundred and one great personalities of past and present. They're not the only candidates I could have chosen. History is crowded. But these are men and women who have impressed or beguiled me for various reasons. They are all charged with The Vital Spark.

LOWELL THOMAS

LIST OF PORTRAITS

SOLOMON

[*d.* 933? B.C.]

SOLOMON succeeded his father, King David, the warrior, as King
of the Jews about the year 970 B.C. and although his long reign
proved peaceful, his advent to the throne was accompanied by not a
little bloodshed. Solomon was the second child of Bathsheba, the
Hittite woman, "very beautiful to look upon," whose husband, Uriah,
had been slain by order of David so that David might marry Bathsheba. David's eldest son had been killed by Absalom, the third son,
who in turn was killed as he fled after revolting against his father.
David's reception of the news of Absalom's death is the subject of
one of the most moving passages in the Old Testament, with its poignant refrain, "Oh, Absalom, my son, my son!"

As he lay dying, David's last days were darkened by domestic intrigues. His fourth son, Adonijah, gave a feast at which he claimed
the succession for himself. He had the support of Joab, commander
of the army, and of the high priest Abiathar, both of whom were
bitterly opposed to the son of a woman who had been the wife of a
Hittite warrior. The pro-Solomon party was headed by Nathan, the
prophet, Benaiah, the second captain, and Zadoc, a priest. At
Nathan's suggestion, Bathsheba went to David and reminded him
that he had once promised her that the first child she bore him after
their marriage should be King. Her influence over the aged King was
still great and he proclaimed Solomon as his heir and successor.

This action seems to have met with popular approval, for after a
brief struggle Adonijah's party collapsed and he himself sought sanctuary at the altar. By Solomon's order he was confined to his own
house, and shortly thereafter put to death. Abiathar was replaced as
high priest by Zadoc. Solomon now felt himself safe except for one
other possibility. Shimei, chief of the few remaining adherents of

Saul, who had been King before David, was still alive and believed
to have aspirations to the throne. So Solomon had him killed.

After this cruel beginning, Solomon entered upon a peaceful reign.
Unlike his father, David, who had spent so much of his life fighting
the Philistines, Solomon believed in making friends and trading with
people. Possibly as part of his peaceful policy, he married the daughter of the Egyptian Pharaoh, and received the Canaanite fortress of
Gezer, recently captured by the Egyptians.

Even more important than his alliance with the rulers of Egypt
was the partnership he entered into with Hiram, King of Tyre. This
enabled him to make use of the great seaport to the north of the
land of the Philistines, gave him free access to the Mediterranean,
and opened up trade with all the then known world. So lucrative did
these ventures prove that as a result of a single voyage Solomon received 420 talents, equal to millions in terms of modern currency.

These enormous profits enabled Solomon to indulge in his love of
building and of display. Not content with the palace of King David,
he spent thirteen years constructing a new royal residence of sur-
passing magnificence in Jerusalem. But the most famous of all Solomon's buildings was the Temple, the central shrine of the Hebrew
people, the place where they all might come to worship their God.
The Temple became the center of their national life.

So great was Solomon's wealth that silver was held of little account, and vessels of purest gold were used for his service. He also
erected a mansion for his Egyptian bride, who had brought a large
retinue of her own people to live with her at Solomon's court. "But,"
says the Bible, "Solomon loved many strange women of the Moabites,
Ammonites, Edomites, Zidonians, and Hittites . . . and he had seven
hundred wives, princesses, and three hundred concubines." So he
thought it right to build places of worship for them, and soon temples
to Astorath, Milcom, Chemosh, Moloch, and other heathen gods arose
around Jerusalem, and, in accompanying his wives to some of these
shrines, Solomon "did evil in the sight of the Lord."

Many stories have been told of the wisdom of Solomon. He instituted regular courts of justice. The old blood feuds of the desert and
the death sentences of tribal sheiks gave way to an ordered administration of law. That he himself decided some legal cases is shown by
the case of the two women who lived together and bore children at

about the same time. When one child died, both women claimed the surviving infant. Solomon said, "Bring me a sword and divide the living child in two, and give half to the one and half to the other." When the one woman begged that the child be not slain, the King ordered, "Give her the living child and in no wise slay it. She is the mother thereof."

We are told that the wisdom of Solomon spread throughout the lands of the Near East. It was thus that the Queen of Sheba heard of the great King of the Jews and traveled to Jerusalem "to prove him with hard questions." She ruled in the land of Ophir whence gold, silver, precious stones, ivory, sandalwood, apes, and peacocks had been brought to the Holy City of the Jews. It is possible that her interest in King Solomon was economic—his trade having been built up at the expense of hers. Solomon's caravans made their way as far as India, and the Queen of Sheba may have hoped by personal persuasion to get him to send more of them to her realm.

In any case, she "came to Jerusalem with a very great train, with camels that bare spices and with much gold and precious stones, and when she was come to Solomon she communed with him of all that was in her heart." Their relationship was more than merely political or economic, and when she returned to the land of Ophir, she bore Solomon a son who was named Menelik, a name used thereafter by the Emperors of Abyssinia who claimed descent from him. They also called themselves by the title of Lion of the Tribe of Judah—a title held today by the Emperor of Ethiopia (Abyssinia), Haile Selassie.

Toward the end of his reign Solomon's desire for peaceful relations with his neighbors caused him to lose part of his domain. The people were restless under the burden of heavy taxation. Solomon had divided the land into twelve districts and made exacting levies on each. As the people paid their taxes in produce or cattle, many of them were reduced to poverty and to slavery. Taking advantage of these conditions, an Edomite named Hadad, who had escaped Joab's slaughter and taken refuge in Egypt, returned to his own country and began to make trouble. As a result Edom became independent. Another part of Solomon's domain passed to Hiram of Tyre, without a war but possibly as the price Solomon had to pay for the use of Hiram's fleet.

Even in Jerusalem an abortive attempt was made to overthrow the

King who dwelt in such luxury and had concentrated so much wealth in this one city. Jeroboam, a man whom Solomon trusted and raised to power, fell in with the prophet Ahijah, who told him about a devine revelation in which the prophet had been informed that because of Solomon's acceptance of foreign deities most of his domain was fated to pass to Jeroboam. The latter now began to conspire against the King until his plot was discovered and he had to flee to Egypt.

The kingdom of the Jews—the only time when they flourished in antiquity as a separate nation and without being subject to anyone —lasted from the advent of Saul, the first King of the Jews, through the reigns of David and Solomon, a period of eighty-six years in all. Upon the death of Solomon, Jeroboam returned from Egypt and led a successful revolt against Rehoboam, Solomon's son—Rehoboam, memorable for his saying, "My father made your yoke heavy, but I will add to it. He chastised you with whips, but I will chastise you with scorpions." This threat to the people of his realm only helped Jeroboam.

The kingdom of Solomon was broken by the rebellion. Rehoboam, leading one tribe only, clung to power in the southern segment of Judah, while Jeroboam took ten tribes and set up the northern kingdom of Israel. A unified Jewish nation was never re-established. In time both parts fell under the yoke of Assyria.

For centuries Solomon was the reputed author of the Book of Proverbs, the Odes of Solomon, the Psalms of Solomon, the Book of Ecclesiastes, and the Song of Solomon. Modern critical research has proved that most of these are of much later date. The Book of Proverbs contains folklore wisdom of a kind that goes back to the dawn of human history, although some of the proverbs could have been set down by Solomon himself—for example, "A soft answer turneth away wrath; but grievous words stir up anger." The Old Testament, however, as we have it, is mainly the work of Jews who lived during and after the Babylonian Captivity. They cast the old traditional lore into literary form, and ascribed its origins to famous figures of the past. The wisdom of Solomon made him a prime candidate for author of lines that he could not possibly have written.

Nor did Solomon write the Book of Ecclesiastes. It shows much Greek influence, and many experts doubt that it could have been put together earlier than the third century B.C. As for the Song of Solomon, that most superb of love poems, its passion sounds Solomonic enough, and it could well describe his feelings during a love affair of his youth, but for various technical reasons we cannot say that Solomon was the author of the Song of Solomon.

These negations do not harm his place in history. Only a great king could have ruled and built as he did. Only a great man could have had so many literary masterpieces ascribed to him. There is no mystery about the influence of Solomon on subsequent generations, an influence felt by the Jewish nation that has been reborn in our time —the state of Israel.

CYRUS THE GREAT

[600?–529 B.C.]

C YRUS THE GREAT, conqueror of the Near East and founder of the Persian Empire, has always been a familiar figure in the West for one special reason. The Old Testament tells how Cyrus took Babylon, released the Jews from their captivity, allowed them to return to Jerusalem, and even paid for the rebuilding of the Temple, opening the royal exchequer for that purpose. Modern historians have another reason for remembering this great King, for he made the Persians the mightiest imperial people before the rise of the Romans.

When Cyrus was born, the Medes and the Persians constituted the most powerful non-Semitic populations of western Asia. The Medes occupied a wide stretch of country below the Caspian Sea. To their south, the Persians held the rugged mountainous terrain toward the Persian Gulf. The laws of the Medes and Persians were common to both nations. They had the same religion, Zoroastrianism, one of the most influential cults of the ancient world. Zoroaster was a prophet who appeared during the lifetime of Cyrus and attacked the old superstitions and idolatries, and taught that the essential religious truth is that the world is an arena where Good (Ahuramazda) struggles against Evil (Ahriman), with every human being forced to take sides with one or the other. This lofty creed spread far beyond the borders of Persia. Its Sun God, Mithra, was worshiped as far west as England, having been carried there by the soldiers of the Roman Empire. In 1954 the world was astonished to learn of the discovery of an underground Mithraic shrine not far from St. Paul's Cathedral in London. And Zoroastrianism is by no means dead: it still has many followers today, 50,000 in Bombay alone—the Parsees.

With good laws and a noble religion to inspire them, the Persians were ready to assume a higher place among the surrounding peoples.

Cyrus appeared just in time to lead them. His birth and youth are shrouded in mystery, and marvelous tales are told of him by Herodotus. Sober history recounts how he inherited the Persian throne, conquered Media in his first campaign, and became King of the Medes and Persians. He founded the Persian Empire in 550 B.C.

Croesus, King of Lydia, whose domain extended all over the west and north coast of Asia Minor, had accumulated vast treasure through his Mediterranean trade and his mines. He was reputed to be the richest man in the world. He felt that Cyrus, young and ambitious, a man of vision and courage, was likely to be tempted by his vast wealth. So he consulted the Delphic oracle and was assured that a mighty kingdom would be overthrown if he, Croesus, marched against the Persians. But the oracle failed to say which mighty kingdom.

Croesus decided to strike first. He invaded Cappadocia, ravaged the Syrian hinterland, and drew Cyrus into a decisive battle on the plain before Sardis, the Lydian capital. The young Persian ruler overwhelmed the Medes, captured their King, stormed into their capital. The fantastic wealth of Croesus fell into his hands. Cyrus ordered Croesus to be burned alive, but as the King was bound on his funeral pyre, a heavy rainstorm prevented its being set afire. Taking this as a sign from the gods, Cyrus ordered his chains to be removed and paid him the respect due to "a favorite of heaven." Ultimately Croesus became one of Cyrus' most trusted counselors.

For the next few years Cyrus was engaged in war with the tribes to his east. He led his armies as far as Afghanistan. But his real enemy lay to the west. It was inevitable that he should ultimately turn toward Babylonia.

The Babylonians had long been convinced that Cyrus would attack their empire and besiege their city. They provisioned Babylon for a siege, and behind their great walls and fortifications waited patiently. When the Persians appeared before Babylon, a fierce battle took place a short distance from the city. As usual Cyrus was victorious. The Babylonian forces withdrew within their walls and made light of the siege because they believed the city could not be taken by assault.

As time went on Cyrus stood frustrated before the city gates. Then he worked out a stratagem based on the fact that the Euphrates River divided Babylon in half, and that the immense walls extended down to the river. Cyrus set his army to digging new channels, turning aside the waters of the Euphrates until they receded to a point where it could be forded. Then the Persians burst into the outlying portions of the city, which fell quickly due to the demoralization of the defenders.

In order to create a friendly buffer between his Empire and Egypt, Cyrus released the Hebrews from the Babylonian captivity, facilitated their return to Jerusalem, and paid for the rebuilding of the Temple of Solomon. We read in Ezra, "Thus saith Cyrus, King of Persia, the Lord God of Heaven hath given me all the kingdoms of the earth; and he hath charged me to build him an house at Jerusalem, which is in Judah. . . . Also Cyrus the King brought forth the vessels of the house of the Lord, which Nebuchadnezzar had brought forth out of Jerusalem, and had put them in the house of his gods; even these did Cyrus, King of Persia, bring forth by the hand of Mithredath the treasurer, and numbered them unto Sheshbazzar, the prince of Judah."

Ever since, Cyrus the Great has had an honorable place in Jewish history. Doubtless his behavior toward the Jews was due to his religion, for he believed as a faithful Zoroastrian that he should live a life of holiness and charity, following Ahuramazda rather than Ahriman.

The rest of Cyrus' reign is obscure in spite of Herodotus and Thucydides. Both authorities agree that he had great ability as a monarch and military leader. It is certain also that he preserved his physical strength and fighting prowess even in his old age; he must have been at least seventy when he fell in battle. The Queen of the Massagetae, Tomyris, foreseeing Cyrus' intention of extending his Empire to the north, as he had done in the west, the east, and the south, sent a mission to ask that he refrain from attacking her people. When her emissaries returned with word that the Persian King would not agree to leave them alone, she collected her forces for war.

The greater part of the Persian military establishment was scattered all over the Empire, occupying conquered countries. The force that Cyrus led was no larger than that commanded by Tomyris. In the course of the fighting Cyrus was killed and his death so disheartened his soldiers that they retreated, carefully carrying his body with them.

The tomb of Cyrus is still in existence. It was discovered by Sir Henry Rawlinson about a hundred years ago at Pasargadae. Composed of immense blocks of white marble, the tomb itself clearly answers the description given by Arrian, the Greek historian and philosopher, who visited the spot when he was appointed Governor of Cappadocia by Marcus Aurelius in 135 A.D. Hence it is beyond doubt that this is the tomb which contained the body of Cyrus the Great when it was visited by that other titan of conquest, Alexander the Great.

BUDDHA

[563?–?483 B.C.]

GAUTAMA BUDDHA was one of the world's greatest religious teachers—and one of its most paradoxical figures. By Indian custom and family tradition he should never have entered religion, for he was born into the caste of warriors. Theology he should have left to the Brahmins. He was marked out to follow the trade of arms, a king leading his soldiers in the never-ending wars of Hindustan. Instead he turned to preaching a doctrine of mystical peace and renunciation. His family hoped that one day he might become a martial hero of India. Instead he became the "Light of Asia."

The later development of Buddhism has so encrusted the life of its founder with legendary tales and outright mythology that it is often impossible to separate fact from fiction. It is historically certain that he was the son of King Suddhodana who ruled at Kapilavastu in the foothills of the Himalayas, and that he received the name Siddhartha Gautama, the latter name being that of the clan to which his family belonged.

We can easily believe the stories of his precocious childhood—how dawning sanctity made him wise and compassionate beyond his years, so much so that his father feared for his military vocation. King Suddhodana determined that young Siddhartha should experience nothing but the luxury of palace life. His most impressionable years were to remain unclouded by the knowledge that for most of humanity life was an unending round of toil and suffering. According to legend, the sentries at the gates to the royal establishment had standing orders to prevent the young prince from passing so that he might not mingle with the seething masses of people who swarmed outside. Thus Siddhartha grew to maturity in princely seclusion, surrounded by servants and royal companions, hunting and racing and following the other pursuits proper to the scion of a royal dynasty.

Finally, to ensure Siddhartha's worldly vocation, King Suddhodana decided that the prince should marry, and for this purpose the most eligible maidens gathered at the palace that he might choose from them. His choice fell upon Yasodhara, most beautiful of all, but she had other royal suitors, and custom demanded that her hand should go to the winner of trials set for that purpose. In the ensuing competition Siddhartha conquered his rivals in horsemanship, swordsmanship, and archery. So he won Yasodhara for his wife, and when a son was born to them it seemed that Siddhartha was ready to accept his royal heritage when King Suddhodana should die.

Nevertheless, the prince was troubled. Buddhist lore tells how he heard celestial voices calling to him to leave his indolent existence and to take up the burden of saving mankind from the scourge of pain and evil. His critical experience came about when he determined to see for himself what lay beyond the palace gates. So he set forth, and wandered through the teeming squalid village of Kapilavastu.

The wretchedness he saw appalled him. Three particular cases of the evils of life remained engraved on his memory—an old man enfeebled and helpless, another tortured with disease, and a corpse. Meditating on the triple phenomena of age, sickness, and death, Siddhartha came to the conclusion that life is essentially evil, and that one who could find a means of conquering evil would be the greatest benefactor of humanity. Sir Edwin Arnold, in his great narrative poem, *The Light of Asia,* makes the young prince express his discovery in these words:

> I see, I feel
> The vastness of the agony of earth,
> The vainness of its joys, the mockery
> Of all its best, the anguish of its worst;
> Since pleasures end in pain, and youth in age,
> And love in loss, and life in hateful death,
> And death in unknown lives, which will but yoke
> Men to their wheel again to whirl the round
> Of false delights and woes that are not false.

Returned to his palace, Siddhartha was unable to forget what he had seen. The royal life of pleasure became as dust and ashes, and

the conviction grew upon him that he was called to embrace a spiritual vocation and to search for a way to the alleviation of suffering,
a way which others might follow. Then came the crisis in his soul and
his momentous decision.

He left the palace secretly by night, not wishing to inflict the pain
of parting on his wife or his parents, and rode away from Kapilavastu.
Tradition records that the heavy gates, which normally required
many men to open, rolled back silently of their own accord, permitting the prince and one servant to ride through. Safely away,
he dismounted. He sent the servant with his horse and his princely
garments back to the palace. Then, after cutting off his long hair,
which was a sign of noble birth, he set out into the forest on foot to
become a monk and to search for an answer to the mystery of life.
This act of Siddhartha Gautama is remembered in the history of
Buddhism as the "Great Renunciation." It was one of the most influential events in the history of the world.

Siddhartha's path first took him to a colony of monks who dwelled
near the neighboring kingdom of Rajagriha. These men practiced a
harsh religious code which later was to astonish the first Europeans who visited India—a code involving such atrocities as self-
mutilation and gazing at the sun until blinded by it. Such fanaticism
was supposed to elevate the soul by degrading the body, so that those
who practiced the worst self-torture were regarded as the holiest of
the monks. Siddhartha thought that the excesses might be merely
aberrations from true mortification, and so he determined to begin
his religious vocation with a discipline of rigorous self-denial. He
fasted until the strength left his body, hoping that his soul might be
purified, and that the truth he was seeking might dawn upon him.
But it was in vain, for his ability to concentrate relaxed as his body
weakened. Finally he became convinced that he had taken a false
path, and decided to abandon it. His fellow monks were scandalized
by his backsliding, but he knew that their way was not the way he
was seeking, so he moved on in his search.

Siddhartha's pilgrimage came to an end in the solitude of the forest,
under a Bo tree, a species of wild fig, in the shade of which he had
seated himself to meditate. He sat there all night, a night of trial and
temptation when Sin and the Powers of Darkness strove to shake his
vocation. Popular belief holds that these were actually existing fig-

ures, that Envy and Anger and Lust appeared in person to tempt the Holy One. A more philosophic explanation is that they were the passions of his own heart. His victory was complete, these enemies disappeared, and Siddhartha came to understand the answer to the riddle of existence. His mind pursued its way unerringly until, with the breaking of dawn, it achieved its final goal—he knew the truth that would save mankind. Thus he had gained a new title, infinitely more glorious than the princely one he had renounced: he would henceforth be remembered among men as the Buddha, or the "Enlightened One."

The knowledge revealed by Buddha after his Enlightenment is formulated in what Buddhists call the Four Noble Truths:

1. Life necessarily involves pain.
2. The cause of pain is the craving for individual existence.
3. There is a cure for pain.
4. This cure lies in the Eightfold Path of right views, right intention, right speech, right action, right livelihood, right effort, right mindfulness, right concentration.

On the basis of these propositions, it follows that the evils of life can be conquered only by the annihilation of individual personality, by eradicating the passions and desires and even thoughts, until the selfless state of Nirvana has been reached. Nirvana is sometimes interpreted to mean "nothingness," but Sir Edwin Arnold expressed a "firm conviction that a third of mankind would never have been brought to believe in blank abstractions, or in Nothingness, as the issue and crown of Being." It probably means the state of absolute quiet when the Four Noble Truths have been grasped and all desire obliterated. Buddha himself attained Nirvana during his lifetime.

Buddha obviously derived some elements of his religion from Hinduism. Both taught the doctrine of transmigration of souls, holding that we live a succession of lives in which each rebirth depends on the character of the one preceding it. The good are reborn on a higher level, while the wicked descend in the scale and may reappear as animals. When the Buddhist saints achieve Nirvana they are not reborn, but have escaped from the evil of existence altogether.

Buddhism is peculiar among religions in that it does not teach the existence of God or the immortality of the soul. For the Buddhist, the only world is this world, and the only hope is to escape its evils by achieving Nirvana. The greatest evil is to be caught in the cycle of birth and rebirth without being able to escape.

According to Buddhist principles, virtue is certain to be rewarded and wrongdoing punished, for every act of man implies consequences in the rebirth to come. Wickedness rivets the individual to the wheel of life with all its attendant evil, but goodness and charity lead to a better existence in life, and finally to Nirvana which is the escape from life. Although the full practice of Buddhist holiness involves monastic celibacy and poverty, nevertheless those not fitted for this type of life are permitted to marry and to possess property. No less than Christianity, Buddhism is a religion of charity and the brotherhood of man.

Buddha lived for more than fifty years after his Enlightenment, and he spent this period wandering about India, preaching his new doctrine and gathering disciples. Among his early converts were the members of his own family. One of the most moving stories of the Buddhist legend describes his visit to Kapilavastu—Siddhartha Gautama, scion of the royal dynasty, returning as the Buddha, the most venerated religious teacher in India. He came back as a monk, clad in the yellow garment of his vocation, and begging alms as he went. King Suddhodana was stricken with shame at the sight, for he knew of his son's reputation as the greatest of sages, and expected that he would appear as the leader of a host of followers and admirers. But Buddha had passed beyond the desire for this kind of individual pre-eminence, and the wisdom of his teaching soon convinced both his father and the rest of his family that he had indeed discovered the truth for which men had so long been waiting.

Buddha continued to preach until the very end, revealing to men the evil of life and the means of conquering it. He died about 483 B.C. when past his eightieth year, still in the midst of his disciples, leaving behind him one of the greatest religious movements known to history.

Buddhism, still a powerful moral force after twenty-five centuries, became the dominant creed of the Far East. It spread to Nepal, Tibet, Japan, Burma, Siam, Ceylon, and even into China, although here its progress has been restricted by indigenous Chinese doctrines like Confucianism. In many places the purity of Buddha's teaching was contaminated by local practices, as in the case of Tibet. When I

visited Lhasa in 1948, officials of the Dalai Lama explained to me
how Buddhism came to the Roof of the World as a conquering creed,
only to mingle with demon worship in the inaccessible parts of the
vast plateau. Since my visit another creed has come to Tibet—communism. Will the gospel of St. Marx finally mingle with demon
worship, and with Buddhism?

Almost as remarkable as the victory of Buddhism elsewhere was its
failure in the land of its birth. It was adopted as the state religion
by King Asoka, who ruled in India during the third century B.C.—
an act which resembles that of the Emperor Constantine in making
Christianity the official religion of the Roman Empire. After a career
of conquest, Asoka decided to abandon the horrors of war for a religion of charity. Accepting Buddhism personally, he imposed it upon
the realm he ruled. He also sent missionaries abroad. They introduced
Buddhism into Ceylon, which is said still to practice the religion in
its purest form.

In spite of Asoka's efforts, Buddhism gradually disappeared from
India, until today comparatively few of its five hundred million adherents are to be found in its birthplace. The reason for this may be
that the practice of Buddhism in India came more and more to re-
semble the Hinduism to which it was related in origin, and that by
degrees it came to merge with the older religion. It is curious to note
that Buddhist tradition relates how the Master himself predicted that
his teaching would fail to last in India because he had been prevailed upon to permit women to enter into the Buddhist community
as disciples. Elsewhere the presence of women has not prevented the
religion from flourishing, and there are Buddhist nuns as well as
monks.

The teacher to whom so much of mankind owes its moral and religious tradition was the greatest Indian, and one of the greatest men,
in history. Excepting Christ, no individual human being has stamped
his personality so indelibly on the conscience of the world.

PERICLES

[490?–429 B.C.]

THE GLORY that was Greece culminated in the age of Pericles. He was born about three years before the battle of Marathon. He was a youth when the victory of Salamis freed Greece decisively from the threat of the oriental despotism of Persia. He grew up while Athens was in the process of founding a great empire of her own. He presided over the greatest days of that empire, led it into the Peloponnesian War that shattered it, and died before he had to face the consequences of his statecraft. While the brilliant Pericles ruled, Athens herself was brilliant. With him gone, her road was downhill to defeat and capitulation.

Pericles' background was aristocratic—his father an admiral who commanded an Athenian fleet against the Persians and took part in the victory at Mycale, his mother a member of the historic and powerful Alcmaeonidae clan. Pericles was born with only one defect, a long head that made him the object of ridicule. To cover this deformity he had the habit of wearing a helmet in public.

His education was all that Athens could offer during the time when Hellenic culture was rising to its greatest heights. He studied literature and music under the foremost masters, and was thoroughly schooled in philosophy, prime occupation of the Athenian intellect.

He entered politics early, associating himself with the popular party, the democratic faction. The Athenian aristocracy, to which Pericles himself belonged, derived from an old land-owning class of Attica, the agricultural region about Athens. The city itself, following the victory over Persia, was booming with the prosperity of maritime trade. The business and worker population of the commercial mart stood posed against the ancient authority of the nobles.

The democratic trend in Athens was to take power away from the older aristocratic bodies and transfer it to the popular assembly, the gathering of all citizens meeting in the Agora, the traditional market place. Pericles caught the ear of the popular assembly, for he excelled in oratory. He advocated and carried through a series of measures to increase the predominance of the democratic masses. He increased the money paid to people of the assembly sitting as a jury. He seems to have established payment for military service, considered hitherto as service to the state. He instigated public works to give jobs to the unemployed. By the time he was thirty, he had become undisputed head of the democratic faction and in control of Athens.

The end of the Persian Wars left Greece with two dominant powers, Athens and Sparta. Athens was a naval power, Sparta a land power. Athens represented democracy, Sparta a military caste. In their dealings with the other Greek city-states and with factional struggles in the city-states, Athens tended to support democracy, while Sparta backed aristocratic parties. Pericles believed that war between the rivals was inevitable, and set about preparing Athens for the conflict.

He built the Long Walls, which at the same time fostered his democratic policy of providing work for the unemployed. The military purpose was to fortify the small peninsula on which Athens stood against attack on the land side. The Long Walls, extending for eight miles, connected the city with its two harbors, Phalerum and Piraeus. Sparta looked upon this fortification of Athens as a hostile act, and war broke out.

The policy of Pericles was now to shun conflict with Sparta on land, and consolidate Athenian supremacy at sea. The Persian Wars had left Athens at the head of an association of Greek island cities, the Delian League. Pericles reduced the allies to the condition of subjects and transformed the confederation into an Athenian sea empire. There were revolts, like that of Samos, which were suppressed, sometimes with great harshness. Eventually the Athenian Empire gained for the Athenian democracy the reputation of a tyrant.

During this period the wealth poured in, and Pericles dedicated the public funds to the highest purposes of civilization: literature, philosophy, and the arts. This was the great day of the Greek drama, Aeschylus, Sophocles, Euripides, Aristophanes. Pericles' life-long friend, the philosopher Anaxagoras, was a guiding spirit, and it was the Athens of Socrates and his brilliant disciple Plato. Pericles labored to make Athens the most beautiful of cities, and used all the genius of Greek artists, all the labor of the otherwise unemployed, in a program for the architectural adornment of the city. The crowning gem was the Parthenon on the Acropolis, with its glorious statue of Athena, the masterpiece of Phidias, greatest of Greek sculptors.

The woman in Pericles' life was Aspasia. He had long been married, but gave up his wife for the woman who represented in such high degree what the Greeks meant by "hetaera." The word signified companion, entertainer, courtesan. Aspasia was beautiful, talented, and trained in rhetoric and philosophy. Allied with Pericles she set the tone of taste and fashion. She joined him in the patronage of art and learning. She advised him about affairs of state. Relying on Aspasia, Pericles consulted Athenian men of affairs less, and people began to complain of his aloofness.

His enemies were quick to take advantage of this and launched a whispering campaign. Pericles was accused of squandering the public funds, of abusing the freedom of speech by permitting licenses to irreligious dramatists like Euripides. Even his friends came under fire. Phidias was accused by the aristocratic party of impiety for having adorned the shield of Athena in the Parthenon with likenesses of Pericles and of himself. The great sculptor died in prison. The philosopher Anaxagoras suffered banishment on charges of irreligion. Most of all, savage denunciations were hurled at Aspasia.

Amidst these dangers to his career, Pericles incurred the one great and serious charge that is made against him to this day. He was and is accused of having brought on war with Sparta for his own political ends. Plutarch says, "He felt his popularity waning so fast that a war was needed to make himself indispensable." In any case, Pericles was foremost in urging Athens to plunge into the Peloponnesian War.

The strategy of Pericles was to hold the Spartans at bay before the Long Walls which he had constructed, while the Athenian fleet reigned supreme on the sea. This worked well enough, but the Spartans ravaged the farm lands of Attica, to the wrath of Athenian landowners.

At the end of the first year of the war Pericles rallied the Athenians with a noble oration in homage of the war dead. It was a call to greatness, with Pericles describing his city as "the school of Hellas," a phrase that was to become classical forever afterward. But the statesman and orator had not much longer to live. A frightful plague broke out, spread like wildfire through the refugees crowded inside Athens, and struck down thousands. Among the first victims was Pericles himself.

He died still hoping for an Athenian victory. But it never came. The Peloponnesian War, with an intervening seven-year truce, dragged on for twenty-five years more, and ended with the utter defeat of Athens. The maritime empire which Pericles had done so much to build was inevitably ruined, but the splendor of civilization that he fostered remains immortalized as the Age of Pericles.

SOCRATES

[470?–399 B.C.]

Socrates stands as one of the greatest figures in the history of philosophy. Yet he wrote nothing. Not a book, not a fragment, not a line, can be ascribed to him. All that we know about this giant of human thought derives from what was written about him. There are two sources chiefly, Plato and Xenophon, and each for one reason or another is unsatisfactory in presenting the life and mind of Socrates.

Xenophon, the famous soldier of the Retreat of the Ten Thousand, who produced an eminent work of literature in the *Anabasis*, was a friend of Socrates, but was too much of a practical man to be at home in the world of ideas and to perceive the intellectual purport of the philosophy he heard.

On the contrary, Plato, himself one of the greatest of philosophers, developed the Socratic ideas to heights of the sublime. Plato's philosophy is presented in the famous *Dialogues*, in which Socrates is the central figure and protagonist. One legend has the elder sage remarking about the strange things this young man put into his mouth. Plato presents his own towering system of philosophy through the medium of Socrates speaking in the *Dialogues*, and the problem is—what is Plato and what is Socrates? Some scholars have thought it is all Plato. But the better supposition would seem to be that the fundamentals derived from the older philosopher who, writing nothing, held forth in speech to disciples and sundry listeners.

Socrates' father seems to have been a man of standing, it being said that he was a friend of the family of Aristides, the renowned statesman called "the Just." Socrates passed his youth during the glorious period of Athens following the Persian Wars. He was born ten years after the decisive victory of Salamis, which set Athens on the road to wealth, power, and the cultural splendor which was to make the name of the city a byword for civilization. He served as a soldier in the occasional wars waged by the rising Athens, and in one battle is said to have saved the life of Alcibiades, the gifted youth whose career of brilliance and instability provides a curious page in Athenian history.

What was it that turned Socrates to his career as a philosopher of the market place and one of the dominant figures in the annals of the human intellect? Plato's dialogue called the *Apology* tells how the Delphic oracle announced that no man living was wiser than Socrates, a judgment that Socrates interpreted to mean that no one else so clearly realized the extent of his own ignorance. But he realized too the need of searching for the truth, and he was something of a mystic about it, being apt to fall into almost trancelike states of thought, even to hearing voices, and he had something of a sense of divine mission. He felt it his duty to enlighten himself if he could, and then to impart his message to his fellow-Athenians.

Thus he came forward, the figure so familiar in the pages of philosophy, Socrates in the market place or in the gymnasium, talking with people, discussing matters of wisdom, asking questions, analyzing replies; not propounding, but developing ideas in a keen type of conversation, the dialectic of question and answer, the Socratic method.

For long years he pursued this way of life, and became one of the most notable figures in Athens, numbering among his listeners and disciples some of the most eminent personalities who lived during the brilliant times of Pericles.

He was short of stature, broad and muscular, and ugly, with a flat face, snub nose, wide mouth, and bushy beard. Even his friends and disciples admitted he looked like Silenus the satyr. He is said to have worn the same coat the year round, with neither shirt nor shoes, summer or winter. Comic writers who ridiculed him presented him as a pauperish figure. He was, in fact, dedicated to poverty as part of his mission of enlightenment, but he was not ascetic and disdained the exaggerated self-imposed rigors affected by some philosophers. In middle life he married, and the name of his wife, Xanthippe has come down to us as a byword for a scold and a shrew. Perhaps she was not quite as much of a termagant as tradition has made of her, for in Plato's *Dialogues* she appears as a sympathetic figure.

Socrates, grotesque figure that he was, belonged to the brilliant circle of Pericles, which was distinguished by the intelligent and cultivated hetaera Aspasia, and the advanced philosopher Anaxagoras. None of them entertained any belief in the old gods of Hellenic polytheism. Yet Socrates was deeply and even mystically religious, holding a belief in an infinite power and the immortality of the soul. In this he may have been influenced by the mystery cults. It was typical of Athens of the great period that, in addition to the official religion of the gods of Olympus and their elaborate mythology, there were cults and brotherhoods that taught a higher doctrine and sought the spiritual goals of immortality and salvation.

But Socrates' great labor lay in the realm of philosophy. His ideas were conditioned by the state of affairs in Greece at that time. Hellenic philosophy had begun with an attempt to apply human reason to the universe, and explained the cosmos by processes of rational thought. This, beginning with Thales of Miletus, who thought that the primordial stuff of the universe was water, had produced brilliant results. The philosophy of Pythagoras held that the essence of things consisted of mathematical relations. The atomic theory of Democritus curiously anticipated the atomic theory of modern chemistry. But that older cosmic philosophy of the Greeks had fallen on evil days; there was a deadlock of rival doctrines and a sterile elaboration of hair-splitting paradoxes.

There had been a reaction. A new school had arisen, the Sophists. They held that all the speculation about the universe was profitless and that reason should be applied to the study of the human being himself. In large part they dedicated their thinking to practical matters, which in ancient Greece meant ways of winning arguments in political debate and in lawsuits. They twisted reasoning to cunning ends, and earned a bad reputation which persists to this day—sophistry meaning false, quibbling logic for an ulterior purpose.

But the Sophists, by applying reason to human problems, turned philosophy inward. In this sense, Socrates follows the Sophists, as may be seen in his often repeated maximum, "Know thyself." He was accused of practicing the disreputable tricks of the Sophists. This is seen in the portrait painted by his greatest antagonist, the comic writer Aristophanes. In *The Clouds,* Aristophanes has a youth sent to school with Socrates to learn how to make the better appear the worse and find a way to cheat creditors. Actually Socrates followed the Sophists only in their concentration on human rather than scientific problems.

Above all Socrates was concerned with the investigation of ideas, the contents of the mind. In this lay his mighty contribution as philosopher of the market place. His method was to ask questions. He liked to appear to be stupid, simple, the better to draw people out and to confound them. The idea behind his questions, as presented so copiously in the *Dialogues* of Plato, was to seek definitions. What do you mean by virtue? Knowledge? The soul? The state? One of the best ways of confusing an antagonist in argument is to make him define the words he uses, and Socrates is represented as winning many a verbal battle in that way. His purpose in demanding clear definitions was to avoid the inexactitude of expression that comes from the ambiguous use of words.

The emphasis on the definition of terms, the insistence on clear precise meanings, was Socrates' greatest contribution to the development of Greek philosophy. That was the glory of the Socratic method, with its questions—what do you mean by this or that? It was the impulse that led to the logical clarity of Plato and the science of logic constructed by Aristotle. In logic, as we have it today, the very first principle is the unambiguous definition of terms. That is the first principle in Aristotle's logic, and we learn from Aristotle that Socrates instituted the art of logical definition.

In politics he was the very ideal of civic patriotism of the Greek city-states, one of his self-prescribed tasks being to expound the dignities and responsibilities of citizenship. As a member of the circle of Pericles, he must have been identified more or less with the political following of that great leader of Athenian democracy. Aristophanes, who lampooned him so mercilessly, was a stalwart of the aristocrats. But Socrates was only too well aware of the faults of the Athenian democracy, the vagaries of the ruling assembly of all the citizens under the influence of ranting demagogues.

He saw much of this during the later years of his life, when Athens was engaged in her mortal struggle with Sparta. Hence it is not surprising to find his great pupil, Plato, theorizing about an ideal republic characterized by an aristocratic class system of an extreme and inflexible sort—government by philosophers. In any case, it was the democratic government of Athens, with a prosecution headed by a popular leader, that decreed the doom of Socrates.

After a final and utter defeat in the Peloponnesian War, Athenian democracy, which had backed the war, was overthrown. Under the dominance of Sparta, an aristocratic government was installed in Athens—the Thirty Tyrants—and there followed a reign of terror against the democrats. Socrates, doing his patriotic duty despite his preference for philosophical speculation, allowed himself to be named one of the Council of Five Hundred, in which capacity he displayed courage by resisting an order to arrest intended victims of the terror. For this he himself might have perished had it not been for the fact that the Thirty Tyrants were overthrown and the democracy took power again.

But the democrats did what the oligarchs had not had time to do—put Socrates to death; it is one of history's great tragedies. He was charged with impiety and the corruption of youth—on grounds of religion, inveighing against the gods, agitating disbelief in the official Pantheon of Olympian divinities, weaning youth away from the creed of their ancestors. There has always been something of a puzzle in this. Religious bigotry was not commonly an Athenian fault, nor were the gods defended with murderous fanaticism. The aristocratic Aristophanes, Socrates' own most notable enemy and the greatest master of Athenian comedy, parodied the Olympian divinities in hilarious style and with what must have seemed to be outrageous blasphemy to any zealous believer in the old polytheism. Yet Socrates was doomed to death on a decidedly nebulous charge of impiety.

The modern scholar can make certain inferences. Socrates had been the close friend and teacher of Alcibiades, who had turned traitor in the war, after being charged with blasphemous outrage against the sacred symbols of the city. Another close friend of Socrates' was Critias. He too has been pictured as a pupil of Socrates, and he was one of the Thirty Tyrants, an extremist in perpetrating the reign of terror against the fallen democrats.

These close associations with hated figures might well have made Socrates extremely unpopular with the newly revived democracy and identified him with the antidemocratic forces. The political angle, however, could not have been conveniently brought up at his trial, because an amnesty had been granted that would have covered Socrates' case. He could not be charged with offenses against the democracy, and so resort was had to the imputation of impiety and the corruption of youth.

There seems to have been no real intention to press the matter to a bitter conclusion. The moving spirit was Anytus, an honest democratic politician, who apparently only wanted to silence the philosopher. The attitude of Socrates, pictured in Plato's *Apology*, was one of scorn and defiance. He ridiculed the accusation, and throughout the trial was unbending. Condemned to death, he might have compromised by accepting a lesser penalty, but he was inflexible, and contended that, instead of being punished for his teachings, he should receive a public award. The only concession he would make was to offer to pay a fine so small as to be ridiculous. His friends offered to increase the amount and pay it, but Socrates' lofty and unbending attitude resulted in a reaffirmation of the sentence. He said he was satisfied and willing to die. A plan to have him escape was arranged, but Socrates refused, saying his duty as a citizen required him to accept the sentence.

The sentence was delayed for thirty days, while a sacred ship was sailing to the island of Delos. During this period of religious grace no death sentence could be executed. Socrates remained in prison, receiving his friends and discoursing with them in the customary Socratic manner of question and answer. He was the same even on the final day, when he drank the hemlock, the deadly potion that was the prescribed means of inflicting the capital sentence. Until the last moment he continued in conversation with his friends, discussing lofty matters of life, death, and the soul. The scene is pictured in the *Phaedo*, a dialogue in which Plato wrote some of the most beautiful pages in all literature.

ALEXANDER THE GREAT

[356–323 B.C.]

ALEXANDER THE GREAT was regent of Macedonia at the age of six-teen, a victorious general at eighteen, King at twenty, and died before he was thirty-three having, in terms of classical geography, conquered the world.

His father was Philip of Macedon, great diplomat, ruler, and military genius, who invented the "Greek phalanx," a solid troop formation that dominated the military tactics of the time. His mother was Olympias, the "witch-woman" who introduced serpents into the mysterious cult of Samothrace. Of a passionate and domineering nature, she sought to fire her son with her own ruthless ambition, and seems to have believed from his birth that he would become a master conqueror.

While still in his early teens, Alexander gave a remarkable display of his courage and will power. Philonicus the Thessalonian offered to sell Philip his horse Bucephalus for thirteen talents of gold (about $8,000), and the King took his son along to see the animal put through its paces. But the stallion proved so vicious and unmanageable that none of the grooms could even mount him. Alexander saw that Bucephalus was frightened by the movement of his own shadow, and quieted him by turning his head toward the sun. Then the young prince mounted the horse, let him run freely, and galloped back to the royal party amid the applause of all those present —including the King of Macedon.

As a tutor for his son Philip chose Aristotle, greatest of philosophers. Aristotle found that although he could furnish the intellect he could not sway the will of his pupil. Anything Alexander wanted to learn, he learned easily; but he was impatient of Aristotle's liberal and democratic views and stoutly maintained that the highest form of statehood could come only from the dictatorship of one man. He told Aristotle that if no other citizen was comparable to him, Alexander, in military virtue or political ability, he would do himself an injustice to consider others his equals. He expected to be held, Plutarch tells us, as "a god among men."

At that time Philip, taking advantage of the quarrels among the Greek cities, was drawing them gradually within the orbit of Macedonian influence. Then it was that Demosthenes at Athens saw the danger that threatened Greece from the north. With all the eloquence at his command he hurled against Philip of Macedon his famous *Philippics,* speeches so filled with fierce denunciation that they have given name to all outpourings of violent invective.

At last the Athenians, roused by further encroachments of the Macedonians, united with the Thebans and challenged Philip. The Macedonian King led his army against them, and the clash took place on the memorable field of Chaeronea. Philip had taken Alexander with him and although he was only eighteen gave his son a key command. The Macedonian phalanx swept all before it. Thebes was taken. Athens lay at Philip's feet. Great statesman that he was, the Macedonian King made no demands upon the city of the Acropolis, but sent Alexander to placate the Athenians.

One thing that could be made to serve the cause of Greek unity was the hatred of the Greeks for the Persians. Therefore Philip pondered an enterprise of unparalleled audacity that was to change the face of the world when carried out by his son, a general attack by the Greeks upon their hereditary foe. In the midst of planning this enterprise, Philip fell in love with a young woman named Cleopatra and decided to get rid of Olympias. A violent scene took place at the banquet following the celebration of Philip's second marriage. The new bride's uncle, Attalus, under the influence of liquor, called upon the Macedonians to entreat the Gods that his niece might bear a son and produce a lawful heir to the throne. Alexander threw a cup of wine into his face, crying, "What! Do you take me for a bastard?" Whereupon Philip drew his sword upon his son, but the wine he had drunk made him stumble and fall. Before the King could be raised from the floor, Alexander shouted, "Macedonians! Look at the man who was preparing to pass from Europe into Asia! He can't even pass from one table to the other without falling!"

Alexander then fled with his mother to her old home in Epirus. Later, at Philip's urging, he consented to return. The King had in mind his Persian expedition, but fell beneath an assassin's dagger before he could set out. The historians acquit Alexander of complicity in the crime. They are not so sure that his mother was innocent. In any case, Alexander was now King of Macedon and heir to his father's anti-Persian policy.

First he had to deal with rebellion in Greece. Thebes had risen against the Macedonians, and Alexander marched on the city and burned it to the ground, sparing only the home of Pindar, the lyric poet, and the temples of the gods. This drastic action caused the rest of Greece to submit. When the youthful King of Macedon turned to the East, he led a host of Macedonians and Greeks combined in one powerful army.

He moved overland, crossed the Hellespont, and entered Asia Minor. Then began a military progress that has no parallel in history, an avalanche of victories, battles won, cities taken; a display of military genius by a magnanimous victor unequaled before or since.

Alexander's first victory was at the Granicus River. The Persian plan was to throw him back before his campaign could get under way, and the battle raged until Alexander led a cavalry charge that broke the enemy line. The Persian horses fled, the Persian feet scattered, every man for himself.

Moving swiftly down the coast of Asia Minor, Alexander captured Halicarnassus, the city containing one of the now so-called Seven Wonders of the World, the Mausoleum or tomb of Mausolus completed only twenty years before. The main power of Persia was still to be met. Alexander hastened forward and forced Darius III into a decisive engagement at Issus. This was a savage contest in which only the spirit and leadership of their commander drove the Macedonians and Greeks forward. Again the Persians broke. Darius fled, leaving his wife and his mother to be captured. Alexander treated the women magnanimously. But he pressed on quickly, dogging the track of the King of Persia.

The strategy of Alexander was dictated now by the fact of sea power. The Persians, allied with the maritime states of Phoenicia, controlled the water route between Asia Minor and Greece. The Macedonians matched land power against sea power, and seized the coast, the seaports, the naval bases of the enemy on the Mediterranean. This meant the conquest of Syria, Palestine, and Egypt. The most difficult task was the siege of Tyre, the great sea stronghold of the Phoenicians, which lasted seven months. Alexander took a terrible vengeance and sold the people of the city into slavery. Then he moved south to the fortress of Gaza, which two months later was in his hands. Palestine and the Jewish nation yielded. Without giving his army time to rest, Alexander hurried on to Egypt. Gaining the submission of that ancient land, he made a hazardous journey across the desert to a famous shrine of Ammon, where the priests hailed him as a divinity. On the Mediterranean he founded the city of Alexandria, the first and greatest of many by that name.

After organizing his government of Egypt and seeing his city laid out, Alexander set his face toward the East. He passed through Damascus and crossed the Euphrates and the Tigris. Darius met him at Arbela with a final rally of Persian power, was again defeated, and again fled before his conqueror. Alexander entered Babylon without striking a blow. He was met by a long procession of priests and nobles who showered upon him gifts of gold and precious stones, rich embroideries and priceless tapestries. As the Lord of Asia, he made a grand gesture, installing the hostage family of Darius in the royal palace. Seated on the throne of Persian kings, he had placed at his feet Greek spoils the Persians had seized years before when they had invaded Greece, the bronzes Xerxes had taken from Athens. These were carried back to Athens by a delegation of Persian nobles.

Alexander then pushed on to Persepolis. He himself ordered the palace there to be burned—it being mere legend that the Athenian hetaera, Thaïs, prompted him to the deed during a drunken orgy. Still pursuing his royal antagonist he made a forced march famous in military annals—more than three hundred miles in eleven days. This time, however, there was no battle. Alexander received word that Darius had been murdered by his own officers.

After setting up his administration in Persia, Alexander continued east, but his army encountered terrible hardships, and there was much discontent among the soldiers, who had been on the march for years and wanted to go home. In no mood to stand insubordination, Alexander had many officers and men put to death. His temper grew worse and he was drinking heavily. In Bactria he captured Roxana, the daughter of a native prince, and against the wishes of his generals, took her for his wife.

They disliked his plan for a mingling of Europeans and Asiatics on a plane of equality, and they were not minded to keep campaigning much longer. This led to many quarrels, in one of which he killed Clitus, his friend and bodyguard, a senseless crime that left him subject to spasms of remorse. His generals followed him into India, and then refused to go any further. He was forced to retreat from the Indus after sending his admiral, Nearchus, sailing back on a memorable voyage by way of the Indian Ocean.

Retracing his path to Persia, Alexander paused at Susa and presided over the marriage of eighty of his commanders to Persian women. It was part of his plan for unity, but after his death many of the Macedonians repudiated their wives. He himself continued on to Babylon, entered the city despite a warning from some Babylonian priests, caught a fever, and died five days later. His generals, bidding for his power, carved out kingdoms for themselves, and began the Hellenistic Age of the Near East.

ARCHIMEDES

[287?–212 B.C.]

FOR twenty-two centuries Archimedes' public fame has been that of the greatest of inventors. In the realm of science his reputation is different: there he is valued for his theoretical physics and mathematics, so modern in conception that they anticipate the thinking of present-day science by more than two thousand years. But for most people throughout the ages he has been the ingenious contriver of wonderful mechanical devices, a wizard of invention.

The great Greek himself held his inventions in small esteem and regarded his mechanical exploits as of little importance. He would have agreed with the learned men who see in him primarily an abstract thinker, for he adopted the typical Greek view that the abstract is nobler and more praiseworthy than the useful. He was accustomed to refer slightingly to his inventions, calling them "the diversions of geometry at play."

Archimedes lived in the full splendor of the Hellenistic world. His birthplace was Syracuse, then the metropolis of Greek Sicily. The family traced an aristocratic lineage, and there are indications that Archimedes was related to Hiero, the ruler of Syracuse.

Archimedes must have shown his ability early in life, for his father decided to send him to Alexandria to be educated. Founded less than a century before by Alexander the Great, the city was the capital of Egypt, and the main seat of learning in the Greco-Roman world. Before the time of Archimedes, Euclid, the great mathematician, had worked in Alexandria where he wrote one of the world's greatest books, his *Elements of Geometry*. In the city of the Nile delta the old philosophic spirit of classic Greece had blossomed into science.

So to Alexandria came Archimedes. He found himself in an atmosphere congenial to his inquiring mind, went through the courses offered. Completing his studies, Archimedes returned to the court of Hiero at Syracuse, where he rapidly came into prominence as a savant, attending on Hiero as a kind of official court scientist. His marvelous discoveries in mathematics, astronomy, and mechanics soon spread his fame far and wide throughout the ancient world.

He did some of his most important work on the principles of the lever. He proved mathematically the great laws of balance, demonstrating, for example, that a lighter weight will always balance a heavier if the lighter is placed far enough from the fulcrum. The principle is exemplified in the familiar fact that a man with a crowbar can lift weights that are too heavy for him to move with his bare hands. This great demonstration was the reason for Archimedes' famous boast, "Give me a place to stand and I will move the earth."

Hiero, struck with amazement, asked to be shown how a small force could move a great weight. The proof, according to Plutarch, was established by the use of a compound pulley, the principle of which is akin to that of the lever. In his demonstration before Hiero, Archimedes moved a large ship, of three masts, loaded with many passengers and full of freight. Such a ship could ordinarily be moved only by the combined labor of many men. But this is what Plutarch tells us of Archimedes: "Sitting himself the while far off, with no great endeavor, but only holding the head of the pulley in his hand and drawing the cords by degrees, he drew the ship in a straight line, as smoothly and evenly as if she had been in the sea."

The exhibition convinced Hiero that the discoveries of Archimedes had a sound practical value. The ruler prevailed on the inventor to build war machines for him. Hiero himself never used the machines, but his republican successors relied on them during the Roman siege of Syracuse, and their astounding success established Archimedes as one of the greatest military engineers of all time.

Still more famous is Archimedes' discovery of the principle which led to the development of quantitative analysis. Hiero possessed a crown which was supposed to be of pure gold; however, he suspected that he had been cheated, that the goldsmith had put a layer of gold over some inferior metal. How could the truth be discovered without damaging the crown? This problem was propounded to Archimedes. For a while he found it a real puzzler. Then, one day, according to the well-known anecdote, he stepped into his bath while he was thinking about the conundrum, and he noticed how the water rose in the tub, his body displacing a certain amount. Whereupon the solution of the problem flashed upon him, and running naked from the bath, he dashed through the streets of Syracuse shouting, *"Eureka!"* (meaning, "I have found it!").

What he had found was a method of determining the relation of volume to weight: he saw that a body displaces its own volume in water, while scales register its weight. Each substance has its own ration of volume to weight, which is its specific gravity. A golden crown and a silver crown, each of the same weight, will have different volumes, and each will displace a different quantity of water. Hence, if Hiero's crown displaced one quantity of water, while an equal weight of pure gold displaced another quantity, the crown could not be pure gold. Conversely, if both displaced the same amount of water, then the crown was genuinely gold all through.

Archimedes' most practical invention was the water screw. This also is said to have followed from a problem put to him by Hiero— how to remove water from the hold of a large ship. Archimedes solved the difficulty by constructing a long, hollow, spiral tube, one end of which was placed in the water and which was turned rapidly by means of a crank at the other end. The rotation of the spiral forced water into the submerged end, and as more and more entered, the rest was forced up the tube until it spilled out at the top. The water screw proved of great value in raising water to irrigate fields, and the same principle is often used today in machines for handling wheat.

Archimedes was an astronomer. He calculated the length of the year, discovered the distances of the planets, and measured the apparent diameter of the sun. In his *On Sphere-Making,* which is now lost, he described how he had constructed an astronomical model, a sphere which imitated the motion of the sun, moon, and planets. Cicero saw this contrivance over a century later, and declared it represented the phases of the moon and the apparent motion of the sun so correctly that it showed eclipses of both the sun and the moon.

The books Archimedes wrote (those that have survived and come down to us) disclose investigations of the mathematics of spheres, cones, and cylinders, the commensurate ratio of the circle, the formula for the parabola, the center of gravity of the plane, the theory of floating bodies, and the principles of hydrostatics. In 1906, a lost treatise of Archimedes' was discovered in Constantinople. It showed that the ancient mathematician had arrived at the elements of what was equivalent to the integral calculus of modern times.

The work of Archimedes astounds us with its variety. But more important, it is all of the highest excellence. It shows him as perhaps the greatest figure in the history of science, a consummate master of both abstract mathematics and laboratory experiment. He was a true mathematical physicist in the modern sense.

Archimedes' career ended in drama—a climax of inventions. The last years of his life coincided with one of history's mightiest conflicts, the Second Punic War—the death struggle between Hannibal and Rome. Archimedes' patron, Hiero, had the wisdom to take the side of Rome in its clash with Carthage, but after his death this wise policy was reversed, with fatal consequence. Dazzled by Hannibal's victories, Gelon turned against Rome, and, in due time, Syracuse was besieged by a Roman army under the Consul Marcellus.

The siege of Syracuse is one of the most famous of all time, marked by its stubborn attack and defense, but distinguished most of all by the inventions of Archimedes. His engines of war are said to have prolonged the siege for three years. He built new and ingenious catapults which hurtled ponderous projectiles for great distances, as well as at short range, with devastating results. He devised machines which discharged showers of missiles upon the enemy through holes in the walls of the city. He constructed mechanisms featuring long poles which reached out and dropped heavy weights on Roman ships and men. Survivors of this havoc reported that huge cranes snatched Roman galleys out of the water, to their total destruction, but the most horrendous tale to confound antiquity relates that Archimedes personally set fire to the Roman fleet with a burning glass—in reality a mirror—by which he focused the rays of the sun on the sails of ships within bow-shot of the walls and set them ablaze. This seemingly magical power terrified the Roman besiegers, who, Plutarch tells us, were so frightened that even so insignificant an item as a piece of rope or wood falling from the parapets was suspect and panic would ensue at the thought that it was another new engine of war invented by Archimedes.

After three years of siege, the Romans stormed the city. Although the Consul Marcellus gave orders that both the life and the house of

Archimedes were to be spared, the great savant, in his seventy-fifth year, fell victim to the fury of a maddened soldier. Throughout the din of battle, while the Romans hacked their way into Syracuse, Archimedes was absorbed in a geometrical problem, a diagram of which he had drawn in the sand, so engrossed in its solution that he forgot everything else. Thus he was when a Roman came upon him. Disturbed in his meditation, the venerable old man told the legionnaire to step aside. Enraged at the order, the soldier killed him with a sword thrust.

Marcellus lamented the death of the man whose genius had kept the Romans at bay for so long. Archimedes' relatives were permitted to give him a funeral of honor. On his tomb was placed, according to his own wish, a representation of a cylinder circumscribing a sphere; and with it an inscription stating the mathematical relation of the one to the other. This formula—that in area and volume the cylinder is 1½ times as great as the sphere—was the discovery which Archimedes regarded as the greatest of all his accomplishments.

HANNIBAL

[247–183 B.C.]

H ANNIBAL was a man who had one compelling idea. The lifework he set himself was easily stated: "Destroy Rome!" Having no other ambition, he personified one side of the great duel of the age, Rome against Carthage.

A glance at the map will show that the central Mediterranean is dominated geographically by the Italian peninsula and the island of Sicily. Across the narrow water, facing Sicily, lies the tip of Africa, what is now Tunis and was ancient Carthage. From that strategic site Carthage, founded by the Phoenicians, for centuries dominated the central Mediterranean, a mighty maritime power. The First Punic War (Punic for Phoenician) was a struggle for the island of Sicily, land power (Rome) versus sea power (Carthage), and the land could not defeat the sea. Rome won the First Punic War only by creating a navy that gained control of the water.

During the last stages of the First Punic War, successes in Sicily were won by a Carthaginian general, Hamilcar Barca. His victories, though futile in the face of the Roman conquest of the sea, gave him a brilliant reputation. After the loss of the war, he took the lead in reviving the power and wealth of his native city. Carthage long had had dealings with Spain, a land inhabited by barbarous tribes but immensely rich in natural resources. Hamilcar planned to create a Carthaginian empire in Spain. Rome hardly knew what he was about, as in less than ten years Hamilcar, with consummate generalship and statecraft, subjugated the Spanish tribes and established a powerful Carthaginian hegemony.

He had several sons, the eldest of whom was Hannibal. Hamilcar educated Hannibal carefully, schooling him in the arts of war, diplomacy, and government. One particular lesson was drilled into the young boy—undying enmity to Rome. At the age of nine he accompanied his father to the temple of the Carthaginian gods, where Hamilcar had him swear a solemn oath to destroy the city on the Tiber. That oath was to dominate the life of Hannibal.

He grew to manhood in a welter of war and power politics in Spain, and distinguished himself as an able leader of soldiers and a player in the game of empire. He was eighteen when his father was killed in battle, to be succeeded by a son-in-law, Hasdrubal. Eight years later Hasdrubal was assassinated; his successor was Hannibal. Now twenty-six, the son of Hamilcar was left with the Spanish dominion his father had established, and with his father's commission to conquer Rome. Hannibal proceeded to honor his vow in a fashion that made spectacular history.

He had under his command a disciplined army consisting largely of Spanish troops, an extremely effective fighting force whose complete allegiance he had won. He could draw on the Iberian Peninsula for reinforcements when he marched against Rome. From Spain a land route led to Italy, and this circumvented the Roman command of the sea. Hannibal could strike at Rome overland. His logic added up to one of the greatest marches in history.

He began by provoking war. He attacked, besieged, and captured Sagunto, an ally of the Romans. Rome demanded redress from Carthage, was refused, and the Second Punic War began.

Hannibal was on his way. In the spring of 218 B.C. he crossed the Pyrenees and marched across Gaul, through what is now southern France. He had 46,000 men and 37 elephants. Rome sent an army by sea to attack Hannibal in Spain, only to find that he had left Spain. The Roman army doubled back, proceeding by ship to Massilia, now Marseilles. The plan was to head him off at the mouths of the Rhone. But the Roman commander soon discovered that Hannibal had crossed the river to the north and was heading for the Alps. August had come and gone, and the Romans believed it utterly impossible for an army to get through the mountains so late in the year.

The crossing of the Alps in the fall of 218 B.C. was a prodigy of history. Hannibal's army traversed high passes at a season when alpine snows were piling high. Glaciers had to be conquered. Avalanches thundered down. Hostile tribes attacked. The warlike natives rolled rocks down on columns toiling through snowy ravines. Worst

of all was getting the elephants across the glacial mountains. It took
fifteen days of nightmare toil and peril, and Hannibal lost twenty
thousand men. He led twenty-five thousand down into the rich plains
of Italy. They were battered and worn, but were able to recuperate
without opposition, thanks to the strategy of Hannibal and to the
surprise of the Romans.

The Carthaginian general maintained iron discipline and forbade
his troops to plunder. This was part of his strategy. A master of statecraft, as well as of war, he planned to use political weapons along
with military might in conquering Rome.

He wanted to attract the other peoples of Italy to his side. Hannibal's great design was to use victory in the field to break her allies
away from Rome, and thereby shatter the Roman hegemony in the
Italian peninsula.

The Romans rushed up an army to oppose him as soon as they
realized what was happening. Hannibal made his stand at the Ticino
River. In the ensuing battle the Romans were defeated, their commander wounded. He was the elder Scipio, now saved from capture
only by the bravery of his seventeen-year-old son, later to become
Scipio Africanus, Hannibal's conqueror. Another Roman army appeared under another commander. Hannibal took up a position on
the Trebbia River. Here he achieved a masterpiece of strategy, concealing part of his army at the start, then hurling it into the battle at
the decisive moment, and winning one of his most brilliant victories
over the Roman legions. The Roman army was destroyed, 30,000
killed and the remainder wounded or scattered.

Hannibal now went into winter quarters. The Gauls of northern
Italy flocked to his standard, hailing him as their liberator from Rome.
The Romans were losing battles, territory, and allies. Hannibal's pol-
icy was working.

Rome raised two new armies, and the first of these moved north
to face Hannibal. Commanded by the Consul Flaminius, the legions
halted, and established camp to wait for the second army. Hannibal
sought to force a battle before the Roman columns could be joined,
so he started on a march into central Italy, ravaging the countryside,
laying waste towns and villages. Flaminius struck out in pursuit. Hannibal led him into a narrow rocky pass near Lake Trasimenus, where
suddenly Flaminius found he was being attacked from all sides. The

SOCRATES

ALEXANDER THE GREAT

legions were caught in a fatal trap; Hannibal's troops closed both bottlenecks of the gorge and closed in on all sides. The Romans fought stubbornly. The battle was so violent that the fighting was not even interrupted by a small earthquake. When it was over, Flaminius' army had been destroyed and he himself slain.

Rome now appointed a dictator, the Roman constitutional device reserved for the gravest emergency. The command with absolute power for one year was given to Quintus Fabius Maximus, after whom Fabian tactics are named. Fabius, unwilling to risk another pitched battle against so formidable an adversary, resorted to guerrilla warfare to harass Hannibal, cut off his supplies and wore his army down in hostile country. In marching and countermarching, Fabius was never far from Hannibal, but refused to be drawn into a decisive test of strength. The Fabian tactics were effective, and Hannibal was hard pressed for supplies. He acted boldly. He pushed south, bypassed Rome, and entered the rich plains of Capua, some twenty-five miles north of Naples.

The Romans followed and almost trapped him between the rocks and marshes. Their troops closed a narrow defile which offered the Carthaginians their only hope of escape. But Hannibal was resourceful. He had a thousand oxen collected, and lighted torches were tied to their horns. At night they were driven against the Roman line. The Romans took the onset of torches for an attack, and in the confusion the defile was left unguarded. Hannibal's army drove through.

The Romans were tired of Fabius. They replaced him with two consuls, who resolved to attack Hannibal boldly. The Consul Varro had 50,000 men as against Hannibal's 40,000 when the two armies met at Cannae. Great as the Roman defeats had been, Cannae was the worst disaster of all. Hannibal's strategy—weakening his front, drawing the Romans forward, hitting them suddenly on both flanks, then forging a ring of steel around them—was so masterly that it stands today as the model of flanking envelopment. The legions were surrounded and destroyed, and Cannae became a byword for a battle of annihilation.

Rome was appalled by the news of Cannae. The flower of her army had perished under the hammer blows of the Carthaginian invader. Only old men and boys remained to defend the city. But there was no thought of surrender. The gates were shut against Hannibal, sur-

vivors of Cannae straggled back to help man the walls, and when
the mighty conqueror arrived, he saw that he could not storm Rome
because he lacked the military engines to breach the defenses.

The Romans rebuilt their forces. Gradually the tide turned. Northern Italy was reclaimed from the Carthaginians. Hannibal remained
in the south. He made no effort to seize more territory, and the
Romans refrained from attacking him. This stalemate prevailed for
nearly four years.

During all this time Hannibal received no help from Carthage. A
faction hostile to him at home blocked measures to aid him. In Spain
his brother Hasdrubal gathered an army and set out overland by
much the same route that Hannibal had taken. He entered Italy, and
sent a message to Hannibal, naming a place for a junction of forces.
The message was intercepted by the Romans, and this enabled the
Consul Claudius Nero to catch Hasdrubal's army at the Metaurus
River and destroy it. Hasdrubal himself was killed and his head was
thrown into Hannibal's camp.

With no hope of aid now, Hannibal retired into Bruttium in southern Italy where he was virtually blockaded by Roman forces. The
Romans meanwhile seized Spain, and planned to strike at Carthage
itself. This was the project of Scipio, the son of Hannibal's first adversary. Scipio took command of a Roman army, and invaded Africa.
Carthage sent frantic appeals to Hannibal to return. This he did and
in the spring of 202 B.C. Hannibal and Scipio Africanus met on the
plain of Zama. The hitherto invincible commander went down to defeat. He lost to Scipio Africanus in one of the decisive battles of history. Carthage had to submit, and Rome imposed the harshest of
terms.

Hannibal became head of the government of defeated Carthage
and set about restoring his country and effecting reforms. But Roman
vengeance pursued him, and he was forced into exile. He went to
the court of the Syrian King, Antiochus. True to his lifelong hatred
of Rome, he persuaded Antiochus to make war. Antiochus, with Hannibal aiding him, was defeated by a Roman army under the command
of a brother of Scipio Africanus.

Hannibal fled, and spent the next few years wandering from the
court of one eastern princeling to that of another. Finally at the court
of Prusias, King of Bithynia, he learned that his host was preparing to

betray him to the Romans. Rather than face such disgrace he ended his own life, in 183 B.C., the year in which Scipio Africanus died.

Little is known of Hannibal's personal life. His character is blemished only by Roman charges of cruelty. We have little description of his appearance, save that he lost one eye campaigning in Italy. He stands a colossal figure, magnified by the fear and enduring respect of Rome.

JULIUS CAESAR

[*100–44* B.C.]

JULIUS CAESAR, one of the world's greatest men of action, acted rashly only once in his life—and it had nothing to do with his wars or his political struggles or even his assassination. He was still a young man when the aristocratic dictator Sulla became master of Rome. Sulla ordered Caesar to divorce his wife since she was the daughter of one of Sulla's enemies. Caesar refused. He thereby took the chance of disappearing in the bloody Sullan prescriptions, a fate from which only the intercession of his aristocratic relations saved him. Sulla spared his life, but is reported to have said, "He has the making of many Mariuses." It was a prophetic remark. Caesar went on to a career that dimmed the memory of the great Marius, the democratic leader who had ruled Rome before Sulla.

Caesar grew to maturity amid savage party feuds—the democrats against the aristocrats, Marius against Sulla. Caesar came from one of Rome's most exclusive families, but he was a relative by marriage of Marius, and he decided to join the popular faction. Hence Sulla's enmity, and his command to Caesar to divorce his wife. Refusing to obey and barely escaping with his life, Caesar went to Asia Minor and served with the legions there, returning home only when he heard that Sulla was dead.

He entered politics but accomplished little. Feeling that he was wasting his time, he left for the island of Rhodes to pursue his studies. On the way he was captured by pirates and held for ransom. As an example of his audacity, history relates that he coolly told the buccaneers he would return and have them executed. Ransomed, he immediately raised a force of ships and soldiers, stormed the pirate stronghold, and carried out his threat. Then he went on to Rhodes to polish his writing and his rhetoric under Greek teachers.

He was torn between war and politics. From Rhodes he went to Asia Minor, where he served in the campaign against the great King of Pontus, Mithridates. Caesar's commander in this war was Lucullus, later to become famous for his (Lucullan) feasts. Leaving Pontus, Caesar returned to Rome, found existence there dull, and volunteered for service in Spain. After that, back to the capital of the world on the Tiber.

At this period Caesar was known chiefly for a wild career of pleasure and extravagance. He indulged immoderately in the Sybarite pastimes of Roman social life, became a carouser and a wastrel. He ran into debt with reckless prodigality, and seemed the kind of financially ruined aristocrat who can readily become a demagogue.

When he sought advancement in the popular party in its feud with the Senate, his spendthrift habits on borrowed money became an asset. He was elected aedile, a municipal office, and courted favor by giving extravagant entertainments for the public, games in the arena, combats of gladiators, spectacular shows for the Roman mob. That won favor with the voters, and he was elected to a succession of offices.

Historians have long debated Caesar's role in the political conspiracies of the time. The most famous of these was the conspiracy of Catiline, which brought Cicero to the heights of fame. The great orator, as Consul, crushed the attempted revolt by desperadoes of the popular faction, delivering in the process his famous orations against Catiline. There were charges that Caesar was involved, and the debate in the Senate saw him accused. Suspicion mounted when he spoke against the severity of the order instigated by Cicero for putting supporters of Catiline to death. It is not clear how much Caesar had to do with the intended insurrection by extremists of his own party, but he probably knew more than he admitted.

The political rise of Caesar now became involved with the famous figure of Pompey, who had made a triumphal progress in the East, taking over where the victories of Lucullus had left off, and completing the war against Mithridates with all the manner of a magnificent conqueror. Pompey returned to Rome in glory, only to meet with the suspicion of the Senate, which always feared a victorious general as a possible dictator. Pompey wanted the Senate to ratify the arrangements and treaties he had made in the East and to reward his legions with lands for their veterans. The Senate was reluctant, and delayed.

Caesar came forward in outspoken support of Pompey, seconding his demands. The two became allies against the Senate, Caesar hoisting himself on Pompey's military reputation, while Pompey, politically inept, was aided by Caesar's position and skill in party matters. There was a third ally, who provided another necessary resource, money. He was Crassus the millionaire, who had large ambitions and played the popular party game against the Senate. Thus was formed an association destined later to overshadow Rome.

When his term in political office expired, Caesar went off according to custom to a military command. He was assigned to Spain. Before going he procured a loan from Crassus to pay off his enormous debts, and is said to have borrowed from Crassus the equivalent of a million dollars. In Spain commanding an army, Caesar strengthened his political position with military prestige. He won sharp successes against Iberian tribes which resisted Roman domination.

After a year of this he returned to Rome, where the Senate was still refusing to grant Pompey's demands for a ratification of his arrangements in the East and for the rewarding of his veterans. The upshot was the First Triumvirate. Pompey, Caesar, and Crassus, already allied politically, concluded an arrangement whereby they together would assume domination, combining Pompey's military reputation, Caesar's leadership in politics, and Crassus' wealth.

According to the arrangement between the triumvirs, Caesar was elected Consul. In this capacity he employed unscrupulous pressure, and forced the Senate to agree to Pompey's demands. He put through, in the same way, a measure giving the rich middle class control of the collection of taxes in the East, which was in the interest of the capitalist Crassus. The year of the consulship of Caesar saw the Triumvirate in full control, and from then on the pages of history are full of the glory of Caesar.

A consul, after his year in office, was by custom assigned to the governorship of a province, as proconsul. Usually he selected a rich province, like Sicily, or Syria, or a wealthy realm in Asia Minor, where he could lay his hands on a fat revenue, and reimburse himself for the heavy expenditures of a political career in Rome. This was an important factor in the looting of great lands during the last days of the Roman Republic. But Caesar, in selecting a province for his pro-consulship, chose another kind of prize. He selected Gaul.

At that time the Roman possession called Gaul consisted of northern Italy, cisalpine Gaul, and a narrow strip along the southern shore of what is now France, transalpine Gaul. To the north lay the principal country of the Celtic tribes, the Gauls, extending from the Rhine to the Pyrenees, generally what is now France. It was a great warlike territory beyond the sphere of Roman domination, an invitation to conquest, which however promised more hard fighting than wealthy loot. Caesar's choice, no rich plum from which to extract a juicy fortune, could be interpreted in terms of lofty ambition.

He was now approaching forty and might well say, as he is reported to have said glumly, that at this age Alexander had conquered the world. In middle life he chose a sphere of action that could lead only to the roughest kind of war as the price of military glory, for military glory he was determined to win.

He took his post as proconsul in command of the legions in his province, and fortune immediately played into his hands, giving him an excuse for intervention in the affairs of the Gauls. A Celtic tribe, the Helvetii, moving from what is now Switzerland, was determined to march across Gaul to Spain. They demanded passage through the strip of territory that Rome held along the southern coast. This Caesar rejected. He defeated the Helvetii, and drove them back into the Alps. Then Germanic invasion threatened Gaul. The Teutons from beyond the Rhine, headed by a warrior king Ariovistus, pressed against the Celtic tribes, and these appealed to Rome for aid. This was Caesar's chance to enter Gaul itself. He answered the appeal of the Celts, attacking Ariovistus, annihilating the Teutonic host, and scattering the survivors back across the Rhine.

Caesar had saved Gaul from the Germans so that he might make it Roman. Knowing that the Gaulish people would fight for their liberty, he prepared for a long hard struggle. First he defeated the Belgae, the inhabitants of what is now Belgium. Other tribes rose against him, only to be put down after savage fighting. He marched into the interior, reached the Loire, and occupied the village that would one day grow to be the city of Paris.

But the conquered barbarians would not remain docile. The year 56 B.C. brought a series of revolts. Peoples in what is now Brittany attacked the Romans, and Caesar had to construct a fleet on the Loire before he could counterattack successfully. Other tribes resisted and were subdued. In suppressing rebellions, Caesar employed merciless severity, executing leaders and selling whole tribes into slavery.

The following year was memorable for the first invasion of Britain. A close connection existed between the British Gauls and those on the southern shore of the Channel, who received aid from the Britons. Caesar took two legions, crossed the Channel, and landed on the coast of Kent. There was some brief, successful fighting by the Romans, who soon departed. Caesar's first invasion of Britain was no more than a raid.

His second landing in Britain occurred a year later, 54 B.C., and was more ambitious. He took five legions, crossed the Channel, and marched on a campaign in southern England. From the coast of Kent the Romans moved along the Thames. They must have passed near the site of what is now London. Heavy resistance was encountered and the legions had trouble throwing back the war chariots of the Britons. The invasion was no great success, and accomplished little. The incorporation of Britain into the Roman Empire was to wait until a later date.

Gaul itself was not really subjugated, and the next two years, 53 and 52 B.C., witnessed a great uprising of the Celtic tribes. This was the time of the great test for Caesar, who hitherto had moved swiftly and with bewildering energy from success to success, but now had to deal with adversity. In surprise uprisings the Gauls destroyed a legion, and besieged another Roman force in what is now Belgium, which Caesar, moving rapidly, was barely able to relieve. He struck again across the Rhine to deter the Germans, while all Gaul was in insurrection.

The Celtic tribes found a great leader to rally them, Vercingetorix, chief of the Arverni. He formed a league of the Gauls and pursued a strategy of holding strong fortified positions instead of challenging the Romans in the field. Caesar had a worthy antagonist, and sustained a defeat when he tried to capture the citadel of Gergovia. Vercingetorix, moving rapidly and spreading the revolt far and wide, struck down toward the old Roman province along the southern coast of Gaul, lost a battle to Caesar, and then threw himself into the stronghold of Alesia, determined to stand siege while the tribes every-where rallied and assailed the encircling lines of the legions.

The siege of Alesia was a classic double siege. Caesar constructed the usual Roman entrenchments around the stronghold, which was situated on a hill and well defended. Thus he held Vercingetorix and his warriors inside. At the same time, knowing that he would be attacked by a relieving army of Gauls, he threw an outer line of earthworks around his own besieging legions.

In due time the relieving force arrived, a huge host of Gauls, who hurled themselves wildly against the outer fortifications. At the same time Vercingetorix ordered a sally from the inside. The legions were on the verge of destruction when the relieving army of Gauls broke in at one point. Caesar was able to save the situation only by leading a counterattack sword in hand. He hurled back the assailants and closed the gap.

Repulsed in heavy battle, the Celtic clans outside settled down to besiege the Romans. So now it was a two-way siege. Caesar's legions encircled Vercingetorix in the stronghold of Alesia, while they in turn were encircled. The issue was decided by factors common enough in the warfare of Romans and barbarians. The legions, pinned between two forces, had a discipline of iron, had organization, food supplies stored and rationed, health guarded by sanitation. The Gauls had a barbarian system of warfare, soon ate the surrounding country empty, and were susceptible to epidemics. With little discipline, they were always impatient of inaction, and tended to break up and go home. The Gallic chiefs staged one more head-on assault, which was beaten off, and then the relieving host marched away. The defenders of Alesia were finally compelled to surrender. Vercingetorix was sent to Rome in chains, later to be strangled in a dungeon.

That was the end of the great insurrection of the Gauls. Caesar made Gaul a Roman province, and in a brief time the Celtic peoples were so thoroughly Romanized that Gaul became a stronghold of imperial power.

Caesar was in Gaul for seven years, and told the story of his campaigns in a memorable work, *De Bello Gallico*. Written with lucidity and strength, this gave him a high place in the history of Latin literature, and for long centuries his *Gallic War* has been a standard text in the study of Latin. He wrote it during intervals between campaigns, and meant it in large part to influence opinion and increase his prestige back in Rome. Yet, despite this political purpose, the correctness of his account has never been seriously shaken.

During the seven years of war in Gaul Caesar had to contend with political affairs back in Rome, which were as perilous for him as any war. With the other two Triumvirs, Pompey and Crassus, left in the capital to keep the situation under control, all at first went well enough.

Then Crassus, the millionaire, set out to win military glory of his own, emulating Caesar in Gaul. He took command of an army against the Parthians in the East, a nation of horsemen who had an empire in Mesopotamia and Persia. Crassus, at the head of his legions, brought about one of the greatest military disasters in history. Caught by the Parthians in the desert, assailed on all sides by light cavalry and a rain of arrows, the army was destroyed and Crassus was killed.

That left Pompey in Rome, and his relations with Caesar now dominate the story. To cement their partnership, the middle-aged Pompey married Caesar's young daughter Julia, to whom he became fondly devoted. But soon Julia died, and Pompey drifted away from Caesar to join the aristocratic party against the popular party led by Caesar. Pompey was essentially a conservative, and his alliance with Caesar had been a matter of political expediency. The central factor for Caesar was the duration of his command. He had been named proconsul of Gaul for five years, and before his term neared an end he had a meeting with Pompey in northern Italy, where it was decided that Caesar's command should be extended for another five years. Later, when Pompey went over to the side of the Senate, the agreement was broken. A clamor was raised that Caesar must give up his command, the well-understood purpose of which was to have him return to Rome as a private citizen, subject to prosecution by his enemies.

Thus it came about that in the month of January 49 B.C., Caesar faced a supreme decision—to submit or resort to rebellion. He was in northern Italy, which was included in his own proconsular province of Gaul. There, at the east, the boundary line was a small stream, the Rubicon. If he crossed it with his soldiers and passed into the territory of Rome proper, that meant a violation of law and a declaration of war. History knows of no more famous incident than when

Caesar, on the northern bank of the stream, made his decision, and spurring his horse into the waters of the Rubicon, cried, *"Alea iacta est!"*—"The die is cast!"

Caesar crossed the Rubicon with one legion, but backed by the veteran army of Gaul, and marched rapidly on Rome. Pompey, possessing no troops comparable to these, fled from Rome, from Italy, and took refuge in the East. Caesar entered Rome and drew up his strategy. First he went to Spain and defeated Pompey's adherents. Then he crossed over to the Balkans where he lost a battle to Pompey at Dyrrachium, and then won the decisive clash at Pharsalia in Greece. Pompey fled to Egypt, where he was murdered, a crime at the news of which Caesar is said to have wept.

After the murder of Pompey in Egypt, Caesar settled the affairs of that fabulously rich but feeble kingdom. And he met the Serpent of the Nile—Cleopatra.

Romantic legend has woven a wealth of fantasy around the relations of Caesar and Cleopatra, including the famed fable of how she, a mere girl, had herself conveyed to Caesar hidden in a roll of carpet. History relates that she captivated him, and persuaded him to establish her as the sole sovereign of Egypt. The middle-aged Roman general dallied with the girl queen for a whole year in Alexandria, while a riot of insurrection broke out against him in the city, and the Romans had a hard time defending their quarters against attack. Cleopatra's royal brother perished in the fighting, and through the favor of Caesar, she ruled as Queen of Egypt.

After romancing at Alexandria, it was high time for Caesar to move against his remaining enemies. In the East a son of the great Mithridates was in arms against Rome. Caesar moved over to Asia Minor, where he met the enemy in a battle that enabled him to send the famous message back to Rome: "I came, I saw, I conquered." Then to Italy, where he had to deal with mutinous Roman soldiers. Next, North Africa, to win the battle of Thapsus against the remaining leaders of the party of the Senate. Another campaign had to be waged in Spain, to which the sons of Pompey had fled and raised an insurrection against Caesar. He defeated them in the battle of Munda, and that was the end of the armed opposition. Caesar was left master of the Roman world.

He was to live for only six months more, and that brief period raises some of the most difficult puzzles in his career. What were his intentions for the Roman political system? Did he plan to overthrow the Republic and make himself King? He ruled in the office of dictator. This was an ancient Roman institution, though only for emergency, but Caesar had himself made dictator for life. He treated the Senate with contempt, adding many new members as he pleased, including provincials. There were many signs that he meditated large changes in the structure of the government at Rome.

The modern historian is tempted to think that Caesar saw the deficiencies of the old Republic more clearly than did his contemporaries, that he saw them somewhat, perhaps, as we can see them two thousand years later. Rome was organized as a city-state. The electorate, for example, was the assemblage of citizens gathered in the Forum. But Rome had become a great empire, destined to become larger. Was the city-state government an adequate instrument to administer a vast realm of many provinces? Today we can answer—no. Caesar seems to have foreseen this answer. He prepared the way for the solution that was to come, one-man rule, the Roman Empire. There were signs that he intended to set himself up as King. His chief lieutenant, Mark Antony, offered him in public a royal crown, which Caesar declined—reluctantly, if we can believe his critics.

Many other stories are told of him. One of the best known is that of the Bona Dea. This was a religious festival at Caesar's house which was supposed to be attended by women only. A notorious rake sneaked in disguised in the garb of a woman and was discovered. The resultant scandal caused Caesar to divorce his wife. To the protest that she had done nothing wrong he replied, "Caesar's wife must be above suspicion."

His second wife enters the Caesar legend in a more poignant way. Calpurnia begged her husband to stay home because she had dreamed of his death. Instead of listening to her, he followed the advice of the conspirators who were waiting with their daggers, went to the Senate House and was struck dead by Brutus, Cassius, and the rest. He fell beneath a statue of his old colleague and adversary, Pompey. It was the Ides of March, 44 B.C.

CLEOPATRA

[*69–30* B.C.]

For almost three hundred years after the death of Alexander the Great, conqueror of the Near East, Egypt was ruled by the Ptolemies, descended from one of Alexander's principal generals. The first Ptolemy made his capital, Alexandria, the great center of Greek culture, and for generations the Greek kingdom in Egypt flourished in wealth, power, and enlightenment. Then decadence set in, and the Ptolemies turned to the rising power of Rome for protection. Egypt became virtually a vassal of Rome.

In 51 B.C. Ptolemy Auletes died, leaving the throne of Egypt to his two eldest children, Cleopatra, who was seventeen, and her brother Ptolemy, three years her junior. They were to be married, brother and sister marriage being ancient royal custom in Egypt. Cleopatra, of Grecian descent, was famous for her beauty and her learning. She was ambitious too. Her brother aspired to rule alone, and so did she. Soon she was out of Egypt and in Syria, going there either to raise a revolt or exiled by her brother. This quarrel was now lost in larger events, the Roman Civil War in which Julius Caesar overthrew Pompey and made himself master of the vast Roman realm. Pompey, defeated at Pharsalia, fled to Egypt to seek refuge there, but was murdered by officials of the boy Ptolemy. Caesar followed, established himself in Alexandria, ready to dictate an arrangement of government affairs in Egypt.

Caesar was soon captivated by Cleopatra. The story that she had herself transported to him in a roll of carpet or in a wicker basket covered with a priceless silken rug is probably apocryphal. But into his presence she came, and the effect of her youth and beauty upon the already aging Roman conqueror was magical. Caesar decided that she should reign together with her brother, as willed by their father. Ptolemy, fearing his sister, refused to accept this decision, and started an insurrection. Caesar had to go through some dangerous fighting in Alexandria, but his Roman legionnaires won out, and Ptolemy was killed. Caesar had Cleopatra proclaimed Queen of Egypt and married to her eleven-year-old younger brother, Ptolemy XIII.

After dallying for some while with her, Caesar left Alexandria to resume his career of conquest in Syria and Armenia. This completed his mastery of most of the known world. Returning to Rome, he sent for Cleopatra, and renewed the love affair. He had her statue placed in the Temple of Venus and recognized as his lawful heir Caesarion, the son she had borne him. She lived openly as Caesar's mistress, a fact which scandalized the Romans. They suspected that she wanted to be Queen of Rome.

Then came the Ides of March, 44 B.C., when Julius Caesar fell victim to republican daggers, and again there was civil war in the Roman realm. A triumvirate was formed, of which the chief members were Caesar's general, Mark Antony, and Caesar's great nephew and heir, Octavian. They defeated the forces of Caesar's assassins, Brutus and Cassius, and divided the Roman world between them. Octavian took Rome and the West. Mark Antony took the East, including Egypt, where Cleopatra reigned.

On Caesar's death Cleopatra had returned to Alexandria. Here she had her young brother-husband poisoned, and remained in sole possession of the land of the Pharaohs. As Queen of Egypt she proved herself an able ruler. During her reign the country enjoyed peace and prosperity. She established law and order, and justice was administered with an even hand. Canals were built to extend the area of arable land. Alexandria flourished anew as the great port of the ancient world, its shipping regulations acknowledged throughout the Mediterranean. Although Cleopatra never hesitated to spend money for public ceremonies or to enhance the splendor and luxury of her regime, she checked up carefully on the revenues and expenditures of her provincial governors and tolerated no abuses. Even Roman writers, who pictured her as a paragon of sumptuous vice, paid tribute to her constructive activity and admitted that Egypt was prosperous under her rule.

A clever politician, Cleopatra was quick to see the danger to which Mark Antony's assumption of power in the East exposed her. Rumor accused her of having given support to Brutus and Cassius when they were powerful. She feared that the murder of her brother-husband might serve as a Roman pretext to deprive her of the crown. So she determined to subjugate Antony as she had Caesar; and the love story of the next fourteen years of her life has inspired artists and writers for twenty centuries.

The way in which Cleopatra came to her first meeting with Mark Antony, who was in Syria, showed her as a genius in practical psychology as well as a glamorous woman. Here is how Plutarch describes the event: "She received several letters, both from Antony and from his friends, to summon her, but she took no account of these orders; and at last, as if in mockery of them, she came sailing up the river Cydnus, in a barge with gilded stern and outspread sails of purple, while oars of silver beat time to the music of flutes and fifes and harps. She herself lay all alone under a canopy of cloth of gold, dressed as Venus in a picture, and beautiful young boys, like painted Cupids, stood on each side to fan her. Her maids were dressed like sea nymphs and graces, some steering at the rudder, some working at the ropes. The perfumes diffused themselves from the vessel to the shore, which was covered with multitudes, part following the galley up the river on either bank, part running out of the city to see the sight. The market place was quite emptied, and Antony at last was left alone sitting upon the tribunal; while the word went through all the multitude, that Venus was come to feast with Bacchus, for the common good of Asia."

Antony's meeting with Cleopatra was love at first sight, shared by two of the most emotional, two of the most dramatic human beings who ever lived. Antony spent the winter in Alexandria with Cleopatra, during which time the Queen never left his side. They hunted, played dice, fished and feasted, till the two lovers seemed utterly detached from the things of this world. One day Mark Antony, humiliated at catching only small fry when fishing with Cleopatra, ordered a diver to attach some of the larger catch to his hook, but the Queen was not so easily duped, and the following day she saw to it that her lover hooked a fine salted cod.

The first phase of their romance lasted only a few months. Antony returned to Rome, where his own faction had fallen out with Octavian. There had been some fighting, with Antony's adherents getting the worst of it. In Rome a reconciliation was effected between the two masters of the Roman world, and was cemented by the marriage of Mark Antony to Octavia, the sister of Octavian. In a new division of empire, Antony again received the East, and returned to Cleopatra's charms.

These were so compelling that he was utterly dominated by the mere thought of her. What was the secret of her fascination? According to Plutarch: ". . . her actual beauty, it is said, was not in itself so remarkable that none could be compared with her, or that no one could see her without being struck by it, but the contact of her presence, if you lived with her, was irresistible; the attraction of her person, joining with the charm of her conversation, and the character that attended all she said or did, was something bewitching. It was a pleasure merely to hear the sound of her voice . . ."

The most famous judgment ever passed on Cleopatra comes from Shakespeare. In his *Antony and Cleopatra* one character remarks that, with Antony's marriage to Octavia, he will have to abandon his Egyptian lover. Enobarbus replies,

> Never; he will not:
> Age cannot wither her, nor custom stale
> Her infinite variety: other women cloy
> The appetites they feed, but she makes hungry
> Where most she satisfies.

And it is in speaking of her appearance at the first meeting with Antony that Shakespeare coined the great phrase, "It beggar'd all description."

Such was Cleopatra. Antony never broke the spell she cast over him, nor did he wish to. For her he repudiated his young wife, Octavia, sister of his partner in empire; and thereby made Octavian his mortal enemy. To satisfy Cleopatra's whim he caroused with her through the streets of Alexandria by night—they and their companions being known as the "Order of the Inimitable Livers." He went on a campaign against the Parthians, barbarians living near the Caspian Sea, and failed to win anything decisive. Having captured an Armenian king, Antony celebrated his triumph by having Cleopatra sit as a Roman magistrate and the captive king brought in chains before her. It was on this occasion that her Roman lover gave a great banquet for the people of Alexandria, at which Cleopatra and he occupied thrones of gold, lower ones being provided for the children she had borne him. He had Caesarion—Cleopatra's son by Julius Caesar—proclaimed King of Egypt and Cyprus to reign jointly with Cleopatra. He began to distribute kingdoms to his and Cleopatra's offspring.

These extravagances led to his downfall. He broke with Octavian; the Roman Senate deprived him of his powers and declared war against Cleopatra. In vain the virtuous Octavia tried to play the part of mediating angel between her errant husband and her brother. Octavian was adamant. He denounced Mark Antony as an enemy of the people and of the Republic, and swore not only to destroy him but to bring Cleopatra in chains to Rome.

While both sides were arming for the decisive conflict, the two lovers spent some twenty months of perfect bliss. One story is that during this time the Queen conceived a bold scheme to build a fleet of 500 vessels which could be dragged on rollers across the sands of the Isthmus of Suez to the Red Sea, whence she and Antony would sail to conquer India.

But the idyl could not last. Octavian had mustered his army and his fleet for the decisive battle, and Antony could not avoid going out to meet him. Antony was not in a hopeless position, for he was the stronger by land. But, yielding to Cleopatra's urging, he decided to place all of his fortunes on a sea battle in spite of the fact that his fleet was inferior. She contributed sixty ships, sailing personally in one in order to be present during the fighting.

The final engagement was fought at Actium, off the coast of Greece, on September 2 in the year 31 B.C. The issue was still in doubt when suddenly Cleopatra summoned her ships and fled. Seeing her go, Antony promptly left the battle to follow her. So victory went to Octavian, now sole master of the Roman world, and soon to become its first Emperor under the title of Augustus.

Antony and Cleopatra went back to Alexandria. They knew that they were lost, and spent the time remaining to them in a typical whirl of licentiousness. They disbanded the "Order of the Inimitable Livers," calling themselves instead the "Diers Together." Then Octavian arrived with his legions, and the end was at hand. Antony thought to retrieve the situation by challenging the Roman master to a personal duel, a challenge which the future Emperor was too shrewd to accept.

The final catastrophe for Antony came when he heard that Cleopatra had committed suicide. The report was false, but the truth arrived too late. He had fallen on his sword, inflicting a mortal wound. He then had himself carried into Cleopatra's presence where shortly afterward he died in her arms.

When the victorious Octavian appeared before Alexandria, Cleopatra, despite her thirty-nine years, again relied on her charm and her beauty, which in their time had subjugated Julius Caesar and Mark Antony. Octavian was thirty-three and his cold virtue was proof against her blandishments. He not only refused to discuss terms with her, but told her plainly that he intended to add Egypt to the Roman Empire and to take her to Rome where she would appear in chains at his triumph.

Cleopatra preferred suicide to humiliation. She managed to have smuggled to her an asp—the venomous adder of Egypt—in a basket of figs. She allowed the reptile to bite her bosom, and a few moments later the most dazzling of all queens lay a lifeless corpse, safe from the pride of her Roman conqueror.

AUGUSTUS

[63 B.C.–14 A.D.]

AUGUSTUS, the first Roman Emperor, was the adopted son and heir of Julius Caesar, his great-uncle. He was a grandson of Caesar's beautiful sister, Julia. Thus he grew up with the knowledge that his family stood at the center of shattering political events, and that he himself would one day be called to participate in such events. All of his education his fond, ambitious mother directed toward preparing him to fill the place destiny had allotted to him. He measured up to her hopes so well that history remembers him not under his given name of Gaius Octavius but under the exalted imperial title of Augustus.

When Caesar crossed the Rubicon, Octavius was fourteen. When the conqueror returned from his Egyptian expedition, his great-nephew was sixteen, mature enough to be introduced to the affairs of war and politics. Hence Octavius accompanied Caesar on his last Spanish campaign, and together they crossed to Carthage, and then returned to Rome.

Octavius was not quite twenty when, on the Ides of March 44 B.C., he received the news that Julius Caesar had been assassinated. Octavius reacted in a way that the world soon would recognize as typical of him. He went into mourning, but made no open attack on the assassins until he was quite sure of the situation. Carefully he gathered information about Brutus, Cassius, and the rest. He learned how Mark Antony had remained loyal to Caesar, and had inflamed the mob against the murderers.

What galvanized Octavius into action was the opening of Caesar's will. Caesar there recognized Octavius as his son, besides leaving him three fourths of his almost incalculable wealth. Octavius now became a legal member of Caesar's family, and took the name Gaius

Julius Caesar Octavianus—or, in English, Octavian. Acclaimed as Caesar's successor by the army, Octavian formed an alliance with Mark Antony. Some months of confused struggles followed, complications involving Octavian, Mark Antony, the Senate, and the assassins of Caesar, Brutus and Cassius.

The Senate, led by Cicero, was hostile to Antony, who joined with Lepidus, a prominent member of the Caesarian faction, in urging Octavian to resist the senatorial oligarchy. Octavian's power was on the rise and he gave proof of his political skill by forming the Second Triumvirate with Antony and Lepidus. A savage blood purge followed. The enemies of the Triumvirate were scattered, and Cicero was among the murdered, a victim of Antony's vengeance.

Brutus and Cassius had fled eastward, and were backed by a strong army. Octavian and Antony crossed over to challenge them, met the legions of the assassins of Caesar at Philippi in Macedonia, and inflicted upon them a crushing defeat in which Brutus and Cassius perished.

Octavian's friendship for Mark Antony was strengthened by the marriage of the wise and beautiful Octavia, his favorite sister, to Antony. But their good-fellowship was not to be of long duration. When Antony was appointed ruler of Asia and the East, Cleopatra, the Egyptian Queen, visited him at Tarsus, making a voyage of extraordinary splendor and magnificence up the Cydnus River. In her girlhood her charms had won Caesar. She was then twenty-eight and in the plenitude of her beauty, and won Mark Antony.

She gained such complete ascendancy over Antony that, in time, he divorced his wife, Octavia, the sister of Octavian. Caesar's heir remained in Rome, strengthening his position, while Antony indulged in splendor, military adventure, and romance in the East. When the inevitable war broke out, the victory went to Octavian, whose admiral destroyed the fleet of Antony and Cleopatra at Actium.

Octavian was now the undisputed master of the Roman world. He undertook great reforms in Rome and throughout the Empire. In everything he fostered the Roman tradition. He upheld the dignity of the Senate, removing unworthy Senators and replacing them by the most enlightened and public-spirited citizens he could find. He restored the temples of the gods and added many new ones. He procured laws to purify the degenerate morals of the times, which was his least successful reform. He revised the administration, especially the fiscal system, and gave much attention to the imperial highways, the historic network of Roman roads. In Rome he built a new Forum, and beautified the whole city. Late in his reign he was able to say with justice that he found Rome a city of brick and left it a city of marble.

He still considered himself merely a citizen, though the first citizen, of the Republic. He united in his own person numerous offices, including those of consul, tribune, and imperator, this last a military title from which we derive the word "emperor." Then he was made *princeps senatus*—hence our word "prince." The ultimate in the honors accorded him came with the title of Augustus, by which he was known thereafter. Following his death the Senate renamed one of the months in his memory, that month becoming Augustus; it remains August to this day.

In spite of all these tributes Augustus carefully avoided calling himself what he was—the master of Rome. He recalled that Julius Caesar had been assassinated because his enemies suspected that he intended to make himself King. So, although Augustus was in fact all-powerful, he kept up the fiction that he ruled in conjunction with the Senate. He was more interested in the realities than in the trappings of power, and cleverly disguising the fact that his authority was more than regal, he never raised up enemies to conspire against him as they had against Caesar.

Officially the new political arrangements constituted the restoration of the Roman Republic as it had existed before Caesar; actually they marked the beginning of a new system, the Roman Empire. The skill with which Augustus drew all the threads of authority into his hands without seeming to do so made him one of the master statesmen of history.

As Emperor he followed the plans of Caesar for strengthening the Roman Empire, but reversed Caesar's policy of expansion. Augustus decided against more conquests, and devoted himself to consolidation. To him the Roman Empire owed its defensive military principle of holding the frontiers of the Rhine and the Danube.

Augustus' generals were everywhere successful, with one notable exception. The great failure came in the German campaign. Gaul had already been conquered by Caesar, and now the plan was to carve out a Roman province on the other side of the Rhine. So to Germany Augustus dispatched the Consul Varus at the head of four legions. Varus proved to be an incompetent commander. He led his forces deep into the Teutoburg Forest, and there the Germans under Arminius surrounded and massacred them, and not even the Roman commander escaped.

This battle was one of the decisive conflicts of history. It caused Augustus to give up any further idea of Romanizing Germany, which remained independent, a land of barbarous wandering tribes, a permanent menace to the civilized world. Out of the Teutonic forests came the war bands which eventually overthrew the Roman Empire. The defeat of Varus kept Germany German, and much of European history since then has developed as a conflict between the Teuton and the Latin, the most familiar antagonism being that between Germany and France. A famous anecdote relates how the Emperor Augustus, upon hearing what had happened in the Teutoburg Forest, cried out, "Varus, give me back my legions!"

Augustus had great interest in and concern for his people, showing to them simplicity, charity, and benevolence. Once at the public games when the audience was seized with panic lest the theater should collapse, he tried to calm them with his voice and, failing, left the imperial loge to sit in the section that appeared most dangerous. He was devoted to his family, and at the death of his mother and that of his sister he went into extended mourning.

The age of Augustus, the Golden Age of Latin literature, was so closely identified with the reign of the first Emperor that it is also called the Augustan Age. For its literary model the period chose Cicero. The great orator gave prose writers their inspiration, and they carried his tradition to a height hardly equaled in the later literatures of Europe. Anyone who can write Ciceronian prose is a true master of his medium, for this is the ultimate test.

At the same time poetry was not lacking. Horace and Ovid belonged to the Augustan Age. But greatest of all was Virgil, the supreme poet of the Latin language, and one of the greatest that any literature can boast. In his *Aeneid* Virgil told the epic story of Aeneas, the Trojan hero who fled from Troy when the Greeks stormed the city, and wandered about until he came to Italy, where he founded the royal line from which the Julian family—that of Caesar and Augustus

—was descended. The *Aeneid* remains the finest example of dignified, cultivated, mature poetry. This is what Tennyson meant when he apostrophized Virgil as the "wielder of the stateliest measures ever moulded by the lips of man."

Augustus himself wrote beautiful Latin. We know this from his *Reply to Brutus* and his *Exhortations on Philosophy*. He wrote his own biography in thirteen volumes, which unfortunately were destroyed during the Dark Ages.

For forty years Augustus was master of the known world. He stands in history as the greatest of all the Roman Emperors. He appears all the more masterful by contrast with the four members of his family who followed him during the next fifty years—Tiberius, Caligula, Claudius, and Nero. This was the Julio-Claudian line of Emperors, beginning with the magnificent Augustus, and ending with the debased Nero. Perhaps the highest tribute to the statesmanship of Augustus is the fact that he laid the political foundations of the Empire so solidly that not even Nero could undermine them. The first Emperor was commemorated by hundreds of monuments after his death, but the finest was the one he himself had erected—the Roman Empire, which was to last for so many centuries, and which produced effects which are still felt in our own day.

JESUS

[4? B.C.–? 29 A.D.]

THE Christian Era takes its title from the most influential figure in all of history. Yet the odd fact is that we don't know the year in which Jesus Christ was born. It was certainly B.C. according to our calendar—probably 4 B.C. in the opinion of most experts.

The time is obscure, but the place is not. Palestine was a province of the Roman Empire, of the single Western realm created by Greco-Roman culture—Greek thought and Roman politics. The affairs of the universal empire provide the setting against which to view the beautiful and poignant stories told in the Gospels. Many of the personalities in the Bible appear in the secular literature of the period.

Thus Herod the Great. Everyone recognizes this man as the one responsible for the Massacre of the Innocents. Hearing that a baby destined to be King of the Jews had been born in Bethlehem, Herod commanded that all the city's children under two years of age be murdered for the protection of his throne. The Massacre of the Innocents failed of its purpose because an angel appeared to Joseph and said, "Arise and take the young child and his mother and flee into Egypt and be thou there until I send thee word: for Herod will seek the young child to destroy him."

Herod's son, Herod Antipas, can be identified from both sacred and secular writings. He ruled the northern part of Palestine, including Galilee. His importance to the story of Christianity is that he married Herodias, whose daughter Salome danced for him and then demanded the head of John the Baptist.

Jesus began life in the humblest surroundings. Joseph was a carpenter living with his wife in the Galilean village of Nazareth. But there was royal Jewish blood of the house of David in this family, and Jewish prophecy foretold that from the descendants of David

CHARLEMAGNE

THOMAS A BECKET

the Messiah would come. Hence the faith and joy with which Mary and Joseph received the revelation that the child born to Mary would be supernaturally conceived and "shall be called the Son of God."

The birth of Jesus, as told in the Gospels, forms one of the most touching idyls in all literature. Caesar Augustus had ordered a census of his Empire, and that included Palestine. In Jewish fashion, Joseph went to Bethlehem, the place of his family's origin, to register, taking Mary with him. Unable to find any other place to stay, they sought shelter in a stable. There Mary "brought forth her first born son, and she wrapped him in swaddling clothes and laid him in a manger, because there was no room for them in the inn." The image of the manger, with the Wise Men from the East guided to it by a star, has been conjured up by a multitude of writers and painters.

Following the birth of her son, Mary went through the usual Jewish purification rites. Joseph, unable to afford anything more, offered a pair of turtledoves in the Temple in Jerusalem. Shortly thereafter Herod ordered the Massacre of the Innocents, and Joseph took his family to Egypt, remaining there until the tyrant's death.

Jesus grew to maturity in Nazareth, where he worked in Joseph's carpenter shop. He received instruction at home and then from the priests in the synagogue. He learned Hebrew, the ancient and sacred language of the Jews, but in everyday life used the common tongue of the area, which was Aramaic. When he was twelve years old, visiting Jerusalem for the Passover, Joseph and Mary found him in the Temple "sitting in the midst of the teachers both hearing them and asking them questions and all that heard him were amazed at his understanding and his answers."

Jesus began his public ministry after meeting John the Baptist, who was baptizing in the Jordan and predicting the advent of one "the latchet of whose shoe I am not worthy to unloose." John hailed Jesus as the man he meant, after which Jesus allowed himself to be baptized. He then spent forty days in the wilderness, fasting and praying, during which time he was tempted by the Devil and emerged to warn men of the wiles of Satan.

It soon became known beyond his family that this carpenter from Nazareth had remarkable knowledge and could do wonderful things. He worked his first miracle at a marriage feast in Cana, Galilee, when he changed water into wine. His great spiritual message he put into the familiar phrases of the Sermon on the Mount. "Blessed are the poor in spirit for theirs is the kingdom of heaven." "Seek ye first the kingdom of God and his righteousness, and all the rest shall be added unto you." "Ye cannot serve God and Mammon."

He preached love and charity, insisting on the Golden Rule and the Brotherhood of Man, but he was not always gentle with sinners. When he attended one Passover in the Temple in Jerusalem, he found it full of money-changers. Dealers had set up their stalls, selling victims for the sacrifice, and exchanging Jewish coins for foreign money. Making a scourge of cords, Jesus drove them out, and overturned their tables, saying wrathfully, "Make not my Father's house a house of merchandise." With human weakness he was always charitable, but not with hypocrisy. He could forgive lust, anger, and envy, but not the covering of worldly ambition with religious pretense.

One of his greatest parables, that of the Pharisee and the publican, concerns this attitude. Both stood praying in the Temple. The Pharisee noted his faithful performance of Jewish ritual, thanking God he was different from other men. The publican "smote upon his breast, saying, God be merciful to me a sinner." Jesus commented on the parable with the words, "I tell you, this man went down to his house justified rather than the other; for everyone that exalteth himself shall be abased; and he that humbleth himself shall be exalted."

He attacked the Pharisees over and over again for pious humbugs, although his remarks seem aimed not at the entire sect but at those of its leaders who were obsessed with the notion of ritualism. He raised up bitter enemies among the priesthood in this way, and made them even more furious by declaring that all men are equal in the sight of God, a doctrine they rejected because of their belief that the Jews were the Chosen People, and loved by their Father beyond all others. They did not appreciate Jesus' parable of the Good Samaritan, for the Samaritans were despised and avoided by the Jews.

Jesus used figures of speech to drive home his points when teaching and preaching. The very names of some of his parables have become common coin: The Good Samaritan, The Prodigal Son, The Wise and Foolish Virgins, The Laborers in the Vineyard, The Widow's Mite.

Besides words, Jesus taught by working miracles. The Gospels tell of his healing many ailments—leprosy, blindness, paralysis, hysteria.

He walked on the surface of the Dead Sea, calmed the elements, and fed a multitude with five loaves of bread and two fish. Most astounding of all, he raised the dead. Told that Lazarus had been buried for four days, Jesus had the grave opened. He cried, "Lazarus, come forth!" Thereupon "he that was dead came forth, bound head and foot with grave-clothes; and his face was bound about with a napkin. Jesus saith unto them: Loose him and let him go."

It is significant that not even Jesus' worst enemies denied that he worked miracles. When he cured a blind and dumb man by casting out a devil, the Pharisees did not question the fact. Their argument against Jesus was, "This fellow doth not cast out devils, but by Beelzebub the prince of devils." To which Jesus responded, "And if Satan cast out Satan, he is divided against himself; how shall then his kingdom stand?"

By now his enemies were ready to destroy him if they could. They tried to trap him with questions about the Law and the Prophets. Asked about the greatest commandment, he replied, "Thou shalt love the Lord thy God with all thy heart, with all thy soul, and all thy mind. This is the first and great commandment. And the second is like unto it, Thou shalt love thy neighbour as thyself. On these two commandments hang all the law and the prophets."

They tried to catch him on the subject of legitimate political authority, and provoked the familiar words, "Render unto Caesar the things that are Caesar's, and unto God the things that are God's."

Some of his acts of mercy and understanding only brought him obloquy from his opponents. This was true of his attitude toward the woman taken in adultery, of whom he said, "He that is without sin among you, let him first cast a stone at her." They claimed he was sanctioning adultery, forgetting that to the woman herself he had said, "Go thy way, and henceforth sin no more."

Of his followers the most important were the Twelve Apostles, the lowly men to whom he would bequeath the task of carrying on his mission. These men, led by St. Peter, gradually came to see in their master the Messiah for whom the Jewish people had been waiting. At first they thought he would become King of the Jews in the ordinary sense of the phrase, and would make them dominant among the peoples of the world. Only by degrees did they come to see that his mission implied much more than this. He would break the mold of sectarian exclusiveness and permit the divine revelation to go out to all mankind.

By what right would he do this? That is the essential question about his ministry. The answer is that he made the astounding claim that he was God: "I and my Father are one." From this line followed the dogma of the Trinity, later defined and formulated by the Christian Church, the argument being that Jesus was the Second Person of the Holy and Undivided Trinity. His claim to divinity was the basic reason why his enemies rejected him. They stoned him "because that thou, being a man, makest thyself God."

Perhaps they would have been willing to let Jesus go his way if he had been without effect on others. But his teaching aroused enormous enthusiasm among the Jews. The high priest, Caiaphas, and the members of the Sanhedrin were afraid that Judaism itself was imperiled by the new doctrine. They did not believe Jesus when he said that he had come not to destroy the Mosaic Law but to fulfill it. Caiaphas stated their argument: "It is expedient for us that one man should die for the people, and that the whole nation perish not."

From this moment on the Gospels describe a darkening tragedy leading to the Crucifixion. The last week in the life of Jesus, Holy Week, is recalled to us each year at Eastertime. The events of those seven days have been enshrined in great art such as Leonardo da Vinci's painting of the Last Supper. This is the week of the Agony in the Garden—and the betrayal of Judas, who, for thirty pieces of silver, led the forces of the Sanhedrin to Jesus. History's arch-traitor told them to seize the man whom he should kiss: "And forthwith he came to Jesus and said: Hail, Master! and kissed him. But Jesus said unto him: Judas, betrayest thou the Son of Man with a kiss?"

Dragged before the high priest, Jesus declared that he was indeed the Messiah looked for by the Jewish people. At this they accused him of blasphemy, and sent him for judgment and punishment to the Roman procurator of Judaea, Pontius Pilate.

Pilate interrogated Jesus, but could not decide the case. The Roman official saw no blasphemy in the prisoner's assertion, "Everyone that is of the truth heareth my voice." Pilate retorted cynically, "What is truth?"—and would have let him go. The crowd demanded a conviction, which Pilate sought to avoid himself by sending Jesus to Herod Antipas in Galilee. Herod, however, would not take the responsibility either, and had him returned to the procurator.

Still unwilling to impose a death sentence, Pilate appealed to a custom of the time of the Passover, which was to release some condemned criminal. He ruled that the crowd might choose between Jesus and a robber named Barabbas. Sure that they would prefer Jesus, Pilate must have been astounded when they shouted furiously, "Not this man but Barabbas!"

That decided the issue. Jesus was mocked, scourged, and crowned with a wreath of thorns. Pilate, disturbed by the noble bearing of the accused, washed his hands, remarking, "I am innocent of the blood of this just man." Jesus, now abandoned to the crowd and the soldiery, was forced to carry his cross up the hill of Calvary, where the Crucifixion took place. At no time did he offer any resistance. His own verdict on his persecutors was, "Forgive them, Father, for they know not what they do." His last words were, "Father, into thy hands I commend my spirit."

The enemies of Jesus were exultant, his followers demoralized, by his death on the cross. Joseph of Arimathea claimed the body and gave it a formal burial. The chief priests, remembering their victim's claim that he would rise from the dead, "made the sepulchre sure, sealing the stone, and setting a watch."

As soon as the sabbath was over, a group of women sorrowfully approached the tomb. They found it empty, with the stone at the entrance rolled back. "And the angel answered and said unto the women, Fear not ye: for I know that ye seek Jesus, which was crucified. He is not here: for he is risen, as he said."

Every year Easter Sunday commemorates this greatest of miracles recounted in the Gospels—the Resurrection. Its meaning for humanity St. Paul expressed in his famous questions, "O death, where is thy sting? O grave, where is thy victory?"

Jesus appeared to his disciples shortly thereafter, lived with them and instructed them for forty days, and then vanished as they listened to his last words. Strengthened to the task by this experience, they immediately took up the burden of spreading Christianity according to his command, "Go ye therefore and teach all nations, baptizing them in the name of the Father and of the Son and of the Holy Ghost."

The missionary work they began has never ceased. It is faithfully carried on today, two thousand years later, by the churches of Christ.

ST. PAUL

[*d.* ?65 A.D.]

THE Apostle to the Gentiles: that title sums up the work wrought by Saul of Tarsus, who became St. Paul. Intensely Jewish, intensely Christian, St. Paul made it his mission to carry to the non-Jewish world the Jewish message of redemption and salvation as taught by Jesus Christ. Clarifying the Christian revelation, systematizing its theology, the Apostle to the Gentiles enlarged a Palestinian creed into a religion applicable to all mankind.

We know that he was educated as a pious Jew, but was also influenced by international Hellenic culture and by the universality of imperial Rome. These three factors are basic.

The Jewish element takes precedence at the start. Saul of Tarsus went to Jerusalem to complete his education. He sat at the feet of Gamaliel, a celebrated Pharisee, who taught him Hebrew orthodoxy and nationalism, both of which the Pharisees championed zealously (hence their persecution of Jesus for minimizing the two props of Jewish particularism). Gamaliel himself was a moderate man, yet his tenets were such that from his tutelage Saul of Tarsus emerged a Jewish extremist.

As such he developed a burning hatred of the Christians who held that the old Mosaic dispensation had been fulfilled in its essentials, superseded in its accidentals, by the life and doctrine of Christ. The claim enraged the pupil of the Pharisees. He took a leading part in persecuting the Christians. He was present at the stoning of Stephen, and guarded the garments of those who carried out the execution of the first Christian martyr. His determination to crush the followers of Jesus became so fanatical, his persecuting zeal so great, that he received a commission to seek and punish Christians outside of Jerusalem. Thus it was that he started for Damascus.

The transition from Saul the Persecutor to Paul the Apostle is one of the most famous incidents in the history of Christianity. In all literature there is nothing more vivid than this passage in the Acts of the Apostles:

"And as he journeyed, he came near Damascus: and suddenly there shined round and about him a light from heaven:

And he fell to the earth, and heard a voice saying unto him, Saul, Saul, why persecutest thou me?

And he said, Who art thou, Lord? And the Lord said, I am Jesus whom thou persecutest."

The familiar story goes on to tell how Paul asked what he should do, and Jesus told him to go on to Damascus and there be instructed. But Paul now was sightless, the vision having blinded his eyes, and he had to be led by companions into Damascus, where for three days he remained in darkness. Then the Lord appeared to a Christian disciple in Damascus, and told him to go to Paul, but the disciple was afraid of the arch-persecutor, who was known to have been sent to oppress the Christians of Damascus. The Lord assured him that Paul had experienced a change of heart, and the disciple went, and laid hands on him. Whereupon Paul regained his sight, and was filled with the Holy Ghost, and was baptized.

The Jews in Damascus were astounded. They knew that Saul of Tarsus had been sent to harass the followers of Jesus. Yet he used the Romanized form of Paul and appeared in the synagogues, preaching the doctrine of Jesus, and announcing that He was the Son of God. Christianized Jews accepted the transformation as a miracle. Orthodox zealots gnashed their teeth and planned to kill him. But friends smuggled him out of Damascus, lowering him from the city wall in a basket.

There was an equal surprise at Jerusalem when Paul appeared again. Instead of bringing disciples of Jesus in bonds, for trial and punishment, he came back preaching Jesus' gospel. His erstwhile fellow-persecutors were taken aback, but their amazement was exceeded by that of the little sect of Christians—who were afraid. When their former arch-enemy came to them as a Christian, they refused to believe him. They suspected it was a ruse to trap them. But one of them, named Barnabas, believed Paul, and took him to the Apostles.

The Apostles were convinced. The onetime persecutor was accepted as a member of the Christian community, and preached the Gospel.

Now the personality of Paul began to broaden in scope. Without ceasing to be a Jew, he showed the impress of Greek and Roman ideas. He became the greatest of all theologians by employing Greek reason to elucidate the Christian revelation. He became the greatest of all missionaries by accepting Roman universality as an ideal, by seeking to extend Christian brotherhood as widely as Roman citizenship. His energy matched his aspirations. For thirty years Paul was on the road, journeying in Palestine, Syria, Asia Minor, Thrace, Greece, the islands of the Mediterranean. Everywhere he founded churches.

But his leadership did not go unchallenged among the Christians. Many felt that they were just another sect of Jews, and shrank from Gentiles who were uncircumcized and did not follow the Jewish dietary laws. Paul saw the faith of Christ as one for all mankind. This followed from the universality of his mind and from his experience with Jews rejecting Jesus while Gentiles accepted him. The decision lay with Peter, chief of the Apostles, and he it was who, inspired by a vision, decreed that, to be a Christian, a man need not be circumcized or observe the Jewish dietary laws. Paul had won in a decision momentous for the future history of Christianity.

There followed the wonderful missionary journey of Paul and Silas. One place they visited was Athens, in which revered center of Greek culture the Apostle to the Gentiles encountered philosophers, Epicurians and Stoics. They questioned him, and he preached to them a famous sermon, saying, "Ye men of Athens, I perceive that in all things ye are too superstitious. For as I passed by, and beheld your devotions, I found an altar with this inscription—To the Unknown God. Whom therefore ye ignorantly worship, Him declare I unto you." But the philosophers ridiculed the doctrine of the resurrection of the dead, and Paul's stay in Athens seems not to have been too successful, though he made some converts among the Jews.

During this trip he became convinced more than ever that Christianity must become a universal religion. For while the Greek philosophers mocked and some Jews were converted, in general the Jews proved hostile, and the Gentiles receptive, to the new doctrine. Usually he would seek out the Jews of a place first, only to be driven away from the synagogue after they heard what he had to say. That would leave him with no one to preach to except the Gentiles.

His third mission took him again on long travels through Asia Minor, which included a memorable stop at Ephesus. In Ephesus one of the most flourishing of crafts was the manufacture of images of the goddess Diana, and the attitude of the practitioners of that trade toward Paul's preaching against idolatry is not hard to guess. A silversmith summoned his fellows and told of the injury the Apostle was doing to their goddess and their profession. Inflamed by superstition and greed, they surged through the streets, shouting, "Great is Diana of the Ephesians!"

At the end of this missionary journey Paul returned to Jerusalem. He had been warned against it because of the fury of the anti-Christian zealots. But he resolved to go. He still considered himself a good Jew. Hence he would make the customary pious observances at the Temple.

As predicted, his appearance provoked a tumult among the zealots. A Roman centurion had Paul seized and was about to scourge him when the prisoner remarked that he was a Roman citizen, therefore immune from such punishment. To get the problem off his hands, and knowing that a band of fanatics had sworn not to eat until they had killed the Apostle to the Gentiles, the Roman centurion sent him under guard to the proconsul at Caesarea. The high priest had sent a request that Paul be returned to Jerusalem for trial, but Paul, as was the prerogative of a Roman citizen, appealed to Caesar. Under the law, to Rome he must go for his hearing.

In Rome, Paul waited for his appeal to Caesar to be heard. He was treated well, living in his own dwelling with a soldier to guard him, and was granted liberty to preach. According to his custom, he brought the Gospel to the Jewish community first, was not received favorably, and turned to the Gentiles. This continued for two years, at which point the *Acts of the Apostles* ends its story.

Later information derives from the Epistles of St. Paul and from ancient tradition. At the end of two years, his appeal to Caesar came to favorable issue and he was liberated. Once again the Apostle went on his travels, visiting churches he had established, founding new ones, renewing former acquaintance with the faithful, preaching and making converts.

The final word we have about the Apostle in the New Testament is in the Second Letter to Timothy. The indication is that he was again a prisoner in Rome, but this time held not under house arrest but in chains like a criminal. There is no definite knowledge of his death. Early Christian writers, however, handed down the tradition that St. Paul, like St. Peter, was murdered in Rome during Nero's ferocious persecution of the Christians.

During the years of his travels and during his imprisonments St. Paul wrote his Epistles, the finest letters in world literature. He employed the vigorous colloquial Greek of the period, and displayed magnificent literary power and intellectual vigor. The Epistles of St. Paul were among the most powerful influences in the beginning of the Universal Christian Church, the cardinal labor of the Apostle to the Gentiles.

NERO

[37–68]

NERO's name has come down through history and legend with a brand of infamy. He stands as the murderous tyrant who, people declared, set fire to Rome and sang while the imperial city burned, and then persecuted the Christians savagely, placing the blame for the fire on them. The odious picture of Nero derives from conservative Roman historians, admirers of the old Roman Republic and hostile to the despotism of the Caesar. Their account of his villainies is perhaps exaggerated, but without doubt Nero was a bloodstained eccentric, unbalanced, possibly insane.

Nero was raised in the strict Augustan manner as a gentleman of the old school. He was a plumpish sort of lad, rather shortsighted, with blue eyes and bronze hair. Even as a child he delighted in drawing and painting, was clever at molding little clay figures, and had a sweet tenor voice. He also began to write quite acceptable Latin verse and would often recite to himself, plucking at the strings of a small harp.

Nero was just seventeen when he became Emperor, a heavy-set youth of medium height with an animated and good-natured face, covered with freckles. The first few years of his reign were excellent. He showed himself anxious for the public welfare and was careful to avoid doing harm or injustice to anyone. Under the guidance of the philosophers Seneca and Burrus, he justified his good reputation.

But Nero had another side to his character. He formed a close friendship with leaders of the Roman fast set. Prominent among these were Salvius Otho, who later for three short months was Emperor; Ofonius Tigellinus; and Petronius Arbiter, the famed "Arbiter of Elegance," who was the acknowledged authority on a way of life that cultivated all the pleasures of a pagan world. Under their influence,

Nero quickly lost all faith in whatever Roman gods there were, and indulged in the maddest pranks. The three friends would disguise themselves and roam the streets at night molesting any good-looking woman they met. Once the husband of one of their victims appeared on the scene and thrashed Nero so thoroughly that it was some days before the Emperor could hold audiences. He had two black eyes.

Nero's first atrocious crime was the murder of his mother, Agrippina, who had smoothed his path to the royal purple by assassinating the claimants who stood in front of him. She made the mistake of trying to control him after he became Emperor, and he decided to get rid of her. An attempt to drown Agrippina by sinking her galley failed because the vessel merely capsized, thus allowing her to cling to it until help arrived. Nero may have been afraid that she had guessed the truth and would revenge herself on him. He sent a band of ruffians to stab her to death. When news that the deed was done reached him, he burst into tears.

After killing his mother, Nero found dealing with his wife easy enough. He charged her with complicity in a plot to revolt, after which he had her executed. Then he married one of his mistresses.

Nero was proud of his singing, acting, painting, chariot-driving—nor was he without talent in any of these arts. He entered public competitions and always won first prize since the judges deemed it wise to humor the imperial performer. His craving for adulation quickly became excessive and then pathological.

In 64 A.D. fire broke out in the poorer section of Rome where most of the ramshackle buildings were of wood. It burned fiercely for over a week. We know that Nero did not set the blaze, but it seems to be true that he picked up his harp and began to chant a dirge. Thus it is a fact that Nero sang while Rome burned.

Nero blamed the fire on the Christians, and instigated a ferocious persecution of the new sect. Christians were hunted down and savagely executed, burned alive as a public spectacle. This was the first of the persecutions, and in it St. Peter and St. Paul are said to have perished.

In 65 a widespread conspiracy was discovered, involving some of the most prominent personalities in Rome. Nero was terrified, and began a reign of terror. Among the conspirators who died was the poet Lucan. Nero's old tutor, the philosopher Seneca, was forced to commit suicide. Nero was now in full career as the suspicious, bloodthirsty tyrant. To excite dislike or misgiving in the Emperor was as good as a death warrant. Nero killed his second wife by kicking her to death.

He went on a triumphal tour of Greece, displaying his poetic talents in the land of classic glory. He entered public competitions, and the supple Greeks knew how to lavish flattery with the prizes. This for Nero was the high point of his imperial career, but he returned to Rome with the warning that trouble was brewing.

The legions in Gaul, Spain, and Africa revolted. Nero's general, sent to put down the uprising, joined it instead. Then the Emperor's personal troops, the famed Praetorian Guard, went over to his enemies. Nero fled, was pursued, and committed suicide. As he lay dying he cried out, "What an artist the world loses in me!" Actually the world had lost the man who stands in history as the prototype of the hideous tyrant—Nero.

TRAJAN

[53–117]

HE Roman Emperor Nerva did one important thing during his otherwise unimportant reign. He adopted a son and successor, and selected the most formidable soldier commanding the most powerful army in the Empire. He named as his colleague and heir the military leader who headed the legions along the Rhine, veteran legions hardened in battle against the German barbarians. The immediate sagacity of this stroke of policy was apparent indeed. Few, even among the arrogant Praetorian Guard, would venture to oppose an Emperor backed by such an adopted son and successor as Marcus Ulpius Trajanus, known to history in English as Trajan.

History gives us an impressive sketch of Trajan's personality. He was tall and had an iron constitution, and was noted for courage and rugged endurance in war. In manner he had the grave dignity considered proper to the Roman. His character was Spartan, with little inclination toward luxurious pleasure. The company he liked was that of his military comrades in arms. He was earnest in devotion to the ancient Roman gods. In an era of dissolute morals, he was conspicuous for family virtue. He married a woman of high moral character to whom he remained faithful all his life.

After his elevation as heir to the Empire, Trajan remained at his post on the Rhine, but the time of waiting was not long. Within three months the aged Nerva died, and Trajan at the city of Cologne assumed the imperial purple. He was the first Roman Emperor to be born outside of Italy. His accession was hailed. No one ventured to dispute the sovereignty of the commander of the legions on the Rhine.

His military character is illustrated by the fact that he did not go at once to Rome to assume his authority in the Imperial City. Instead he made an inspection tour of the frontiers, the Rhine and the Danube, which were ever in danger from the barbarians beyond. The tour lasted for two years, after which he made his entrance into Rome.

He did it unostentatiously, entering on foot. He followed the usual custom of presenting gifts to soldiers and citizens, but refrained from showy display, which he disliked. Members of the imperial court were reduced in number, and a regime of economy put into effect. Old Roman laws were revived in the interest of public order and decency, though Trajan, like other Emperors, found it impossible to arrest by laws the progress of degeneration in a wealthy society. The Praetorian Guards were curbed. They would have liked nothing better than to break out into violence, but were intimidated by the veteran commander of legions.

Trajan's works of peace were impressive. In Rome he was a great builder, providing edifices, libraries, bridges. He set up a fund for the rearing of destitute orphaned children in Italy. He devoted great effort to the reconstruction of the army, improving the morale and discipline of the legions.

One of his great friends was Pliny the Younger, whom he named to official position in Asia, and with whom he corresponded in notable letters. To these epistles we owe some of the earliest information about the Christians, who were becoming numerous. Trajan opposed them as enemies of the ancient gods, but advised leniency toward them as long as they did not disturb the peace.

Trajan was the last of the great Roman conquerors, and brought about the final expansion of the Empire, extending its boundaries to their farthest limit. Augustus had set a terminus to the march of the legions, which had encompassed so much of the then known world. He had established a policy of consolidation, and placed the frontiers of the Empire on the Rhine and the Danube in the west, natural lines of defense, with a more ambiguous border facing Parthia in the east. Since then there had been some extension of territory, such as the conquest of Britain. But the new acquisition had been, for the most part, a rounding out of the Augustan frontiers. Trajan, however, embarked on great campaigns north of the Danube and in the East.

In what is now Romania was a realm of warlike barbarians, the kingdom of Dacia. The Dacians even exacted tribute from the Romans. Trajan decided to end the tribute, and embarked on his Dacian War, the outcome of which was the complete subjugation of the barbarians. Today the monument to the Dacian victory can still be seen in Rome—the great Column of Trajan, with its bas-relief sculpture depicting the campaign. Dacia became so thoroughly Romanized as to be called Romania, its people speaking a language descended from Latin.

Eight years of peace followed, and then the Parthian Wars began. The kingdom of Parthia, in what is now Mesopotamia, had inflicted a notable disaster upon the Roman legions by defeating and killing Crassus. Later the Roman power prevailed, but in Trajan's reign the Parthians rebelled. The Emperor at once invaded Armenia, turning it into a Roman province. In a second campaign he made a Roman province of Parthian territory along the river Tigris. Then he turned upon the Parthian capital, Ctesiphon, and captured it. Trajan marched down the Tigris to the Persian Gulf, and there stood on the shore gazing out upon the sea that led to India. He exclaimed, "If only I were younger!" What he had in mind was the memory of Alexander, who had marched to conquests in fabulous India.

He installed a Parthian king over the remnants of Parthia. Starting back for Rome, now feeling the pressure of the barbarians along the imperial frontiers from Britain to Africa, Trajan died en route. He ranks as one of the greatest of the Roman Emperors, and as the last of the mighty Roman conquerors.

CONSTANTINE

[280?–337]

T HE great historic fame of Constantine lies in the fact that he was the first Christian Roman Emperor, the man who established Christianity as the religion of the Roman Empire. The story of his life is interwoven with the complexities and confusions of the Roman imperial system, also with those of the growing Church.

The Emperor Diocletian, who re-established a strongly organized government, after a long period of turmoil, thought the Roman Empire too large to be administered by one man. He therefore appointed a second emperor, Maximian, to reign jointly with him, both having the supreme title of Augustus. He created, likewise, two subordinate emperors, each with the title of Caesar. Thus, with two Augusti and two Caesars, the Roman Empire now had in effect four rulers, each administering some one section of its realm.

The arrangement promised to promote efficiency, but in the end it resulted in a series of dreary struggles between the emperors and subemperors, the Augusti and the Caesars. They intrigued, plotted, and fought wars, overthrowing each other and naming successors, usurping the imperial rank, and promoting or opposing the usurpation of others. Names flashed and vanished in bewildering complexity.

Prominent among these names is that of Constantius Chlorus, an able military commander, a native of Illyria, in the modern Balkans. Under the scheme of Diocletian, he was made one of the Caesars, and was given the administration of Gaul and Britain. He was the father of Constantine the Great.

Constantine was born about 280 A.D. at Naissus in Upper Moesia, now Yugoslavia. His mother was Helena, described as the daughter of an innkeeper, a woman of great beauty and saintly virtue. She was a Christian, later to be canonized by the Church as a saint and

legended as the discoverer of the Sepulcher of the Savior. Helena in-
stilled in her son an inclination toward Christianity which became a
dominant theme in his career.

Constantine was a boy when his father, Constantius, received the
title of Caesar and gained a share in the imperial sovereignty. Constantius, adopted by Maximian who ruled with Diocletian, divorced
Helena, Constantine's mother, and married Maximian's daughter.
Helena remained on terms of lifelong affection with her son, and he
in turn raised his Christian mother to the highest honor.

This was an element in the greatest phenomenon of those centuries, the rise of Christianity. In spite of repeated persecution the
once obscure sect had spread throughout the Roman Empire. Diocletian determined to extirpate what he considered a subversive cult.
He launched a ferocious persecution, and the Christians endured
their culminating ordeal. Meanwhile, the young Constantine, reared
to Christian sympathies by his mother, was placed in gilded captivity.

When his father, as Caesar, went to assume the administration of
Gaul and Britain, young Constantine was left at the court of Diocletian, ostensibly to be trained in imperial duties, but actually as a
hostage for his father's good behavior. It is related that Diocletian
thought well of the youth, and that Constantine accompanied the
Emperor on a military campaign in Egypt. But otherwise little is
known of his early years.

Eusebius, Bishop of Caesarea, who wrote the life of Constantine,
provides the earliest description we have of him. At about twenty he
was tall and handsome, of graceful carriage and commanding presence. He impressed everyone by his tremendous strength. His powers
of mind and ample education are stressed by his biographer.

Diocletian abdicated, and went into retirement. His place was
taken by Galerius, the first of the many shifts in the divided administration of the Empire. Constantius, attending these events, asked to
have his son with him. Galerius reluctantly gave his consent. Constantius had to hurry to Britain to deal with a threatened invasion of
the Picts of Scotland. His son followed and caught up with him at
Boulogne. Together they crossed the Channel, landed at Dover, and
hurried north. They won a brilliant victory over the Picts.

Under Constantius, Britain was happier and more prosperous than
any other province of the Roman Empire. He refrained from perse-

cuting the Christians, and established a wise, mild administration. He was immensely popular, and his legions were devoted to him. With the applause of people and soldiers he was proclaimed Emperor of the West at York, but died the following year, after a solemn ceremony at which Constantine was named his successor.

These events were bound up with the intricacies of the imperial system, as Constantine now claimed to be an Augustus instead of a mere Caesar. There were disputes for seven years, during which he ruled Britain with conspicuous success, much to the benefit of that Roman province. Constantine granted full toleration to the Christians, as befitted the son of St. Helena.

There was another shift of politics, and Licinius became Emperor of the East. Constantine was acknowledged as Emperor of the West.

He married Fausta, daughter of Maximian. His new father-in-law was the onetime partner of Diocletian as Emperor. Maximian had retired from power with Diocletian but could not stay retired. He now appeared on the scene as a gross, intriguing troublemaker.

Maximian had a son, Maxentius, who seized power in Rome. The once imperial city was now neglected, the seat of the rulers being transferred elsewhere, to Asia Minor, to the Balkans, to Milan, to Britain—wherever trouble threatened around the frontiers of the Empire. The Roman populace, discontented by the perpetual absence of their Emperors, welcomed Maxentius and enabled him to hold power in the city. Maximian supported his son in this bid for power. But even so the two soon came to a disagreement, Maxentius accusing his father of causing trouble for him. Driven out by his son's soldiers, Maximian was forced to seek refuge with his son-in-law, Constantine, and to plead for clemency.

He was received with hospitality; but, still the troublemaker of old, he requited Constantine's generosity by trying to overthrow him and seize power. This attempt was unsuccessful, but Constantine forgave him. Even so signal an act of mercy could not change Maximian. He tried to persuade his daughter, Fausta, to join a plot against her husband's life, a suggestion that she promptly reported to Constantine. Maximian had gone too far. The sources differ on how he met his end, one telling us that he committed suicide, another that he was found with a broken neck, the cause being unknown. At any rate the archtroublemaker had come to the end of the road.

Constantine now marched against Maxentius in Rome. The campaign culminated in the Battle of the Milvian Bridge, 312 A.D. At a critical moment in the conflict at the bridge leading to Rome, Constantine is said to have seen a cross in the sky with the words, *"In Hoc Signo Vincis"*—"By this sign thou shalt conquer." Maxentius was defeated and killed, and tradition holds the operation at the Milvian Bridge to be the turning point in the triumph of Christianity.

The victory, which made Constantine the undisputed master of the West, was followed by the Edict of Milan in 313, which guaranteed religious liberty to the Christians throughout the Roman Empire. It was signed jointly by Constantine and Licinius, who was still the ruler of the East.

The imperial picture, after kaleidoscopic changes, was now simplified so that there were only two rulers. In 314, Licinius attacked Constantine, making a bid for the mastery of the entire Empire, but was defeated. For the next nine years peace reigned, and Constantine devoted himself to reforming the administration, correcting abuses, strengthening his frontiers, and holding the barbarians at bay. During this period he built the Arch of Constantine in Rome. In 323, Licinius made another bid for supreme power and without warning launched an attack. He was repulsed, and Constantine pursued him to Adrianople where he won a decisive victory. Licinius surrendered and was executed. From then on to his death in 337 Constantine the Great was sole master of the Roman world. The remainder of his reign was largely peaceful.

The Empress Fausta, by whom Constantine had three sons, became jealous of Crispus, the Emperor's eldest and illegitimate son of whom he was extremely fond. She persuaded Constantine that Crispus was plotting against him, and brought so much false evidence to bear that the Emperor authorized the execution of his son. After this sentence was carried out, Constantine entered on a period of depression and deep remorse, during which he had Fausta's charges investigated. He became convinced that Crispus was innocent. Fausta was condemned, and was smothered in her bath.

More and more Constantine became devoted to Christianity, and many of the legal reforms he introduced throughout the Roman Empire show the Christian influence. He never made any attempt to persecute the pagan worship of old, but exerted himself to strengthen the Christian Church. He was interested in church administration and in theology, seeking to promote conformity and uniformity of belief. In 325 he convened a great council of the whole Church at Nicaea, a city of Asia Minor, the site of which lies today within Turkey.

About three hundred bishops, and many other leaders of both church and state, attended the council. The great problem laid before them was theological, the mystery of the Incarnation, how to understand the two natures of Christ, the divine on the one hand and the human on the other. This problem had produced the Arian heresy, which took its name from its author, Arius, who held that Christ the Man was not truly God but an inferior creation of God. Arianism at once produced serious disputes among the theologians since it denied one of the fundamental articles of faith. It was to still these disputes that Constantine called the Council of Nicaea. After listening to all sides of the question, the members agreed to state as dogma that Christ was truly God because he was of the same substance as God the Father. The formulation of the dogma is known as the Nicene Creed, and it marks an epoch in the development of Christian doctrine. Arius was of course condemned, but nevertheless his heresy remained strong among certain peoples, particularly among some of the German tribes which later burst into the Empire. One reason for the triumph of Clovis in Gaul was that he was a Catholic fighting against Arians, and therefore had the backing of the Church.

Next to his part in the establishment of Christianity, Constantine's most enduring accomplishment was the creation of Constantinople, capital of the Eastern Empire. Rome, situated in central Italy, had little strategic relevance for the vast sprawling Empire, and for a long time the Emperors had set up their courts at places of better military location. Constantine had a further reason for moving. He wanted his capital to be a Christian city, a thing impossible at Rome which was traditionally pagan and hostile to the new religion. He fixed his eye on the straits between Europe and Asia, where there was an ancient Greek city, Byzantium. There he resolved to establish a mighty capital named after himself. His judgment was so excellent that Constantinople remained a citadel of imperial power for centuries, the Eastern Empire standing for nearly a thousand years after the Western Empire had fallen; and the metropolis on the straits, now called Istanbul, is still one of the greatest centers of strategic importance in the world, guardian of the route through the Dardanelles and the Bosporus into the Black Sea. Periodically the Russians start an international crisis by attempting to snatch the Dardanelles from Turkey.

When Constantine began the construction of the city, which was to be unique in the world, he pushed forward the work with every resource at his command. In 330 Constantinople was officially inaugurated and dedicated to the Blessed Virgin. Its specifically Christian character made the new capital distinctive, but nevertheless it was an imitation of Rome in many ways. It had its own Senate, its Forum, its "bread and circuses." In fact, Constantinople was also known as New Rome to indicate that, as far as the Empire was concerned, it was picking up where Old Rome had left off. In this it was successful, later Emperors living there and beautifying the city until it became one of the most splendid in the world.

The foundation of Constantinople strengthened the Empire in the East, but it had a bad effect on the West. The whole imperial structure was now permanently divided, and the part headed by Rome, gravely weakened and with lowered prestige, was left to fend for itself. As time passed the city on the Bosporus rose in power, and the city on the Tiber sank, one reason being that frequently barbarian invaders, foiled by the fortifications of Constantinople, moved up through the Balkans to strike into the provinces of the Western Empire. This happened in the case of Alaric the Visigoth, who took Rome itself in 410.

During the rest of his life Constantine remained sole master of the Roman world, but for administrative purposes he divided it among three sons and two nephews, a move which worked all right in his own time, only to cause a later fight for power in which most of his family was massacred. When the smoke cleared, Julian was Emperor —Julian the Apostate, who made a vigorous, although vain, attempt to undo Constantine's religious policy by uprooting Christianity. The religion of Constantine proved too strong for Julian.

Oddly the champion of the Christian faith waited until he lay on his deathbed before he would consent to be baptized. He died shortly afterward, whereupon his body, in a casket of gold, was taken to Constantinople and buried in the Church of Peace, now the Church of the Apostles.

ALARIC

[370?–410]

ELEVEN HUNDRED and sixty-three years after the foundation of Rome, the Imperial City, which had subdued and civilized so considerable a part of mankind, was delivered to the licentious fury of the tribes of Germany and Scythia."

With these memorable words Edward Gibbon, greatest of English historians, mourns the moment of the year 410 when Alaric the Visigoth carved his place in history with fire and sword. The Roman Empire lingered on for another sixty-six years, but it was never the same after the barbarians of the north penetrated the defenses of the Eternal City under the command of Alaric.

The Romans were not without warning that catastrophe was coming their way. For centuries the barbarians had been pressing against the northern frontiers along the Danube—Goths, Vandals, Lombards, Franks. Behind, pushing them west, were the hordes of central Asia, especially the Huns. Roman legions stood on guard along the perimeter, trying to contain this threat to the civilized world.

In the last quarter of the fourth century A.D. the Goths held what is now Hungary and Rumania. Allied with the Roman Empire, they acquired some tinge of culture blended with the persistent warlike hardihood of the barbarians. Suddenly they were assailed by the Huns, who overwhelmed the Gothic armies. The eastern Goths or Ostrogoths submitted and remained where they were as vassals of the Huns. The western Goths or Visigoths fled across the Danube into Roman territory.

The Romans allowed them to stay as refugees, but soon disputes between the two peoples began, war broke out, and the Visigoths defeated the Romans in the decisive Battle of Adrianople. When peace was made, the Visigoths received land in the Balkans, where they were settled when the greatest of the Visigoths appeared.

Alaric came of an ancient noble family, members of which had often been raised to the kingship of the Visigoths. The practice of the Romans at that time was to accept the barbarians into the imperial armed forces, and so young Alaric went to Constantinople to be trained as a general of the Visigothic auxiliaries. Already a Christian of the Arian sect, he now learned the graces of classical culture along with the strategy and tactics of Roman military science. A typical Teuton, he was tall and fair with blue eyes. He shaved his head according to the fashion of the day, sported a sleeveless coat of fur dyed a brilliant scarlet, and became immensely popular with both Visigoths and Romans.

When Alaric was twenty he accompanied the Emperor Theodosius on a military campaign in which the youthful Visigoth so distinguished himself that he was marked as a rising commander in the imperial service. But promotion did not come quickly enough for him. He and his Visigoths were often left unemployed because the generals in Constantinople were jealous of him. Finally he asked to be given a command that would have allowed him to win the laurels of victory and his men to reap the plunder of war. His request went unanswered.

Theodosius died in 395 A.D. He had divided up the Roman Empire between his two sons, making Arcadius Emperor of the East and Honorius Emperor of the West. Alaric hoped to be appointed to one of the high offices of the Eastern Empire, but was disappointed. To secure the succession of his two sons who were minors, Theodosius had named Rufinus as regent of the East, and Stilicho, a Vandal military commander in the service of Rome, as regent of the West. The events that ensued were to be dominated by the rivalry between Stilicho the Vandal and Alaric the Visigoth, both German barbarians, both great generals.

Alaric, furious with thwarted ambition, marched on Constantinople. Unable to capture the powerfully fortified city, he turned southwest into Greece. There his Goths gratified their love of pillage. Plundering and destroying, they drove toward Athens. But Alaric sent a message to the archons, the city magistrates, saying that his mission was one of peace, that he had long admired Athens and all

JOAN OF ARC

COLUMBUS

she stood for in art and letters. He was met outside the walls by the archons, who were amazed to see a mild-mannered affable man dressed like a Greek of the time of Pericles.

Alaric, ordering his army to remain outside Athens, visited the shrines of the Acropolis, and then attended a magnificent banquet in his honor. At his request, excerpts from Plato were read so that he might listen to words of wisdom rather than to postprandial oratory. He saw Aeschylus' *The Persians* performed at the theater. He listened to readings from the poets Homer, Sappho, and Anacreon. The next morning he took leave of the archons and rode off.

When he rejoined his army, Alaric was confronted by an almost mutinous horde. His Visigoths had looked forward to looting Athens. To satisfy them, to restore his authority, Alaric started off on a march through Greece, a march of rapine and looting. Much as he regretted it, he had to abandon the holy site of Eleusis to his followers. The great shrine venerated throughout the ancient world was violated, the priests beaten to death, the temple and the altars wrecked. Then the Visigoths pushed on to Corinth.

But now Stilicho was in Greece. The great Vandal commander for the Western Empire came with an army to overthrow his Gothic rival. Outgeneraled and outnumbered, Alaric burned Corinth and withdrew to avoid defeat. Then came a sudden transformation. The regent Rufinus had been murdered. The Eastern Empire needed an army commander. Alaric appealed to the Emperor Arcadius in Constantinople and was appointed *magister militum* and given charge of the province of Illyricum (modern Yugoslavia) next door to Italy. His enemy Stilicho left Greece for Rome. The secret of these bewildering changes is to be found in the growing hostility between the Eastern and Western Empires.

As the commander of a Roman province Alaric adopted the Roman uniform with tunic, instead of the barbarian dress of the Visigoths. He reorganized the army of the Eastern Empire, into which he integrated forces of his own Visigoths. In Constantinople he "lived apart from his wife and children." Of them nothing is known except that Alaric's wife was a Greek. The dawn of the fifth century saw Alaric, a man of thirty, rising rapidly to be the most influential personality in the Eastern Roman Empire. This great realm extended from the Adriatic to the Tigris, from Scythia on the north to the southern boundary of Egypt. The young Emperor Arcadius, now twenty-three, ruled in oriental splendor.

But Alaric had determined to be more than an official of the Empire. When his men raised him on their shields in barbarian fashion and hailed him as King of the Visigoths, he told them he was ready to direct another campaign of conquest and plunder. The target this time—Rome. From Illyricum he marched as far as Milan. It was this invasion of Italy by Alaric that caused the withdrawal of the legions from Britain and left that island to be conquered by the Anglo-Saxons. Then Stilicho the Vandal crossed his path again and won the Battle of Pollentia, forcing the Visigoths back across the Alps.

As long as Stilicho lived Rome was safe. But the Romans thought the great Vandal too ambitious, and he was murdered at the climax of a plot in which the Emperor Honorius took part. The road to the Eternal City now lay open to Alaric and his Visigoths, and they took it.

The capital of the Western Empire had been transferred from Rome to Ravenna, a powerful fortress on the Adriatic, where the Emperor Honorius held his court. Alaric bypassed Ravenna, headed straight for Rome, and besieged the city on the Tiber. The ambassadors of the Senate visited his camp. Alaric assured them that, if they paid subsidies and furnished him with gold, silver, silk, and spices in quantities sufficient to defray the cost of his expedition, he would raise the siege and place himself and his forces at the disposal of Rome. These terms were accepted, after which Alaric sent in wagons of food for the starving people, thus demonstrating that a barbarian commander could be humane. He entertained Romans of distinction and withdrew his forces so that the inhabitants of the city might not feel humiliated by the presence of their conquerors.

At Ravenna, the Emperor Honorius and his court were amazed that the Visigoths had not seized the city. Alaric asked for an alliance with the Emperor, and the people of Rome sent an envoy named Attalus to Ravenna to support his demand. The Emperor refused, but appointed Jovius, long a friend of Alaric, to take charge in Rome. Jovius wrote to the Emperor urging compliance with the demands of the Visigoth King. The Emperor's reply was a flat refusal, couched in insulting terms and calling Alaric "an impudent barbarian."

This led to a cleavage between Rome and Ravenna. Alaric, to force the issue, cut off the food supply of Rome. Once more the ambassadors of the Senate visited him. Alaric now demanded the Senate depose Honorius and elect a new Emperor. He made it clear that he did not mean himself, and suggested Attalus, who was pleased and flattered. The people, disgusted with Honorius, proclaimed Attalus Emperor. At first he took orders from Alaric without question. Then he discovered that he had a mind of his own. He determined that, if he was to be Emperor, it would not be as the mere puppet of the Gothic King. Alaric, who had made Attalus, stripped him of power.

Then, after discovering a plot hatched by Honorius to kill him, Alaric marched on Rome again. He was tired of the Senate's indecision and lack of ability to set up an effective government.

On August 24, 410, as a violent thunderstorm broke over Rome, Alaric led the attack. After piercing the city's defenses, he allowed his troops to pillage the city for three days. They looted most of what they could lift or carry, but there was no extensive destruction of buildings. The churches, in particular, were spared at Alaric's order. These facts are recorded in various ecclesiastical documents still preserved in the Vatican library.

When the Visigoths captured the city, Rome was not all it once had been, but it was still the magnificent metropolis of the Western world. It lay in a shambles by the time the victors grew tired of looting. Placidia, daughter of Theodosius and sister of the Emperor, was among the spoils. She was given to Athaulf, Alaric's brother-in-law.

The only person left unconcerned by the sack of Rome was the Emperor Honorius himself, living in luxurious ease at Ravenna. When news was brought to him that Rome had been taken, he replied, "It's impossible! I was feeding her only a few minutes ago!" For he was a chicken fancier and had named his favorite pullet "Rome!" The rest of the civilized world groaned. St. Augustine wrote *The City of God* to show the faithful that they need not despair since the Church remained even though Rome was shattered.

Alaric marched south through Calabria, his intention being to gain control of Sicily and invade Africa whence the imperial forces at Ravenna drew their main supply of corn and other foodstuffs. A storm wrecked many of his ships, and he contracted a malignant fever from which he died late in 410 at the age of thirty-nine or forty. He was buried with a great treasure in the bed of the Busento River, which was turned from its course to permit the interment and then restored to its normal channel. The workers who had deflected the course of the river to dig Alaric's grave were all put to death, so as to hide forever the site where lies buried the first blond barbarian to stand as conqueror of imperial Rome.

After Alaric's death his successor, Athaulf, made peace with the imperial government. According to the terms, the Visigoths were granted lands in southern Gaul and across the Pyrenees, where during the following century they established a flourishing realm, which, after many vicissitudes, became the Visigothic kingdom in Spain.

ST. PATRICK

I T IS generally agreed that the Patron Saint of Ireland was a native of Britain, but in his family the names are Roman. "Patrick" is a later version of the stately Latin "Patricius." The saint's father was Calpurnius; his grandfather, Potitus. All this reflects the fact that at the time of his birth Britain was still Roman, a province of the Empire of the West. The barbarian invasions were on, and eventually Roman Britain would be overrun by the Anglo-Saxons and transformed into England. But in the later part of the fourth century, Roman Britain was flourishing. There were cities, estates, villas, exactly as in Roman Gaul across the Channel. Today an endless abundance of archaeological remains portray elaborate buildings, well-developed agriculture, and the characteristic Roman roads.

Patrick's father is described as a landowner of medium property, from which we can assume well-tilled acres cultivated likely enough by a few slaves. It would seem, however, that the education of the future saint may not have been great. In later times it was said that he was unlettered, and the writings attributed to him have a crude Latin style. He himself seems to have admitted that he lacked literary learning.

Roman Britain had long since accepted Christianity, which had become the official religion of the Empire, and it seems clear that Patrick was reared as a Christian. His father is called a deacon, his grandfather a presbyter. As a boy, therefore, he would have attended a church of the ancient basilica style, still so familiar among the oldest churches in Rome, and likely enough heard his share of the religious disputes in that era of heresies and controversies.

The determining event for Patrick's future career came about when he was sixteen. He was seized by raiders from Ireland, and taken to that neighboring island as a slave. This accords with the general history of the time. The Empire was sinking into the ruin of barbarian conquest, and the protection of the legions had been withdrawn from Britain, leaving that corner of Roman civilization with little defense against barbarian threats from all sides. It is a famous page in history how the Roman Britons called in their future conquerors, the Angles and Saxons, for protection against the Picts and Scots who raided the civilized country from the bleak mountains of Caledonia. But, in addition to forays from the north, there were raids across the water from Ireland. The Irish of the period, primitive and warlike, landed on expeditions of destruction, looting, and slave-catching. During one of these they captured Patrick the Briton.

He remained in servitude for six years, during which time little is known about him save that he turned ardently to religion. The slave boy doing menial chores in Ireland experienced spiritual ecstasies and visions. He may well have been in contact with Christians in Ireland, communities of whom have been known to have existed, before the great conversion of which St. Patrick was the apostle.

The story relates that, after six years, Patrick escaped from slavery, made his way to the seashore, and was able to get aboard a ship sailing for Gaul. There were trade connections between pre-Christian Ireland and the lands of the Roman Empire, and it is characteristic that the vessel on which Patrick sailed is said to have carried a cargo of Irish wolfhounds.

Landing in Gaul, he turned to religion, in accord with the spiritual fervor that had come upon him in Ireland. He went to a monastery, where he became a member of the community of monks. Presently he returned home to Britain, but this was not to be his residence for long. His religious enthusiasms were combined with recollections of the land where he had been enslaved. He had a dream, in which a heavenly visitor bade him go as a Christian missionary to Ireland and take the Gospel to pagans there.

He journeyed to Gaul, to the city of Auxerre, and there prepared himself for his mission. He was not alone in his plan to Christianize Ireland. In Rome the Pope mooted a similar project, which would seem to have looked forward not only to the conversion of the heathen but also to the combating of heresy. The Pelagian heresy, the idea that men can win their own salvation without divine grace, appears to have spread to Christian communities in Ireland. These were to be brought back to orthodoxy.

Thus far Patrick's history is relatively clear, but his future career as the Apostle of Ireland is involved in a wealth of legend spun by the Celtic imagination. The information we have is from the *Book of Armagh*, a confession attributed to St. Patrick, and a letter handed down by tradition.

From amidst embroideries of Irish fancy we can glean the fact that Patrick, with two companions in his mission, went first to southern Ireland, but that was not to be the scene of his fame. He proceeded north to Ulster, and there began those missionary exploits which were to bring all of Ireland under the sway of Roman Christianity.

The pagan High-king was not pleased with this intrusion of a foreign religion. When Patrick boldly defied the royal authorities by lighting a fire as part of the ritual on Easter Eve, he conflicted with a pagan festival during which time it was forbidden to light a fire. The Irish Druids, priests of the old paganism, were angered, but Patrick vanquished them in religious argument. As a result, the High-king granted Patrick his protection, though he himself remained a pagan. Tradition tells how, later, the saint overthrew an idol of great renown, continuing his missionary contests with the Druids.

The saint journeyed far and wide, preaching, founding churches, making marvelous conversions, bringing chiefs and clans into Christianity. He built a church and a monastery at Armagh, where he presided as bishop. To this day Armagh, in Ulster, is the Primatial See of the Irish Church.

Legend credits him with many wonders, the favorite being how St. Patrick drove the snakes out of Ireland. For long years he continued to preside over the Irish Church, which he had founded and brought into full communion with Rome. He spent his last few years in pious retirement, and by the time the end came for him he could see Ireland as won to Christianity.

He was, perhaps, the most successful of all missionaries outside of the apostolic era. Down the centuries the Irish have held him as the saint who Christianized their land. He started Ireland on its way to becoming the Medieval Island of Saints and Scholars. Seldom has any one individual made such an impression on a people. You can see the effects of this Roman Briton every time you watch the Irish parading on March 17—St. Patrick's Day.

ATTILA

[406?–453]

For a brief period of some ten years Attila, King of the Huns—
the Scourge of God—ruled a vast empire from the Caspian to the
Rhine, from the Baltic to the Danube. Although he never entered
Rome, he did more than any other man to destroy the power and
prestige, the culture and civilization, of the Roman Empire. He struck
just when the grandiose imperial structure was tottering to its final
collapse under the hammering of repeated barbarian invasions.

There were actually two Empires, one in the East and one in the
West. The Eastern Empire stood until 1453, when it fell to the Turks.
But the last of the Western Emperors disappeared less than twenty-
five years after Attila had led his ferocious horde through Europe as
far as France. Europe has never forgotten Attila. Since his time the
word "Hun" has been a synonym for wanton savagery.

The Huns were a Mongolian people whose original home was in
the Far East. Defeated by the Chinese, they began to move westward, driving other barbarians before them into the Roman Empire.
By the fourth century one group of Hunnish tribes had taken over
what is now Hungary, and were threatening both the Eastern and
Western Empires. Brutal in appearance and action, mounted on
tough wiry ponies, and swinging sharp swords, they soon became a
terror to their neighbors. Whole populations fled at their approach.
Before Attila, the two Roman Emperors were accustomed to pay
tribute to the Huns in order to save their provinces from devastation.
Even this was not enough to satisfy the greatest of the Hunnish Kings.

The date of Attila's birth is not known, but it was about the year
406. He became King of the Huns on the death of his Uncle Rugilas in
433 A.D. As he shared his power with his brother Bleda, it was assumed by some writers that they were twins. From Rugilas they in-

herited the war of nerves which he had waged against the Eastern
Empire, and which compelled the Emperor Theodosius II to pay a
yearly subsidy of 350 pounds of gold. Theodosius also had granted
to Rugilas the title of Roman general.

Attila and Bleda possessed all the typical Hunnish arrogance.
When they became joint kings in 433, they received the ambassadors
of Constantinople on horseback. As they refused to dismount, the
Roman envoys—Plinthas, a general of Scythian extraction but of con-
sular rank, and Epigenes, a wise and experienced statesman—likewise were unwilling to appear before the Huns on foot. The meeting
was held on horseback.

The Huns demanded that the Romans denounce an alliance they
had with Germanic tribes along the Danube; that they double the
annual "tribute"—a word that elicited an angry protest from the
Romans; that they pay a "fine" of eight gold pieces for each Roman
captive escaping from the Huns; and that they return to the Huns all
fugitives who sought refuge with the Romans. From these humiliating and insolent terms Attila and Bleda refused to depart, and the
ambassadors returned to Constantinople. Theodosius II favored ap-
peasement of the Huns, and met all their demands. He allowed the
pacifist views of his sister, Pulcheria, and his mother, Queen Eudocia,
to override the advice of his statesmen and generals. The latter
argued that the Roman armies, with their superior equipment and
discipline, should be used to destroy the power of the Huns while
there was yet time.

Attila now proceeded to consolidate his power in the North, bringing virtually the whole of Germany and eastern Europe under his
sway. He subjected the Teutonic tribes of the forests of Germany,
establishing such dominion over them that he became formidable in
Germanic legend, King Etzel of the Nibelungenlied. It was during
this period of northern conquest that Attila had his brother Bleda
slain, and thus became sole ruler of the Huns.

His ferocity was augmented by weird religious symbolism. The
ancient Scythians, barbarians inhabiting what is now the Ukraine,
had worshiped a sword as an idol, hilt buried in the ground, blade
pointing toward the sky. The Romans called it the Sword of Mars.
So now a Hungarian shepherd came forward with a strange story.
He told how one of his sheep had gone lame from a cut and left a

trail of blood. This trail he had followed, and it had led him to a half-buried sword. This, he said, was the symbol of the Scythian war god—the Sword of Mars. He presented the blade to Attila, who accepted it as a divine omen, a sign that he was to conquer the world: as the possessor of the Sword of Mars his was the dominion of the entire earth. With superstition thus inflaming his sanguinary instincts, he was to sally forth in the civilized realms of the Roman Empire as the Scourge of God.

A contemporary Gothic observer describes this Mongol conqueror as follows:

"His features bore the stamp of his national origin—a large head, a swarthy complexion, small deep-seated eyes, a flat nose, a few hairs in the place of a beard, broad shoulders, and a short square body, of nervous strength, though of a disproportioned form. The haughty demeanor of the King of the Huns expressed the consciousness of his superiority above the rest of mankind; and he had a custom of fiercely rolling his eyes as if he wished to enjoy the terror which he inspired."

In 441, Attila turned against the Roman Empire of the East. His pretext was that the Bishop of Margus had crossed the Danube and stolen some of the Hunnish royal treasure. He ordered the prelate to be seized and put to death. To save his life, the bishop turned his city over to the Huns, and fled. So began the ruthless invasion of the Eastern Empire. The Huns swept through the Balkans causing devastation that brought about the saying that grass did not grow where Attila's horse had trod. More than seventy cities were utterly destroyed, Macedonia and Thrace ravaged. When the Huns reached the outskirts of Constantinople, the feeble Emperor sued for peace.

The terms Attila imposed were harsh and humiliating: the surrender of territory south of the Danube, leaving the delta of that great river entirely in the hands of the Huns; a war indemnity of six thousand pounds of gold payable immediately; the raising of the annual tribute from seven hundred to twenty-one hundred pounds of gold; the return of all Hun prisoners of war and of all deserters and refugee slaves. Thereby he showed that the Roman Empire could not protect those to whom it had given refuge. The Eastern Empire was ruined, its fiscal system disrupted, and every attempted recovery blocked by fresh demands from a ruthless enemy. Finally the Romans decided to have Attila assassinated. The plot failed, and brought final disgrace to Theodosius II, who shortly afterward fell from his horse and was killed.

Having no children, Theodosius was succeeded by his sister, Pulcheria, who chose as her consort Marcian, a Thracian general of humble birth. He became Emperor of the East. Although his material resources were at a low ebb, he had a proud fighting spirit, and when Attila arrogantly ordered his annual tribute paid, the new Emperor replied that Rome was to be insulted no longer by barbarians. He said he would be liberal to allies, but if attacked he would fight.

This firm attitude surprised the Huns and made them hesitate. Attila had to make up his mind whether to chastise the defiant Emperor of the East or to ravage the Empire of the West. The latter alternative seemed the easier and the richer prospect, and Attila decided on the rape of Gaul, which was rich, peaceful, and lightly garrisoned by the Romans. He had little to fear apparently. He had strong barbarian enemies in the West, notably the Franks and Visigoths, but he knew that they could not stop him without forming a coalition with the Romans.

Another and more romantic cause for war against the Empire of the West was an affair that had come to pass some time previously. When she was sixteen, Honoria, sister of the Western Emperor Valentinian, had thrown herself into the arms of her handsome chamberlain, Eugenius. Whereupon she was exiled in disgrace to Constantinople. Held a prisoner of her family and faced by long and hopeless celibacy, she took a bold course. To secure her freedom she offered herself to Attila as his wife and sent him her ring to bind the bargain. At the time Attila thought nothing of the matter, but now years later, he demanded of the Emperor of the West a fulfillment of the pledge, requiring that Honoria be sent to him. His ultimatum firmly but diplomatically rejected, the invasion of Gaul was begun.

From all of eastern Europe, from the shores of the Baltic to Hungary, Attila moved his barbarian hordes to the Rhine and assembled them at its juncture with the Moselle, where Coblentz now stands. There he was joined by more allies, and the crossing of the Rhine by a quarter of a million men was effected without opposition. Their march across Gaul—now the sunny land of France—was one of terror and wanton destruction, of rape and murder, of fire and sword, so atrocious that it left scars that time has been unable to heal and that are visible today, fifteen hundred years later.

Every city and town was overrun and sacked, its inhabitants murdered, before the torch was applied, and the barbarians swept on leaving only smoking ruins in their wake. Vienne, just a few miles south of Lyons, famous for its beautiful temples, was utterly destroyed and the charred ruins still stand as silent witnesses of atrocious deeds. The beautiful Roman theater at Orange still shows traces of the flames that ate their way through the wings and up the outer wall of the stage. This orgy of bestial lust finally brought the Huns to Orléans.

It was June of 451, and the critical moment for Europe had arrived. The affairs of the Western Empire, over which the weak Valentinian reigned, were largely in the hands of Aëtius, the last great Roman general. From an old patrician family, he provided a striking exception to the rule that barbarian generals commanded the armies of the falling Empire. Of great administrative, diplomatic ability, he knew the Huns well, having spent years of his youth at the Hunnish court. He now persuaded Theodoric I, King of the Visigoths, who were established in Gaul with a kingdom there, that Attila's threat to the Romans was of equal danger to him. The same argument caused Meroveus, King of the Franks, to bring in a contingent. Thereby Aëtius mustered a combined army of Romans, Visigoths, and Franks which reached Orléans just as the city was about to be looted by the Huns. Faced with the first armed opposition he had encountered in Gaul, Attila was quick to recognize the advantages of retreat to more favorable ground. The Huns withdrew to the northeast and halted on the Catalaunian plain, near Châlons, where the Hunnish horsemen would have the advantage.

"Ruthless, manifold, immense, obstinate" is the description that Jornandes, the Gothic historian, has left of the Battle of Châlons. The open plain where every enemy maneuver could be seen, lent itself well to the prolonged hand-to-hand fighting that was the feature of this, one of the decisive battles of history. From dawn to nightfall the carnage went on as fresh units were thrown into the struggle. The Gothic King, Theodoric, was killed. The day seemed lost for the Romans, but victory was finally snatched from the jaws of defeat by the valor and discipline of a few of their military formations. During the night Attila retreated toward the Rhine. The victors were too exhausted to follow him and he crossed the Rhine with what was left of his forces.

Having re-formed his hordes, Attila struck southward into Italy, in 452 A.D. In Venetia, after a siege, he devastated the beautiful city of Aquileia, sacked and burned to the ground, and dealt likewise with Concordia, Altinum, and Padua. Fugitives from the Huns fled to the marshes and founded Venice. Upon Milan and the cities of the Lombard plains, the blows of the Huns fell more lightly. No attempt was made to destroy them after they had been plundered. Then Attila set out for Rome. The Romans sent a delegation headed by their bishop, Pope Leo the Great, to sue for peace.

The Scourge of God and the Vicar of Christ met near the confluence of the Mincio and the Po. Legend tells of a miraculous vision that deterred the pagan Hun. In any case, by a miracle of persuasive eloquence the Pope induced Attila to turn back and leave Rome unharmed—other factors being the payment of an immense dowry for Honoria, the imperial bride whom Attila claimed, and the growing incidence of disease among the Huns, who were unaccustomed to the climate of Italy. Threatening to return more terrible than ever if Honoria was not delivered to his ambassadors, Attila withdrew to Pannonia (now Austria), taking to wife in 453 a young and beautiful girl named Ildico. This wedding was celebrated by a great feast and during the night he collapsed suddenly and died in his young bride's arms. With him died the Empire of the Huns.

MOHAMMED

[570–632]

Long before the birth of Mohammed, the city of Mecca was the most sacred place in Arabia. From time immemorial the pagan idol-worshiping Arabs had revered the shrine of the Kaaba, with its magical Black Stone, a wonder-working fetish. The Bedouin of the desert carried out pilgrimages to Mecca to pray before the Kaaba. Mohammed took advantage of past history, centered his new religion at the old city, and made Mecca a byword in most of the languages of the world, a byword for a spot where people gather regularly.

He was born into one of the chief clans of Mecca, the Koreish, who administered the cult of the Black Stone of the Kaaba and the exploitation of the pilgrim traffic. He seems to have been a serious youth, little inclined to frolic and carouse, and did not make friends easily. The future prophet was foreshadowed in the brooding, introspective youth. The family relations in whose charge he was left were not rich, and at seventeen he had to go to work.

Young Mohammed became a caravan leader, a profession typical of the desert, where communications, trade, and transport were held together by strings of camels wending their way across the sands. Mecca itself, not far from the coast of the Red Sea, was a center of caravan traffic in southern Arabia.

Mohammed's travels took him afar, to the Yemen in the south, and northward into Syria, toward Asia Minor. His caravan journeys brought him into much contact with Jews and Christians and their religious beliefs, theological ideas that already had made their way vaguely among the Bedouins. Meeting Jews and Christians, Mohammed was influenced deeply and intensely by their monotheism, the worship of one God.

Mohammed had for an employer a rich widow, Khadija. She was

not displeased with the ability or the person of her caravan leader. He was of middle height and muscular, bearded and meditative, with large thoughtful eyes. Although he was twenty-five, while she was forty, the widow thought of matrimony, and Mohammed was agreeable to an alliance with his wealthy employer. Entering married life with a woman fifteen years his senior, he found it a successful and happy union. Four daughters and three sons were born to them. The sons all died. Of the daughters, one continued the lineage of Mohammed—Fatima, whom Islam venerates next only to the prophet himself.

Mohammed now quit his caravan job and settled down at Mecca. Marriage to a rich wife gave him a good position, and he set up as a man of business affairs, earning a reputation for sound ability and practical good sense.

Years went by for this businessman of Mecca, and he had reached middle age before he came to the turning point that set him on his great career. A flourishing citizen in commerce, he had another side— religious, brooding with mysticism, inclined to solitude and reflection on spiritual matters. One account relates that he retired to the desert for contemplation and prayer, and in a cave had a vision of the archangel Gabriel. Famous in the Moslem legend is the story of how the archangel told Mohammed that there was only one God, the same God as was worshiped by the Jews and Christians, and that Mohammed was to be his Prophet. The Judaic and Christian ideas with which Mohammed had come into close contact as a caravan driver were thus dramatized in a vision. Some speak of him as being subject to epileptic seizures. Suffice it to say that he was subject to visions, and the appearance of the archangel Gabriel in the cave was the most decisive of all—setting Mohammed on his mission.

His wife became his first convert, dedicated to the doctrine of one God with Mohammed as his Prophet. Next was a cousin, young Ali, whom he adopted as his son and who in turn was to marry Mohammed's daughter Fatima. One of the most influential of the first converts was Abu Bekr, later to become father-in-law and successor of Mohammed. Another was Omar, likewise to be a successor to the Prophet, and one of the greatest. Mohammed continued to have visions, and announced revelations to his followers. This habit continued all his life. His revelations had a way of answering the need and convenience of the moment, and sometimes were contradictory. Thus

early the pattern was set whereby actions and policies were sanctioned by timely and convenient revelations. Later they were written
down and became the Koran.

Mohammed was forty years old when he began his religious missions, and at first the formation of a cult centered around himself was
peaceable. Yet trouble was bound to come as the new religion spread
among people in Mecca. The doctrine of one God provoked the hostility of the devotees of older cults, the more so as Mecca was the city
of the worship of the Black Stone and benefited by the streams of
desert pilgrims to the Kaaba. There was a financial as well as a religious angle, and here was a citizen of Mecca preaching a new creed
which, it seemed, could only injure the long established and most
profitable cult. There were disputes and recriminations, especially as
the disturbing gospel of one God spread like a theological epidemic.
Riots broke out in Mecca, followed by persecution of the new religion.

Violence increased to such a point that Mohammed and his followers were besieged in the quarters they occupied in the city. His
antagonists were resolved to kill him, and it became necessary for
him to flee. He had many followers in the nearby town of Yathrib.
Because of what now ensued, that place became known as Medina,
which means "the city." The converts to Mohammedanism at Medina
invited their Prophet to join them.

A band of killers assigned to take his life found that he had fled
secretly. The date of Mohammed's escape to Medina is July 16, 622
A.D., the year of the "hegira," or flight, which is the central date in the
Moslem calendar, as the birth of Christ is in the Christian reckoning
of time. Mohammed was then about fifty-two.

At Medina, where he was accompanied by a number of fellow-
exiles from Mecca, his following was numerous and powerful enough
for him to take control and establish a theocratic regime. Consolidating the faithful under his own authority, he set what was to be the
pattern of future Mohammedan policy—a despotism, civil as well as
religious, under a combined spiritual and political autocrat. At Medina opposition was suppressed, and the city became Mohammed's
own miniature state.

The Prophet continued his method of shaping his new religion by
the authority of frequent revelations. Bit by bit he accumulated and

developed the tenets and practices that were to spread across continents as the institution of Islam. The revelations dictated theology, the routine of piety and prayer, civil institutions, political policy, actions of personal expediency, every sort of thing.

Mohammed's wife had died before his flight to Medina, and he now took other wives. Polygamy was common enough among the Arabs, and Mohammed sanctioned and at the same time limited the practice. With a series of revelations on the subject of marriage, he established the doctrine that permits a Moslem to have four wives. Mohammed himself, however, had many more than four. He married the daughters of his influential adherents, Abu Bekr and Omar, and indulged in a degree of polygamy that is to be explained largely by policy—taking a wife as a means of political alliance.

Inevitably he got into war with Mecca. His fellow exiles raided caravans of their native city. Mecca, in any case, could not look with equanimity on the rise of a hostile power at neighboring Medina, which stood to the north along the caravan route that brought Mecca so much of its prosperity. Sporadic fighting broke out, which in no wise diminished the spread of Mohammed's doctrines among the tribes of nomads that roamed the desert. War, in fact, was an aspect of religion that they could understand best. The Prophet's revelations established the connection between belief and the sword, with the doctrine that the Moslem who died in battle was assured of instant entrance into paradise, and this became the mighty force that sent Islam on the way to world conquest.

A truce was arranged, whereby the Prophet was permitted to make the traditional pilgrimage to the Kaaba. When he appeared in Mecca with a suitable display of piety, it made a favorable impression, and aided the cause of the Prophet among the people of the city. The result was that, shortly afterward, Mohammed was able to launch an attack against Mecca and take the city with little resistance. He made the holy city, with the Kaaba and the Black Stone, his religious center, while Medina was his political capital.

To the One and Only God he gave the Arabic name of Allah, and it is characteristic that to this day Moslems of all nationalities use that same Arabic word for the Deity, calling him Allah. Mohammed continued the pilgrimage to Mecca, but he removed all vestiges of polytheism and idol worship, and dedicated the Kaaba and the Black Stone to the worship of Allah.

In this manner arose one of the great religions of the world. Mohammed founded a creed separate from Judaism and Christianity and hostile to both. He acknowledged the truth of the Old Testament, the validity of the patriarchs and prophets, and revered Jesus as one of the greatest of the Prophets. He held that his own religion of Islam fulfilled and completed the truths of Judaism and Christianity.

He sent emissaries to countries bordering Arabia, the Greek Empire at Constantinople, the Persian Empire to the east, bidding them accept his revelation. These envoys were received with ridicule by imperial officials who little dreamt of what was to come.

During the final years of his life, Mohammed brought about the unity of the Arabs, hitherto a welter of feuding tribes, rallying them to the cause of his religion and launching that vast surge in the desert peoples under the gospel of spreading Islam by the sword. He was preparing an expedition against the Greek Empire when he died. He had started a fire that was to sweep much of the world, the vast conquests that were to be directed by his immediate successors, his father-in-law, Abu Bekr, his great lieutenant Omar, and the others of the mighty caliphs of Islam.

He left a book, though he did not write it. His sayings and revelations were remembered and cherished and finally written down. Then they were assembled in an official account, the Koran, the Bible of Islam, and one of the most potent books this world has ever known.

CHARLEMAGNE

[742-814]

CHARLEMAGNE followed all three paths to eminence prescribed by Shakespeare in the famous lines from *Twelfth Night:* "Some are born great, some achieve greatness, some have greatness thrust upon 'em." He was born King of the Franks. He conquered a vast empire. He was, although apparently he did not will it, crowned Roman Emperor by the Pope.

Charlemagne did not descend from a long dynasty. His ancestors had been mayors of the palace under the feckless Merovingians. Charlemagne's grandfather, Charles Martel, was only a mayor of the palace when he checked the sweep of Islam that threatened all Europe. The Moslems, having conquered Spain, pushed on into France, and the Battle of Tours was decisive in stopping them once and for all. Charles Martel's successor, his son Pepin the Short, made an end to the myth of the do-nothing Merovingians, deposing the last of these and having himself crowned King of the Franks. This he did with the sanction of the Pope, who gave a memorable opinion that the title of king should belong to the one who exercises the power of king. Pepin earned the blessing of Rome by going to the aid of the Pope against the Lombards, enemies and oppressors of the Papacy, overthrowing them in war and curbing their power.

King Pepin left two sons, Charles and Carloman, between whom he divided his kingdom, according to Frankish custom; but Carloman died presently, and Charles took over the entire domain. Thus he fell heir to the power and prestige of the Franks—the greatness he was born to.

He won for himself the mightiest epithet that history bestows. To the centuries that followed him, he was Charles the Great, Carolus Magnus, Charlemagne. His achievements were a turning point in the history of the West. He shaped the things that were to come, things military and political, affairs of empire and world culture. With Charlemagne, history enters upon a new era, because of his triumphs in war, in statecraft, and in the advancement of civilization.

He was one of the greatest of conquerors, his reign of forty-three years presenting an interminable series of invasions and campaigns, bewildering in their multiplicity, monotonous in their almost unvarying success. His most desperate wars were those against the Saxons, kinsmen of his own blond Germanic Franks, as warlike and as stubborn. The Saxons were still Teutonic pagans, worshiping Wotan and Thor, and seeking the embattled delights of Valhalla. Charlemagne mingled motives of empire with those of religion and civilization, his cardinal demand upon the Saxons being that they accept Christianity, which meant their entrance into civilization—such civilization as had descended from classical Rome to mingle with Germanic ways and customs to become the Middle Ages.

But the actual events of war had little semblance to anything either Christian or civilized. The struggle was stubborn and ferocious, and Charlemagne had to undertake fourteen campaigns before the Saxons were subjugated. On one day alone he had 4,500 beheaded. In the end, he moved them in mass deportations from their original territory between the Elbe and Weser to other parts of Germany. The Saxons were crushed and Christianized, and Charlemagne extended his conquests to include most of Germany. He seized Bavaria, and obliterated the robber kingdom of the Avars on the Danube.

Of high political consequence were his campaigns in Italy, where he continued his father's action against the Lombards, who were enemies of the Papacy. Sweeping through the passes of the Alps, he overthrew the Lombard kingdom for all time, and had himself crowned with that diadem historic and legendary, the Iron Crown of the Lombards. This attached northern Italy to the Frankish kingdom, and Charlemagne, confirming a previous grant made by his father, bestowed upon the Papacy sovereign title to the city of Rome and adjacent territory, long to endure as the Papal States. In this he forged the final bond between the Frankish monarchy and the Western Church.

It is a moody irony of history that, in the campaigns of this prodigiously successful commander, the one event that rang the loudest in subsequent song and story was a defeat. It was a minor mishap, a thing of little consequence, but it became the most beguiling theme in the legend of Charlemagne that filled the Middle Ages. Europe for centuries was haunted by the mournful echo of Roland's Horn.

It was inevitable that Charlemagne, the paladin of Christendom, should dream of driving the Moslem out of Spain, and rescuing the Spanish Christians from the infidel. He never did accomplish that, but he marched beyond the Pyrenees in campaigns which, while fairly indecisive, did allow him to seize part of northern Spain. During one such foray occurred a minor action, hardly more than a skirmish. A rear-guard force of the Frankish army, retiring from Spain, was cut off in a defile of the Pyrenees, trapped by Basque mountaineers. In command was Roland, nephew of Charlemagne and warden of the marches of Brittany. The rear-guard detachment was destroyed by the Basques, and Roland fell. In his last stand, he blew a vainly imploring note on his horn, calling for rescue that never came. So said the later legends of the Middle Ages, which magnified the minor defeat of Roncesvalles into epic tragedy, commemorated by a favorite masterpiece of medieval literature, the *Song of Roland*.

Charlemagne was, in personal appearance, the typical barbarian monarch. Of great stature and physical strength, with blue eyes and blond hair and beard, he cut the figure of the Frankish warrior. He was a devotee of the hunt, which he pursued with his Teutonic boon companions in the forests around Aachen. In dress he preferred the rude costume of the Franks, rather than the robes of the Romans, and he dined in the style of the barbarians, banqueting on huge joints of game and disdaining the more delicate cookery of the Romans. In his domestic life he was no model. He had a succession of four wives and a sequence of mistresses, which was in accord with the dissolute ways of the barbarians who settled down amidst the ruins of Roman culture and its corrupt morals.

He was dedicated to the ancient Germanic traditions, and had the ancient heroic sagas of the Germans collected and written down so they might not be lost, and caused the laws of the Franks to be collated, and those of the Saxons, Thuringians, and Frisians. He had the barbarian statutes assembled and written down in emulation of the codification of Roman law by the Byzantine Emperors.

But this Frankish King, so simple and rude in many ways, was no mere barbarian. In his person he united the great trend of his era, the fusion of Germanic customs with Roman and Christian culture. He adopted what was left of the Roman science of statecraft, and organized his vast empire thoroughly and methodically, sending royal representatives to every part to administer, supervise, gather information, and promote order and system. He regulated the Church in his domains, convoking ecclesiastical councils and giving them advice and direction. A devout Christian, this mightiest monarch of his time never submitted his secular power to the rule of the Church. On the contrary, he felt it his duty to supervise it, and see that theology and clerical administration were sound. As complete a theocrat as the Byzantine Emperor, who ruled over the Eastern Church in Constantinople, Charlemagne rather regarded the Pope as his private chaplain.

He was a friend of scholars, and learned men from every part of Europe were attracted to his court. The most famous, the Saxon Alcuin of York, reorganized the palace school, where the children of the nobility were educated with those of the Emperor. Many schools were founded in monasteries and cathedral establishments, and the arts of the past were revived. To Charlemagne's scholars we are indebted for the oldest existing manuscripts of Caesar, Virgil, Tacitus, and other masters of Roman literature. Grammarians patronized by this Romanized German King made Latin once again a vehicle of precise literary expression, and one of the finest Latin productions of the time was the biography of Charlemagne written by the monk Einhard, a friend and confidant of the Emperor. The Latin translation of the Bible was worked over and improved. Illuminators and goldsmiths plied their crafts, and handwriting was raised to an art. The ancestor of our modern printed type is the calligraphy developed in that period, known as Carolingian minuscule. So brilliant were the art and literature of the reign of Charlemagne that the era is known in history as the Carolingian Renaissance.

The great Frankish King, an unlettered Germanic soldier to begin with, undertook to master some of this learning himself. He studied grammar with Peter of Pisa and rhetoric, dialectic, and astronomy with Alcuin. He was accustomed to have passages from St. Augustine's *City of God* read aloud to him. Yet he really never learned to write. Though he entered avidly into the learned discussions and debates of his scholars, he was never able to form letters with ease. His hand, schooled to the use of the sword and not of the pen, could not acquire the dexterity necessary for handwriting. It is related that at night Charlemagne would take pad and pen and practice patiently, but he never got beyond the laborious forming of rude letters.

At Christmastime in the year 800, Charlemagne was in Rome on affairs of the Papacy. A sedition against Leo III, with charges of misconduct against him, had driven that pontiff to flight, and he had barely escaped with his life from the fury of the Roman mob. He had sought sanctuary at the Frankish court, where the accusation of his enemies followed him. Charlemagne, as chief of western Christendom and guardian of the Church, determined to make an inquiry on the papal scene and pass judgment in Rome. With Leo III as a suppliant and an honored guest, he led an army across the Alps to the Eternal City. There, after much discussion, the pontiff was permitted to exonerate himself by swearing an oath of innocence. Such was the setting for a fateful ritual.

On Christmas Day, in the basilica of St. Peter, Charlemagne knelt before the altar in prayer. Pope Leo III stepped up behind him, and crowned him with the diadem of Roman Emperor. Thus, with sacrosanct symbolism, the pontiff proclaimed a revival in the West of the ancient authority of the Roman Empire, with the great Frankish King as a latter-day successor to the Caesars.

This is one of the most debated events in history. Was Charlemagne aware in advance that this coronation was going to take place? Or was he taken by surprise? His biographer, Einhard, who had intimate knowledge of the Emperor's affairs, quotes Charlemagne as saying that had he known of the Pope's intention he would not have entered the church on that Christmas Day. Historians are still debating the probability of that statement.

Legally the Roman Empire was still in existence, represented by the Byzantine Emperor at Constantinople. The fall of the Western Empire, more than three centuries before, was regarded as having transferred the sovereignty of the West to the head of the Eastern Empire. The people of the time could not believe that the mighty regime of old, which had given unity and order, had vanished forever, and in a formal way the potentate at Constantinople, legal successor to the Caesars, was recognized as having universal authority as the

Roman Emperor, a shadowy fictitious authority to which the barbarian Kings of the West had never given more than polite recognition. Now, by crowning Charlemagne as Roman Emperor, the Pope presumed to transfer the imperial title from Byzantium to the great King of the West.

In Constantinople a woman had seized power, the Empress Irene, after blinding her son. This had created widespread indignation, and it could be argued that the imperial succession at Byzantium had actually lapsed. The throne of the Caesars, occupied thus criminally by a woman, might be considered vacant. The Byzantine court could not, of course, be expected to yield to the will of the Western Papacy, and Charlemagne, crowned with the imperial diadem, had to be concerned about possible Byzantine reprisal.

There was no great danger. The Eastern Empire was helplessly immersed in upheavals of intrigue and palace revolution. Still, Charlemagne found it expedient to offer marriage to the Empress Irene, but she was overthrown before any such plan could go far, and under her successor there was some desultory warfare between the Franks and Byzantines.

More important, Charlemagne may have noted the profoundly significant fact that the pontiff of the Western Church had assumed the right to transfer the imperial authority and crown an Emperor. Leo III had, in fact, laid the legal foundation of the Holy Roman Empire, which was to continue for a thousand years, and through the centuries the Papacy was to claim the power of granting or withholding the imperial crown, of annointing and dethroning Emperors. This was the central fact in the subsequent long conflict between the Papacy and the Empire. Charlemagne may well have looked askance at an unexpected papal coronation, but the thing was done. Greatness was thrust upon him, as we may believe from the statement of his own friend and biographer.

The mighty Emperor lived beyond his seventieth year in the full tide of his threefold greatness, and after his death became a fabulous legend. During the long period of the Middle Ages, the imagination of that credulous era transformed him into a giant myth, the subject of unending songs and epics. All the luxuriance of medieval fantasy was woven around Charlemagne and his paladins, like the valorous Roland who perished at Roncesvalles. The great Emperor and his

MICHELANGELO

HENRY VIII

Twelve Peers were rivaled only by King Arthur and the Knights of the Round Table.

All this is illustrated vividly in one of the dazzling pages left from medieval literature. In the latter part of the ninth century there was a monk in the monastery of St. Gall who set down stories of Charlemagne. The precise identity of the writer is unknown. History calls him "the Monk of St. Gall." He writes of the Emperor's expedition across the Alps to attack the Lombards. The Lombard King, Didier, is described as waiting in his powerful fortress of Pavia, and with him Count Ogger, a Frank who had fled from Charlemagne. The Monk of St. Gall pictures King Didier standing on the walls of Pavia, watching the approach of the army of the Franks. Beside him, Count Ogger, who knew Charlemagne. Here is the passage:

First of all, he saw only a thick cloud of dust; it was caused by the engines of war by which the walls of the capital were to be battered. "Here is Charles," cried Didier, "with this great army!" "No," answered Ogger.

Then there appeared a huge crowd of common soldiers. "Surely Charles advances triumphant in the midst of this host!" "Not yet," replied Ogger.

Next there appeared the body of guards, veteran warriors who never knew rest. "Now Charles is coming!" said Didier, full of terror. "No," answered Ogger, "not yet."

After these came the bishops, abbots, clerks of the royal chapel, and counts. Then Didier cried, choking with fear, "Let us go down and hide ourselves in the bowels of the earth, far from the face of this terrible foe!" "When you see the harvest fields shaking with terror," said Ogger, "then you may believe that Charles is approaching."

As he said this, a dark cloud appeared, driven by the east wind, which converted the day into night. But the emperor advanced a little nearer, and the gleam of his arms lightened over Pavia a day darker than the darkest night. Then Charles himself appeared, clothed from head to foot in steel armour, a lance on his left hand, his right resting upon his invincible sword.

Ogger recognised him, and struck with terror, trembled and fell, crying, "It is he!"

ALFRED THE GREAT

[849–899]

ALFRED THE GREAT was the first King of all the English. It was he who saved the final remnant of England from the Viking invaders, began the counterattack against them, and laid the political foundation on which his successors built a unified state. His work as soldier and statesman lifted him to the rank of the world's greatest men.

In the fifth century A.D., the Roman province of Britain was overrun by Germanic peoples, the Angles, Saxons, and Jutes, who in time were Christianized and divided into contending kingdoms. This was the heptarchy, or seven kingdoms, a term loosely applied to the early English principalities, although their number was seldom exactly seven. They had very nearly been united into one kingdom, Angleland or England, by Egbert, Alfred's grandfather, who spent much of his youth at the court of Charlemagne, where he learned the ABC's of war and government. During his reign the Danes, the Vikings, invaded the country. Robbing, murdering, and pillaging, they laid waste the land, destroyed the churches, and terrorized the people. Egbert defeated them in 837 at Hingston in Cornwall, but his death two years later prompted the Danes to renew their depredations.

His son and successor was Ethelwulf, who, when he died, was succeeded in turn by four of his sons: Ethelbald, Ethelbert, Ethelred, and Alfred. Ethelred became King of Wessex, which comprised all England west of Sussex and south of the Thames River, except Cornwall. He fought to stem the Viking tide, and then left Alfred to carry on the struggle.

Alfred was twenty-two when he succeeded his brother in 871. Within a month of his coronation at Winchester he was forced to fight the Danes. The year 871 became known as "Alfred's Year of

Battles." After inconclusive warfare the invaders retired north of the Thames, and Wessex for a time was secure against Danish attack, but the rest of England remained in Viking hands.

Then in 877 the Danes, under Guthrum, renewed their attacks, killed many of Alfred's men, and captured Chippenham where the King lived. According to legend, Alfred, disguised as a peasant, sought refuge in the home of a cowherd who formerly had tended his cattle. Unrecognized even by his loyal servant, Alfred remained there for some time, spending his days planning how best to launch a counterattack against the enemy.

This is the setting for the famous anecdote of the burned cakes. The legend has it that one day the cowherd's wife asked their guest to keep an eye on some cakes she was baking. Alfred agreed absentmindedly, but his thoughts were on plans to regain his kingdom. Suddenly the mistress of the house smelled something burning. She rushed in, to find the cakes ruined, and Alfred sitting idly by gazing into the fire. Without realizing what she was doing, the woman upbraided her King for his negligence, and Alfred accepted the rebuke without revealing his identity.

The story of Alfred and the cakes is one of the great anecdotes of history, but no one knows how much truth there is in it. Actually almost nothing is known of Alfred's life at this period. That he was forced to adopt a disguise is probable. That he spent his time planning his next move is fact. When he completed his plans he rallied his followers and with them built a fort on a few acres of firm ground in the center of a bog. He called it Athelney, the Isle of Nobles. Gradually the Wessex forces were re-formed. They renewed the fight against the Norsemen. The tide began to turn when, in a chance engagement that was little more than a skirmish, Alfred's men captured the famous war flag of the Danes, "the Raven." This was of special significance, for the Danes believed the flag to be magical, expressing by the flapping of its wings the success or failure of any enterprise. Hubba, their commander, was routed and killed.

Alfred's next move was to find out how things stood with the enemy. According to an old story, he entered their camp dressed as a minstrel. He played before Guthrum, the Danish prince, and during his two or three days' stay found out all he needed to know. Encouraged by these observations, he secretly sent word throughout the land summoning all who would join him to meet with their followers at Brixton, on the edge of Selwood Forest, to fight the Danes.

He trained his men carefully all winter long. Then, with the last of the cold weather behind, he led his forces through Wiltshire. The Danes were strongly entrenched at Edington, but after a siege of fourteen days Alfred won a decisive victory. The enemy was forced to sue for peace.

The first proof of Alfred's real greatness was demonstrated by the terms he laid down. It was clearly impossible to expel all the Danes then in England. Much of the north as well as East Anglia had been devastated by the invaders and was virtually unpopulated. Alfred, therefore, made a bold and successful attempt to convert his mortal enemies to friendship and confederacy.

By the Peace of Wedmore the Danes were allowed to remain in England on condition that they surrender their arms and adopt Christianity. Guthrum, their leader, was the first to be baptized. He was then adopted by Alfred and renamed Athelstan. Under the Danelaw, as it was called, the erstwhile enemy settled down among the native population, thickly in the north and east, and thinly in the midlands, but they were not allowed south of the Thames. It is not difficult to trace even today the difference between the English of the north country from those who live in the south. The peace seemed to be a surrender of the major part of Britain to the Danes, but in saving Wessex, Alfred saved England, for the reign of terror was over at last.

With the restoration of peace in 878 began the noblest reign in the long history of the English monarchy. It has been rightly said that what lifts Alfred to the level of the world's greatest men is the high moral character of his life and rule. With the Peace of Wedmore, Alfred the warrior became Alfred the Great. At thirty he gave up all ambition of conquest. He secured the peace he had won, and devoted himself to initiating sound laws, educating the people, and preparing for the future.

He collected all the laws promulgated by his predecessors, selected the best, and humanized, reformed, and codified them. Justice was administered by regular courts. Alfred appointed sheriffs to help him with local government, and the shires of present-day England follow closely the lines of those which he established.

More than four centuries of barbarian turmoil had destroyed the civilization of Roman Britain. Few indeed were the Englishmen who could understand a word of the Latin they heard at mass. There was no literature to speak of and almost no one could read or write.

To remedy this Alfred established schools and invited scholars from all parts of Europe to visit England. Every landowner who held two hundred acres was obliged by law to have his children educated. Alfred set up a school for young nobles at his own court. He surrounded himself with tutors, for in spite of all his accomplishments he had never learned to read Latin. Now, in middle age, he mastered the classical Roman tongue. When he was proficient he translated into Saxon: Bede's *Ecclesiastical History of the English People, Aesop's Fables, Epitome of History* by Orosius, and Boethius' *Consolation of Philosophy;* and he did a free translation of Gregory the Great's *Pastoral Care.* It is believed that the *Anglo-Saxon Chronicle,* the most important source of early British history, was compiled during his reign. These translations mark the origin of English prose literature.

Alfred steadily built up the defenses of the country. In 886 he began the fortification of London. This year also marked the beginning of his reign as King of all the English, the year in which the Angles and Saxons, the remaining kingdoms of the heptarchy not under his control, spontaneously recognized him as King.

Alfred realized the necessity of controlling the sea as a means of preventing invasion. He devoted a great deal of his energy to building ships of improved design, adding to the number of oars for the sake of speed and maneuverability.

Alfred's interest in other lands was wide and varied. He was never too busy to listen to the accounts of foreign visitors. His questions were searching and pointed. He encouraged foreign trade and his own envoys were known as far as Jerusalem.

A methodical man, Alfred divided his day into three parts: one for conducting business of state, one for study and religious devotions, while the third was for sleep and recreation. To keep an accurate record of his division of time, he had special candles made which burned exactly one inch in twenty minutes. It is said, too, that he carried with him always a small notebook in which he jotted down ideas and suggestions. Even during his busiest days he made time for learning old Saxon songs, and he ordered them taught at the palace school as a means of keeping alive the ancient culture of his race.

When the Vikings invaded England again in 893, Alfred's system of warfare proved effective. In a great battle near Chester, the English King destroyed the main Danish force. The remnant that was left fled to the coast and re-embarked. But the Norsemen never reached home. Alfred's ships caught them on the North Sea, destroyed some vessels and chased the others down the east coast to the Channel, where they were wrecked on the Goodwin Sands.

Alfred spent his remaining years in peace, consolidating his gains. He died in 899, having reigned as King of Wessex for twenty-eight years and as King of all the English for fourteen years. He is buried at Winchester in the great cathedral he began to build and which was completed by his son and successor, Edward the Elder. He stands forth in history as one of the best and wisest of Kings—Alfred the Great.

WILLIAM THE CONQUEROR

[*1027–1087*]

T HE Norman Conquest of England is a leading example of the medieval love of legality. William, Duke of Normandy, did not simply overrun territory belonging to someone else. He claimed to be the rightful heir to the English throne, and he stuck to his claim long after his power in England was such that he needed no apology for his position.

His attitude seems the more striking in that his own origin was clouded by illegality, illegitimacy. His father was the rough, energetic, belligerent Duke of Normandy, who before he came into his Norman inheritance was already known as Robert the Devil. William's mother was Arletta, daughter of a tanner, and she never married the father of her son. Hence the son became known as William the Bastard. The medieval theory of legality was wide enough to take account of such cases, especially where nobility or royalty was concerned. It allowed a certain amount of freedom to a ruler in making his own selection. When Robert the Devil went on a pilgrimage to the Holy Land, having no other male children he named William the Bastard his successor, and the decision was honored by the barons of the duchy. Robert the Devil never returned from his pilgrimage. William the Bastard became Duke of Normandy, his place acknowledged by the men who had followed his father, although he had to defend it in arms against claimants who hoped to overthrow him.

Those who tried to beat him in war were the first to learn of his special ability at it. He was physically vigorous, a real leader of men, one given to the application of the mailed fist, who would not remain quiescent under insult or injury, but rather satisfied his followers that they could count on him to defend his and their rights in the rough-and-tumble activities of the time. William the Bastard was, to this extent, a true Norman duke, a true son of Robert the Devil.

He was also a man of exceptional piety and morality. He married Matilda, daughter of the Count of Flanders, and remained faithful to her throughout their existence together. He scrupulously practiced the religious devotions of the Catholic church, even undertaking to enforce the Truce of God in Normandy, something that won for him the favor of the Holy See and later papal backing in his expedition across the Channel. William was no St. Louis, but in the decency of his private life and the control of license at his ducal court, he stood out among the feudal magnates of the eleventh century.

The legalities of his claim to the throne of England came about in this way. The King of England, Edward the Confessor, was his cousin, a man without children and therefore concerned for the inheritance of the English crown. Edward the Confessor undoubtedly wished that William of Normandy might follow him as King of England, and seemingly had promised him the succession in explicit terms. But Harold of Wessex, Edward's brother-in-law, got himself recognized as King by the nobles gathered in London. On Edward's death Harold was crowned in Westminster Abbey by the Archbishop of York. Such was the background for the Norman Conquest.

William had long been familiar with the situation in England. He had crossed the Channel in 1051 to visit Edward the Confessor, at which time the famous promise was said to have been made that the Duke of Normandy should become King of England on Edward's death. At the same time William met Harold of Wessex on friendly terms.

A few years later Harold, who was destined to dispute William's claim, suffered a shipwreck on the Norman coast. Rescued and treated with every respect by William, Harold was persuaded to swear on holy relics that he would support William's claim to the English throne. Harold later charged trickery, saying he didn't know about the relics on which he swore.

For the next decade William devoted himself to strengthening his Duchy of Normandy and preparing for the day when he would become King of England. Then early in 1066 came the news from London. Edward the Confessor was dead. He had named Harold as his successor. The English assembly called the Witenagemot had approved the choice. The coronation had taken place. Harold of Wessex was King of England.

The historians will always argue about the status of King Harold in terms of medieval thinking. It is clear that the Witenagemot considered binding neither the promise of Edward the Confessor nor the oath of Harold, in which they had pledged support of William's candidacy. The argument was that the people of England, represented by their council of elders, had a right to a voice in selecting the man who would rule them. Since most of our information comes from the side that won, the Norman side, the surviving literature speaks mainly of the perfidy of Harold in accepting the crown in spite of his solemnly plighted word.

William's reaction at the news from England is indisputable. He was beside himself with rage. The man who had posed as his friend, accepted his hospitality, and made him promises, now was discovered to be a hypocrite, and a hypocrite sitting on William's throne. In typical Norman fashion, the Duke of Normandy fell into a fury, berated his rival in fierce tirades, and went into action.

To his side he summoned his barons, his knights, and their followers. He had huge forests cut down to be made into ships, and his province rang with the noise of his preparations. He appealed to the Pope, to the King of France, to the chivalry of Christendom, arguing that the laws of God and man made him the rightful King of England. His claim was accepted. Pope Alexander II sent him a consecrated banner. Soldiers of fortune flocked to his banner. When he crossed the Channel with his armada and went ashore at Pevensey on the southern coast of England, he was at the head of some ten thousand men.

Harold was unfortunate from start to finish in his efforts to meet the Norman attack that he knew was coming. Shortly before William sailed, an army of Vikings landed in the north of England. Harold quickly marched against the Vikings and defeated them, but in so doing he was compelled to leave his southern coast open to the Norman invasion. The English King turned back and hurried to the scene of the landings, but these were already accomplished by the time he arrived.

Everything was now set for the climactic battle that would decide the issue between two men, each of whom regarded himself as King of

England. Harold chose to meet the attack on Senlac Hill, just outside Hastings in the Sussex Downs. As the two armies grappled with one another, two different methods of battle strove for supremacy. The English fought on foot, protecting themselves with a wall of heavy shields, hurling javelins at long range, then coming to close quarters with the battle-axes they had copied from the Vikings. The Normans, more advanced in their style of fighting, had a strong cavalry arm, while their men on foot wielded the longbow and the terrible crossbow.

Harold, a foeman worthy of William's steel, understood perfectly well what the difference in armament and tactics meant. He chose Hastings because the hill and the English javelins would stop the charge of the Norman cavalry. He depended on his Saxon shields to ward off the arrows of the enemy, whereupon he would send his troops hurtling down the hill with their battle-axes. He felt confident because his numbers were somewhat greater than those of the enemy.

Harold held a strong position as the Norman knights advanced. In their van a minstrel sang the *Song of Roland,* the saga of chivalry surrounding the venerated paladin of Charlemagne. The first part of the Battle of Hastings went as Harold had planned it. William's cavalry, slowed up by the hill and galled by English javelins, were repulsed in their charge and forced to fall back. This was the critical moment for the Duke of Normandy, but he had the answer in the form of a strategem. He ordered his army to withdraw to level ground. Harold, thinking it was a disorganized retreat, ordered his soldiers to charge. Then the Normans wheeled around and met them head-on. The cavalry created havoc among the English thanes. As the melee was at its height, the bolt to a Norman crossbow struck Harold in the eye, killing him and leaving the English without a leader, without a king. Soon the defenders of Hastings were flying in utter rout.

William of Normandy—now William the Conqueror—marched on London to enforce his claim to the throne. There he fulfilled his great ambition by becoming King of England. The nation did not accept him at once. Rebellions broke out in many places, all of which he ruthlessly put down. He made himself absolute master of England, and his men an aristocracy ruling over the subject English, a sociological pattern that existed for centuries afterward and may be seen in Sir Walter Scott's novel *Ivanhoe.* Modern England is a compound of old English and later Norman ingredients; this applies to the English language as well, with its Teutonic base and the Latin additions brought over in the French of the Norman knights.

Our knowledge of England under the Normans is very extensive because William the Conqueror ordered the compilation of the Domesday Book in 1085. A survey of most of the country, it gives the size of every important estate, the name of the owner, the nature of the land—arable, pasture, or forest—and its value in the time of Edward the Confessor. The Domesday Book, still preserved in the Public Record Office in London, shows that in William's time there were 300,000 families owning land in England and the total population of the country was about 2,000,000. William the Conqueror set up the feudal system, and instituted the right of primogeniture, the inheritance of the throne by the eldest son of the reigning monarch, which exists in England to this day.

On William's death his body was returned to Normandy, where it was buried in the Abbey at Caen. In the nearby town of Bayeux may be seen the celebrated Bayeux tapestry, a wonderful work of the time that tells the story of the Battle of Hastings from the sailing of the Norman armada to the rout of the English at the hands of William the Conqueror.

GODFREY OF BOUILLON

[*1061?–1100*]

O N July 15, 1099, Godfrey of Bouillon directed the placing of a movable wooden tower against a wall of Jerusalem, mounted it to the top, fought his way across the wall, and was the first knight to enter the Holy City. The Moslem defenders were overpowered, and a massacre followed. But even before the fighting had ceased, Godfrey divested himself of his coat of mail, and barefoot, clad in a penitential shirt, made the rounds as a pilgrim and then knelt in prayer beside the hollowed rock where the body of Christ is reputed to have been laid after the Crucifixion. In Godfrey were united the violence and piety of the typical Crusader.

He refused the title of King of Jerusalem, proffered by the assembled chivalry of Europe after the victorious First Crusade, on the ground that his humility forbade him "to wear a crown of gold where his Saviour had worn one of thorns." Godfrey of Bouillon contented himself with the title of Guardian of the Holy Sepulcher. He was, however, the ruler of the new Christian state.

As Chaucer said, Godfrey was "a very parfaite and gentil knight" but he had not always been so humble and religious. A direct descendant of Charlemagne, he inherited authority in Belgian Brabant where he was Count of Bouillon. He received a better education than most European nobles of the Middle Ages, and could read, write, and speak Latin, French, and German. He resembled the others of his class in his belligerence. At the age of eighteen he was already schooled in deciding differences of opinion at the point of a sword.

The era was dominated by the great struggle between the Empire and the Papacy. Godfrey of Bouillon, a vassal of the Empire, had to choose between Emperor and Pope. The future leader of the First Crusade elected against the Pope. Emperor Henry IV was compelled to make his submission to Pope Gregory VII at Canossa, but renewed his defiance, and was excommunicated. Godfrey, supporting his feudal sovereign against the Bishop of Rome, received the Duchy of Lorraine, and entered into the possession of the richest fief of the Rhineland.

The Emperor led an army against the Pope, captured Rome, and drove Gregory VII into exile. Godfrey was foremost in the assault. He killed Rudolph of Swabia, at the foot of the high altar of the Lateran basilica, which was sacrilege. Then he rode in the imperial cavalcade when Henry IV entered Rome in triumph, to be crowned by an antipope he appointed.

But, stricken with malarial fever, so common in Rome, Godfrey fell gravely ill. He looked upon this as divine punishment for the sacrilege he had committed, and vowed that if restored to health he would do something pleasing to God in atonement. Recovering from his illness he abandoned arms, returned home, and interested himself in the welfare of the people dwelling on his vast estates. Then he resolved to make a pilgrimage to Jerusalem.

Upon the death of Gregory VII, Pope Urban II was raised to the throne of St. Peter. He preached the First Crusade. For centuries the Moslem Arabs, in possession of Palestine, had permitted the Christians to make pilgrimages to Jerusalem and the Holy Places. But now the Seljuk Turks had seized control, and they, being more fanatical Mohammedans, were maltreating the pilgrims. Their strength, moreover, was a menace to the Christian world.

The Papacy took the lead, Urban II summoning the chivalry of Europe to march against the infidel. At Clermont the assembled nobles and knights answered his great eloquence with cries of *"Deus vult"*—"God wills it!" The call of the Crusade aroused intense enthusiasm throughout Christendom.

Godfrey of Bouillon, who had already made a vow to perform a pilgrimage to Jerusalem, gladly embraced the opportunity to go as a soldier of Christ. He set out with an army of forty thousand fighting men, of whom more than three thousand were knights. They went by land, through Germany and Hungary and the Balkans, territories of the Byzantine Empire. Their first destination was Constantinople, the common rendezvous for various of the crusading princes.

Godfrey's crusaders reached the valley of the Danube in September of 1096 and passed through Hungary without let or hindrance, paying for everything they took. Then they crossed into the territory of the Byzantine Empire. The Byzantine Emperor was in a quandary. He wanted the Moslems defeated. He had appealed for the crusade after the Byzantines had been defeated by the Seljuk Turks and lost Asia Minor. But he could only look with misgiving at the powerful host rallying at his capital. Alexius demanded that Godfrey of Bouillon swear fealty to him and march on, removing the crusading army from Byzantine territory. Godfrey was in a quandary. How could he, a leader in a crusade preached by the Pope and a vassal of the Holy Roman Emperor, swear allegiance to the Eastern Emperor? All winter long Godfrey maintained his point of view and refused to swear fealty to Alexius.

Alexius lost patience and cut off the supplies of the crusaders. This forced their hand. Godfrey of Bouillon solemnly did homage to the Emperor of the East and promised to restore to him any of the imperial possessions that might be taken from the infidels. When the great Count of Toulouse arrived, Godfrey induced him to do likewise. The example was followed by all the other Christian princes who passed through Constantinople. Had it not been for this wise piece of diplomacy, the First Crusade might have had a very different ending.

Godfrey, who became more and more religious, looked upon himself as a pilgrim rather than a political and military leader. He left the conduct of the crusade to his brother Baldwin, Count of Flanders; to Bohemund, chief of the Italian-Norman contingent; to Raymund of Toulouse; and to Tancred, the nephew of the Norman King of southern Italy, Robert Guiscard.

During the crossing of Syria, Godfrey was seriously hurt while hunting but this did not prevent him from acting as mediator when the leaders of the crusade quarreled among themselves over spoils. He himself gave up a castle his own followers had taken, and thus appeased Bohemund at the siege of Antioch. Near Antioch, Godfrey, with only twelve knights in his train, charged and put to flight 150 Turks. The capture of Antioch was vital to the crusaders, for it gave them a great city and made them all the more certain of victory.

They marched on their ultimate destination—Jerusalem. Ferocious fighting took place as they encircled, blockaded, and then stormed the Holy City. Many historians have wondered how Godfrey could have been responsible for so much bloodshed and then have turned so fervently to his role of pilgrim. But for medieval men it was normal to fight for their faith, and the crusaders were furious about the way their coreligionists had been oppressed by the Moslems.

As Guardian of the Holy Sepulcher, Godfrey had a short reign of a year, but it was an eventful reign. He fought the Arabs of Egypt, and won the great Battle of Acalon which for eighty-seven years made secure the Christian kingdom. He was beset by the jealousy of Raymund of Toulouse. He was opposed by the patriarch Dagobert who had been ordered by the Pope to see that a theocracy was established in the Holy Land. He rebuilt Joppa (Jaffa), which became the port of arrival for new crusaders and pilgrims who made their way to the new kingdom of Jerusalem. He signed a treaty of alliance with Venice by which its fleet undertook to safeguard shipping on the way to and from the Holy Land.

Godfrey of Bouillon was stricken with the plague at Caesarea. He returned to Jerusalem, and there he died amidst all the consolations of his Catholic religion. No place could have been more appropriate for the passing of the Guardian of the Holy Sepulcher.

THOMAS À BECKET

[1118?–1170]

THE majestic pile of Canterbury Cathedral was still incomplete and men were at work on the Norman Tower four days after Christmas in the year 1170, when a small body of knights, attended by their squires, rode through the ancient city. They were seeking Thomas à Becket, Archbishop of Canterbury and Primate of all England. Four of them alighted and entered the Archbishop's quarters. Finding him at his meal, they began an abusive dispute with him, calling him a traitor and an enemy of the King. Then they went outside, crying to the followers of the Archbishop that they were absolved from allegiance to him.

It was clear that the knights were bent on violence, so the others present urged Thomas à Becket to enter the cathedral for sanctuary. He did so, but only with great reluctance, for he was not a man to fear his enemies.

The doors were barred, a useless measure which merely held up the knights momentarily as they battered their way in.

Furiously they rushed upon the Archbishop, seized hold of him, and attempted to drag him out of the building. He was too strong for them, and sent them reeling as he twisted free. Then he said calmly, "I will not leave the cathedral. If you want to kill me, kill me here." As they pulled their daggers from their belts, he bowed his head and covered his face with his cloak. Four times they struck him before the Archbishop collapsed and lay dead in his own cathedral.

"Will no man rid me of this haughty prelate?" King Henry II had exclaimed in a fit of temper, and four of his courtiers, taking his words too literally, had ridden off to do their monarch's bidding. The story is told in T. S. Eliot's famous play, *Murder in the Cathedral*.

Thomas à Becket was of pure Norman stock. His parents were both born in France, his father at Rouen, his mother at Caen. The elder Becket was a wealthy man when Thomas was born, an official of the port of London who wielded considerable influence.

Thomas was sent to school in Surrey and then in London. A quick tongue, a nimble mind, and a long memory won him high praise from all his teachers. Among his fellow-pupils he distinguished himself in the sham fights between boys of different wards who fought with wooden swords and shields for supremacy in the streets, a form of sport then as popular as football is today. At eighteen he was a good-looking youth devoted to cockfighting and tilting (sometimes on horseback, sometimes from punts on the river), and forever dancing with girls or running to help extinguish fires, which were numerous in medieval London. He competed in verse-making contests, and was in all respects a gay young fellow of the time. On the other hand, he was immersed in theological studies, and went to Paris to continue them, drinking deeply of the learning, lore, and legend of the Church.

His father being in financial difficulties, Thomas took employment as a clerk. There is a story from this period of his life that while he and a friend were riding along a country road one day Thomas fell from his horse into a millstream, and was miraculously saved from death because the miller (knowing nothing of the accident) chose that very moment to stop the mill wheel.

Thomas soon gained a reputation as an administrator. At the age of twenty-four he was noticed by Theobald, the Archbiship of Canterbury, who took him into his service.

In an Icelandic saga there is a description of Thomas in his youth: ". . . slim of growth, pale of hue, dark of hair, long nose, straight features, winning and lovable, frank of speech, slightly stuttering, keen of discernment, wondrously strong memory, with unusual aptitude for making difficult questions plain." Such was the young man who was favored with ecclesiastical employment in the establishment of England's highest ranking prelate, Theobald, Archbishop of Canterbury.

The key to his character and career is to be found in his whole-hearted dedication to whatever cause he served, his gift of loyalty, his genius for partnership. His nature was made up of opposites: gay, carefree roistering on the one hand and religious fervor on the other. Now going into the service of the Archbishop and the Church, he did

so uncompromisingly. He turned from secular pleasures to spiritual
ardors and a zeal in the cause of the Church.

In the entourage of the Archbishop he encountered enmities, got
into quarrels, probably because of that inability to compromise which
distinguished his character. He was twice dismissed, as a result
apparently of the influence of an enemy he made in the Canterbury circle, but was taken back by the Archbishop, who had an abid-
ing regard for him. Thomas went to France and Italy, especially to
Bologna, to study canon law (the law of the Church) and the newly
revised Roman law.

England at the time was torn by a dispute for the succession to the
crown—the war of Stephen and Matilda. The direct line of William
the Conqueror, who was succeeded by two of his sons, ended when
King Henry I died without a male heir. The throne was claimed by
his daughter Matilda and his nephew Stephen of Blois. Stephen was
crowned King, and civil strife ensued in behalf of Matilda and of her
son, Henry of Anjou. Archbishop Theobald opposed Stephen and
supported Matilda and Henry. In this he had the valuable aid of his
able adjutant Thomas.

The Archbishop went to the Council of Rheims in defiance of the
King's orders. He was accompanied by Thomas. In 1151 Theobald
sent Thomas to Rome to dissuade the Pope from approving the
coronation of Stephen's son Eustache. Thomas was then thirty-three.
He carried out the mission with consummate ability, the Pope sanctioning everything he had been sent to obtain. On Thomas' return to
England, King Stephen had the Archbishop of Canterbury arrested
and thrown into prison. Theobald escaped, and fled to France.
Thomas accompanied him.

The quarrel for the succession ended with a compromise whereby
Stephen remained King but recognized Matilda's son Henry as his
successor. Thus, in time, the candidate supported by the Archbishop,
and by Thomas, would come to the throne. This occurred on Stephen's
death in 1154. Henry, Count of Anjou, became King Henry II of England. Theobald, Archbishop of Canterbury, was restored to influence.
Thomas was promoted to be archdeacon of Canterbury.

The new King was twenty-one, Thomas was thirty-six. The two
men became fast friends. The following year, Archbishop Theobald
recommended Thomas for appointment to the high office of Chancel-

lor of England. Henry was pleased to have his bosom friend as chief official and adviser. The old Archbishop was delighted to have his stalwart follower placed in the most important position in the government of the King, supposing that he would support the privileges of the Church. Never was an archbishop more mistaken.

Having enlisted in the service of the King, Thomas was now the King's man. With his habit of uncompromising adherence, he turned from the ecclesiastical to the secular cause, as became Thomas à Becket, Chancellor of England. He laid heavy taxes on the Church to pay for Henry's foreign wars. Of still greater consequence, he pressed the case of the crown in a dispute over civil and ecclesiastical courts. This was a dominant controversy of the time. Ancient custom was that clerics accused of crime were tried by the Church in its own courts. But the times were changing and the increase of royal power required that criminal clerics should answer to the King's courts of justice. The Church was violently opposed, and Thomas à Becket pressed the cause of the King.

Becket's transition to the secular cause of the King was complete. Not content with serving in a civil capacity he studied military science, and played an active part in King Henry's warlike expeditions. In 1159, he organized the campaign against the Count of Toulouse, who was encroaching upon Anjou, Henry's hereditary domain in France. The Chancellor accompanied the English forces to France, arrayed himself in armor, and charged at the head of a company of knights. The enemy defeated, he took command of the army when the King returned to England.

Again when there was war on the Norman border of Henry's French domain, the Chancellor served in warfare against the King of France. He engaged in single combat with a French knight, and unhorsed his opponent who had to pay a heavy ransom. Finally when the war was won, Becket was sent to make peace with the French King.

Accompanied by a sumptuous retinue, he discharged the duties of an ambassador with dexterity, magnanimity, and splendor. He negotiated terms of peace and also a dynastic marriage uniting the French and English royal houses. His personality was attractive, his demeanor proud, his military reputation great.

Thomas à Becket was now at the zenith of his secular power. He was the King's closest companion in the council chamber, in court pageantry, in forest hunts. As Chancellor he presided with a busy hand over the King's affairs, and defended the King's cause against all comers, including the Church. He rebuilt the Tower of London which had fallen into disrepair. He entertained lavishly and kept open house. His generosity was proverbial, and legend relates that when riding with the King he had been known to give his own rich warm mantle to an old man who had none.

It was then that Henry II made the same mistake that Archbishop Theobald had made before him. The aged Primate of England died, and the King proposed to make Thomas à Becket his successor as Archbishop of Canterbury. He took it for granted that his friend as archbishop would continue to be the King's man. Becket was reluctant. He had a genuine friendship for Henry, and knew what his new elevation would mean. He protested against it, and is said to have warned Henry that as Primate of England he would be on the side of the Church. But the King insisted. Thomas à Becket became Archbishop of Canterbury in 1162. The new Primate of England was forty-four.

The clergy of England regarded him coldly. He was only an archdeacon, so he had first to be consecrated as a priest before being raised to the dignity of archbishop. The bishops acquiesced in silence. The King expected the Church to be brought to a state of dependence on the Crown, and it could only be supposed that Thomas the Archbishop would lend himself to this as Thomas the Chancellor had done.

Thomas à Becket, becoming the Primate of England, was transformed. He rid his life of all things secular. Although he had a special dispensation from the Pope to remain Chancellor, he resigned that high office. He discarded all rich raiment and, except when officiating in the cathedral, wore only the simplest ecclesiastical attire. He doubled the income of the bishops. He clung with the utmost tenacity to all the Church's legal and property rights which the King was so anxious and determined to reclaim. He would allow no cleric to appear before the King's courts, even to answer a criminal offense. He became as violently pro-Church as he had been pro-Crown. Before a year had elapsed Thomas à Becket, Archbishop of Canterbury, was on the worst possible terms with King Henry II.

The Pope seemed willing to compromise with the King of England. But Becket would listen to no one. The open break with the King came at the Council of Woodstock in 1163. The Archbishop successfully opposed the King's proposal that a land tax should be paid by the Church into the royal exchequer, and excommunicated a tenant-in-chief who had challenged his authority over some land in Canterbury. Then he bluntly refused to allow a charge of assault upon one of the King's officers.

A council was called at Clarendon to settle the points of authority in dispute between the Church and the Crown, and the Archbishop promised, at the urgent request of the Pope, to obey the laws and customs of England. Whereupon Henry II caused to be drawn up the Constitutions of Clarendon, one article of which proposed a compromise in the dispute over the ecclesiastical court. This compromise provided that an accused cleric should be tried by a church court, but should be punished by the King's justice if found guilty. The Archbishop of York and the bishops in general were in favor of accepting the compromise. Henry demanded that the Archbishop of Canterbury sign, but Thomas à Becket refused.

Having thus defied the King, the Archbishop stopped saying mass in public, and withdrew into private devotions. At the insistence of friends who feared for his life, he decided to leave England for France. His first two attempts failed, the first time because of unfavorable winds, the second because the sailors, fearing the King's vengeance, mutinied. Finally he got across the Channel in November 1164, and from French soil continued his fight against the King.

After two years of persuasion Becket induced the Pope to let him excommunicate the King's principal counselors, then two of the bishops who had accepted the Constitutions of Clarendon. It would seem that his zeal for the Church had become confused with bitter resentment and a personal grudge against the King. The story of the two one-time bosom friends was now to run its tragic course.

After the primate had been absent from the see of Canterbury for six years, Henry II undertook to depose him and replace him. The King had his son crowned by the Archbishop of York. This was a grave infringement upon the rights of Canterbury, and the Pope gave Henry the choice between being excommunicated and effecting a reconciliation with the exiled archbishop. The King was forced to accede. Thomas à Becket returned to Canterbury. Before leaving France he said, "I go to England to die." The reconciliation with the King was a hollow truce. The Archbishop immediately declared the Constitutions of Clarendon to be null and void, and suspended the bishops who had rendered service to the King. It was an open declaration of war. Within a month of his return to England, Thomas à Becket, at the age of fifty-two, was murdered in his own cathedral.

No one regretted the crime more than the King, who had inadvertently caused it. Faced with excommunication by the Pope and the possible loss of his crown, he had to make atonement with personal penance, scourged by monks of Canterbury at the place in the cathedral where the Archbishop had fallen under dagger strokes.

Two years after his death, Thomas à Becket was canonized a saint, and his tomb became an immediate object of pilgrimage. For centuries afterward the Canterbury pilgrims were a feature of English life; more than two hundred years later they gave Chaucer the idea for his *Canterbury Tales,* one of the greatest works in the history of English literature. Then came the era of Henry VIII, who desecrated the tomb, ended the pilgrimages, and brought to a summary conclusion the long contest between Church and Crown, in which the story of Thomas à Becket was the most dramatic episode.

SALADIN

[1138–1193]

T HE outstanding figure on the Mohammedan side during the
Crusades was the man known to the West as Saladin. In original Arabic his name meant "he who reverences the creed"—meaning
the Moslem creed. Yet this pious son of Islam gained the admiration
and respect of the Christian crusaders who fought him.

Raised in Damascus, the center of Arabic culture, Saladin as a
young man proved that he was a genius at both war and politics. He
was only in his mid-twenties when he received the post of second-in-
command in Egypt. Within a few years he had become vizier in the
Land of the Nile. Then he led his army to Damascus to put down an
insurrection against the reigning family, and after a period of anarchy
and military rule, emerged as Sultan. He was the only one who could
control the rebellious Arab chieftains. Two years later he had united
the Mohammedan world in an imposing empire.

Facing Saladin's empire stood the Christian kingdom of Jerusalem,
founded by the crusaders. The rival religions had produced rival
political powers that contended for mastery of the Middle East. But
the kingdom of Jerusalem was an artificial creation of mail-clad
knights from Europe. One disastrous defeat would topple it into
extinction.

Saladin determined to win such a battle. He laid siege to Tiberias,
thus drawing the crusaders under Guy de Lusignan into an attempt
to relieve the city. The crusaders got as far as Hattin and then
camped. Before they knew what was happening, Saladin had maneuvered his army into position during the night, so that by morning
they were surrounded.

Hastily the Christians closed their ranks, setting up a wall of
spears. Four times their armored knights thundered against Saladin's

lines, only to be beaten back. Then the Saracens set fire to the brush on the sides of the hill and swarmed up to the attack. The crusaders fought with great valor, but the odds were hopelessly against them. Except for a few knights who cut their way through the throng of assailants, the rest died where they stood, sword in hand.

Saladin entered Jerusalem, then overran all Palestine. But in 1191, Richard Coeur de Lion, King of England, arrived on the Third Crusade and landed at Haifa. The crusaders marched to Acre, besieged it, and took it about a month after their arrival. Richard the Lionhearted fought four campaigns in Palestine. He won brilliant victories. He gained the admiration of his great opponent, Saladin. But the Moslem kept the Christian from reconquering Jerusalem. After a lingering stalemate the two sides patched up a truce that left Saladin with the upper hand in Palestine. Only a tiny strip of coast was granted to the Christians, along with permission to visit Jerusalem unarmed for purposes of trade and devotion.

The two great leaders never met face to face. Richard soon left for home, the situation in England cutting short his crusading effort. Saladin died within a year of the truce. The storytellers, however, would not leave it at that; anecdotes were handed down about the vigorous, foolhardy, quick-tempered crusader confronting the lithe, intelligent, self-controlled Moslem. Sir Walter Scott has Saladin meet Richard the Lionhearted in his novel *The Talisman*. But the "meeting" remains fiction rather than fact.

Saladin died on a pilgrimage to Mecca. He left to succeeding sultans an empire firmly established. He left to Moslem commanders the tradition of victory in the field, the tradition of Hattin. He left the crusaders the dispiriting doubt that Jerusalem would ever be theirs again. He left to Palestine, to Europe, to the world, the memory of the chivalrous Saracen. Some of the most splendid events of world history are evoked by the name of Saladin.

IVAN THE TERRIBLE

QUEEN ELIZABETH

RICHARD THE LIONHEARTED

[*1157–1199*]

To THE modern mind the life of Richard the Lionhearted was one
of senseless, incessant fighting. For us there is little meaning in
the unending battles in which he delighted, and in which he engaged upon the slightest excuse. Save for the Third Crusade, in which
he performed wondrous prodigies, his other excursions and campaigns appear to have had little point. Yet he was hailed as the ideal
of his era. To the belligerent Middle Ages he was all that a hero should
be. He waged war for war's sake, but in the days of chivalry and
knighthood that was the thing to do. He was admired as the paladin
that no man wanted to encounter in a hand-to-hand affray.

Richard was the third son of Henry II and Eleanor of Aquitaine.
He grew up more French than English in those times when king and
nobility were French, and when so much of the royal dominion was
in France. At the age of eleven, as a younger son, he was invested
with the lordship of a suitable inheritance, his mother's own Aquitaine. She took him to be installed there, and he assumed the lordship
with all pomp and pageantry. In the semi-independence of Aquitaine
he grew to maturity. Unwilling to accept the authority of anybody,
he took the field against both his father and his brothers when they
demanded a vassal's oath from him. He acted the more boldly because he was helped by the King of France, Philip Augustus, and
managed to save the integrity of his realm south of the Loire.

Henry II's last invasion of France ended in defeat. He fell ill and
died in a fury because, his two elder sons being already dead, the
throne must pass to Richard. The rebellious lord of Aquitaine went to
London for his coronation. He was now his own master. It was as
King of England, but holding extensive territories in France, that he
turned his mind to the Crusades.

In the Holy Land the Christian kingdom of Jerusalem had fallen to the Moslems. The crusaders held no more than some strong points along the coast of Palestine. Christendom was crying out for a new expedition against the infidel. The new King of England, renowned for his valor, trained to love fighting by a youth in which he had to fight repeatedly for his land and his position, was eager to be off for the Holy Land. With Philip Augustus of France he was leagued under oath to undertake the Third Crusade.

On his way to Palestine, Richard made the first foreign conquest in English history. One of his ships was wrecked on the island of Cyprus, the ruler of which, King Isaac, maltreated crusaders and sailors, and the islanders plundered the vessel. Richard, battle-axe in hand, landed at the head of his army and conquered the island. Then he celebrated his wedding to Princess Berengaria of Navarre. Richard was crowned King of Cyprus and his bride Queen of England and of Cyprus.

Twelve months after he had left England, Richard joined the Christian besiegers of Acre. It was here that during a misunderstanding in surrender negotiations, Richard committed a barbarity for which he has been greatly criticized. The crusaders held five thousand Saracen hostages to guarantee a truce. The defenders of Acre broke the terms of the truce, and Richard ordered the hostages to be massacred.

Philip Augustus left the crusade and returned to France on a plea of ill-health. He was much affronted by Richard's marriage to Berengaria and by the repudiation of his sister Princess Alice. But he swore peace and friendship and left a few thousand men of his army under Richard's command.

Richard then fell out with Leopold, Archduke of Austria, another of the top leaders of the Third Crusade. When Acre surrendered, the Archduke placed his flag over the gate of the citadel. Richard arrogantly tore down the Austrian standard with his own hands. The feud that resulted was destined to have far-reaching effects on Richard's life.

The departure of Philip Augustus left the Christian army weakened, but Richard was in command of the knights and fought for Jerusalem. His antagonist was one of the great figures of Mohammedan history, the princely Saladin, chivalrous warrior and statesman, whose name the legends of Christendom raised as high as that of Richard the Lionhearted himself. The contest between the two provided material for centuries of medieval storytelling.

Richard won battles at Ascalon and Joppa, the ponderous charge of the mail-clad knights crushing the more lightly armed Saracens. He himself was always in the forefront with his men. But the crusaders were divided by quarrels among the leaders who disputed for possession of the crown of the Christian kingdom of Jerusalem, which was to be re-established upon the capture of the Holy City. The Duke of Burgundy drew off with his knights, and was joined by Germans and Austrians, forces of the affronted Archduke Leopold of Austria.

The crusading army was disrupted, and Richard, moreover, heard of intrigues against him by his brother John back in England. With heavy heart he had to give up the hope of capturing Jerusalem, after having arrived in sight of the Holy City. It is said that he refused to gaze on Jerusalem, which he could not capture.

He retired to the coast, and negotiated a truce with Saladin. Richard was so delighted with the gallant bearing of his great enemy that he declared he would rather be the friend of the brave and honest infidel than of his own false Christian allies. The terms they made were that the Christians should retain the coast towns and pilgrims might visit the Holy Places without molestation.

Richard's attempt to get home by way of Europe resulted in one of history's most romantic stories. While crossing Austria he was recognized in spite of a disguise. The vengeful Leopold, remembering the animosity that had developed in Palestine, had him immured in a castle. No one knew where he was, or whether he was dead or alive.

One of Richard's companions on the hopeless homeward journey had been Blondel de Nesle, a troubadour knight and poet. This faithful friend sought the King throughout Austria, singing from castle to castle. When he reached the right one he sang beneath the tower a song which he and Richard had composed together. Scarcely had he finished the first verse when Richard answered back with the second. Blondel hurried to England with the news of Richard's imprisonment. Eventually the King of England was ransomed from the Holy Roman Emperor.

Arriving home, Richard forced the submission of John and the rebellious barons. Soon afterward he led an invading army into France.

He was as belligerent as ever, and the rest of his life was spent in campaigns and battles—endless, fruitless war with Philip Augustus.

Richard's penchant for war destroyed him. While besieging a castle in France he was hit in the shoulder by an arrow shot from the ramparts. He tore the arrow out himself, then refused to allow the wound to be dressed until he had ridden around the walls. Infection set in and killed him at the age of forty-two. His influence lingers on in the motto of England—"Dieu et mon droit!"—which was first shouted by Richard the Lionhearted when he was fighting in Palestine on the Third Crusade.

GENGHIS KHAN

[1162–1227]

HISTORY rates Genghis Khan as the greatest and most terrible of all conquerors. His armies overran a larger part of the earth, subjected more peoples far and wide, and wrought a more destructive havoc and slaughter than is recorded in any other page of the grim annals of mankind. In the memory of terrified nations, Genghis Khan seemed less like a mere human being than a diabolical power of some devastating force of nature. He was, indeed, the supreme personification of one dominating fact of human dynamics, the hosts and hordes that have been discharged from the vast spaces of central Asia. Time and again, explosive invasions have come out of the immense heartland. History notes especially the Huns and the Turks, and, most of all, the Mongols.

For ages, central Asia, from the Urals to the borders of China, had been the spawning ground of tribes and nomad horsemen, living in tents, driving their herds of cattle from one pasture to another, fighting against each other in petty ferocious warfare. From time to time, masses of these wandering clans had coalesced, and become formidable predatory forces, a menace to civilized neighbors, raiding into settled agricultural countries and ravaging cities. For the central Asian nomads, the nearest and most accessible neighbor, with its teeming population and wealthy culture, was China, and Chinese history presents a series of nightmares in the ravaging assaults of the barbarians of the vast outer plain. Further off on the other side were Persia, India, the Near East, Europe, and all were reached at one time or another by the horse-riding tribes rallied for systematic warfare. The climax came in the thirteenth century with Genghis Khan.

This ferocious conqueror, son of a petty Mongol chieftain, was named Temuchin. He inherited a kingdom when he was thirteen, along with the kind of trouble customary with so young a ruler trying to govern turbulent subchiefs. A number of them withdrew from their allegiance, but Temuchin's mother, a nomad queen, was not one to sit by while the patrimony of her son vanished. She directed war against the rebels, year after year, until Temuchin himself had reached the age of a warrior and was able to complete the task of restoring the consolidation of tribes that his father had ruled. He enlarged his nomad empire, overthrew every rival who dared to face him, and emerged from his wars as master of nearly all of Mongolia.

Temuchin decided to confer on himself a title suitable to his dignity. Far and wide among the tents of the central Asian herdsmen he was famous as a brutal warrior and a merciless enemy. He summoned an assembly of Mongol chiefs, proclaimed an empire, and assumed the name of Genghis Khan, meaning "the mightiest lord." He was now ready for his career as the most terrible of conquerors.

He looked to a new theater of war, and had his choice between East and West. In time he was to strike in both directions, his career divided between China and the countries that reached far toward the setting sun. The nearest place of wealth and loot and easy spoils was China, while the road to the West was longer. The campaigns of Genghis Khan alternated. First he struck into China, and then he embarked on ventures that led him westward.

The state of affairs in China, at the beginning of the thirteenth century, was a graphic example of the peril to which that great land had long been subjected, menaced by the barbarians of the vast plains. Not long before this time northern China had been conquered by a nomad tribal power, the Chin Tartars, who were akin to the Mongols. The Chins had assailed the Sung dynasty of native Chinese emperors who once had reigned in glory. The Sungs had been driven into southern China, where they still held sway, while the Chins ruled over the northern part of the country.

Genghis Khan attacked the Chins, drove beyond the Great Wall, and invaded northern China. His armies reached the sea, resistance collapsed, and the commanders for the Chin Emperor came over to the side of the Mongols. The defeated sovereign sought peace, but his actions aroused the suspicion of Genghis Khan, who struck again, destroyed the Chin dynasty, and made himself master of northern

China. In the south, the native Chinese Sung Emperor still remained. The fate of the Sung dynasty was to await another day.

It is in such fashion that Chinese history recalls Genghis Khan and the Mongols. On the other side of the great Eurasian land mass there is a similar story. The Arabs and Islam have one page of this history, Christendom another, both vivid with the terror. An Arab chronicler says that the immense western conquests of the destroyer were the result of accidents. This is true in the sense that Genghis Khan's great marches and devastations westward were not the result of a plan of widespread dominion, but were brought on by circumstances, one thing leading to another.

In winning the hegemony of the Mongols, the terrible Khan subjugated the Nimans, led by their chief Kushlek. The Nimans were utterly defeated in battle, and Kushlek fled. But this chieftain did not give up easily. While his conqueror was campaigning in China, Kushlek gathered an army, and set about restoring himself to power over his people. This brought Genghis Khan out of China. He defeated Kushlek, sent him in fugitive flight again, and then returned to overrunning the great land to the east.

Kushlek, still undaunted, embarked on schemes and treacheries that enabled him to seize the throne of a central Asian prince, which gave him the command of military forces for a renewal of the war. He allied himself with the Shah of Khwarizm, a powerful kingdom in the southern part of central Asia. This was in the general region of what is now Russian Turkestan, and included such great cities as Bokhara and Samarkand. Genghis Khan hastened from China to meet Kushlek once more, and crushed him finally and completely.

These campaigns against his bitter enemy had taken Genghis Khan westward, and his armies now stood at the border of Khwarizm. He had no desire to go further. Western conquest was not in his mind. So he sent an emissary to the Shah of Khwarizm, suggesting peace and amity. The Shah was agreeable, and matters might have ended there had it not been for a mistake made by the governor of one of the provinces of the principality of Khwarizm. Into his territory came a party of merchants sent by Genghis Khan. The governor thought they were spies, and had them killed.

The Mongol conqueror did not take an injury lightly. He sent emissaries to the Shah of Khwarizm, demanding that the offending governor be turned over to the Mongols for punishment. Whereupon the Shah made a second mistake. Taking this as an insult, he had the chief of the Mongol deputation decapitated, cut off the beards of the others, and sent them back. This outrage brought about results that spread waves of terror as far as western Europe.

Genghis Khan set out on a march with a kind of army and a style of military action that baffled the countries to the west. The Mongol hordes were light cavalry, swarms of horsemen with a mobility unknown elsewhere. They were well organized for campaigns of bewildering swiftness. They had transport, communications, and brilliant leadership. Their sovereign himself was a consummate master of an art of war as he developed it out of the traditional tactics of the central Asian nomads, and he had a number of sons who were as able as himself. They led the wings of the mighty host that now poured into countries of the West.

The Shah of Khwarizm was utterly defeated. He is said to have had an army of 400,000 men, of whom 160,000 were killed in a disastrous battle. Oriental figures are likely to be exaggerated, but the path of Genghis Khan was certainly one of wholesale slaughter. The cities of Khwarizm were captured and devastated, their inhabitants massacred. In those days Bokhara was a great center of the arts of civilization. Bokhara was captured after a short siege and given to flames and slaughter. Then the same fate befell Samarkand, equally a center of population and culture.

The Shah of Khwarizm fled, and was pursued by the vindictive Mongols. He reached the Caspian Sea, where he died. His son and heir continued the flight, the Mongol horsemen on his trail. This pursuit led them all the way into India. Cities were taken and burned, and the people killed. The Mongols pushed down through what is now Afghanistan, and ravaged the northern provinces of India.

Such atrocities were the customary pattern of events in the vast sweep of the central Asian hordes. Modern historians wonder at the incredible horrors perpetrated by Genghis Khan and his sons and other commanders. It was a studied policy to exterminate the people of cities, who were systematically massacred.

Yet Genghis Khan seems to have been human and reasonable enough in many instances. The Mohammedans, upon whom he inflicted such monstrous atrocities, were religious fanatics and oppressors. The Christians, whom he slaughtered, were persecutors too. But the Mongol chieftain himself was tolerant, without religious animosity. He himself was a devotee of primitive superstitions. (The Mongols later were to become Buddhists.) He displayed a rather enlightened interest in various religions and philosophies. Yet he was the arch-exterminator. One theory is that the Mongols, cattle-driving tribes of the plains, looked with innate hostility upon cities and agricultural communities, which constantly impinged upon grazing lands of nomad herdsmen. Therefore the systematic obliteration of settled communities was a part of the herdsmen's ancient vendetta.

The original feud of Genghis Khan against the Shah of Khwarizm had led the Mongols to Turkestan, Persia, Afghanistan, and into India, and it seemed they would go on without end. Armies commanded by sons of Genghis Khan swept around the northern shore of the Caspian Sea, and into the Caucasus and Russia, defeating all enemies along the way. At that time the most powerful state in Russia was the principality of Kiev, which mustered its power against the plague of central Asian horsemen. There was a rally of the Christian Slavs, and they made a mistake reminiscent of previous events. The Mongol commander sent envoys to them, and these were murdered. The Mongols accepted the barbarous challenge in the usual way. A host of Russians were utterly defeated, and rapine and slaughter were spread to the borders of central Europe.

The subsequent history, following the death of Genghis Khan at the height of his power, continues the story of invasion. Under his sons the Mongols poured into the heart of Islam, made an end to the caliphate of Baghdad, and went on to the Mediterranean, ravaging and slaying. In Europe they subjugated Russia, which long remained oppressed by Mongol tyranny, harried Poland, and drove into Hungary. They even reached the Adriatic, the borders of Italy. This final thrust into Europe was halted only because of a dispute among the heirs of Genghis Khan back home, which persuaded the Mongol princes to withdraw and return to central Asia.

On the eastern side of Asia, the original conquests were continued. The Sung dynasty in the south of China was overthrown, and all of China came under the sovereignty of a Mongol emperor, the grandson of Genghis Khan, the renowned Kublai Khan.

ST. FRANCIS OF ASSISI

[1182–1226]

A KEY to the life of the most beloved of Christian saints is to be found in the fact that his real name is forgotten. He was baptized John, but we remember him as Francesco, which means "little Frenchman." It was odd to be called that in the medieval Italian city of Assisi. One theory is that the mother of St. Francis was from the south of France, and she gave her son his nickname and taught him her speech. We know the future founder of the Franciscan order learned to love Provençal, the language of southern France, the tongue of the troubadours.

In Italy at the time, the approach of the thirteenth century, French manners were much esteemed and the poetic style of the troubadours was cultivated. Minstrels from southern France were favorites. Many wandered across the Alps and brought to Italy their code of chivalry, romantic courtesies and the troubadour gallantry of dedication to a lady. Later in the thirteenth century, Dante, the greatest poet of Italy, was to be much influenced by the chivalric lyrics of France.

Hence the significance in the name Francesco, the "little Frenchman," betokening a youthful fondness for the troubadour way—caroling songs of gallantry, frolicking in the manner of the minstrel, dancing in the courtly style. This was the way of St. Francis of Assisi all his life. He called poverty his bride and cherished her as a knight cherished his lady. He called her his Lady Poverty.

The life of Francis of Assisi is so wreathed in legend that it is often impossible to disentangle fact from pious imagination. He was the son of one of the chief merchants of the town. He grew up an elegant youth, much given to the luxuries and festivities of the time, a leader in circles of sumptuous merrymaking. Later legend attributes to him something of a dissolute early life, but there seems little evidence that he was any worse than the son of an affluent merchant of the period was likely to be. He was conspicuous in pleasure-seeking revelry, but it is also noted that he was always charitable to the poor.

One day Francis was in his father's shop attending to business when a beggar came in pleading for alms—in the name of God. The merchant's son told him roughly to get out, but then immediately asked himself, "What wouldn't I have done if he had asked me in the name of some great nobleman? How much better should I have received him in the name of God?" Instantly the youth ran after the beggar, and pressed money into his hand and vowed that thereafter he would always help the poor.

At about his twentieth year he went on a military expedition, was taken prisoner, kept in a dungeon until he became ill, then released. His body recovered but his spirit was troubled. For a time he alternated between his accustomed role as a leader of gay youth and a new life of tranceful prayer and service to the poor. He made a trip to Rome, and on the way gave to a beggar the rich mantle that his father had provided for him. He was ambitious for a military life, but in the Eternal City he had a mystical experience and heard a voice bidding him to enter the service of God. He returned home profoundly changed. The true bent of his nature is pictured in a familiar story. On the highway one day he passed a leper. He had an especial horror of the wretched victims of the loathsome disease, but he went to the leper, embraced him, and kissed him in a heroic effort of charity. Arrived home, he gave alms insistently to the poor, and devoted himself especially to kindness to lepers.

His father's response to all this was typical. The wealthy merchant was outraged at the extravagant behavior of his son, and was afraid the bemused youth would throw away the family wealth. He did what he could to persuade Francis to return to his senses, and then tried to disinherit him. Taking the necessary legal measures, he brought the youth before the Bishop of Assisi. A hearing was held, and the son said to his father, "Until now I have called you my father, but now I am a servant of God." He renounced his inheritance, discarded his rich apparel for a humble robe, and went away into the woods to pray and meditate.

He established himself at an old chapel, St. Mary of the Angels, which had long fallen into wreckage and disuse, and there he gave himself over to religious austerities. He called himself the Poverello, the Little Poor Man. For three years he lived as a hermit, sallying forth to minister to the poor. He begged for bread, and devoted himself to the care of the most wretched of paupers, the broken and fallen, and most of all he ministered to lepers, nursing them, feeding them, praying with them.

After three years of this solitary labor of charity in the countryside, he went into Assisi with a ministry to the needy and outcast of the town. He felt impelled to preach, though he was a layman with no church connection. He preached in praise of poverty, and with prayer and song extolled the joy of giving up all worldly possessions for the sake of Lady Poverty. Companions joined him, and presently he had about him twelve devoted followers, converted to his pattern of a life of humility and a disdain for wealth and earthly goods.

Francis, now at the head of a group, bethought himself of the wisdom of regularizing his position with the Church. He led his band of twelve disciples to Rome, and went to the Pope to request permission and sanction for his mission. In those early years of the thirteenth century the Papacy was at the height of its power and authority, and Innocent III was the very figure of the proud pontiff ruling an all-powerful Church with vast possessions. To him came Francis with his gospel of humility and poverty.

Innocent III might well have found something revolutionary in this. There were currents of hostility toward the splendor and authority of the medieval Church. Zealots had arisen, teaching doctrines of apostolic poverty and simplicity and advocating the humble ways of the early Church. Some of these had turned into dangerous heretics. Yet others, attacking ecclesiastical wealth, had been great saints.

The pontiff received St. Francis and his followers in kindly fashion, and listened to what they proposed. The Little Poor Man wanted authority for his group to preach and work among the poor. They themselves would eschew all possessions, and preserve an absolute poverty. Innocent III expressed his doubts about the feasibility of an organization based on complete nonpossession. The regular monastic orders of the Middle Ages were founded on the vow of poverty, individual poverty. The monk himself possessed nothing, but the group of monks did. Individually they were consecrated to nonpossession, collectively the monastery had vast possessions. Francis, however, proposed not only individual but also collective poverty.

Though doubtful of the practicality of this, Innocent III granted his sanction. He laid down a condition that Francis and his followers be taken into the ecclesiastical organization. They were to constitute a new religious order, with the Poverello of Assisi as their head. They were to pledge allegiance to him, while he pledged allegiance to the Papacy. This was the foundation of the Franciscan order.

The Little Poor Man and his companions returned to Assisi and began their labors. Their doctrines had a magical appeal. New followers flocked to them, renouncing worldly hopes, living in huts, begging sustenance for themselves and the poor, preaching, praying, singing. At their head Francis rejoiced as a troubadour of the Lord. Everywhere in the countryside were seen the Friars Minor, the Little Brothers.

Francis had a great desire to convert the infidels of Islam, a common ambition in the medieval church. So he went to Moslem lands, on journeys wreathed with legend. Historians have difficulty in estimating the facts, so marvelous were the stories that sprang up. Francis is said to have set out for Syria, and another story pictures him on a mission to convert the Moors in Spain. Still another places him in Egypt.

He returned to Italy, and found great changes in the order he had established. The movement was spreading far and wide in Italy, and soon there were Franciscans in other countries—France, Germany, England, Spain. Francis had started a world movement far beyond anything he had dreamed. But Pope Innocent III had told him that his ideal of perfect poverty would be too rigorous and extreme for a religious order of large numbers. And this was proving to be the case.

Francis found his friars putting up buildings, convents, churches, which violated his own principle of utter nonpossession. The way of Francis and his original companions, to live in rude huts and beg their bread, was not being carried out in a religious organization which was rapidly becoming one of the great institutions of the later Middle Ages.

Francis disagreed with the trend, but matters were out of his control. It became clear that he lacked the administrative ability to rule the Franciscans. His character was that of the saint, the troubadour

of Lady Poverty. With his profound humility, he gave up the leadership of his order, resigning it to other hands.

He went into the mountains, and devoted himself to fasting,
penance, and prayer. His health was failing, and the severe rigors he
inflicted on his body enfeebled him more and more. It was now that
the most miraculous visitation of all came upon him, the Stigmata.
In a mountain retreat he went into a spell of suffering and exaltation,
and on his body appeared the signs of the Crucifixion, on his hands
and feet the marks of nails, and in his side the wound of the lance,
such as the Saviour had suffered. Ever since, pious Catholics have
loved to dwell on the Stigmata of Francis of Assisi as among the greatest of miracles.

During this period he sang the "Canticle of the Sun," one of the
wonderful literary productions of the Middle Ages. With a sensitive
love for nature and a pious intoxication in natural scenes, he praises
God for the sun, the moon, the stars, the wind, the elements of water
and fire. He calls these his brothers and sisters. He even calls death
his sister, and praises the Lord for it. The canticle was one of the first
great expressions in the Italian vernacular, as opposed to learned
Latin, and foreshadowed the establishment of the Italian language
as a literary vehicle and the national speech.

The final years of the life of Francis of Assisi were brightened by
the creation of the Franciscan nuns. These were founded by a woman
of rank and station in Assisi, who abandoned the world to follow the
life of poverty. St. Clara became the devoted disciple of Francis, and
her labors resulted in the Franciscan nuns, who still flourish and
whom the English Middle Ages knew as the Poor Clares.

Francis of Assisi died at the age of forty-five. His personality left
a profound impress on subsequent times. People never grew weary
of the legends about the Little Poor Man. The favorite story told of
St. Francis preaching to the birds as they bowed their heads in reverence, the most exquisite idyl of the Middle Ages.

In the centuries that followed, the dissensions evident among the
first Franciscans increased. The final settlement was a compromise,
odd and typical of the epoch, a middle road between the ideal of a
religious order with no possessions whatever and the actual fact that
the Franciscans owned large properties. Formal title to these was
vested in the Papacy, while the Franciscans retained the use of them.

There was a similar movement away from Francis' idea that worldly learning should be abandoned for piety and prayer. The Franciscans, spreading throughout Europe, became famous for scholarship. One of their number was Roger Bacon, the English Franciscan, whose erudition was a wonder of the thirteenth century. It was a far cry indeed from the Little Poor Man, who inveighed against worldly knowledge, to that Roger Bacon who, in such remarkable fashion, adumbrated the coming of modern science.

ST. LOUIS

[1214–1270]

To THE Middle Ages, Louis IX of France was the ideal Christian sovereign. To the modern student he stands as a notable example of how medieval religious zeal could shape noble conduct and enlightened benevolence in a ruler. His place in history is that of *Saint* Louis.

Despite the fact that he was born to be a king, St. Louis's determination was to live a blameless life and to ensure his eternal salvation. He ruled firmly as a monarch, but he practiced Christian humility in dealing with his subjects. He made justice and charity the aims of his administration. He brought hope to the downtrodden, fed the hungry, defended the weak, restrained his barons when they would have tyrannized in the provinces. The classical image of St. Louis pictures him dispensing justice to his people under the oak at Vincennes.

An intensely faithful son of the Church, he never missed his religious duties. He had priests with him wherever he went. He fasted, wore a hair shirt, and scourged himself for his sins. He lectured his friends about their obligations to their Creator. He would permit no license at his court.

For all this, St. Louis had a more worldly side. He was gay by nature, fond of convivial company, not at all averse to living in the style of a king. He spent money freely when there was a building to be put up or a war to be fought, although his use of his royal treasury was so wise that he never suffered from the financial worries that beset so many of his brother monarchs.

After a serious illness in 1244, St. Louis determined to go on a crusade. He wanted to bring succor to the Christian knights who, after winning and losing Jerusalem, barely clung to fortresses on the coast of Palestine. Actually the end of Christian power in the Near East was in sight, and the crusading idea was now obsolete. But it lingered on, and could not fail to attract the saintly and knightly King of France.

Louis was resolved to take the cross. He ordered the sacred symbol to be sewn on the shoulder of his cloak, and then by a stratagem drew his knights into the crusade with him. At Christmastime he distributed among them cloaks to which the cross had been secretly stitched. These cloaks they put on in the dark, attending Christmas Mass at dawn. Then, in the lighted chapel, seeing themselves arrayed with the cross, they were ashamed to put it aside.

At the head of his knights, the King of France invaded Egypt, a dominating center of Moslem power. The crusaders landed and captured the port of Damietta. Then St. Louis led them on a march to Cairo. They were halted by the Arabs before Mansura and had to retreat. The enemy in numbers far superior to the crusaders pressed home their advantage, and the retreat became a rout. Louis fought valiantly, but was taken prisoner and put in chains.

He accepted this fate like a saint. His Christian piety even struck the Moslems, one of whom brought him his breviary so that he might perform his offices. Resigned to ending his days in captivity, he was released after the payment of an enormous ransom. He immediately went on to the Holy Land, where he remained for four years. He accomplished nothing because no help came from Europe, where the great powers were caught in the conflict between Pope and Emperor. St. Louis returned home and resumed his rule of France.

He soon signed treaties with England and Spain. In these he gave up French territory and was much criticized for it, but in fact he thereby consolidated central France, welding the northern provinces into a powerful unit. This achievement was typical of St. Louis. Keeping peace with his neighbors, he at the same time and with great political acumen strengthened his own kingdom. His sense of justice was so well known that he was selected as mediator in some of the worst disputes of the time, notably that between Henry III of England and his barons. The King of France decided in favor of the King of England.

St. Louis still wanted to go crusading. Again he fixed his attention on North Africa. But this time his counselors were set against the idea. It was with difficulty that he raised an army. He landed at the site of ancient Carthage, only to have the plague break out among his soldiers. St. Louis went among them fearlessly, nursing the stricken, fortifying the souls of the dying. The inevitable happened. The King caught the dread disease, and it carried him off in the prime of his life. He died as he had lived—a king, a crusader, a saint.

MARCO POLO

[1254?–?1324]

The Middle Ages were fascinated with the Orient. Europeans knew that far across the steppes and mountains of central Asia there stood a mighty kingdom, old, cultured, quite unlike anything known to the West. Cathay—the very name rang with romantic overtones. The land of mandarins and silk and delicately wrought miniatures of gold and ivory. By the thirteenth century, trade with China, moving by way of Constantinople and Bokhara, was already well established.

The tales and rumors about Cathay created intense interest in Europe. The first man to visit the land of Confucius and to write a travel book about it would, therefore, have a large audience. Such a man was Marco Polo, a young Venetian, son of a merchant who traded with China and had traveled as far as Peking in search of merchandise.

Marco Polo was enchanted by stories of strange people his father had met, the exotic lands he had seen, the weird customs of races that differed from Europeans in the color of their skin and the slant of their eyes, and among whom women had their feet bound so tightly in infancy that they could hardly walk. When his father began to talk of setting out again, young Marco begged to go with him, overcame all objections, and made one of the party when the elder Polo and his brother started for the East again.

It was a long, weary, arduous journey—through Europe and the Near East, across Armenia and Persia and central Asia, and on into the realm of Kublai Khan. Marco Polo was excited by almost everything he saw—by the burning oil (petroleum) that gushed out of the earth in Persia, by the titanic peaks of the Himalayas, by the harsh dry sands of the Gobi Desert. Most of all, the young Venetian traveler was struck by the great cities of China, with their populations so different in appearance from any people he had ever seen before.

Three days' journey from Kublai Khan's palace the Polos stopped and sent messengers ahead to announce them. The Khan sent a cavalcade of nearly a thousand horsemen to escort the distinguished travelers.

Kublai Khan, grandson of Genghis Khan, was the founder of the Mongol dynasty in China. Inheriting the vast domains of the conqueror Genghis, he expanded them by conquering southern China. He treated all conquered peoples humanely and although himself an ardent Buddhist, was greatly interested in other religions, especially the Christian and Mohammedan. He reigned in undreamed-of splendor, his palace a factory of golden luxury and pageantry.

This lordly potentate made the Venetians welcome. He took a particular fancy to the junior member of the expedition, and even allowed Marco Polo to give him lessons in Italian. Marco, for his part, learned the Tartar language and adopted the dress and manners of the people. While his father and uncle continued to trade, constantly improving their stock of precious stones, diamonds from the Golconda mines in India and rubies from Burma, young Marco entered the diplomatic service of Kublai Khan. He was sent on missions throughout the empire, even into Tibet. He sailed to Japan for Kublai Khan, becoming the first European to visit the strange island kingdom off the coast of Cathay. He saw the spice islands of Indonesia. He reached Ceylon and Madagascar and Abyssinia.

The years slipped by with Marco Polo serving the great Khan, and with the elder Polo engaged in trade. When they began to talk of returning home, the Emperor of Cathay appointed them to escort his daughter to Persia where she was to marry the Shah. This was the last duty performed by Marco Polo in the Chinese service. From Persia he, his father, and his uncle continued on back to Venice.

When they reached home, after an absence of so many years—Marco was now forty-one—wearing oriental clothes with queer shoes that turned up at the toes, no one recognized them and they had a hard time convincing people who they really were. A great banquet was ordered, to which they invited all their relatives and old friends. The three Polos received their guests attired in rich robes of crimson satin, and after dinner they ripped open the seams of their traveling clothes and spilled out a fortune in diamonds and rubies upon the table.

The elder Polos settled down to a life of luxury and rest, but Marco, who was in the prime of life, began to take part in Venetian politics and became a popular hero. The tales he told of his travels seemed so exaggerated that the Venetians called him Marco Millions. He commanded a Venetian galley in the great sea battle of Curzola, in which the Venetians defeated the fleet of Genoa. But Marco Polo was taken prisoner and thrown into prison in Genoa. He quickly made friends with his captors and, when they learned who he was, he was given a house which he shared with a fellow-captive, Rusticano of Pisa, a scholar who urged Marco Polo to tell of his experiences in detail and he would write them down. It is said that as Marco knew only the Venetian language and Rusticano spoke Tuscan, they could not understand each other's Italian; but both knew French and in that language *The Book of Marco Polo* was written. This helped to pass the year Marco spent as a prisoner and gave to posterity a minute and vivid record of the wonderful experiences of the world's ranking figure in travel and adventure.

Rarely has the imagination of man been stirred as it was by *The Book of Marco Polo*. The glowing description he gave of fabulous Cathay, of the huge expanse of fertile and fruitful country, roads dotted with wayside inns linking prosperous towns and great cities, rich Buddhist monasteries, artists expert at the carving of jade and the weaving of silk shot with gold thread—all this deeply interested the Mediterranean world and the thought of all Europe. To *The Book of Marco Polo,* and the impulse it gave to travel in distant lands, we owe a dominant inspiration for the great explorations of the Portuguese and the discovery of the New World.

After Marco had been eleven months in prison, Genoa and Venice made peace, and he was free to return home, marry, and settle down in a home of his own. At forty-five he was still a dashing hero and a handsome man. He married Donata Loredano, whose father was a member of the Doge's council and one of the richest nobles in Venice. He took over his father-in-law's business, lent money to foreign princes, financed merchants and ship owners engaged in foreign trade. Before his death he had become one of the richest and most prominent men of his time, a great banker and merchant prince.

But his greatest fame was—and is—in his travel story. To this day the name of Marco Polo stands for the classical tourist of all time, the leading authority on the Cathay of Kublai Khan.

ROBERT BRUCE

[1274–1329]

I N 1298, King Edward I of England crossed the border into Scotland, seized Edinburgh and Stirling, forced the Scots to capitulate, and had himself declared King of Scotland. Then, leaving a viceroy to rule in his name, Edward returned to England. With him he took the Stone of Scone, on which Scottish Kings were crowned, carried it to London, and placed it in Westminster Abbey where it is still used for the coronation of British monarchs.

Among the many knights to accompany Edward I on this expedition to Scotland was Robert Bruce, a Scotsman who had become a prime favorite of the English King. Bruce remained in Scotland. Edward had not been away long when he received word of a Scottish uprising led by Sir William Wallace. He learned, moreover, to his utter amazement that Bruce had joined the insurgents. Edward hurriedly marched to Scotland and defeated the Scots at the Battle of Falkirk. Sir William Wallace, "the hammer and scourge of England," was captured and barbarously executed.

Robert Bruce escaped under an amnesty. But he was not reconciled to English rule of Scotland. The example of William Wallace had stirred his patriotism so deeply that from then on he planned to set his country free. One of his first moves was against Scottish traitors who had helped the English with information. The worst of these Bruce himself stabbed to death before the altar of the church in Dumfries, for which crime of murder and sacrilege he was excommunicated.

Openly committed to the Scottish cause, Bruce gathered followers and marched to Scone, where on March 27, 1306, he proclaimed himself King of Scotland and was crowned by a woman, Lady Macduff, Countess of Fife, who used as a makeshift crown a small circlet of gold. At the coronation was a young lord who became the most romantic and devoted of all his knights, James of Douglas, afterward known as the Black Douglas.

Edward, hearing of Bruce's coronation, sent an army to destroy him. Bruce was defeated. He escaped into the highlands, but most of his devoted followers were either killed in battle or else hanged after they had been captured. Even Bruce's wife and children fell into the hands of the English.

This was the period of despair of which the legend of Bruce and the spider is told—how the dejected fugitive hiding in a cave watched a spider doggedly spinning a web, often falling back but always climbing up again and finally succeeding. Like the spider, the King of Scotland could be patient too. He continued the struggle with new raids and insurrections led by himself and his followers. His fortunes were about to turn.

Edward I of England died, one of England's most powerful kings and Scotland's most formidable enemy. He was succeeded by a weak and incompetent son, who was no match for Robert Bruce. The Scottish patriots began to harry the allies of the English. Bruce won a decisive battle near Carrick. The Black Douglas seized Arran. Recruits began to flock to their banner.

Early in 1309, the Scottish King held his first parliament at St. Andrews. The next year he was recognized by the Scottish clergy, in spite of his excommunication by the Pope. This brought the Scottish people almost unanimously to his side. He continued to storm English strongholds: Linlithgow, Dumbarton, Perth. Two successful raids into England were followed by the capture of Roxburgh and Edinburgh.

Edward II now roused himself to counterattack. He led his armed host into Scotland and met Bruce at Bannockburn. The result was the greatest military triumph in Scottish history. First Bruce killed one of the English leaders in single combat. Then he directed the strategy by which the Scottish pikemen stood firm and piled up the charging English. Edward II fled from the field.

In the exchange of prisoners that followed, Bruce was at last reunited with his wife and children after eight long years of separation. The Scottish parliament met at Ayr and unanimously settled the succession to the crown of Scotland on Bruce and his heirs.

Inspired by the success of the Bruce and the establishment of Scottish independence, the Irish rose against the English and offered the crown of Ireland to Robert I of Scotland. He declined, but he campaigned in Ireland with his brother Edward, who accepted the Irish crown after victories over the English, only to be killed in battle a year later.

Immediately after his return from Ireland, King Robert was approached by the envoys of Pope John XXII to arrange a two-year truce with England, but he refused to accept the letters from the Pope because they were addressed to "Robert Bruce, governing in Scotland," instead of to Robert Bruce, King of Scotland. Fighting continued for five years more, until finally the King's position became so strong that he was recognized by most foreign monarchs. In 1323 his title of King of Scotland was at last confirmed by the Pope. The English were obliged to recognize it.

Bruce was stricken with leprosy and, early in the summer of 1329, he summoned Black Douglas to his bedside. Froissart, the great French chronicler, describes the scene. The dying King embraced Douglas and said, "Sir James, my dear friend, I wish as soon as I be dead that my heart be taken out of my body and embalmed, and that, taking as much of my treasure as you think necessary for yourself and the retinue suitable to your rank which shall accompany you on your journey, you convey my heart to the Holy Sepulchre in Jerusalem where our Lord lay." He died on June 7, 1329.

True to his oath, Black Douglas removed the King's heart and encased it in a large silver locket which he wore around his neck. However he never reached the Holy Land, but was killed fighting the Moors in Spain. His body was found on the battlefield and, with the silver locket still around his neck, was sent back to Scotland by the King of Spain, on a Spanish ship, guarded by Spanish noblemen.

Bruce's heart was buried at Melrose Abbey, and the body of his faithful friend, Black Douglas, was entombed in St. Bride's Chapel of Douglas.

MARY QUEEN OF SCOTS

SIR WALTER RALEIGH

BOCCACCIO

[1313–1375]

G IOVANNI BOCCACCIO, immortal in literature as the author of the *Decameron,* was an illegitimate child—his father an Italian merchant, his mother a French widow. Born in Paris, the infant was taken by his father home to Florence. His stepmother grew to hate him, especially after she had a son of her own, and she created so much unpleasantness that at the age of eleven Giovanni was sent to Naples to live with and work for a merchant of that city.

He had no taste, however, for trade or bookkeeping. Without any instruction or advice from others, he acquired a liking for literature and poetry, despite everything his father and employer had to say about such "useless pursuits." He always claimed that he could have become a great poet if he had been allowed to start early enough. In this belief, he hated his father.

Boccaccio often wrote about the joys and pleasures of his early life in Naples, a gay and beautiful city, then at the height of its splendor under the beneficent rule of Robert the Wise. When the boy was sixteen, his father came to Naples, presented him at the court of the King, and, finally convinced of his inaptitude for trade, agreed to his taking up law.

When Boccaccio was eighteen he saw Maria d'Aquino for the first time. It was in the Church of San Lorenzo on Holy Saturday 1331. He returned next day, Easter Sunday, and stayed till she arrived for High Mass. She was only seventeen and the belle of Naples. Although she was already married to an old and wealthy husband, the fact did not prevent her from having a large following of admirers, of whom Giovanni Boccaccio became one. He courted her with all the ardor of youth, gained her favor, spent two passionate years with her, then tired her with his constant jealousy, so that two years later she refused to have anything more to do with him. But she had left upon his heart an imprint that time could not efface. She was his Fiammetta. It is typical that the three great literary lights of the era, Dante, Petrarch, and Boccaccio, had the worship of a woman as a dominant influence in life and art—Dante with Beatrice, Petrarch with Laura, Boccaccio with Fiammetta.

Shortly after their separation Boccaccio wrote to Fiammetta that he was "thinking of past joys in present misery." He was indeed miserable. In addition to his loss of Fiammetta, blow after blow fell upon him in the space of a few months. Disappointed love, poverty, the loss of friends, devoted in days of prosperity, drove him from Naples to Florence with nothing left but his art. He began the ungrateful labor of earning his bread by writing.

In Florence he wrote three books all inspired by his consuming passion: the *Ameto,* in prose interspersed with verse; the *Amorosa Visione;* and the *Fiammetta,* the first psychological novel in European literature. In this the story of their idyl is told by Fiammetta, but it ends the other way around—with the torment and despair that she suffers when abandoned by him. It was followed by Boccaccio's last and best work in verse, the *Ninfale Fiesolano,* which captures in words the beauty of the Italian countryside.

Unsuccessful in Florence, Boccaccio returned to Naples. The following year he was in Ravenna, where he talked at length with Dante's daughter Beatrice, and actually lived in the house of Ostasia da Polent, who had befriended Dante. He was collecting material for his *Vita di Dante,* which was written several years later. Boccaccio was the earliest man of letters to show real appreciation of the author of the *Divine Comedy,* who was the first great writer in the Tuscan tongue, which became modern Italian. Boccaccio's own poetry was in Tuscan, and Dante had a great influence on his style of verse.

Then came the Black Death, which swept from southern Italy up to Florence. In Naples, Fiammetta was among the victims, as was Boccaccio's stepmother in Florence, where three fifths of the people died. Boccaccio himself saw the horrors of the plague in Naples. The scourge forms the background for his *Decameron,* the first prose work in the Tuscan tongue. It is beyond all question the best collection of stories that ever issued from the pen of man.

Not so long as the *Arabian Nights,* it is at least an equal as a work of art. Chaucer borrowed from it, as did Marguerite of Angoulême, and Balzac. The *Canterbury Tales,* the *Heptaméron,* and the *Droll Stories* all bask more or less in the reflected glory of Boccaccio.

The *Decameron* tells how in Florence three young men and seven women, fleeing from the Black Death, seek refuge in the gardens of a stately villa beneath Fiesole. There the fugitives from the plague divert themselves by relating stories. Each tells ten of the hundred tales over which the civilized world has laughed and wept for six hundred years. The *Decameron* is a priceless mirror held up to life, to life as it was in what was then the most polished society in the world. Portraying a civilization, the book is no abstract history, but captures the attention of the reader with a series of independent stories, each an artistic gem in its own right. The characters live as they do only in the best of writers.

Tuscan, the language of Florence, had been brought to a high state of perfection by Dante, and became almost exclusively the language of literature. It was the first written departure from Latin in Italy, and as early as 1212, Florentine bankers kept their accounts and wrote their letters in Tuscan, which bears an even closer relation to modern Italian than Chaucer does to the literary language of postwar America. What Dante began in verse, Boccaccio completed in prose: the establishment of the Italian language.

The *Decameron* was followed by the *Corbaccio,* a satire against women, savage and scathing, in which all the praise Boccaccio had lavished on Fiammetta is reversed in a vitriolic denunciation. This was Boccaccio's last work of literary creation. From there he turned to scholarship.

In 1350 a new influence had come into his life. He was sent as an ambassador for the Florentine Republic to invite Petrarch to return to Florence, and for the rest of his days he was the disciple of Europe's first Humanist. Because Petrarch was unacquainted with the work of Dante, Boccaccio with his own hand copied out the whole of the *Divine Comedy* and sent it to "his illustrious and sublime master." After finishing his *Vita di Dante,* the earliest life of the poet, Boccaccio forswore his beloved Tuscan and wrote in Latin, the only language Petrarch used. Under the latter's guidance he accumulated an immense store of classical knowledge, and learned Greek, which enabled him later in life to assist the scholar Pilatus in translating Homer's *Iliad* and *Odyssey* into Latin.

Boccaccio's Latin works did not have a large circulation during his life but after the invention of printing went through numerous editions and became standard textbooks of the Renaissance all over Europe. Before he was forty-five, Boccaccio was beginning to show signs of age. No longer the handsome young giant of his youth, he was fat and heavy and his hair was gray. He had many passing love affairs, and was the father of five children. But after Fiammetta his heart was never again involved in romance.

Gradually Boccaccio drifted into age and poverty, the friendship of Petrarch and the love of little children being his only consolations. When he was sixty and in dire need, his friends came to his assistance and in order to relieve his want founded the Cathedra Dantesca, a series of lectures he was paid to deliver on the author of the *Divine Comedy*. A year later he was dead. They buried him wrapped in a warm winter cloak that Petrarch had left him fifty florins to buy.

EDWARD III

[*1312–1377*]

E DWARD III of England is remembered for two things: he started the Hundred Years' War; he founded the Order of the Garter, which remains to this day one of Britain's highest and most coveted decorations.

There were many reasons—social, political, economic—for the Hundred Years' War, but the occasion that moved Edward III to action was a dynastic quarrel. He had a claim to the throne of France through his mother, a French princess. With a typical medieval love of legality he pushed his claim, while the French on their side retorted that by the Salic Law of France royal inheritance was restricted to the male branch. They acknowledged another claimant, who became Philip VI.

Edward, in a culminating affirmation of his pretension, proclaimed himself King of France, and had the golden lilies of France quartered on the royal arms. At the same time, he adopted the motto, *"Dieu et Mon Droit!"* He would make good his right and take the French throne by force.

In 1346, after some desultory fighting, Edward III of England began one of the glorious military campaigns of English history. He landed in France with the flower of his chivalry. By his side he had his son, the Prince of Wales, called the Black Prince from the color of his armor, whose heroics would live in the annals of both England and France.

Edward would have driven through to Paris, but the French destroyed the bridges over the Seine to hold him up while they marshaled an army. When he finally got across the river into Flanders, the enemy was hot on his heels.

With a battle now imminent, the English King forded the Somme, continued on toward Amiens, and selected the field of Crécy as the place to make his stand against a force three times the size of his own. He formed three lines, the first led by the Black Prince, the second by great lords of England, Arundel and Northampton, the third by the King in person. Behind the first line the English bowmen were massed in serried ranks, with gaps to permit the passage of the knights in the second and third rows.

It was the archers who saved the English from being overwhelmed. These overmatched the crossbowmen of the French, and as soon as the French knights came within range, thousands of arrows were showered upon them. They rode gallantly in a series of senseless assaults, and were riddled by the storm of arrows. Horses reared, riders fell, panic ensued. Then the Black Prince led a cavalry charge, followed by the remainder of the English army. The nobility of France was decimated. The survivors reeled back in utter defeat.

Among the slain was the blind King of Bohemia. Led by two of his knights, the sightless monarch spurred forward into the melee and was killed. One story relates that his crest of three ostrich plumes and his motto, *"Ich Dien"* ("I serve"), were taken by the Prince of Wales to celebrate his great victory. They have been used by every Prince of Wales since.

Edward III now laid siege to Calais. That city only twenty-one miles from England across the straits of Dover could be a permanent bridgehead, the possession of which would enable England to invade the Continent any time at will. Calais was well defended, but after a year had to surrender. Angered by the stubbornness of the people of Calais, Edward granted terms only on condition that the lives of six leading burghers be forfeited. In the city six volunteered, offering their lives to save their fellow-townsmen. They appeared before the English King with bare heads, bare feet, and ropes about their necks. This scene provided Rodin, the nineteenth-century sculptor, with the theme for one of his greatest masterpieces, the tableau called "The Burghers of Calais."

The English and the French agreed to a truce that allowed Edward III to return to London. He celebrated his victories in France with magnificent tournaments, and founded the Order of the Garter. The manner of its origin is one of the amusing curiosities of history. The King was dancing at a court ball with the Countess of Shrewsbury, his mistress, when she lost a garter. The King picked it up and fastened it around her knee. Some of the courtiers present could not repress their smiles, and the King rebuked them with the phrase, *"Honi soit qui mal y pense"* ("Shame upon him who thinks evil of it.") He took the garter as the symbol of his new order of knighthood and made the famous saying its motto. The order has never been enlarged from its original number of twenty-five besides the monarch.

Edward was soon again involved in war. He himself entered Scotland and harried the Scots, while the Black Prince campaigned in France and won the Battle of Poitiers. This Prince of Wales, the most feared champion in Christendom, even captured the King of France and took him to London, where he was lavishly entertained by King Edward. In medieval fashion, the French sovereign was ransomed for three thousand crowns of gold.

That was the end of the Hundred Years' War as far as Edward III was concerned. Signing a peace with France, he began to think more about domestic improvements than foreign conquest. He built the Round Tower of Windsor Castle, endowed King's Hall (now Trinity College) at Cambridge, and patronized Chaucer. He would have done more for his realm had it not been for the fearful scourge of the Black Death which cut the population of England by about a third.

Edward's reign was clouded over at the end. The Black Prince predeceased his father, dying of dropsy when he was only forty-six. This left the throne to the Black Prince's son, the child who would be the unfortunate Richard II. Edward III had begun the Hundred Years' War triumphantly. It would end with the defeat of the English at the hands of Joan of Arc, a debacle leading England straight into the cruel civil strife called the Wars of the Roses.

TAMERLANE

[*1336–1405*]

"IF I were alive today, mankind would tremble!" Such was the legend found on the tomb of Tamerlane when it was excavated at Samarkand, in central Asia. No more fitting epitaph ever commemorated a more ferocious destroyer.

He claimed to be a descendant of Genghis Khan, and his life was governed by this notion of ancestry. The horror he wrought was in emulation of that Mongol exterminator, whose very name stands for merciless slaughter on the largest scale. Genghis Khan in the thirteenth century, and Tamerlane in the fourteenth, were typical of the waves of terror that came out of the vast Asiatic land mass and struck into China, into India, and into the lands of the West.

Genghis Khan was a Mongol from a land bordering on China. Tamerlane was a native of Turkestan, much farther to the west, and was probably of the Turkish race, though with some Mongol blood. Oddly his father was of a scholarly sort who gave himself over to learned pursuits and works of religion. He became a convert to Islam, and his son was reared in fanatical devotion to the creed of the Koran. This was a dominant factor in the career of Tamerlane, who held his life to be dedicated to the spread of the true belief of Islam. His father may have been a pious scholar, but his mother excited him with tales of the savage exploits and conquests of their ferocious ancestor, Genghis Khan.

He was given the name of Timur. He injured a leg in a wrestling match, limped for the rest of his life, and became known as Timur-i-leng—Timur the Lame. This European writers turned into Tamerlane.

He first appears in history as a tribal chieftain, fighting, conspiring, murdering, rising to power at Samarkand. His story thereafter is one of many years of interminable marches, battles, conquests, in the course of which Tamerlane won possession of Turkestan, most of Persia, and lands extending as far west as Mesopotamia, Kurdistan, the Caspian Sea, and the River Volga.

He was a master of the art of war. He organized his troops with sound method and strict discipline, had experts for officers, and was a progressive in the art of battle. He is said to have formed a unit of mobile artillery, in advance of his time. He made ruthless use of diplomacy, and had an elaborate network of spies in countries on which he had designs. He worked by intrigue and falseness, using cajolery and seeking to strike terror. He sent agents to spread reports of the terrifying vengeance he inflicted on those who defied him, and of his magnanimity toward those who yielded. In this he was served well by his pretension to be the heir to the terrifying Genghis Khan. One chronicler relates how, when a deputation would come and implore his mercy, Tamerlane would turn to his advisers and ask, "What did Genghis Khan do in such a case?" The answer was only too easy, and this later destroyer would then bid his commanders to be as merciless as his ancestor of the previous century.

Historians tend to interpret the mass murders and destruction wrought by both Genghis Khan and Tamerlane as a manifestation of the nomad mind. In central Asia there was interminable war between the wandering tribes of herdsmen and the settled populated areas of cities and farms, and the nomad conqueror saw urban and agricultural civilization as something merely to be wiped out. Tamerlane destroyed cities, and extirpated populations by a systematic program of obliteration. He destroyed irrigation works and aqueducts that had existed for long centuries, as in Mesopotamia, for example, where he mined the canals built by the Babylonians of remote antiquity. Deliberately he reduced rich and heavily populated countries to a desert, a kind of terrain fit for nomads.

He lives in history most evilly as the builder of pyramids of skulls. When a city had been sacked, he would have a pyramid erected of the heads of tens of thousands of massacred victims. The horror in which his memory was held arose most of all from the trail of hideous monuments he left along his line of march.

Tamerlane's palace was a tent almost 1,800 feet long, and furnished with the utmost magnificence of central Asia. He liked circuses and kept a troupe of performers, complete with a menagerie of elephants and tigers, which gave performances for his guests. In spite of his ferocity, he fancied himself as a patron of the arts, and was generous to musicians and poets. He prided himself on his piety, though the role he affected as a pillar of Islam did not prevent him from smiting Moslems, as well as infidels, with murderous fury.

Thus his greatest victory was over Mohammedans—the Ottoman Turks. With a powerful army Tamerlane marched into Asia Minor. He could have picked no more formidable adversary. The Turks were then at the height of that warlike vigor which was to make them the terror of Europe. Half a century later they were to capture Constantinople, and go on with the conquest of the Balkans and Hungary, all the way to Vienna. They were in the midst of their career of almost uninterrupted victory, and it is an eloquent sign of their stamina and strength that they were able to rise again and go on after what Tamerlane did to them.

In the Battle of Angora he completely defeated the Turkish army, the military power that might well have considered itself invincible, and captured Sultan Bajazet and his family. Mohammedan historians dwell upon the terror of the event. The story long was famous—how the captured Sultan was kept in an iron cage, displayed as a trophy on the march of the great Tamerlane. There is a story that every day at an appointed hour, one member of the family of the unfortunate Bajazet was slain in front of his cage. However, the truth seems to be that Tamerlane took the captive Sultan along in a litter fenced with bars, thus giving rise to the story of the cage, and boasted of his magnanimity in not putting Bajazet to death. This, he explained, was because the Turks were Mohammedans, and the captive Sultan had fought bravely against the Christians, so that he had earned the regard of Tamerlane, the pious Moslem.

Tamerlane's victory at Angora opened the way for him to push into Mesopotamia and Syria, where he captured Baghdad and Damascus. His power was at its apogee, his devastations extending from China deep into Russia, which land of the Slavs his commanders raided in hard-riding forays. The list of cities he destroyed, the myriads he massacred, the pyramids of skulls he built, made him the terror of the world.

From the defeat of the Turks he returned to Samarkand and was preparing to strike out at the other side of his vast dominions with an invasion of China. But he was stricken down by fever and died in the sixty-ninth year of a life that well earned the epitaph inscribed on his tomb at Samarkand: "If I were alive today, mankind would tremble."

JOAN OF ARC

[*1412–1431*]

I N ALL history there is no more wonderful story than that of the
Maid of Orléans, and no tale of marvel is better authenticated
even in details. A sixteen-year-old peasant girl, humble and illiterate,
convinced nobles and prelates that she had been sent by God to save
France. She raised the siege of Orléans, drove the English before her,
and led the Dauphin to Rheims where he was crowned King, she
standing beside him, a banner in her hand.

Joan was born at Domrémy in Champagne. Her father, Jacques
d'Arc, was a man of some consequence in Domrémy. He collected
taxes, inspected weights and measures, and represented the village
in lawsuits. He had a four-room house, a good piece of land, and a
few cattle. Not being destined for a clerical career, none of his children received any education. Joan could neither read nor write. She
learned her prayers from her mother, also how to spin and sew. She
tended the cattle in the pasture, and played with other children.
She was a pious child and went to church regularly.

Joan was a normal girl, healthy in mind and body. She was strong
and well built, very earnest, and had no lack of shrewd peasant
humor. There is no doubt that she did have visions. She was sincere and no trick was played upon her. Her own account, given
at her trial, relates that about noon one day in the summer when she
was thirteen, as she stood in her father's garden, near the church, she
saw a great light and had a vision of the Archangel Michael, surrounded by other angels. She was frightened, did not know what to
make of it, and soon the vision faded away. In the weeks that followed, the vision returned, and her fear gave way to a feeling of
comfort. The archangel bade her be a good girl, told her that St.

Catherine and St. Margaret would soon visit her, and told her to obey them as they were sent by God to guide her.

During the next three years, Joan heard "voices" regularly. Both St. Catherine and St. Margaret appeared to her, in the guise of queens, wearing rich and precious crowns. They bade her go to the aid of the King of France, who needed help because the English invaders were deep inside his kingdom and in control of strategic strong points from the Channel to the Loire. Domrémy was sacked in 1428. The villagers, who had fled before the raiders, returned and rebuilt their cottages. The blackened ruins of the church stood near where Joan had heard the voices. Now the voices became specific. They told her she must save Orléans and have the Dauphin crowned King at Rheims, then in English hands. Joan was sixteen.

She told her family, and was laughed at. Her father said he'd drown her if she didn't stop the nonsense about going to save France. Orléans was not yet besieged when she made her first attempt. In May 1428, she set out for the local fortress of Vaucouleurs, where Robert de Baudricourt had a castle. Joan told Baudricourt that she was sent by God, and bade him write to the Dauphin (the title for a King of France who had not yet been crowned) that she would lead him to his coronation. Baudricourt thought she was crazy and sent her back to her father.

In October the siege of Orléans began. Joan renewed her pleadings with Baudricourt. Even considering the medieval fondness for wonder and legend, what happened was remarkable. Joan, announcing that she would raise the siege of Orléans, was able to persuade Baudricourt and his military entourage to such a degree that they sent her to the Dauphin, who was at Chinon. They gave her money for the journey, and the people of Vaucouleurs provided her with a horse. She exchanged her kirtle of red cloth for the dress of a page boy.

At Chinon she was brought into the presence of the Dauphin. Although she had never seen the Dauphin and he purposely kept back in the midst of his courtiers, Joan recognized him instantly. She went to him and said, "Most noble Dauphin, I have come from God to help you and your kingdom." Charles talked with her for two hours, and ordered her to be examined by a theological commission, which, after making inquiries at Domrémy, pronounced in her favor.

In April 1429, Joan of Arc set out for her great exploit. She was clad in male attire, wearing a suit of white armor, and carried a banner sewn with the golden lilies of France and bearing an image of God holding an orb and supported by two archangels, with the motto Jesus Maria. She led a force of four thousand men to the relief of Orléans.

Although the city was well fortified and had more than two hundred cannon, it was invested by an English army of ten thousand men who had surrounded the town with a dozen fortified redoubts. However, French reinforcements were able to get in, and along with them Joan of Arc. She now collaborated with Dunois and La Hire who commanded the garrison.

Two days later she ordered the English to withdraw. When they paid no attention to the proclamation, she led a sortie of the garrison which stormed a key redoubt. Then she went on to capture the stronghold of Tournelles, which commanded an all-important bridge. In this assault Joan herself placed the first scaling ladder and was wounded in the shoulder by an arrow. The loss of the forts put the English in an untenable position. They had to withdraw. Orléans was saved. Sir John Fastolf, a foremost English commander whom Shakespeare turned into a comic figure under the name of Falstaff, was beaten.

Then Joan went back to the Dauphin and persuaded him to march on Rheims and there be crowned King of France. With the fortunes of the English failing, this was accomplished without much difficulty. So Charles VII was crowned in the great Cathedral of St. Remi. The Maid was at his side, her banner in her hand. She knelt before him and said, "Gentle King! Now is fulfilled the will of God that I should raise the siege of Orléans and lead you to the city of Rheims to receive holy unction and be crowned to show that you are indeed the King and rightful lord of the fair realm of France."

Joan remained with the army. The cities of Compiègne, Senlis, and Beauvais fell to the royal forces. From the last-named town the French drove out the bishop—Pierre Cauchon. Then, leaving the King at Compiègne, Joan went on to attack Paris. Marching from St. Denis, she herself led the attack on the Porte St. Honoré. At the bottom of what is now the Avenue de l'Opéra, on the south side of the Place du Théâtre Français, Joan was wounded in the thigh by an arrow and had to be dragged back to safety. The attack failed.

The English and their Burgundian allies decided to recapture Compiègne, in order to prevent another attack upon Paris. Joan at once went to the assistance of the threatened town. She entered it and on the following day, leading a sortie against the Burgundians, she was dragged from her horse and taken prisoner. Bishop Cauchon of Beauvais, who had been driven from his see by Joan, went to the camp of the Burgundian commander who held the Maid. He persuaded the Burgundians to sell Joan to the English.

The English believed her to be a witch—how else explain their defeats at the hand of a peasant girl? With Joan their prisoner, they could have destroyed her, but wanted to discredit her with the multitudes in France who believed her to have been sent by God. To that purpose they wanted her condemned by ecclesiastical authorities as a witch.

They took Joan to Rouen, their military headquarters, and handed her over to Bishop Cauchon who was to be her judge. They declared that if she were not convicted of witchcraft and burned, they would seize her again and inflict their own punishment. Cauchon appointed the ecclesiastical court that was to try Joan: ten members of the University of Paris, twenty-two canons of Rouen, and eight monks of various orders.

The original transcript of the trial is preserved in the library of the Chamber of Deputies in Paris, and four authentic copies are still in existence. No better source of information about Joan could be imagined, for she was questioned at length about her childhood, her visions, and her every action from the time she left Domrémy until her arrest at Compiègne.

The trial lasted from the end of February to the beginning of May. Her demeanor in the face of her judges was such as to win the admiration of the English, who hated her. One of them exclaimed, "God, what a pity she isn't English." Her condemnation was a foregone conclusion. Cauchon pronounced her guilty of heresy. He declared her visions worthless, and condemned her for wearing male attire, for not having obeyed her father, for an attempt to escape, for the sin of pride, and for declaring that her responsibility was to God and not to the Church as represented by her judges. Joan then asked to be sent to Rome, that she might appeal to the Pope. This request was refused, and every effort made to obtain her submission.

Finally when the sentence of the court condemning her to be burned alive was read to her, this nineteen-year-old girl, exhausted by her long trial, abandoned by the King she had crowned, alone and without friends, weakened and signed an abjuration, the terms of which she did not understand. She was taken back to prison and given a life sentence.

The English were furious. They threatened to recapture her. Bishop Cauchon, fearful of the consequences to himself, visited her in prison and declared that she had relapsed. She was delivered to the secular arm on May 30, 1431, in the Old Market Square in Rouen.

Dressed as a woman, Joan was tied to the stake around which the wood was piled. She listened to a long sermon, and then Bishop Cauchon read the sentence. The Maid asked all the priests who were present to say a Mass for her soul. An English soldier gave her a cross made of two pieces of wood. She kissed it as the smoke rose from the fagots and the wood blazed up around her. In a loud voice she cried, "Jesus! Jesus!" When it was all over, her ashes were thrown into the Seine.

Later Charles VII reopened the case, allowing her family to send evidence to Rome. The Pope appointed three bishops to hear testimony and they held sittings at Domrémy, Orléans, Paris, and Rouen. Their findings blamed Bishop Cauchon for an atrocious miscarriage of justice, and on June 16, 1456, the judgment of 1431 was annulled.

Joan was beatified in Rome in 1909 and canonized by Pope Benedict XV in 1920 as St. Joan of Arc. The French Republic declared the fete of Joan of Arc to be a national festival of patriotism. It is celebrated on May 8, the anniversary of the relief of Orléans.

COLUMBUS

[1451–1506]

THE most important voyage ever undertaken by man can be precisely dated. It began on August 3, 1492, at the Spanish port of Palos. It ended on October 12, 1492, at Watlings Island in the West Indies. The distance covered was the width of the Atlantic. The accomplishment was the discovery of America.

Yet the admiral of the expedition believed that he had done something less significant. Christopher Columbus identified his landfall as part of Asia, for the Far East had been his destination, and to the day of his death he would not let himself be disabused of the notion that he had done what he had set out to do—find a new route to lands already on the map.

Most of the early life of the Great Navigator is shrouded in obscurity. We know he was a native of Genoa who began as a merchant and then went to sea. We have no idea when he became obsessed with the idea of reaching the Spice Islands of the East by sailing west, but his imagination must have been moved by the age he was living in—the Age of Discovery. Stories of the westward voyages of the Norsemen were current in Genoa. Columbus had heard about Marco Polo's travels overland to Cathay. He would have learned that the Portuguese sea captain, Bartholomew Dias, had recently rounded the Cape of Good Hope and set the stage for Vasco da Gama to push on to India. Columbus' idea was to reach the same place by a more direct route—by sailing boldly across the Atlantic to the coast of Asia.

With the help of his brother, who taught him about maps and their use, Columbus devoted himself to the acquisition of information that would be useful to him on his voyage of exploration. He traveled widely. He studied Spanish as well as Portuguese, and read the works of the Portuguese navigators. He boned up on the things to take on a long sea voyage, how to deal with savages or with civilized people in other countries, what ships were most seaworthy. He read the classical geographers avidly, searching for every last bit of information about the size of the earth. Thus primed, he began to look for a royal patron, beginning with King John II of Portugal.

King John was sympathetic to the arguments Christopher Columbus presented in favor of a westward journey to Asia, but he felt it necessary to submit the plan to a board of experts. They reported adversely, on the grounds that Columbus was not a skilled navigator—he was more of a merchant trader—and that it would be unwise to entrust a foreigner with an undertaking of this magnitude, especially as Portugal had many able seamen who could lead such an expedition. The King sent out ships of his own, trying to anticipate Columbus, but the attempt was a failure, the Portuguese admiral soon returning home.

Disheartened but not deterred, Columbus set out to find other backers. He sent his brother Bartholomew to England and France to plead on his behalf, and himself started for Spain with his son Diego. He arrived there at a time when Ferdinand and Isabella were engaged in the final struggle to conquer the Moors, and the finances of the country were being taxed to the utmost to keep the Spanish troops in the field.

But Isabella of Spain was no ordinary woman. She received the tall, handsome, thirty-four-year-old Italian, listened to what he had to say, and was quick to see what immense advantages would accrue to Spain if the voyage of discovery succeeded. Explaining to Columbus that it was impossible to finance his project, she suggested that he wait till the Moslem war was over, when she would see what could be done. Meanwhile she provided him with a comfortable income and living quarters in the palace, and sent his young son Diego to be taken care of by the Franciscan monks. Columbus became a courtier.

Again and again during the next few years Columbus pressed Queen Isabella to help him go ahead with his plan; again and again she put him off because the war was still on and the treasury almost empty. In despair, Columbus decided to go to France to seek the support of Charles VIII. On his way he stopped at the monastery where he had left his son. The monks were disappointed to see him leaving Spain, and the provincial of the Franciscans, Father Juan

Perez, who had been the Queen's confessor and who had much influence with her, told Columbus to wait while he tried to intercede for him. Ecclesiastics were interested in expansion and exploration, for it enhanced the glory and broadened the influence of the Church as well as of the country undertaking the mission.

Father Perez was successful. The Queen sent for Columbus and promised to support him on his own terms if he would wait till the war was over. In January of 1492, Granada, the last stronghold of the Moors, fell. Spain was free.

The Queen kept her promise, and Columbus drove a hard bargain. It says a great deal for his strength of will and persuasive powers that he was able to get the shrewd and hardheaded Queen to agree that he be made an admiral—Admiral of the Ocean Sea was the title— and have privileges similar to those of the Lord High Admiral of Spain; that he and his heirs be the governors of any lands he might discover, with three assistants, two to be appointed by him and one by the Crown; that after deducting the costs of the expedition he be allowed to retain one tenth of all the wealth obtained; that he be supreme judge in all disputes between Spain and the new lands; and that he and his heirs forever should provide one eighth of the cost of outfitting all future expeditions of discovery and receive one eighth of all the profits.

The Queen's council flatly refused to approve these terms, but by this time Columbus had won the support of many influential noblemen, churchmen, and some of the richest merchants, who pointed out that the terms were contingent on the success of the expedition. The council finally agreed.

One point in all this should be noted. No one opposed Columbus on the ground that the earth was flat. Every influential Spaniard knew it was a globe, the real question being the size of the globe. Ironically the opponents of the idea were right. They said that Columbus had grossly underestimated the distance from Europe to China, as indeed he had. The only thing that saved his expedition from failure was the accident of his coming across an unknown land mass on the other side of the Atlantic.

Royal approval and royal money now supporting him, Columbus plunged furiously into the labor of organizing his expedition. On August 3, 1492, after an impressive ceremony in the Church of St.

George, Christopher Columbus set sail from Palos, with the parting blessing of his friend Father Juan Perez. Three caravels, the "Nina," "Pinta," and "Santa Maria," steered westward into the depths of the Atlantic.

Columbus was about forty-one years old, quiet, dignified, yet powerfully dominating his men. He made them sail on and on, day after day, not knowing what lay ahead, with nothing to break the monotony of the endless sea, nothing to quiet their fears. He used persuasion, dominance, trickery to prevent them from turning back. The three small ships kept moving forward, their bows pointing west. Then came the most dramatic moment in the history of exploration: in the early morning hours of October 12, 1492, Rodrigo de Triana, a simple sailor aboard the "Nina," spotted a light. The expedition was close to land. As dawn broke they saw it was an island, one of the West Indian chain, that is known today as Watlings Island. Columbus, carrying the royal flag of Spain, led his men ashore. He named the island San Salvador, and claimed it in the name of King Ferdinand and Queen Isabella. Thus was founded the Spanish claim to the New World.

Continuing his voyage, Columbus now sailed among the islands of the West Indies. Believing that he had reached Asia, he sought for spices and gold. He reached the large island that is now divided between Haiti and the Dominican Republic, and named it Hispaniola. Here he built a fort, La Navidad, to garrison which he disembarked a force of forty men. He was tactful with the natives and careful to keep them well disposed and friendly by giving them presents. He called them Indians because he believed that he was on an island not far from the coast of India.

Columbus remained in the Caribbean Sea for several months before deciding it was time to return home. The "Santa Maria" had been wrecked when she piled up on the shore, so the Admiral of the Ocean Sea transferred his flag to the "Nina." The "Nina" and the "Pinta" then set sail for Spain.

Reaching Palos, Columbus proceeded in triumph to the Spanish court where he made a report of his wonderful voyage to the King and Queen, and obtained their approval for another expedition to undertake the colonization of the newly discovered lands.

Six months later Columbus sailed again, this time with seventeen

ships and more than 1,500 men well supplied with arms and ammunition. After a successful crossing of the Atlantic, he sought out the fort
he had established, only to find that the garrison of La Navidad had
been massacred by hostile Indians. He immediately founded a settlement at Isabela, some thirty miles from La Navidad. This was the
first European town in the New World. Columbus then sailed westward and discovered Jamaica. On his return to Isabela he found
the Indians hostile, but, landing a large force, he easily defeated
them.

Meanwhile Columbus' opponents in Spain had induced the authorities to send out Juan Aguado to inquire into Columbus' dealings with the natives. Columbus had no difficulty in convincing
Aguado that his administration, if not perfect, was as good as possible
under the circumstances, and they returned to Spain together. Columbus himself presented his case to the King, received a favorable
hearing, and all charges against him were dismissed.

After a prolonged rest, much of which he spent in writing of his discoveries, Columbus set out on his third voyage in May of 1498. This
time he steered farther south, and became the first white man to land
in South America. He was convinced that he had reached India.
During the next two years of his third voyage, Columbus discovered
virtually all the Leeward and Windward Islands.

Then reports of further trouble in the administration of Spain's
new possessions brought out another investigator, Francisco de
Bobadilla. Lusting for power and anxious to usurp Columbus' place,
Bobadilla threw the Great Navigator into chains and sent him back
to Spain to answer charges of oppressing the colonists, of unjust wars
against the Indians, and of withholding gold and other valuables
instead of sending them home to the King and Queen.

This was too vastly different a homecoming from the triumphant
returns from the first two voyages, and the people of Spain were
aroused to indignation. Columbus got his own report of the affair into
Queen Isabella's hands before Bobadilla's official dispatch arrived.
She was shocked and ordered his immediate release.

Again displaying his dynamic personality, Columbus dressed
richly, surrounded himself with a retinue of servants, and proceeded
to court. He explained his actions with pride and conviction. Ferdinand and Isabella believed him and agreed to recall Bobadilla. It was

arranged for an administrator to be sent out to take over the work of government. Columbus was to devote himself to exploration, at which he had scored such triumphs.

He set out on his fourth voyage. Sailing from Spain in March of 1502, he landed on the mainland of Central America in what is now Honduras and, following the coast to the south, reached the Isthmus of Panama, seeking a westward passage in an apparent effort to sail around the world. Convinced that there was no passage and that he had reached the mainland of Asia, he returned to Jamaica, whence he sailed for Spain.

He was now weary and exhausted by illness. Queen Isabella had just died, and, although a great deal of money was owing to Columbus, King Ferdinand was in no hurry to settle the explorer's claims. What strength he had left, Columbus spent in endless and fruitless trips to court to plead for his rights. He was reduced to borrowing money to live and moved to Valladolid, where he took lodgings and was attended by only one servant. He died in obscurity on May 20, 1506, at the age of fifty-five, never dreaming that he had discovered a New World.

VESPUCCI

[1451–1512]

I N THE year 1507 a new book of geography was being prepared at a small university in Lorraine. It was badly needed. Fifteen years previously Christopher Columbus had discovered the New World, and great explorations were sweeping along on the opposite side of the Atlantic. New lands were being reported in rapid succession, and the map of the globe was changing from day to day.

At the small university of Lorraine, the professor of cosmography was a learned scholar named Martin Waldseemüller, and he had the task of preparing the new geography. We can imagine the problem he faced in plotting the recent discoveries on his charts. But Professor Waldseemüller felt himself fortunate, no doubt, to be in the possession of a document that had just come to hand.

This was a letter written by an Italian, a Florentine named Amerigo Vespucci, who told of voyages he had made. His epistle circulated widely, and had been translated into French and Latin. Waldseemüller had the Latin translation, with the author's first name of Amerigo Latinized as—Americus, or, in the feminine form, America.

There was one thing remarkable about this Vespucci: he insisted that the lands he had visited across the Atlantic formed a hitherto unknown expanse of the surface of the earth. Columbus, the original discoverer, claimed to have voyaged to India. He died in that belief. Had Columbus realized that he had, in fact, discovered a New World, America would undoubtedly have been named after him, as Columbia. But now it was becoming gradually understood that the new lands were not outlying parts of Asia but islands and continents unknown and undreamed of. In this view Vespucci was foremost. He stated his opinion strongly and persuasively in writings that attracted much attention, and one of these was the letter that Professor of Cosmography Martin Waldseemüller had before him.

Thus while Columbus claimed he had sailed to the Indies, Vespucci said it was a New World. Some might have surmised that both were right—that Columbus had indeed reached the coast of Asia, while the lands described by Vespucci were something else.

However that may be, Waldseemüller included in his new geography the places described by Amerigo (Americus) Vespucci, which were actually the northern coast of South America, and marked them down as "New World." To which he added the opinion that this territory should be called "America, because Americus discovered it." This christening caught on, and that is how America got its name, applied at first to the part of South America described by Vespucci and later extended to North America.

There is one point to notice in this performance by cosmographer Waldseemüller, his phraseology—"America, because Americus discovered it." Vespucci never did claim that he had discovered the continent of which he told, South America. In fact, he was no expedition leader but a geographer-navigator, and could not properly claim to have discovered anything. Columbus, after his voyages among some of the West Indian islands, was the first to reach the mainland of South America. This was in 1498, after John Cabot, the Genoese sailing for England, had reached North America in 1497. But the dates set down by Vespucci would indicate that he was in South America before Columbus, and had reached the New World mainland some days before John Cabot. Vespucci's claim on this point is usually considered false, but the truth is not easy to get at.

The namesake of the New World was, in fact, very much of a mystery man. Some have called him a great liar, while others have defended the veracity of his narratives. In his life much is vague and contradictory, with the one outstanding feature—that he was active in furthering the idea that this was a New World, and the New World was given his name.

He was born in the glowing Florence of the Medici, his family history closely connected with that fabulous clan of bankers and princes. As a partisan of the Medici, his grandfather, after whom he was named, was for thirty-six years secretary of the Florentine Senate. The explorer's father, Nastagio Vespucci, filled that highly honor-

GALILEO

CARDINAL RICHELIEU

able and lucrative office for another four years, and became head of several of the great guilds.

As soon as Amerigo was old enough to go to school he was sent to his uncle, Fra Giorgio Antonio Vespucci, dean of the cathedral, who conducted a school for the education of noble youths. Uncle Giorgio was a scholar who collected maps and manuscripts, and taught his nephew to love them. He encouraged the boy to study astronomy, navigation, map making.

A famous painting by Ghirlandaio on the wall of a chapel built by the Vespucci shows the whole family, and portrays Amerigo at the age of about seventeen or eighteen. It pictures him as a vigorous and intelligent youth of medium height, with dark wavy hair, dark eyes, and strong chin, a fine oval face.

Young Vespucci entered the service of the Medici, and rose to a trusted position. His letters hint that he was on terms of intimacy with the princely bankers, living with them, virtually a member of the family.

But this period of Vespucci's life is mostly a blank, and it is not until his early forties that he emerges clearly. We find him now in Spain, to which country he had probably gone on business for the Medici banking house. We see him engaged in large commercial affairs at Seville and Cadiz, and one of these is on record as having to do with the new lands beyond the Atlantic.

Gianetto Berardi, a fellow Florentine, who had provided ships and provisions for Columbus' second expedition, had an order to supply twelve ships fully equipped for the King of Spain. He died, and the contract was turned over to Vespucci. Columbus had been granted a monopoly of voyages to the lands he found, but this had been revoked, and the field was open to others such as the King of Spain might commission. The result was a rush of expeditions, and Amerigo Vespucci, by his own account, was foremost in this work.

He says he went on four voyages, the first of which is the chief cause of controversy—the one in which he claims to have reached South America in June of 1497, which was before Columbus saw the mainland on his third voyage, and before John Cabot found the mainland of North America. The account given by Vespucci made the critics argue that, if it were true, he must have sailed in the Pacific, and so his narrative is generally discounted.

His third voyage, begun in 1501 in the service of the King of Portugal, is likewise a subject of skepticism. He left two accounts which contradict each other in dates and distances, and would make it seem that he had sailed to the Antarctic continent. This completes the belief of some that he was a great liar.

His most famous accounts are contained in two letters written in 1503 and 1504 respectively. Both were circulated widely, and featured Vespucci's contention that he had visited a New World, as against Columbus' claim of finding a sea route to India. The second was the letter that Waldseemüller had before him when he named America.

The cartographer argued that the newly discovered fourth part of the world—Europe, Africa, and Asia being already known—should be called America "because Americus discovered it." Of course Amerigo Vespucci did nothing of the kind. America was discovered by Christopher Columbus, who reached Watlings Island in the Bahamas on October 12, 1492. Giovanni Caboto, a Genoese pilot naturalized at Venice, who settled in Bristol, England, about 1490 and was called John Cabot, is known to have reached the mainland of North America on June 24, 1497. Nearly all authorities disagree with Vespucci's statement that he had hit the mainland of South America six days earlier. But it is quite certain that Vespucci was the first of the explorers to realize that this was indeed a New World and not the coast of Asia.

Amerigo Vespucci spent the remainder of his life in Spain. He visited Christopher Columbus in his retirement, and became a good friend of the Discoverer's. What did they talk about? Did Vespucci argue that Columbus had uncovered a totally fresh field for exploration, while Columbus insisted that it was Asia, the Indies? Nobody knows, but it is a fascinating picture, this meeting of the one who discovered America and the other after whom America was named.

Columbus is immortal as the Great Navigator. Vespucci is immortal because a German cartographer attached his first name to the lands Columbus discovered. All of which means that it is only by a strange twist of fortune that we call ourselves Americans.

FERDINAND AND ISABELLA

[*1452–1516*]   [*1451–1504*]

I N 1469 a great new power appeared in Europe. With the marriage of Ferdinand, the seventeen-year-old King of Aragon, to Isabella, the eighteen-year-old heiress to the crown of Castile and León, Spain was transformed from a heterogeneous group of conflicting principalities to a powerful unified government.

Ferdinand was the son of King John II of Aragon and his second wife, Juana Enriquez. Ferdinand, succeeding to the throne in 1469, appeared older than his seventeen years. He had a high forehead, bushy eyebrows, and was becoming bald. He was unemotional, dignified, sober in his tastes, simple in his dress. His life up to that point had been uneventful.

Isabella's childhood had been stormy and hectic. She was the daughter of King John II of Castile and León, who married twice. His heir was the son of his first wife. Isabella and a brother were children of his second marriage. On King John's death, his eldest son, Isabella's half-brother, ascended the throne as Henry IV of Castile and León. He hated Isabella and her brother because they stood in line to succeed him. Ordering them to remain at his court, he kept them under close surveillance.

The new King, feeble, vicious, irreligious, dissolute, married the daughter of King Alfonso of Portugal. After seven years a daughter was born. Baptized Juana, she promptly got the nickname of "La Beltraneja," in pointed reference to Don Beltrán de la Cueva, a swaggering cavalier who was believed to be her father.

The power of Don Beltrán aroused the hostility of the nobles of Castile, who sent a protest to the King stating that "Donna Juana, the one called the Princess, is not your daughter." Facing revolt, the King was forced to recognize as heir to the crown his half-brother Alfonso,

Isabella's younger brother. When Alfonso died suddenly, with assassination by poison suspected, the revolt broke out. The nobles offered their allegiance to Isabella, who had retired to a convent. She refused, saying that Henry IV was still their King. Whereupon they forced the monarch to acknowledge Isabella as the heiress to his throne.

An attempt was made to marry her to Alfonso V of Portugal, but she preferred Ferdinand of Aragon. Defying both Henry and Alfonso, she fled to Valladolid, where Ferdinand joined her. They were married shortly afterward.

We have no portrait of Isabella, but those who knew her say she was delicately beautiful, with blonde hair and a fair complexion. Her voice was musical, her bearing queenly. She was highly intelligent and strong-willed, and her partnership with Ferdinand was that of an equal. She seems to have fallen in love with him at first sight and, although she insisted always on her own inherited royal prerogative, she was a devoted wife the rest of her life. At Isabella's request, Ferdinand signed a statement that he would respect Castilian laws and customs, that he would live in Castile and leave only if she permitted him to, that he would allow her to pass on his appointments. But no real friction ever came between them.

Upon her coronation as Queen of Castile and León following the death of Henry IV, she and Ferdinand took up residence in Madrid, the capital of Castile. Sweeping reforms were begun immediately to assert the supremacy of the crown in Isabella's turbulent realm. Men of ability were put into office, the old crowd of hangers-on was swept out. It was a bitter struggle and the young rulers made many enemies. They put down rebellion in the provinces. They threw back an attempted invasion by the Portuguese.

Ferdinand and Isabella had to deal with the final phase of a problem that had beset Spain for centuries, the Moors. Early in the eighth century the Moslems had conquered the country. For more than seven hundred years there had been continuous warfare as the Christian principalities had slowly regained their freedom. In the south of Spain the Mohammedan stronghold of Granada still held out against the Christian monarchs.

Among the Moorish population of the Spanish lands were those who had been Christianized, Moriscos. Closely allied, in Spanish eyes at least, were the Jews, including the Maranos or Christianized Jews.

Many Moriscos and Maranos were accused of being converts in name only. The persistence of Moslems in Spain was considered a peril to unity and a source of disorder. The Spanish were inclined to link the Jews with the Moslems because of the support given to the Moorish conquest by the Jews. Isabella, moreover, is said to have been prejudiced by her experiences at the dissolute court of her half-brother Henry IV, at which Moors and Jews were both prominent.

The Spanish Inquisition was one result of this attitude. In 1478, Ferdinand and Isabella obtained authority from Pope Sixtus IV to appoint three inquisitors whom they could remove or replace at will and who were independent of the bishops. The Inquisition was employed to seek out pretended conversions, and did this in such fashion as to win its evil reputation as an instrument of terror. By a general edict the Moors and the Jews were expelled from Spain in 1492, the year of the fall of Granada and the discovery of America.

When the troops of Ferdinand and Isabella entered Granada, the story of the Moors in Spain ended. Almost immediately the story of America began.

Isabella was personally responsible for the great voyage. She listened to Christopher Columbus and supported him against the advice of learned counselors. Despite the depletion of her treasury due to the war against Granada, she made the discovery of America possible. That she financed Columbus by pawning her jewels seems to be only a pleasing fiction. But it is true that she saw to it that the money was found. When Columbus returned with the first gold ever brought from the New World to the Old, she had it melted into a life-size image of the Christ child, which was placed in the arms of a silver statue of the Virgin Mary. This beautiful work of art is now in the treasury of the cathedral at Toledo.

Every expedition to the New World had her enthusiastic aid. Every conquistador who returned to Spain was obliged to describe his adventures and discoveries to her. Ferdinand, on the other hand, saw only the material gain to be derived from Spanish possessions in the New World and little of the glory of magnificent achievement. After Isabella's death he allowed Columbus to die in poverty, and was never satisfied with the enormous wealth that flowed into his treasury.

In the politics of Europe, Ferdinand was a master of statecraft, and played a shrewd cold game. He laid the foundation for the great power which Spain was to have in European affairs for more than a century. His army won brilliant successes in Italy and, under Gonzalo de Córdoba, El Gran Capitan, who led the expedition, began the dominance of Spanish infantry over all other fighting men of the epoch.

To history Isabella is known as Isabella the Catholic, the Pope having granted her and her husband the title held thereafter by each Spanish sovereign—the Catholic King. Isabella died when she was fifty-three, leaving behind her a reputation of lofty virtue both as a woman and as a sovereign.

Her morals were above reproach and she made the Spanish court "the nursery of virtue and of generous ambition." From her own private funds she founded the famous palace school, and her intelligence and foresight are illustrated by her support of Columbus. Her part in the establishment of the Inquisition and the expulsion of Moors and Jews is attributed to her belief that the non-Christians were a threat to the integrity of Spain—a fixed idea of the time, when so much emphasis was placed on religious unity.

The death of Isabella left her inheritance of Castile and León to her daughter Juana, married to Philip the Handsome of Austria. Technically the union of Spain through the marriage of Ferdinand and Isabella was dissolved, but this was only temporary. There was a dispute between Ferdinand and his daughter's husband; then Philip died and Juana became insane. Their son Charles came into the inheritance of both his maternal grandparents, Ferdinand and Isabella. From his paternal grandparents he was to inherit Austria and the Low Countries. In the boy heir the dynastic unification of Spain became permanent. Ferdinand now ruled as regent for his grandson over Castile and León, as well as over his own Aragon.

He survived Isabella for twelve years. His death in 1516, and the succession of his grandson, Charles I of Spain, who was elected Holy Roman Emperor as Charles V, placed Spain under the aegis of the Hapsburgs and dragged the Iberian Peninsula into the politics of central Europe. A new Spain, a new Europe, a New World were in the making—all largely due to Ferdinand and Isabella.

FRANCISCO PIZARRO

[1470?–1541]

ESTREMADURA, a province of Spain lying between Andalusia and Portugal, was the birthplace of the conquistadores who gave to Spain the richest spoils of the New World—Balboa, Cortez, and Pizarro. Of the three the last was the most ruthless, the most perfidious, but he carved out for his country a Pacific empire covering all that is now Peru, the northern lands of Chile, and the southern part of Ecuador. His loot was greater than that of his rivals. His achievement was the more fantastic as he could neither read nor write, and he could only scrawl a fancy flourish or rubric under his name that had to be written in by a secretary.

Tired of being a swineherd, he had enlisted in Balboa's first expedition and was with him again when from a height in Darien he first caught sight of the Southern Sea. Pizarro was more than fifty and possessed of nothing but an old soldier's allotment of land near Panama City, when he started on the expedition that was to give him a place in history as the destroyer of a purely American civilization, higher in some ways than that which Spain herself could boast.

Pizarro's reputation for perfidy is enhanced by the story of the downfall of Balboa. The discoverer of the Pacific had ousted the official leader in Panama, and another functionary, Pedrarias, was sent by the authorities in Spain to look into matters. Pedrarias brought about the condemnation and execution of Balboa, and Pizarro was found on the side of the winner. In the service of Pedrarias, he distinguished himself by leading several expeditions against the warlike tribes to the north, and gained a reputation as a tough competent soldier.

At this time in 1522 an expedition returned from the coast south of Panama with more glowing accounts of the wealth of that area than any yet received. Pizarro formed a project with Diego de Almagro, also an old soldier, for fitting out an expedition of their own to conquer these unknown lands for the King of Spain. Almagro was rough, honest, and of a frank hasty disposition. To obtain funds they turned to Father Hernando de Luque, Vicar of Panama, whom the historian Prescott describes as "a man of singular prudence and knowledge of the world." Pizarro and Almagro put in all they had, but by far the greater part of the expense was borne by the Vicar. It was agreed among them that Pizarro was to be in command of the expedition, Almagro to look after equipment and supplies. All profits were to be equally divided among the three partners.

Pizarro sailed southward, reached Peru, and found ample evidence that at last he was in the fabulous land of the Incas. He returned to Panama to tell of his discoveries. The governor of Panama, however, refused to be convinced and denied permission for any further voyages. That incited Pizarro to go to Spain with a personal appeal to the King. Illiterate though he was, he presented so forcefully the golden promise of the lands he had reached that he won the favor of Charles V, King of Spain and Holy Roman Emperor. The sovereign knighted him with the Order of Santiago, and commissioned him to continue his ambitious plans with the title of Captain General of the new lands he might conquer. He was granted the rank and authority of viceroy, while his partners Almagro and Luque were assigned to subordinate positions. This, connived by Pizarro, was a prime example of his ruthlessness and perfidy.

However, he managed to mollify his partners on his return to Panama, and soon set out for another visit to Peru. The expedition landed at the Bay of St. Matthew in Peru, and marched along the coast, plundering villages. Before they had gone far reinforcements joined them, landed from two ships commanded by Hernando de Soto, later to become immortal as the discoverer of the Mississippi River.

The Inca civilization was then at the height of its glory, with superb architecture, great engineering works, a remarkable system of terracing of fields, skill in weaving and pattern making, no method of writing but an ingenious system of recording with knotted cords, a communal village system, an absolute state with a hierarchy of nobles and a supreme sovereign. The religion was sun worship, which brought about the development of the science of astronomy. It was a culture imposing, splendid, and wealthy.

Pizarro landed just as a civil war had ended. The Inca Atahualpa, Prince of Quito, the northern part of the domain, had gained absolute control of the empire. Atahualpa sent an invitation to the strangers to be his guests. That was exactly what Pizarro had in mind. He quickly advanced with 110 foot soldiers and 67 cavalrymen.

Pizarro and his officers were received by the Inca who promised to visit them in their camp the following day. It was during the night apparently that the conquistador formed his plans. The disparity of forces was so great that the only way he could obtain control was to seize the person of the Inca by treachery. The next day the unsuspecting Atahualpa arrived at Pizarro's camp accompanied by a retinue of nobles and an escort of several thousand. The Spaniards cut down the Inca sovereign's bodyguard and made him their prisoner.

Atahualpa bargained for his freedom and, playing on the Spanish lust for treasure, promised to fill a room full of gold as high as he could reach and fill another room twice with silver. Pizarro agreed to the ransom terms. Atahualpa sent out couriers and actually collected gold and silver to the value of millions of dollars in present-day money. But, instead of releasing the Inca, according to the bargain, Pizarro had him put to death. The Spanish commander feared for the safety of his small force in the midst of a hostile empire. But his treachery aroused indignation even among the Spaniards.

Pizarro set out to march to Cuzco, the Inca metropolis. The Indians, rallying from their stupor, harassed his march continually but could not stop him. Cuzco was pillaged of a vast amount of treasure and turned into a Spanish city. The Incas rose in revolt, only to be put down with savage cruelty.

Pizarro now had only his old partner to worry about. Almagro entered Cuzco at the head of a large force and claimed the city. Soon war broke out between the two Spanish leaders. Almagro lost, was taken prisoner and executed. But Pizarro too was destroyed by the feud, for three years later a band of Almagro's men forced their way into his palace at Lima and murdered him. The Incas were saved from rule by Pizarro, but their subjection to Spain, which was the work of Pizarro, became permanent.

WOLSEY

[1471?–1530]

ENGLAND, having emerged enfeebled from the shattering civil
strife known as the Wars of the Roses, was not a great power
when Henry VIII came to the throne. That the kingdom rose swiftly
to international influence was because of the virtuosity of Thomas
Cardinal Wolsey. With the artistry of an earlier Richelieu, he played
the game of international politics to such good effect that he gave
England a deciding weight in a European balance of power, the historic position of Great Britain in subsequent times.

The son of a grazier, young Thomas Wolsey showed so much intellectual promise that he was marked down for the priesthood. At
eleven he entered Oxford, emerging with his degree four years later.
He was ordained, began to teach at Oxford, received ecclesiastical
preferment, and became chaplain to the Archbishop of Canterbury.
Wolsey's next step took him into the court of Henry VII, where he
cultivated the friendship of the heir to the throne.

After Henry VIII's accession, honors came to Wolsey in quick succession. Entering the Privy Council, he took upon himself most of the
work of governing, thus allowing Henry to spend his time hunting,
dancing, carousing, eating. Wolsey stood beside the throne as the
trusted confidant and instrument of the King of England.

The preferment already given to Wolsey was as nothing compared
to what he aspired to. He wanted to be a cardinal, to be Lord Chancellor of England, and doubtless already dreamed of becoming Pope.
To that end he plunged into international politics, urging Henry VIII
into an alliance with the Holy Roman Emperor, Maximilian, in a war
against France because of the Emperor's influence in Rome. The
campaign was successful; Henry was pleased, Wolsey hopeful. His
hope did not end in disappointment. Six months later he became

Archbishop of York, second only to the Archbishop of Canterbury in the English hierarchy.

Then he persuaded the King to demand for him a cardinal's hat. The papal messenger bringing the hat to London was met on Blackheath by a great number of prelates and nobles, who conducted him in great pomp and triumph to Westminster Abbey; there eight mitered abbots received the sacred hat with due solemnity and conveyed it to the high altar whereon it was set. The following Sunday, Wolsey repaired to the abbey and knelt before the Archbishop of Canterbury, who, after the benediction and prayers, placed the hat on his head. Within weeks Wolsey mounted to the highest seat of English politics, becoming Lord Chancellor. In the entire realm he now had no master excepting the King himself.

In 1516 the Pope appointed Cardinal Wolsey papal legate to England, with extensive authority over the English clergy. Wolsey established a legatine court to inquire into clerical conduct and pass judgment and inflict penalties. Most of the fines imposed went into Wolsey's pocket, and it is said that, with all the revenues that he acquired, the Cardinal had an annual income as great if not greater than that of Henry VIII.

Cardinal Wolsey now obtained a ninety-nine-year lease of an estate near Hampton, fifteen miles southwest of St. Paul's Cathedral, whereon he erected Hampton Court Palace, one of the finest specimens of Tudor architecture. It was more splendidly furnished than any of the royal palaces, and at Hampton Court Wolsey lived in state.

At this juncture, the Emperor Maximilian died, and Charles of Spain, Francis of France, and Henry of England were all candidates for election as Holy Roman Emperor. Since Henry really had no chance of being elected, both Charles and Francis showered gifts on Wolsey in the hope that he would persuade his King to withdraw in their favor. Charles V promised Wolsey to make him Pope. Charles was elected, the King of Spain becoming the Holy Roman Emperor Charles V.

This was followed by the prolonged wars between Charles V and Francis I. Both sides wooed the support of England, which gave Wolsey great opportunity to apply the policy of the balance of power. Under his supervision King Henry crossed the Channel and met

Frances I in great splendor on the Field of the Cloth of Gold. Then
Henry conferred with Charles V. The magnificence was less, but the
effect was greater. Wolsey kept England to its alliance with the
Emperor.

The next year Pope Leo X died, and Wolsey counted on the aid of
Charles in the papal election. Had Wolsey succeeded, England might
well have assumed first place among the European powers. But
Charles V had become suspicious of Wolsey. Secretly he ordered his
ambassador in Rome to press for the election of Adrian, a venerable
Flemish prelate who had been the Emperor's tutor. At the same time
Charles wrote a warm public letter in favor of Wolsey's candidacy.
Wolsey was too wise to be taken in, and told Charles's ambassador
that his master could procure Wolsey's election if he were in earnest
about it. Adrian was chosen Pope.

The war between Charles and Francis turned in favor of the Empire. The French King was defeated and made prisoner at the Battle
of Pavia. Wolsey, having failed to become Pope, now also saw the
balance of power upset. He reversed the alliance with Charles, and
took England to the side of France.

In pursuit of his complicated policy and to finance the extravagance of the King, Wolsey resorted to forced loans from both laity
and clergy and the imposition of additional heavy taxes on the clergy,
and was becoming unpopular at home. To strengthen his position, he
in 1525 presented Hampton Court Palace to Henry VIII, who gave
him Richmond Palace in exchange. To ingratiate himself further, he
produced a will making Henry his sole heir. The mighty Cardinal
lorded it over England. But his nemesis was approaching.

Henry VIII was tired of his wife, Catherine of Aragon, who had
not given him an heir. He decided to get rid of her and to marry his
mistress Anne Boleyn. Hence upon Cardinal Wolsey fell the task of
arranging a royal divorce.

Wolsey wanted the divorce since it was a blow at Charles V, who
was Catherine's nephew. Pope Clement VII, who had succeeded
Adrian, sent Cardinal Campeggio to London to try the divorce action, but Charles brought pressure to bear and the Pope recalled
Campeggio. The motives in the affair have been debated endlessly
on the score of both morality and international policy. In the end the

plans of Henry and Wolsey miscarried completely. The divorce was disallowed by the Holy See.

Anne Boleyn blamed Wolsey. Henry VIII furiously demanded that the Cardinal surrender the Great Seal and retire to Esher to await the King's pleasure. Parliament debated whether to try him on the grounds that he had abused his power as papal legate, had made treaties without the King's knowledge, and had committed sundry other misdemeanors. The charges were thrown out, but Wolsey was a ruined man. He had made too many enemies during his rise from obscurity to power, and they brought pressure to bear on the King.

The Cardinal was in York when Henry VIII had him arrested for high treason. Wolsey—broken, dispirited, ill—began a slow, painful journey to London. He got no further than Leicester Abbey. Knowing he had come to the end of the road, he remarked to the head of the abbey, "Father Abbott, I am come hither to leave my bones among you." He made his confession and died soon afterward. The last words of Cardinal Wolsey were "If I had served my God as diligently as I have done the King, He would not have given me over in my gray hairs."

VASCO NUÑEZ DE BALBOA

[1475–1517]

W HEN in the late afternoon of September 25, 1513, from Mt. Quaragua, a peak in Darien—the exact location is uncertain— Vasco Nuñez de Balboa saw shining below him the Pacific Ocean, he knew that his quest for the South Sea was at an end. He had with him only 190 men, their Carib porters, and his faithful war dog Leoncico, a fine Spanish bloodhound. A few hours later the sun dropped below the horizon.

> "Not as in northern climes obscurely bright
> But one unclouded blaze of living light."

Had the trail of the first European to reach the placid waters that bathe the western shores of the New World been a little further north, had he climbed the hill at Ancon, where the Panama Canal now ends, he would have been a sorely puzzled man. For there the narrow strip of land between the two oceans bends like a swan's neck, the coast line faces east, and the sun rises over the Pacific.

Balboa and his men carved the name of the King of Spain on the tall coconut palms that fringe the shore, and a notary was witness to the ceremony of taking possession of the land in his name. Then, after the soldiers had tasted the water and found it salt, Balboa, resplendent in full armor, strode into the sea and holding aloft his naked sword claimed the ocean as the property of Ferdinand the Catholic, King of Aragon, Castile, Granada, and Navarre, Sovereign Lord of Sicily and Naples.

Balboa came from the village of Jerez de los Caballeros in southern Spain where he grew up on a small estate which his family owned and where they grew grapes and made wine. A "hidalgo" or gentleman, Balboa was anything but a typical Spaniard. He stood a full six feet and his flaming red hair and blue eyes told of a Vandal ancestry. As his people were undistinguished and far from wealthy, he took service before he was seventeen as squire to Don Pedro Puertocarrero, a noble Spanish cavalier, under whom he served for eight years, rising to the rank of captain. He was acknowledged to be one of the finest swordsmen of his day. Peter Martyr, the historian, describes him as being "bold and somewhat boastful, a rashe Royster rather than a politike Captayne."

It was lust for gold rather than any interest in geographical exploration that led Balboa and many another conquistador to face the perils of the Atlantic in their frail caravels and to discover much of the New World. His imagination had been fired by the voyages of Christopher Columbus. After discovering the Tierra Firme or coasts of Central and South America during his third voyage in 1498, that great navigator wrote to Ferdinand and Isabella of the quantities of gold and pearls to be found in South America which he then believed to be the east coast of Asia. Exaggerated accounts of the fabulous wealth of the Spanish Main passed from mouth to mouth and lost nothing in the telling.

Balboa determined to get his share. In 1500 he set out with Rodrigo de Bastidas, a notary, for Hispaniola, by then called San Domingo, with two caravels and a company of cavaliers and soldiers. When they arrived Balboa, who had been brought up on farm land, settled down to raising food for the small Spanish colony established there. As he was without business experience, at the end of eight years he found himself hopelessly in debt.

Then Don Alonzo de Ojeda, a great Spanish cavalier who had accompanied Christopher Columbus on his first voyage, returned to the New World with an expedition of his own. Arriving at San Domingo, Don Alonzo, before continuing onward, left orders for Martin Fernando Enciso, his notary, to follow him with two ships of supplies. Enciso was warned that many debtors, to evade their creditors, were planning to stow away on his vessels. There was a law on the island that no debtor might leave without the permission of his creditors, so Enciso took every precaution. But no sooner were the two supply ships under way than out of one of the large casks supposed to be filled with provisions there stepped a tall redhead dragging after him a bloodhound. The man was Balboa and the dog his faithful war companion Leoncico. In those days many Spanish officers had their own war dogs, which wore armor the same as their masters. A complete set of such canine accouterment is preserved in the Royal Armory in Madrid.

At this time Balboa was in the full strength of his manhood and just the kind of fighter any conquistador would be glad to have with him. So he had little difficulty in persuading Enciso to take him along. In spite or perhaps because of his free and rather reckless manner, Balboa had the gift of making friends and winning confidence, and Enciso relied a great deal upon him for the rest of the expedition.

When they reached their destination they found no sign of Ojeda, who had been shipwrecked and later made his way back to San Domingo. The Spanish settlement he had founded was in ruins, the survivors dying of hunger and privation. Supplies were left with them, and then Balboa persuaded Enciso to continue on along the coast. They came to Darien, Panama. There, after beating off various attacks by hostile Indians, they built a town and called it Santa Maria del Antigua. They prospered beyond expectation as food was plentiful, and they took much gold from the natives. Being a lawyer, Enciso, as governor and chief judge, made so many laws and regulations that the soldiers grew restive and finally deposed him and made Balboa governor in his stead. Eventually Enciso returned to Spain and lodged a complaint against Balboa with the King.

Balboa began to conquer and settle the surrounding country. Through his justice and humane treatment of the natives, he secured the friendship of many Carib tribes. Although he was ruthless with hostile Indians, he never practiced, or allowed his men to indulge in, the cruelties that have blackened the names of other conquistadores. Indeed Balboa took an Indian princess to wife. She was the daughter of Careta, a cacique or chief of one of the most powerful tribes in Darien. Another cacique, Comogre, chief of a prosperous territory, invited Balboa to visit him and make a treaty of peace. It was through this man's son, Ponca, that the Spaniards first heard of a wonderful land to the south, beyond a great body of water, where the people ate and drank out of vessels of pure gold. It was the first time any European had heard of Peru and the Pacific Ocean.

After concluding the treaty, Balboa returned to his headquarters at Darien where he found letters from Spain warning him that Enciso had undermined his authority at home, that King Ferdinand was sending out a new governor to Darien, and that Balboa would probably be arrested. Balboa had just written to the King, telling him of the great South Sea and the golden land beyond it, begging for reinforcements and permission to set out in quest of these riches. But when he got the warning letters, he decided to start without awaiting word from Spain.

So on September 1, 1513, he set out with 190 men and a party of native bearers to find the South Sea. Among his followers was Francisco Pizarro, later to become famous as the conqueror of Peru. They had only one ship and ten native canoes, and they hugged the coast on the first leg of their journey. At Acla they left the sea and marched south to the cacique Ponca's territory, from which they hoped to cross the isthmus. Ponca gave them directions and told them of a peak from which they would be able to see the South Sea. The Spaniards resumed their trek, making their way by compass. There were no trails through the tropical forest. They had to chop their way with machetes foot by foot. The heat by day was terrific, at times as high as 120 degrees, but the nights were cold, and swarms of mosquitoes and other insects, not to mention snakes, impeded their progress. Many of the men contracted severe chills and fever. Worst of all they were hungry, as Balboa, not realizing how long it would take him to reach his objective, had underestimated the amount of food necessary.

But Balboa was a real leader of men. Sharing all their hardships, coaxing and swearing by turn, he pushed them on and on till they came to the foothills of the range that Ponca had described. There they found nearly a thousand Indian warriors drawn up to defend their territory. The Indians rushed forward to attack the Spaniards, but one volley from the matchlocks that Balboa's men carried terrified them so that they fell back. Tired as they were, the Spaniards pursued them, killing six hundred and taking many prisoners. In the Indian village they found gold and pearls and, even more valuable, a plentiful supply of food. The next day, they climbed the mountain from which they saw "El Mar del Sur"—the South Sea.

Balboa and his men stayed on the shores of the Pacific for some time, explored the surrounding country and made friends with the local caciques. One of these, Tomaco, told them of the Pearl Islands and presented them with several hundred fine pearls. After another terrible trip across the isthmus, Balboa returned to Darien. He immediately wrote to the King telling him of his great discovery, of the gold and pearls he had brought back, and of the even greater quantities still to be had. King Ferdinand was so pleased he decided that the reports made by Enciso must have been false. He appointed Balboa Admiral of the South Sea and Governor of Panama and Coyba.

However, before receiving Balboa's letter, the King had already sent out a large fleet with fifteen hundred men under the command of Don Pedro Arias de Avila, who had served with great distinction against the Moors in Spain and in North Africa. The King had charged Don Pedro to inquire into Balboa's administration. While this was happening Balboa made several trips across the isthmus, visited the Pearl Islands, and would have sailed down to Peru but for adverse weather and lack of adequate shipping. As soon as Don Pedro arrived, he had Balboa arrested pending his investigation of Enciso's charges. But Balboa was so popular with his men, and had such a record to show, that he was soon released.

The truce did not last for long. Don Pedro was conspicuous for cruelty, and his policy of torture and pillage resulted in continuous warfare between the Spaniards and the Indians. Before his coming Balboa had been on the friendliest terms with the natives, but now when they captured a Spaniard they dismembered him or poured molten gold down his throat, crying, "Eat, Christian, eat your fill of gold!" Seeing that his own affairs were in a bad way, and jealous of Balboa who was preparing to set out for Peru, Don Pedro charged him with treason to the King. After the semblance of a trial, the man who had discovered the Pacific was beheaded in the public square at Acla.

Balboa had developed from a "rashe Royster" into a "politike Captayne," he had made one of the greatest geographical discoveries of all time, and had founded a flourishing colony against great odds. His execution can be added to the long list of crimes that we call "judicial murders."

MICHELANGELO

[1475–1564]

THE greatest genius in the history of art, Michelangelo Buonarroti, was born into an aristocratic Florentine family that considered the vocation of the artist beneath its dignity. The boy's native ability had to struggle against family tradition, and only won in the end because he attracted the favor of the most powerful man in Florence, Lorenzo de' Medici, familiar to us as Lorenzo the Magnificent. Even Michelangelo's father had to admit it was no stain on the escutcheon of the Buonarrotis for his son to be patronized by Lorenzo the Magnificent.

At that point in the Italian Renaissance, Florence already boasted many of the finest masters of painting, sculpture, and architecture—Giotto, Masaccio, Ghiberti, Brunelleschi, Donatello, Fra Angelico, Botticelli. Michelangelo joined their ranks and surpassed them all. He was on his way to the top shortly after Lorenzo the Magnificent found him sculpting a faun in the Medici gardens, and undertook to help him.

Michelangelo performed commissions for Lorenzo and for his son after him. Then, when the Medici fell from power, the painter wandered around Italy, working at Venice, Bologna, Rome. He was solitary and unsociable, always ready to get into a brawl with other artists. In one such fracas he received the broken nose that shows up in his portraits.

The fury of his personality was reflected in his work, which always gives an impression of power and deep emotion. He went to great lengths to make his productions authentic. While in Florence he frequented San Spirito, a religious establishment that ran a hospital for the poor of the city, and was permitted to dissect unclaimed cadavers. He persisted stubbornly, making drawings of the human

organism, bones and muscles, which gave him a profound knowledge
of anatomy, later to be disclosed in the mastery with which he depicted the human body.

Two early sculptures reveal the new power he had brought to
Renaissance art—the emaciated figure of John the Baptist, and the
"Sleeping Cupid" which was so classically perfect that an unscrupulous dealer sold it as a Greek antique. At twenty Michelangelo went
to Rome and chiseled one of his best-loved works, the *Pietà*, depicting the Virgin holding the dead body of her Son after the descent
from the Cross.

Back in Florence, Michelangelo accepted commissions to paint,
but he always insisted that he was primarily a sculptor. His supremacy in the latter art he proved with his heroic figure of "David," which
succeeding centuries have reckoned as one of the greatest of sculptures. The work took two years, and then the statue, weighing ten
tons, was moved from Michelangelo's studio to a public square, where
it was to be set up. The moving job required forty men, working with
special equipment that operated on greased beams. For four days the
forty men dragged the mighty "David" through the streets. Armed
guards were posted over it at night. The Florentines hailed it as one
of the glories of their city. Michelangelo received four hundred
ducats for the "David," and his reputation was made. Commissions
poured in on him.

The most important of these commissions came from Pope Julius II,
who assigned him to decorate the ceiling of the Sistine Chapel.
Michelangelo did not want to paint, but he accepted the task and
plunged into it with his customary fury.

The pictures were done in fresco, by applying paint while the plaster was still wet. There were ten thousand square feet to be covered,
and the ceiling was in the form of a vault, which entailed difficult
problems of draftsmanship. The Pope wanted paintings of the twelve
Apostles, but Michelangelo decided on scenes from the Old Testament, beginning with the creation of man. Julius II let him have his
way, but the two had endless arguments.

The labor was monumental. The artist worked on a tall scaffold,
and lay on his back as he applied plaster and paint to the ceiling.
Near by, decorating rooms in the Vatican, Raphael had competent
assistants whom he had trained. But Michelangelo, always impatient

and inclined to work alone, found his assistants unsatisfactory. He locked them out, and worked with only one boy to mix his paints. At times he slept on a pallet on the top of the platform, and often worked through the night by the light of candles. He stuck to it with unrelenting toil for four years. He painted 343 figures, most of which were from ten to fifteen feet in height, until, in October of 1512, the platform was finally taken down, and people jammed in to see the masterpiece.

Today the world gazes in awe and admiration at the pictures on the ceiling of the Sistine Chapel, so often reproduced. One, "The Creation of Adam," might well be reckoned as the most stupendous presentation of a great idea ever achieved by means of draftsmanship and paint.

The Sistine Chapel might have exhausted a lesser man. But Michelangelo now turned back to his first love, sculpture, and produced many more masterpieces. Probably the grandest is his representation of Moses, something unsurpassed in the entire history of art. When we think of the mighty Lawgiver of the Jews, the image that comes to mind is the huge marble into which Michelangelo put all of his energy and intensity. His leaning was to grandeur and violence, which, properly controlled, were the essence of his genius. He had absolute control of his idea and his chisel when he wrought his "Moses."

During his later years Michelangelo was at work in Rome and Venice, but mainly in Florence whenever the politics of his native city would permit. The Medici were locked in a constant struggle with the opposition. They returned to Florence in triumph, fell again, then returned again. Michelangelo espoused the cause of the opposition, for he had come to regard as tyrants the family of his original patron. But the Medici loved art too much to hold it against him. From a Medici, Pope Clement VII, the artist received a commission to decorate the tomb of the Medici.

This led to new figures in marble that rank beside the "Moses." Michelangelo turned out a "Madonna and Child," and two great portrait statues with attendant figures. One is a vigorous representation of Giuliano de' Medici, symbolizing action. The other is a tremendous brooding figure in a helmet, picturing Lorenzo, not the Magnificent, but a later member of the Medici family. The figures that accompanied these, two for each, are themselves masterpieces, called "Night" and "Day," and "Morning" and "Evening." But Michelangelo never completed the tomb of the Medici, just as he left so many other huge projects unfinished.

Approaching sixty, Michelangelo was summoned to Rome once more. A new Pope, Paul III, wanted the Sistine Chapel finished with a fresco on the rear wall. The space was large, and Michelangelo painted his tremendous "Last Judgment." He created an immense composition of 200 figures, one of which included a portrait of himself, so cunningly incorporated that it was not discovered until centuries later. The "Last Judgment," one of the most familiar of pictures, shows Michelangelo in an extreme display of his knowledge of anatomy and his gift for violence and terror.

The last phase for Michelangelo was achievement as an architect, when he was in his late sixties. The building of St. Peter's, the largest church in the world, was still going on, with a succession of architects. Michelangelo now took command, and his contribution was the famous dome. He designed that monumental cupola familiar to all the world. The work dragged, but the great dome of St. Peter's was finally constructed in accordance with his design, and stands as a tribute to his gifts as an architect.

During the later years of his life, he achieved eminence in still another art, poetry. He wrote sonnets, full of his inner broodings, which have their place in Italian literature. When he died at the age of eighty-nine he left many dreams unaccomplished, many works half-completed. But no man in history ever wrought so many masterpieces infused with such majesty and power.

CAESAR BORGIA

[1476?–1507]

THE name of Borgia stands for villainy. In a peculiar degree it symbolizes the crimes of perfidy and assassination that accompanied the intellectual and artistic brilliance of the Italian Renaissance. The Borgia family gave to the Roman Church two pontiffs. The second, Alexander VI, was the most notorious of Renaissance popes, condemned even by Catholic historians. His son, Caesar Borgia, became the personification of crime and murderous falseness in the game of power.

The Borgias were Spanish by origin. The first to attain eminence was a learned ecclesiastic who became secretary to the King of Aragon and through royal influence rose to the highest rank. He was made a cardinal and elected Pope, succeeding to the throne of St. Peter as Calixtus III. The principal thing to be noted about Calixtus III was the practice of nepotism. He placed the interest of family before all else. Soon after he became Pope he sent for his favorite nephew, who was studying law in Spain, and created him Cardinal and Vice-Chancellor of the Church although he was only twenty-five. The Cardinal used bribery to further his ambition, and was elected Pope Alexander VI in the fateful year of 1492.

Enlightened and cultivated, the new pontiff was a patron of learning, literature, and art, but his life was one of open scandal. Before he became Pope he had three sons and a daughter. As pontiff he continued in his flagrant ways, made the Vatican a scene of disgraceful revelry, then turned to crime itself, especially to the removal of his opponents by poison. Poisoning was, in fact, the atrocity that became associated particularly with the name of Borgia. Much of this infamous reputation was founded in the malevolent gossip of embittered political enemies, but enough of it was true to make Alexander VI the worst of the secular popes of the Renaissance.

Caesar Borgia was sixteen when his father became pontiff. Alexander VI immediately moved to improve the lot of his family, committing simony and nepotism, both violations of the canon law of the Church. Caesar was appointed first Bishop of Valencia and then a cardinal. Strong and self-willed, he began to lead a profligate life at the Vatican.

One of the first things Caesar Cardinal Borgia did was to have his elder brother murdered in order to become next in line to the Pope as head of the family. Alexander VI, stricken by the crime, refused to let it be investigated. Instead, he now placed his secular hopes in the son guilty of fratricide, freeing him from his religious vows and returning him to the status of a layman. Caesar Borgia was ready for his career of glory and crime.

He set out with a gorgeous retinue as papal emissary to Louis XII of France, who was seeking an annulment of his marriage. Caesar Borgia had the necessary decree in his pocket. In return, the French King created the Pope's handsome son Duke of Valentinois.

The mission of Caesar Borgia to France included negotiations in matters of far-reaching import. The time had come when Italy was about to be torn by repeated foreign invasions, French, Spanish, German. Already, in the year of the accession of Alexander VI, Charles VIII of France had swept with an army down into Italy to assert a claim to the crown of the kingdom of Naples. That attempt had been futile, but now the new French King, Louis XII, was meditating similar designs on the dukedom of Milan, and the Pope and Caesar Borgia were scheming to use the French invasion to further their own interests.

Louis XII took Caesar Borgia with him when he marched into Italy. Milan was captured, its duke made a prisoner, Lodovico Il Moro, a famous Renaissance figure. The papal policy developed with an assertion of authority over cities in the province of Romagna, cities that owed some sort of allegiance to the Church but were actually under the rule of local despots.

Alexander VI published a bull depriving the city states in Romagna of their rights on the ground that they had failed to pay their taxes to the Church. This amounted to a declaration of war. Caesar

OLIVER CROMWELL

PETER THE GREAT

Borgia, with papal and French forces, attacked Imola, which surrendered at once, and then besieged Forli, held by Caterina Sforza. One of the formidable women of her time, a warrior princess, she made a brave defense but was finally forced to yield.

Caesar now paused long enough to commit another crime within the bosom of his family, the murder of the husband of Caesar's sister Lucrezia. The two men had quarreled violently and had even come to blows. In consequence the brother-in-law was waylaid and stabbed to death by masked men in the neighborhood of Caesar's palace.

This incident fostered rumors of an incestuous relationship between Caesar and Lucrezia. Although constantly repeated by enemies of the family, the story is probably without foundation. Later on Lucrezia Borgia was married again, this time to Alfonzo of Este, who became Duke of Ferrara. She set up a brilliant court at Ferrara, and brought there Ariosto, Cardinal Bembo, Titian, Aldus Manutius, and many other men of letters. She did not escape the rumors, but ended by winning general esteem.

Caesar Borgia continued his conquest of Romagna, where the Pope had made him duke. Malatesta of Rimini and Sforza of Pesaro fled before him. Faenza held out under Manfredi, who surrendered only on a promise that his life would be spared. His conqueror honored the promise in Borgia fashion by having Manfredi put to death.

Caesar Borgia, seeking to strengthen his position as ruler, gave the captured cities a good administration. He was wise enough to employ Leonardo da Vinci, whose multiple genius accomplished for him everything from inventing weapons to restoring buildings. But he used terror freely, and, now a tyrant at the height of his power, he cowed much of Italy. Some cities opened their gates to him simply out of fear. His success in Romagna helped Machiavelli formulate the political theory of ruthless realism that has been so effective in the modern world.

Caesar Borgia was threatened by a conspiracy, but this he overcame with a display of Machiavellian guile. Some of his principal captains turned traitor. There were concerted uprisings, and Borgia forces were defeated. Caesar invoked the aid of the French, and that was enough to daunt the conspirators, who were willing to betray each other. His false captains sought to go back to his side. He, with a more sinister treachery than theirs, enticed them with promises of forgiveness and friendship, lured them into his house, and had them killed.

There was one foe, however, that he could not conquer by violence or treachery—the plague. This scourge, ravaging Rome, carried off Alexander VI and left his son struggling for his life. By the time Caesar Borgia was back on his feet, his enemies were ready for him. The new Pope, Pius III, was a peaceful man who left the Borgias alone. After him came an implacable enemy, Julius II, a man as ambitious as the Borgias and not inclined to let them stand in his way.

Caesar Borgia, with his power in Romagna now undermined, was arrested by Julius II and turned over to the Spaniards at Naples. They considered him a menace to their position in Italy. Closely guarded, he was sent to Spain where he remained in prison for nearly two years. Then he made his escape and took refuge with his brother-in-law, the King of Navarre. Placed in command of a force attacking a castle, Caesar Borgia died in battle while leading his men to the assault.

There is an incongruous epilogue to the story of the Borgias. After Alexander VI and Caesar Borgia and Lucrezia Borgia, after the immorality, nepotism, ferocity, stabbings, and poisonings—after all this there comes a saint.

The eldest son of the Pope, the one whom Caesar Borgia caused to be murdered, had a grandson named Francis Borgia, who rose to eminence in the service of the Emperor Charles V, became a duke, and then, on the death of his wife, entered the Society of Jesus. At the behest of St. Ignatius Loyola himself, Francis Borgia refused a cardinal's hat and took to itinerant preaching. On the death of Loyola's successor, he was elected general of the Jesuits, whom he ruled with such vigor that he has often been called the second founder of the order. Canonized a hundred years after his death, he closes the great annals of the family on an exalted note—as St. Francis Borgia.

THOMAS MORE

[1478–1535]

Nothing is known of Sir Thomas More's early childhood. He recalled in later life how his nurse sat on the floor with the children, telling them stories, and no doubt he had heard his family talking about the terrible tragedy in the Tower of London when Richard III had his two nephews murdered. Perhaps it was the impression this made that led him to write his vivid history of the reign of that tyrant king. His father sent him to the best school in London, where he proved an apt pupil. His intelligence and pleasant demeanor gained him a place in the household of John Morton, Archbishop of Canterbury, Primate and Lord Chancellor of England, closest adviser of King Henry VII.

Here Thomas acted as page and cupbearer. He continued his studies under the most favorable conditions, and wrote some light humorous verse and comedy sketches in which he acted. His sense of drama and command of language developed rapidly. The house was always full of prelates, dignitaries of state, and men of letters, and Thomas was exposed to the keenest minds and the latest information.

When he was fifteen the Archbishop sent him to Oxford with a special letter to the scholar and humanist John Colet urging that he be taught Greek. At Oxford, as Thomas More said later, "I had no love or even thought of anything beyond my studies." He was enchanted with the new classical lore of the Revival of Learning, and became England's greatest Humanist and the close friend of Erasmus.

After Oxford, More studied law, which eventually led him into the government and high position. He himself always preferred scholarship to the career of lawyer. Erasmus urged him to give up the law and give himself entirely to the humanities and pure learning. This

More could not do, but he did devote much of his spare time to books on literature, history, philosophy, and theology. And he began to write serious literature.

His *Adages* were published and well received. He became known as an eloquent speaker, and made frequent addresses on learned subjects. When he was twenty-five he lectured on St. Augustine's *City of God* in one of London's largest churches. He entered Parliament, where he acted independently enough to oppose financial demands made by Henry VII.

Despite his success as a barrister and scholar, Thomas More felt himself drawn to a life of religious contemplation. Although he took no vows, he voluntarily followed the Franciscan way of life, fasting, keeping vigil, repeating prayers, and wearing a hair shirt. He continued to wear the hair shirt for the rest of his life. He felt tempted to join a religious order, but was too much a man of the world. He married twice and had a large family.

More tutored his children in Latin, divinity, astronomy, natural history, and music. When absent he kept up an active correspondence with them, asking questions and criticizing their letters to him. The family picture is one of the most attractive. Outsiders described his second wife as blunt and sharp-spoken, but More eulogized her as a good mother to the children.

In 1509, Henry VII, with whom More had been in disfavor, died and was succeeded by Henry VIII, who was only eighteen. He was a prince of scholarly cultivation. A man of the Renaissance, he fancied learning and the arts, and sought to surround himself with foremost figures in the new revival of the ancient classics. Of these Thomas More was one of the best known in England, and a top-ranking practitioner of the law in addition.

The King determined to make the scholar one of the inner court circle. More resisted as long as he could, but Wolsey, Cardinal and Lord Chancellor, persuaded him to give way. More received an appointment to the Privy Council. He mounted the bench as a judge of the Court of Requests, the poor man's court. He was knighted, becoming Sir Thomas More, and offices and honors were heaped on him.

His relations with the King grew so close that they could be seen walking arm in arm through More's garden, to which the King came frequently. But Thomas More must have had forebodings that royal tyranny was about to raise its ugly head in England. He disapproved of the highhanded ways that Henry VIII soon displayed. The situation passed from difficult to intolerable.

It was during this time that More produced his masterpiece, in which he gave free rein to his idealism, humanism, and love of his fellow-men. *Utopia* purports to be a conversation between More, his Flemish friend Peter Giles, and a Portuguese sailor, Rafael Hythlodaye, who had sailed with Amerigo Vespucci, after whom America was named. Written in Latin, *Utopia* was a skillful blending of fact and fancy. Its atmosphere of reality was enhanced by obvious references to the England and the Europe in which More lived.

Utopia was free of all crime, because it was free of greed and vanity. No jewels or adornments were worn and private possessions were minimal. There was communal ownership of land, meals were taken in common, and there were no class distinctions. Religious freedom prevailed, and war was unknown. *Utopia* was centuries ahead of its time, and contained much food for thought on social subjects—unemployment, education, equality of women, the trend toward urban concentration of population, marriage, divorce, suicide, slavery, crime, reformation of criminals, public health, sanitation, all the way down to the incubation of chickens. The book's penetration and wit made it a great success, and it ran through four large editions in two years, and was translated into English, French, German, Italian, Flemish. It remains a classic and a byword for the unattainable ideal.

The road to doom for Sir Thomas More began when Henry VIII resolved to divorce his Queen, Catherine of Aragon, and marry young Anne Boleyn. The Pope refused the divorce, and this caused the downfall of Cardinal Wolsey. Sir Thomas More was named to take Wolsey's place as Chancellor, the first layman ever to occupy that post. More accepted only on condition that he not be asked to do anything about the divorce.

As Lord Chancellor, he set an example of honesty and diligence. He sought to reform the monastic orders, upheld the Church of Rome and sought to curb heresy. Then, as Henry VIII persisted in divorcing the Queen and marrying Anne Boleyn, Sir Thomas More resigned as Chancellor. The King obtained from Parliament the Act of Supremacy, making him head of the Church of England. Sir Thomas More openly opposed this, and refused to take the oath acknowledging the supremacy of the sovereign in matters of religion.

The King had him arrested and thrown into the Tower of London. He was treated well, and received visits from his family. His friends urged him to yield, and the King gave him a final opportunity to take the oath renouncing the authority of the Roman Church. Sir Thomas More steadfastly refused. He was tried and found guilty of high treason and sentenced to be hanged. Henry VIII commuted this sentence to the more honorable death by decapitation, and Sir Thomas More was beheaded.

His last words were, "I die in and for the faith of the Catholic Church; the King's loyal servant, but God's first." In history he stands as the greatest Humanist of sixteenth-century England. In political theory he remains the creator of *Utopia*. In the Roman Catholic Church he is a saint, canonized in 1935.

MAGELLAN

[1480?–1521]

IN THE year 1504 an armada set sail from Portugal and steered down the coast of Africa, bound for the fabled lands of the East. Columbus had discovered America. Vasco da Gama, sailing around the Cape of Good Hope, had reached India, and had begun the Portuguese Empire in the Indies. Now the King at Lisbon was sending a viceroy, Francisco de Almeida, to govern that empire and expand it. One of the members of the expedition, a mere apprentice or cadet, was the future circumnavigator Ferdinand Magellan. Beginning his career, he was following the lure that had set the Great Discoveries in motion, the lure of the Spice Islands.

Viceroy Almeida was an energetic empire builder, as was to be his greater successor Albuquerque, soon to take his place. Enforcing commercial interests and seizing coastal possessions, the Portuguese struck in India and Malaya. Cadet Magellan took part in these operations and became an able soldier. He landed at several points in India, was wounded twice, and won the rank of captain. After distinguishing himself in the capture of Malacca in Malaya, he was sent on an expedition to explore the Spice Islands.

These were the present-day Moluccas, between the Celebes and New Guinea, the tropical land from which came the vast abundance of spices that Europe craved. Magellan and his companions, in a squadron of ships, coasted along northern Java, skirted Celebes, and sailed to the Banda group. This section of the Moluccas was the heart of the Spice Islands. The Portuguese explorers found such a wealth of spices that they went no further. They took aboard cloves and nutmegs, and returned.

Such was Magellan's experience with the Spice Islands. Shortly afterward he returned to Portugal, having spent eight years in the

East. He was now a thoroughly experienced sailor and soldier, ready for a top command of his own, anxious to get back to the job of exploration. Promoted in rank, he next led an expedition against the Moslems in Morocco. There he received a wound that left him with a limp for the rest of his life. He was invalided out of the army, his soldiering career over when he was thirty-four.

With nothing much to do, he reflected on his experiences in the Indies, his voyage of exploration to the Spice Islands. He studied accounts of other explorers, Portuguese and Spaniards, who were discovering new wonders every day. Columbus, seeking the Indies by sailing west, had found a New World. But could not the Orient really be reached by sailing that way? Magellan became convinced that there must be a southern passage for sailing west to the Spice Islands, a passage through or around South America. This he determined to find, no matter how far south he had to sail.

He approached the King of Portugal, only to be rebuffed. Next he turned to Spain—which had financed Columbus. Friends brought Magellan to the notice of the Emperor Charles V and his minister Fonseca. It was to Fonseca's discredit that he had consistently opposed Columbus, but now he just as consistently supported Magellan. Spain and Portugal were rivals. Portugal had reached the Spice Islands by sailing east, and it would be in the interest of Spain to do the same by a westward route.

The minister and the Emperor saw the advantages, and an agreement was signed whereby Magellan was named Captain General and was granted a share of the profits that might accrue from the voyage. Five ships were provided for the trip around the world.

At dawn on September 20, 1519, Magellan sailed from the port of San Lucar, and steered for the Canary Islands. From there he and his men sailed south but were becalmed off the west coast of Africa. Then they ran into terrible storms. Food and water began to be scarce and had to be rationed. Murmuring broke out among the crew, but the Captain General put a stop to it by clapping one of his disaffected officers into irons. The flotilla turned west and crossed the Atlantic.

The coast of Brazil was reached just before supplies gave out. The Spaniards filled their water tanks. They obtained fresh fruits and vegetables from the Indians. Thus replenished, they coasted southward and came to the mouth of the Rio de la Plata, which Magellan was convinced was the strait he was looking for. He sailed up the great waterway for three weeks before he found it was only a river.

The strait, he surmised, must be farther south. He sailed down the coast of Patagonia, where the weather turned so bad that the ships were forced to anchor in the harbor of what is now Port St. Julian. It was Easter Eve, and the cold season of the Southern Hemisphere was coming on. Magellan announced his intention of spending the winter there to overhaul the ships, an announcement that provoked a mutiny among his men, who doubted that any strait into the Pacific existed. Magellan suppressed the rebellion by hanging fourteen mutineers.

In August the ships set sail again. Again they were beset by storms, blown out to sea, and struggled back to the coast. About the middle of October they rounded a headland and found themselves in a large bay, that narrowed as it went inland. Some thought it was just another river but Magellan never doubted that he had found his strait at last.

The ships entered, and for thirty-eight days sailed inland through winding passages. The water remained deep and salt. There could no longer be any question. They were in the tortuous passage between Patagonia and Tierra del Fuego, now known as the Strait of Magellan.

But food was running short, and the captains held a council to consider the continuation of the voyage. Magellan was his usual uncompromising self. He was going on to the Spice Islands. He ordered the captains to conceal the lack of supplies from the crews, and sent them back to their ships. During the night one deserted and returned to Spain.

The remaining ships rounded Cape Deseado, the western outlet of the strait, and entered the great South Sea, which Balboa had sighted from the Isthmus of Panama seven years before. The great ocean was so mild and tranquil, in contrast to the tempestuous Atlantic, that Magellan named it the Pacific. The natives of the coast proved friendly, and helped the Spaniards bring supplies aboard.

A northwesterly course was set, and for ninety-eight days they sailed the vast expanse of the Pacific, discovering only two islands, sterile and uninhabited. The food gave out. They chewed pieces of leather to allay their hunger, when they had eaten the last rat on board. Nineteen men died of scurvy and the rest were so weak they could not have survived much longer. The last drop of water was distributed the night before they reached the Ladrones.

The islands were so named by Magellan because the natives who came on board, although friendly, tried to steal everything they could. However, fresh water and food were obtained. Three days later the ships reached the Philippines.

Magellan's early journeying in the East had never taken him to the Philippines. But he had been to the Moluccas, the Spice Islands of Banda. These were some hundreds of miles south of the Philippines, and a little to the east. So now Magellan himself had actually passed the longitude he had attained on his exploring trip to the Spice Islands nine years before. Counting his early travels, he had circumnavigated the globe.

It was clear that he was not far from the Moluccas, and all he had to do was to set sail for them. His goal was near. He could proceed to the Spice Islands, to Banda, where he had seen the treasures of cloves and nutmegs. Then westward, by the route he had sailed before, back to Spain, completing the circumnavigation in a single voyage. Spain, where he could claim the glory and the reward for his exploit. Spain, where his wife awaited him with a child born after his departure.

But Magellan had the heart of the explorer and conquistador. He must see more of these islands he had reached. He must bring Christianity to them, and add them to the Empire of Spain. So his ships struck out among the islands. They came to Cebu, a large island in the middle Philippines. There Magellan became involved in a local war. Deciding to win friends on one side, and at the same time show his power, he went ashore with only sixty men to face a horde of natives.

The disproportion of numbers was too great. In the fight more than half of the little band of Europeans fell. The remainder retreated to their boats. Behind they left their Captain General, who had been struck down during the melee. What became of his body no one could tell.

Thus perished Magellan, just as he had come to the success of his stupendous adventure. Having brought his dream to reality, having discovered the strait between the Atlantic and the Pacific, and then sailed west to the Orient, he was killed in a petty skirmish. The leader of the first expedition to sail around the world did not make it himself.

The remainder of the story is the voyage home. One ship, the "Victoria," was left. The others had either deserted, been abandoned, or beached for repairs. The "Victoria" headed west, rounded the Cape of Good Hope, and crossed the Equator. Sailing north, she touched the Cape Verde Islands, and then continued on to Spain—the first ship in history ever to circumnavigate the earth. It was Magellan's hour of triumph, although he was not there.

MARTIN LUTHER

[1483-1546]

IN THE breakup of the Middle Ages there were two phases, the Renaissance and the Reformation. They were interrelated, but distinct. The Renaissance, originating in Italy, revived classical models and produced an outburst of humanized art and competing nationalisms as against the medieval past of mysticism, disciplined theology, and one universal Christendom. The Reformation, beginning in northern Europe, was a religious revival against church abuses, against the elaborate ecclesiasticism of the Middle Ages. But the Reformation also opposed the classical spirit of the Renaissance, which infiltrated the Church and was cultivated by the Papacy. The Renaissance is symbolized by Pope Leo X, the Reformation by his great adversary, Martin Luther.

Luther was a German living far from the artistic brilliance and polished vices of Rome. During his student years there was no hint of his coming breach with the Church. The education he got was intensely religious, which accorded with his mood. He was taught logic, rhetoric, scholastic philosophy, theology. His peasant origins made him susceptible to legends and superstitions, and he lived in a state of religious fantasy. But he liked to sing and learned to play instruments. There was an abundance of broad jollity in him.

Young Luther was a brilliant university student, but haunted by religious anxieties, and especially devoted to the saints. His first spiritual crisis came during a journey in a thunderstorm, when a stroke of lightning knocked him from his horse. In fear he called on St. Ann, vowing that if his life was spared he would become a monk. He kept his vow and entered the Order of St. Augustine.

Luther was not one to do things by halves. Preparing for his vows as monk and priest, he practiced harsh austerities to overcome the lusts of the flesh. For the sake of humility he went begging through the streets with a pack on his back. He fasted until he was too weak to stand, and fell unconscious. Later in life he referred to his monastic preparation as his martyrdom.

He plunged into theological studies, the Bible, St. Augustine, St. Bernard. His books with notes on the margin still exist. He struggled with the problems of predestination and free will. Fears beset him, fears for his own salvation. But his abilities attracted the notice and friendship of his superiors. He was transferred to Wittenberg, where he became a professor of theology and scholastic philosophy. There, too, his spiritual turmoil continued, his agitated preoccupation with salvation. He was tormented by a consciousness of sin.

When he was twenty-seven, Luther accompanied a mission sent by the monastic authorities to Rome. At the seat of the Church he beheld the luxury of great ecclesiastics, the laxity of the papal court. Rome presented the glories of art and the moral evils characteristic of the Italian Renaissance, popes dedicated more to classical culture than to zeal for religion, prelates given over to lives of elegance and pleasure. In the splendor of Renaissance Rome the austere, soul-tortured monk from Germany saw iniquity and corruption. This visit was to be reflected in his future tirades against the abuses and iniquities in the Church.

One story tells how he climbed the Scala Santa, the Sacred Stairs. Popes had granted indulgence from sin for the ritual of ascending the Sacred Stairs. As Luther climbed, the Biblical text flooded into his mind: "The just shall live by faith." He turned and walked down. This is said to have signalized Luther's revolt against the Church of Rome.

Returning to Wittenberg, he plunged into the study of St. Paul, and found his solution of the problem of salvation, the doctrine that overcame guilt and sin. This was justification by faith instead of works. By works was meant good deeds, right conduct, religious observances. Luther now believed that salvation could not be won by any of these, but only through faith in the redemption of Christ.

During this transformation he was elected subprior of the Wittenberg monastery, received the degree of Doctor of Theology, and was admitted to the Senate of the University. This meant that his lectures would no longer have to be submitted for approval and that he could teach as he pleased. He was appointed vicar of monasteries in Meissen and Thuringia, which necessitated an inspection of eleven monasteries at least once a year.

He preached in his monastery and in the Wittenberg parish church, his sermons couched in language the common man could understand, in German as well as in Latin. He denounced ecclesiastical corruption. He preached the doctrine of salvation by faith, condemned belief in the spiritual powers of relics, and denounced the misuse of indulgences.

At this time it happened that a sale of indulgences was being preached in Germany. The practice was old. It had begun as a remission of penance granted by the Pope. Pious practices were counted as earning the forgiveness of sin, and these included the contribution of money. Strictly the indulgence had to be earned also by prayer and repentance, but in fact many regarded it as a spiritual benefit that could be bought and sold.

The circumstances of the indulgence were these. The Archbishop of Magdeburg had paid to the Pope various sums for high ecclesiastical offices. The sum of ten thousand ducats was advanced by the German banking house of Fugger. To enable the Archbishop to repay the bankers, the Pope authorized him to sell indulgences, all sales in excess of the ten thousand ducats to go toward the rebuilding of St. Peter's in Rome. The indulgence was preached by Tetzel, prior of the Dominicans at Leipzig.

Luther did not know this background of facts, but the arrival of Tetzel aroused him to drastic action. On October 31, 1517, he nailed to the church door at Wittenberg his Ninety-five Theses questioning the value of these indulgences and condemning their sale. The original theses were in Luther's own handwriting. Wittenberg printers got out both Latin texts and German translations, and these circulated all over Germany. They gained wide popular approval, and there was a flare of discontent against the Church.

Luther was astonished by the uproar that ensued, but in fact the Reformation was on. He by no means thought to disrupt and divide the ancient Church. But the time was ripe for religious revolt, and he was the leader.

Luther's Ninety-five Theses got him into angry controversy with Tetzel, who was preaching the indulgence. Luther wrote to the Archbishop asking him to stop the sale. His letter was immediately forwarded to the Pope with a complaint. The Pope, Leo X, dismissed the commotion in Germany as a monks' quarrel. He merely sent Luther's letter to the general of the Augustinian order, telling him to settle matters.

The controversy came before the Augustinian chapter at Heidelberg. Before appearing, Luther resigned as vicar so as not to involve the order. He spoke at length in defense of his theses, after which he returned to Wittenberg.

Later he went to Augsburg to be examined by Cardinal Cajetan, general of the Dominican order. They had three meetings. The result —an impasse. Luther was still a Catholic. But his position in the Church became impossible when he went to Leipzig for a public debate with Johann Eck, professor of theology at the University of Ingolstadt.

In the debate Eck skillfully pressed Luther into a position of defending previous heresies, and drove him to the admission that not only popes but the councils of the Church could err. Luther left Leipzig branded as a heretic.

He now published a series of memorable writings, in which he went far beyond his original position in opposition to the sale of indulgences. He called upon the German people to liberate themselves from the authority of the Pope. He denied the superior position of the clergy over the laity. He rejected any sacrament not based on the evidence of the New Testament.

Leo X issued a bill of condemnation, which decreed the excommunication of Luther unless he recanted in sixty days. Luther publicly burned the papal bull in Wittenberg together with other church documents. He was now formally excommunicated, and the Pope called upon the Emperor Charles V to proceed against him as a heretic. But Luther had powerful friends and supporters, and the Elector of Saxony persuaded the Emperor to less drastic measures.

Charles V summoned the Diet of Worms, an assemblage of the notables of the Empire, and ordered Luther to appear before it, giving him a safe conduct. As he was under the ban of excommunication, friends tried to dissuade him from attending, but Luther would not listen. "I shall go to Worms," he said, "though there were as many devils there as there are tiles on the roofs." He appeared before the diet on April 17 and 18, 1521.

Charles V, who was only twenty, presided in person over an enormous crowd of princes and prelates, learned men and great landowners. The representative of the Pope demanded that, before being heard, Luther should recant the position set forth in his books. He refused. When called upon by the Emperor to disavow his previous utterances, he replied, "I neither can nor will recant anything since it is neither right nor safe to act against conscience." He ended with the words, "Here I take my stand. I can do naught else. So help me God, Amen."

According to the Emperor's safe conduct, Luther was allowed to depart, but stood in grave danger. His friend the Elector of Saxony gave him a refuge in Wartburg Castle, where Luther grew a beard and posed as a knight. The concealment was prudent, because Charles V now condemned him, placing him under the ban of the Empire.

Luther remained in Wartburg Castle for eleven months, during which time he issued a series of polemical writings that set forth a charter of the Lutheran Reformation. He was joined there by Melanchthon, one of the foremost of German Humanists, whom Luther had met at Wittenberg. Melanchthon, classical scholar, aided Luther in the translation of the New Testament from Greek into German.

The Reformation made rapid progress in Germany. Emerging from Wartburg, Luther asserted his leadership. He declaimed against the sacrament of penance, the absolution of sins, the celibacy of the clergy. From far and wide came tidings of revolt against the old religion. Luther applauded.

But the reform agitation brought about a wild Peasants' Revolt, a ferocious rebellion against the oppression of the rural population by the nobles. Luther had defended the rights of the common people, but now he drew back. He issued manifestoes explaining that liberty applied to religion, not politics, and stated a characteristic doctrine that people owed obedience to princes, despite injustice. His appeals to the peasants to yield had little success, and he put forth a demand for ferocious war against what he called "Thievish, Murderous Hordes of Peasants." They were crushed and slaughtered by the landowners.

Monks and nuns, converted to the Reformation, were leaving monasteries and convents, and were marrying. In 1523 the citizens of Torgau brought to Luther nine nuns who had escaped from a convent. He aided them. Among these nuns was Catherine von Bora, who had been smuggled out in an empty beer barrel. He found a place for her as a maid in the household of a wealthy burgher of Reichenbach, and married her "to please his father, tease the Pope and spite the Devil."

Martin Luther's life now settled itself into a pattern that remained unchanged until his death. He carried on an unrelenting fight against the Papacy and the Church of Rome. He built the Protestant Evangelical Church and prepared a new divine service. He had a conference with Zwingli and other Swiss Reformed divines. They were unable to agree on doctrinal points and from then on the Reformation movements in Germany and Switzerland continued on separate lines.

Luther did not attend the Diet of Augsburg, which brought forth the Augsburg Confession, thereafter the official statement of Lutheranism. The Reformation was now taking on political aspects, a struggle for power between the Emperor and the Protestant princes. This left Luther in the background.

He continued to write, and completed his greatest work, the translation of the Bible into German. Theological and polemical pamphlets came from his pen in a steady stream, along with hundreds of letters. He wrote hymns for use in Lutheran churches. The most popular hymn in Germany today, one sung everywhere in the world, is Luther's "A Mighty Fortress Is Our God."

To the day of his death the earth-shaking Reformer never called himself a Protestant. That term, so familiar now, had its origin when some other religious rebels presented to the Holy Roman Emperor protests against measures to which they objected. It was only gradually that the word Protestant came into general use.

ST. IGNATIUS OF LOYOLA

[1491?–1556]

IGNATIUS LOYOLA was born at the castle of Loyola, near Guipuzcoa, probably in 1491, or some twenty years after the marriage of Ferdinand and Isabella had unified Spain. Of his youth we know only that he was a page at the Spanish court and later an officer in the army of the Duke of Najera. The life he led was no different from that of other young officers of his station in society. In his later deeply religious years he looked upon those young years as incredibly sinful, but it is probable that his sins were no more than the usual roistering and gallantry of the time.

His personal bravery was proverbial. Wars between Spain and France were on, and at seventeen he distinguished himself under the Duke of Alba in the conquest of southern Navarre. By the time he was thirty he held a command in the garrison of Pampeluna, capital of Navarre, when it was besieged by the French. In the bombardment a cannon ball broke Loyola's right leg. The town surrendered. The French treated their captives well. A surgeon set the young officer's broken leg, and they sent him back to his castle of Loyola. There the Spanish doctors found that the bone had not been properly set, and broke it again in an effort to lengthen the injured limb. This was a very painful operation, and for a long time the young officer was confined to his bed and suffered agony.

During his convalescence he did a great deal of reading. Among the books brought to him were the *Life of Christ* by Ludolf of Saxony and *Amadis of Gaul*, a tale of a famous hero of chivalry much admired in Spain (and satirized by Cervantes in *Don Quixote*). Thus Loyola's feverish visions fluctuated between earthly and spiritual glories. Finally, in February 1522, after much soul searching he decided to abandon the military for a monastic life, and to make a pilgrimage to Jerusalem.

When he announced this decision to his family, his eldest brother tried hard to dissuade him. He pleaded that it was nonsense at his age to renounce the world, and that Spain was full of promise for so distinguished a young soldier. But Ignatius had his way and after taking leave of his family, left the castle of Loyola and went to the famous Benedictine monastery of Montserrat about thirty miles north of Barcelona. Here in the ancient church built in 880 A.D. he made his vows, stripped off his gay cavalier clothes, and took the pilgrim's dress of sackcloth, staff, and gourd. He hung up his sword and dagger by the altar of the Mother of God, dedicated himself to a life of poverty, and gave his mule and all he had left to the monastery.

From Montserrat, Loyola went to Manresa, a shrine a few miles to the north, where he devoted himself to religious exercises and penances, spending many hours of the day on his knees at prayer, scourging himself, taking meat and wine only on Sundays. Gradually he forged an iron mastery of his thoughts and volitions. He stayed a year at Manresa, where he made the first draft of his *Spiritual Exercises.* He began to gather a few disciples.

This period in his life over, Loyola set out on his pilgrimage to Jerusalem, and sailed from Barcelona to Italy. He went to Rome and then on to Venice. The Doge granted him passage on a government ship bound for Cyprus. He fell desperately ill, but when he sailed he felt much better after a spell of seasickness. In this he saw the hand of God.

In Jerusalem, Loyola incurred the disapproval of the Franciscan monks because the excessive zeal he displayed threatened to draw the anger of the Turks, whose regulations he violated. On a visit to the Mount of Olives he had a vision of the Saviour. Another time he saw the Virgin and Child, after which he never again felt the lure of carnal temptation. He spent much time in prayer and in gazing at the stars: "How contemptible the world seems when I look up to the sky."

He now realized that he must study, and the next period of his life was one of books and scholarships at seats of learning: Barcelona, Alcala, Salamanca. Finally he went to study at the University of

Paris in 1528. He remained there for seven years, during which time the Jesuit Order had its genesis.

The cardinal factor was the formation of a group. Loyola banded together with a few fellow-students, most of them Spaniards, who were impressed by his ideas of mystic piety as expressed in the *Spiritual Exercises*. One was Laynez, who was to succeed him as head of the Society of Jesus. Another was to become the great missionary to the Orient, Francis Xavier, "Apostle of the Indies."

Their first plan was to go on a mission to the Holy Land, to aid the sick and convert the infidel, just as Loyola's own first impulse had been a pilgrimage to Jerusalem. If they could not get to Palestine, they would go to Rome and offer their services to the Pope. They proceeded to Italy and found that war with the Turks made their journey to Palestine impossible, whereupon they went to Rome and placed themselves at the disposal of Pope Paul III.

In Rome, Loyola expanded the idea of his band of companions into a program for a new religious order. He drew up a plan for the structure of the society, the rules of conduct. This constitution, together with the *Spiritual Exercises*, set forth the corporate existence and the way of life of the Jesuits. Loyola and his companions had encountered hostility, and papal sanction was gained only with difficulty. But they finally were given approbation by a papal bull on September 27, 1540. The following year Loyola was elected first general of the Jesuits, which office he retained until his death in 1556.

His essential idea was expressed in the name he chose for the order. He called it the Company of Jesus. "Company" was a military term, reflecting the founder's own training as a soldier. Latinized from the Spanish, "Company" became Society, but the military connotation tells the story. Loyola saw his followers as soldiers of the Church, and military notions of discipline were the key to the Jesuit spirit. Obedience, as of a soldier to the command of an officer, was sublimated into an abnegation of will. The supreme renunciation of self and pride was accomplished by the discipline of the will in obedience to the leader of the society.

The exterior history of the society was conditioned by two great facts. The original goal of Loyola and his companions was the Holy Land and the conversion of the Moslems, but that never came to pass. The two dominant facts of the era, the sixteenth century, were the great explorations and the Protestant Reformation, and these set the course of the Jesuits.

Under the administration of their founder, they sent famous missions along the two great trails opened on the oceans, around Africa to India and the Far East, across the Atlantic to the New World. Loyola's companion, Francis Xavier, won sainthood and historic fame for the missionary work he inaugurated in China and Japan, and a host of Jesuits labored with brilliant success and sometimes martyrdom in the Christianization of the Indians of North and South America.

In Europe, Ignatius Loyola was a contemporary of Martin Luther, and his company of soldiers of the Church was immediately engaged in the great religious strife. The Reformation seemed at first to sweep all before it, but soon there was a reaction, the Counter Reformation, which regained much of the lost ground in countries like Austria, southern Germany, Hungary, Bohemia, Poland. In this the Jesuits were predominant. It is hardly too much to say that they *were* the Counter Reformation.

Their achievement was twofold. They took the lead in the correction of church abuses that had incited the Protestant Reformation, the transformation of the secular-minded Papacy of the Renaissance, the elimination of corruption and abuses, the reforms effected by the Council of Trent. They were foremost in the task of bringing Protestant areas back to Rome. Their most effective weapon was their schools, which became famous all over Europe, and played a great part in the growth of the art of teaching.

After the formation of the order, Ignatius Loyola spent the rest of his life directing it. Stationed in Rome, he saw the Society of Jesus well on its career of overseas missions and leadership in the Counter Reformation. In 1556, Loyola fell ill and retired to a small villa in the Aventine. As his end neared he returned to his house in Rome, and there, on July 30, 1556, this great saint passed away. But his work did not pass away. The Jesuits, who are so influential in the modern world, who labor in Europe and America and at the ends of the earth, look back with reverence to the Spanish soldier who mapped out the mode of life they follow.

Two portraits of Loyola exist, one by Rubens, the other by Titian. They bear out the descriptions we have of him as a dashing young officer. He was of a little less than medium height, slightly built, with masses of dark hair and large dark eyes and a rather pale complexion. The face that looks out from Rubens' portrait, while benevolent, is ascetic and austere, the mouth firm, the lips thin, but the large eyes tell of the visions of a seer. All his life he walked with a barely perceptible limp from the injury he incurred in the siege of Pampeluna, the injury that sent the young soldier on his religious career.

JACQUES CARTIER

[*1491–1557*]

How Canada got its name is one of the curiosities of history. In 1536 three ships sailed up the St. Lawrence River and approached the site of modern Quebec. The commander of the expedition, Jacques Cartier, asked his Indian guides the name of the place. They told him that he was now in Canada. Actually the word "canada," in the Huron-Iroquois language, meant merely "village." Cartier took it to mean the whole territory. The name stuck, and the Indian word for "village" came to signify all of what is now the great nation to our north.

Jacques Cartier lived in the age of the great discoveries. The year after his birth, Columbus discovered America, and the Spaniards were on their golden career of exploration and conquest in the New World. In the East, the Portuguese were building an empire in the Indies. In the West, they discovered Brazil.

Cartier, a sea captain of St. Malo, brought France into the field of exploration. He sailed to Iceland and Greenland. Then he branched out and made trading voyages to Brazil, sharing in the mercantile spoils of glittering colonial empires that were being established in the New World. Finally he decided to look for the Northwest Passage.

If a way could be found to navigate around the north of the New World, just as Magellan had sailed around the south of the Americas, a trade route to the Orient and the Indies might be established out of the reach of the power of Spain and Portugal. The quest for the Northwest Passage was to attract seafaring men for generations, a sort of oceanic Eldorado, and one of its first proponents was Jacques Cartier. He never found that will-o'-the-wisp, but he did find Canada for France.

The coast of Canada had been reached thirty-eight years before by John Cabot, the Genoese navigator sailing for the King of England in the wake of the discoveries of Columbus. But that had been followed by little or nothing in the way of exploration. For many years, in fact, the chief result of voyages to the northern part of North America was an exploitation of the Newfoundland fishing banks. In this seafarers from St. Malo played a large part, as they still do. Cartier of St. Malo would go further—beyond the fishing banks and, if it existed, into the Northwest Passage.

It was April 20, 1534, when Jacques Cartier sailed from St. Malo with two sixty-ton vessels and crews made up of hardy mariners and adventurers out for excitement and plunder. In middle age he was on his way to immortality.

He sailed to the west for twenty days, and came to the northern tip of Newfoundland. The reader might well consult a map and follow the general course of the voyages of Jacques Cartier to gain an interesting, if not amusing, idea of the gropings of the first navigator in a region now so familiar. Like a blind man he poked into the maze of waters around Newfoundland, Nova Scotia, New Brunswick, and the Gulf and River of St. Lawrence, always hoping that the next inlet would turn out to be the Northwest Passage.

He proceeded around the northern tip of Newfoundland, and then through the straits of Belle Isle, which separates the large island from the mainland. He coasted down the western shore of Newfoundland, until a storm drove him out into the Gulf of St. Lawrence.

Cartier sailed south to Prince Edward Island. This he considered to be a part of the mainland, and turned northwest to find the passage. Coasting along what is now New Brunswick, he came to Chaleur Bay, and thought that this great inlet reaching to the west might be the goal of dreams, leading to the Pacific Ocean and Asia. Disappointed to find it was only a bay, he continued along the coast and put in to what is now Gaspé Harbor.

There he went ashore, planted a cross, and claimed the land for the King of France. He made friends with a tribe of Indians from whom he hoped to get information about the interior of the continent. He persuaded the chief to send his two sons to accompany the expedition, promising to bring them back the following year. Cartier sailed north again, and the two Indians told him of a mighty river and tremendous lakes that lay to the west. There were indications of great new lands and waters, hints of wonders and wealth.

But winter was now closing in, and Cartier decided to return home. He set sail for France, following the course by which he had come, through Belle Isle Strait and around the north of Newfoundland.

Back in France, Cartier made a report to King Francis I, who was impressed by the account of a strange continent, prospects of the Northwest Passage, and indications of wealth to be gained. The two Indians were eloquent evidence, and their own thoughts must have been interesting as they compared sixteenth-century Paris with their native aboriginal village on the shore of the wilderness. The King ordered a larger expedition to be prepared.

The sailing this time was impressive, a sign of the importance attached to the venture. There was a stately religious ceremony in the cathedral of St. Malo, where Cartier and his captains and crews were blessed by the archbishop. Cartier sailed just two years after his first voyage. Following his previous course, he crossed the Atlantic, rounded Newfoundland through the Strait of Belle Isle, and proceeded south to the large island of Anticosti. There he bestowed a name on the great inland waters that were to be the scope of his explorations. He called them after St. Lawrence, which name in time came to apply not only to the gulf, but also to the river.

His two Indians had told him about the St. Lawrence River, and now Cartier sailed up the broad waters which were thereafter to be the French gateway to the heart of the continent. He anchored at the mouth of the Saguenay, which flows into the St. Lawrence. His Indian guides informed him that beyond its banks lay a realm of wealth and gems. Actually, of course, he faced an unbroken wilderness as bare of golden cities and bejeweled potentates as any place could be. Cartier had fallen in with that curious phenomenon often found elsewhere, Indians telling fables of treasure that dazzled the white man.

Cartier now entertained two illusions. In addition to his dream of the Northwest Passage, he had a vision of a northern Mexico or Peru with the riches of Montezuma or the Incas lying just over the horizon of the wilderness. Sailing on, the three ships came in sight of the island of Orleans, near the present-day metropolis of Quebec, and there occurred the misinterpretation by which the Indian word for "village" became the name for half a continent—Canada.

In the St. Charles River Cartier left two of his ships at anchor and proceeded up the mainstream in the smallest, a forty-ton sloop. When that vessel went aground, he continued in a long boat until he reached a place which the Huron-Iroquois called Hochelaga. This, because of a prominent hill overlooking the area, Cartier named Le Mont Royal, now Montreal. The hardy navigator would have gone further in the long boat, but was checked by the Lachine Rapids.

He made his way back to the ships waiting for him, and found affairs going badly. It was winter now, the first winter spent by the French in Canada. The weather was bitter cold, with great snows, and scurvy had broken out among the crews. Twenty-five died, the rest were disabled. In this crisis the expedition was aided by the Indians, who brewed a broth from the bark and leaves of a tree and gave it to the sailors as a medicine. The primitive remedy relieved the scurvy.

Cartier was still fascinated by the tales of the splendid realm of Saguenay, and sought what information he could about that mythical kingdom. More to the point, he did some bartering with the Indians for their furs, in this discovering the real source of immediate wealth—not the Northwest Passage, not the fictitious gold of a mythical Eldorado of the north, but the fur trade. He sailed back to France, once more taking Indians with him.

The result of his second voyage was amply satisfactory to King Francis I. The Indians and the stories of the wealth of Saguenay were impressive. Even more so was the reality of the rich furs that Cartier brought back. He was commissioned to make another voyage, this time to open the new land in the name of the King of France. Five ships, together with materials for a settlement, were provided, and Cartier was to be followed by a high-ranking noble, who would assume the command of the new province.

The veteran navigator could not have been pleased by being superseded in authority, but he sailed back to the Gulf and River of St. Lawrence, and made his way upstream to the Lachine Rapids. Still pursuing the dream of gold, he sent a party up the Ottawa River, which he was told was the best way to reach the kingdom of Saguenay and its treasures. He explored as much as he could, and then decided to return home to France.

He had reached Newfoundland when he encountered the Seigneur de Roberval, assigned to take command of the territory. This dignitary arrived in state, accompanied by a number of gentlemen, adventurers, and courtiers. Roberval ordered Cartier to accompany him back up the St. Lawrence, but the captain from St. Malo refused, probably because his men had done their work and could not be expected to start all over again without a rest.

As far as we know, that was the end of Cartier's career. He may have sailed to Canada once more to help get Roberval's expedition out. If so, it was but an epilogue to his work as discoverer and explorer in the New World.

Jacques Cartier won a vast northern realm for France, although long years were to go by before the first actual settlements were made. During that interval the principal Canadian activities of the French were fishing and fur trading. The Northwest Passage was an illusion, Saguenay a mirage, but the cargoes of pelts that Cartier brought back showed the treasure trail that led to the development of French Canada.

HENRY VIII

[*1491–1547*]

HENRY VIII was a Dr. Jekyll and Mr. Hyde of European royalty. Mr. Hyde combined despotism with crime, murdered Sir Thomas More, and left behind him a trail of marriages, divorces, and decapitated wives. Dr. Jekyll was the first King of England to receive a classical education according to the cultural standard of the Renaissance. He was an accomplished scholar, knew Greek, had a complete mastery of Latin and French, was able to converse in Italian, Spanish, and German. An excellent musician, he composed many songs and had a fine resounding baritone voice.

Few men in his kingdom were as handsome as Henry VIII in early manhood. Of commanding presence, he was, to quote the Venetian ambassador, "exceedingly fair and as well proportioned as possible." His fair hair and beard, with a touch of red, shone like gold in the sun. His bright blue eyes were somewhat small, and set well apart. His face was broad and heavy.

The King's whole appearance gave the impression of great strength. As horseman, bowman, and wrestler he was a match for any of his subjects, and was a great bowler. But the chase was Henry's favorite sport. He loved to hunt down the magnificent stags that roamed the royal forests, shooting them on horseback with his bow and arrow.

His father, Henry VII—the most avaricious of monarchs—left him an enormous fortune of more than two million pounds that made him virtually independent of parliamentary grants of money. He was surrounded by wise, prudent, and experienced counselors. Henry's own industry, his acute political mind, his indomitable will power, his subtlety of intellect, his rough-and-ready manner gave stability to his government.

In June of 1509, Henry VIII married Catherine of Aragon, daughter of Ferdinand and Isabella of Spain. Catherine had been married to his elder brother, Arthur, a sickly youth of fifteen who died less than six months later. The King, Henry VII, shocked at the idea of losing the dowry of 200,000 ducats—about $14,000,000—and the advantages of the Spanish alliance, secured the permission of Pope Julius II to marry young Henry to the widowed Catherine.

The day before their coronation in Westminster Abbey, King Henry and Queen Catherine, attended by a throng of nobles and all their court, made a royal progress through London amidst great pageantry and rejoicing. The city was draped with costly hangings, bunting flew everywhere, and along Cheapside and the approaches to Guildhall, maidens with long tresses hanging down their shoulders poured wine free to all who wished to drink the health of the royal couple.

The young King's handsome person, cheerful disposition, jovial manners, his open-handed, hearty, and good-humored way, made him the idol of the people. They called him "Bluff King Hal." Tilts, tournaments, dances, pageants, hunting, wine, women, and song filled his days and occupied his nights.

Henry had able assistants in the work of government. More and more he turned to Thomas Wolsey, a churchman who had served his father, and in Wolsey found a remarkable counselor ready to serve his every whim. Soon Wolsey was the King's Almoner and a member of the Council. Although twenty years older he became the King's close friend and intimate adviser. Henry made Wolsey Archbishop of York and Chancellor of England, and showered lucrative benefices and sinecures upon him. Pope Leo X created the Archbishop a Cardinal, then in 1515 appointed him papal legate. The Cardinal's splendor and magnificence were unbounded. His retinue numbered eight hundred persons, including many nobles and knights. He celebrated High Mass with a pomp equal to that of the Pope, assisted by bishops and mitered abbots and with noblemen serving as altar boys. This gorgeous display appealed to the young King and pleased the people, from whose ranks the great Cardinal had risen.

As Wolsey's star rose, Queen Catherine began to lose the royal favor. Henry wanted a son and heir, but all of their children died in infancy. Whispers of the King's desire to divorce Catherine of

Aragon were heard, but the birth of Princess Mary in 1516 kept alive the hope of a male heir and the rumor ceased.

Then the throne of the Holy Roman Empire, which was elective, fell vacant. Both Francis I, the new King of France, and Henry VIII of England aspired to the dignity of Holy Roman Emperor. But Charles, grandson of the late Emperor and of King Ferdinand too, won enough support to be elected. Thereupon Francis I courted the alliance of Henry VIII, fearing the power of the new Emperor Charles V who ruled Spain, Austria, Naples, and the Netherlands and had golden possessions in the New World.

So Francis I arranged to meet the English King in France to conclude an alliance. But before Henry left England, Charles V paid him a visit. In confidential talks, the Emperor offered to make Cardinal Wolsey pope if he would stop the French alliance. This Wolsey promised to do. Henry VIII crossed over to Calais on the day of the Emperor's departure. He was accompanied by the Queen and the whole court.

The meeting between the kings of England and of France took place on what became known as the Field of the Cloth of Gold. Magnificent temporary buildings and banqueting halls had been erected for the two rulers. Their retinues were housed in tents covered with splendid tapestries and cloth of silver and gold. Tournaments, banquets, and festivities continued for two weeks, and many nobles ruined themselves to outshine the others in splendor of equipment. Wolsey kept his promise to Charles. No Anglo-French alliance came out of the Field of the Cloth of Gold.

Immediately on leaving Francis, the King and Queen, accompanied by Wolsey, went on to Gravelines, near Calais, where they met Charles V again. He renewed his promise to make Wolsey pope, adding to this a substantial present of money. The four-year-old daughter of Henry and Catherine was secretly betrothed to the twenty-year-old Emperor. England's support was pledged to Charles should hostilities break out between him and Francis I.

Less than two years after the Field of the Cloth of Gold, Charles V was at war with Francis I. True to his promise at Gravelines, Henry VIII went to the aid of the Emperor and the Earl of Surrey invaded France and ravaged the country as far as Paris. But Charles did not keep his word to make Wolsey pope. The Cardinal was put off, and at length resolved to wean Henry away from the Emperor's cause and effect a new alliance with France. In 1525, Francis I was defeated at Pavia and taken prisoner. His conqueror, Charles V, became supreme in Europe. In 1527, Charles's army sacked Rome and the Holy Roman Emperor made the Pope a virtual captive.

Meanwhile Martin Luther was beginning the Protestant Reformation in Germany. Henry VIII was much opposed to the Protestant doctrines, and wrote a book in Latin defending the Church against the attacks of Luther. He sent a copy to the Pope, who was so pleased with it that he conferred upon the King and his heirs forever the title of "Defender of the Faith," which is used by the sovereigns of England to this day. But the Reformation was welcomed by many people in England.

By 1526 it seemed fairly certain that Queen Catherine would never produce a male heir. Henry remembered that in marrying his brother's widow he had gone against the canon laws of the Church, although a special papal dispensation had permitted the marriage. He had notions that he was left without a son and heir as punishment for an unlawful marriage. Moreover, he had fallen violently in love with Anne Boleyn, a maid of honor to the Queen.

The King told Wolsey to obtain a divorce. There were moral scruples about this, in addition to which the Pope was held by Charles V, Catherine's nephew. His Holiness feared to offend Charles by granting the divorce, or Henry by refusing it. He finally commissioned Cardinals Wolsey and Campeggio to open a court in London to inquire into the validity of the King's marriage with the widow of his deceased brother. Before the court Queen Catherine threw herself at her husband's feet, begging him to have pity on her. But Henry was determined on the divorce. The trial dragged on; the King was kept in suspense. Then suddenly the Pope ordered the proceedings transferred to Rome. Henry's rage knew no bounds.

It was on Wolsey that the King's wrath fell. The Cardinal was stripped of his offices and honors and went into retirement. His enemies succeeded in having him arrested for high treason. On the way to London to stand trial he was taken ill and died. His last words were, "If I had served my God as diligently as I have done the King, He would not have given me over in my gray hairs."

It was then that Thomas Cranmer suggested that the question be put to the universities of Europe: "Whether it was lawful for a man to marry his brother's widow." This was done and the decision was in the King's favor. Cranmer was made Archbishop of Canterbury.

Henry would wait no longer. He married Anne Boleyn and had her crowned as his Queen. They were already expecting an heir. Catherine of Aragon, cast aside, spent the remaining three years of her life in seclusion at Kimbolton Castle.

When Henry's marriage was reported to the Pope he threatened excommunication if the King did not put Anne away. These threats only made Henry VIII more furious, and he now made the definite break with Rome. The clergy in convocation declared the Church of England independent of papal authority. Parliament passed the Act of Supremacy declaring the King to be "the supreme Head on earth of the Church of England." The suppression of the monasteries began.

Anne Boleyn did not enjoy her majesty for long. Her child was a daughter, Elizabeth, who was later to become the Virgin Queen. Anne's failure to produce a son caused Henry's affections to cool, and her own misconduct made it easy for her enemies to get rid of her, all the more so as the King was already in love with one of her maids of honor. She was confined in the Tower of London, charged with infidelities, tried by a court of twenty-six peers, and found guilty. This beautiful woman of twenty-nine was beheaded in May 1536. The following day Henry married Jane Seymour. She gave birth to a son, who later reigned as Edward VI. She died twelve days later.

Henry VIII was now the Tudor despot. His break with Rome and the pillaging of the monasteries provoked popular revolts, which were savagely crushed. The great scholar and humorist, Sir Thomas More, and the saintly Bishop Fisher refused to recognize the King as head of the Church. They both died under the headsman's axe.

But Henry VIII still opposed the Reformation, and had Protestants burned at the stake. Tyndale was executed for publishing an English translation of the Bible. Henry wanted Catholicism without the Pope.

Though opposed to Luther's doctrines, he took as his next wife a Lutheran from Germany. He selected Anne of Cleves on the basis of a portrait, only to be disappointed and humiliated when he saw a stockily built German Fräulein without a trace of beauty. It was with the greatest difficulty that he could be persuaded to go through with the marriage.

Henry's wrath turned on Thomas Cromwell, his minister, who had negotiated the match. Cromwell was hated by the nobility as an upstart, by the Catholics for his part in the suppression of the monasteries, by the Protestants for the burning of their fellow-believers at the stake. His enemies took advantage of the King's displeasure. Cromwell was seized at the council table, taken to the Tower, and beheaded. Then Parliament declared the obnoxious marriage null and void on the ground that the King had entered into it against his will.

Henry's fifth wife was Catherine Howard, the niece of the Duke of Norfolk, head of the Catholic nobility. But the marriage had not lasted six months when it became known that she had been unchaste. The scandal infuriated the King and aroused his lust for vengeance. The men involved were executed after Catherine had confessed. The Queen herself was beheaded.

Three years later Henry VIII married Catherine Parr, a widow who had buried two husbands. She was a cultured woman, educated far beyond her times, with plenty of good common sense. She secretly favored the reform party and carefully instructed Prince Edward and Princess Elizabeth in her principles.

The last years of Henry's life were marked by a change in his attitude toward the Reformation, undoubtedly due to the influence of Catherine Parr. In 1546 he offered to unite with the Lutheran princes of Germany in a Protestant League. The following year he ordered the arrest and execution of the Catholic leader, the Duke of Norfolk, and of his son, the Earl of Surrey. The son was beheaded but the father escaped, his execution having been fixed for the day that followed, as it turned out, the King's own death.

During his final period Henry VIII was a gross creature, corpulent and unwieldly, with a great festering ulcer on one leg. He had to be carried from one apartment to another in a chair. On the day of his death he was well enough to transact public business with his ministers and give them good advice on the future policy of the government. Toward evening he collapsed and sent for Archbishop Cranmer. Speechless when the prelate reached him, he was able only to make a sign with his hand to answer the question whether he put his trust in God. He died on January 28, 1547, in his fifty-sixth year, having reigned for thirty-eight years.

CHARLES V

[1500–1558]

THE Emperor Charles V was the product of the most extraordinary series of dynastic marriages that history records. Ferdinand of Aragon married Isabella of Castile, and thereby unified Spain. Their inheritance of Spain and the fabulous New World went to a daughter, Juana. The Holy Roman Emperor, Maximilian, possessor of the Austrian domain of the Hapsburgs, married Mary of Burgundy, heiress of the dukedom of Burgundy. Mary brought Flanders and the Netherlands to her husband. They had a son, Philip the Handsome, heir to the combined domains of his parents. Philip married Juana, and *their* son Charles came into the greatest inheritance of all time. From his father he derived Austria and its possessions, together with the Low Countries; from his mother, Spain and the Spanish empire in America.

Charles came into his Burgundian inheritance when he was only fifteen. He became King of Spain the following year. He now had only to wait for his Austrian inheritance, which would be his upon the death of his grandfather, the Emperor Maximilian. He had been most carefully trained for his heavy responsibilities by the prelate Adrian of Utrecht, from whom he derived his lifelong devotion to the Catholic religion; by Henry of Nassau, who brought him his love of history and gave him a clear insight into the intricacies of European diplomacy; by William of Croy who, as Charles's governor and Lord Chamberlain, introduced him to court ritual and the shady side of politics.

When the Emperor Maximilian died in 1519, Charles entered upon his Austrian inheritance, and became a candidate for the throne of the Holy Roman Empire, an elective office. He had rivals, Henry VIII of England and Francis I of France. Charles remained in Spain, and sent William of Croy, well supplied with money, to do whatever was necessary to ensure his election. The fact that he was devoted to the Church and made huge contributions to their exchequers won over the three archbishop electors of Trèves, Mayence, and Cologne. Three of the four princely electors were promised protection against any encroachments on their domains by the fourth, the Hohenzollern Margrave of Brandenburg. The latter was unwilling to vote for Francis I because he hated the French. He was suspicious of Henry VIII of England. So Charles won the election by unanimous vote on the first ballot.

On July 23, 1520, Charles V was crowned Emperor at Aix-la-Chapelle. He had made his grand entry the day before, and in the cathedral where Charlemagne lies buried had taken his solemn oath and kept his vigil. He was the Holy Roman Emperor with domains that ranged from the fields and forests of central Europe to the gold mines of Peru, yet the imperial crown brought to the twenty-year-old youth the supreme problem of the age. In Germany he was faced with the beginning of the Reformation.

Three years before, Luther had posted his world-shaking theses on the door of the church at Wittenberg, signaling revolt against the Catholic Church. Protestantism was spreading through Germany. To deal with this great religious disturbance, Charles V summoned the Diet of Worms. He furnished Luther with a safe conduct to attend and defend his views. The great Protestant leader maintained his point of view, despite all the opposition of the Catholic clergy.

Luther's was a momentous decision, and Charles had to make one equally great. He cast the weight of his authority as Emperor against Luther, and decreed, "It is certain that a single monk must err if he stands against the opinion of all Christendom. Otherwise Christendom itself would have erred for a thousand years. Therefore I am determined to set my kingdoms and dominions, my friends, my body, my blood, my life, my soul upon it. For it were a great shame to us and to you, members of the German nation, if in our time and through our negligence, we were to let even the appearance of heresy and denigration of true religion to enter the hearts of men. Ye all heard Luther's speech here yesterday, and now I say unto you that I regret having delayed so long to proceed against him. I will not hear him again! He has his safe conduct, and may return whence he came. But from now on I regard him as a dangerous and notorious heretic, and trust that you all, as good Christians, will not be wanting in your duty." Charles refused all conciliation and the edict against the reformer was signed and published.

While Charles was busy with the religious problem in Germany a storm had broken over Spain. Resentment against the absence of the sovereign, against rule by Flemish foreigners, and against heavy taxation flamed into open rebellion in Castile. The regent, Charles's old tutor, the prelate Adrian of Utrecht, was unable to stem the tide. Peasant revolts broke out in Valencia and Majorca. Fortunately for Charles, dissension shattered the ranks of the insurgents and brought about their defeat. The repression was ruthless. Then, after order had been restored, its maintenance was assured by the appointment of two Castilians as co-regents with Adrian.

Pieces were being shuffled on the European chessboard. War broke out between Charles V and Francis I. Milan fell to the imperial and papal arms. Pope Leo X died before the end of 1521, and Charles V had enough influence to secure the election of his old tutor and friend, Adrian of Utrecht, who became Pope Adrian VI. The venerable prelate tried in vain to compose the differences between the two great Catholic powers, France and Spain. He died within two years of his election, and was succeeded by a new Medici Pope, Clement VII.

Meanwhile Charles V had paid a state visit to Henry VIII and signed the Treaty of Windsor under which they planned a joint invasion of France. The Emperor then left for Spain, and busied himself with strengthening his hold on the Spanish throne and sending out conquistadores to the New World. Invasions of France in 1522 and 1523 failed. Pope Clement VII reversed the policy of his predecessor, and gave his support to France.

The war of the two great Catholic powers came to a climax at the Battle of Pavia in Italy, where the army of Charles V won an overwhelming victory. Francis I was taken prisoner. He secured his release by signing a treaty, which imposed humiliating terms on France. In Italy the troops of Charles V, commanded by Charles of Bourbon, the Constable of France who had turned against his King, marched on Rome to punish the Pope. The imperial army, which included many German Protestants, stormed Rome and the sack of the city lasted for months. Clement VII was a prisoner and powerless.

Safe in western Europe, Charles declared war against the Turks and pushed them back to the Danube. He conquered Tunis, but failed to take Algiers. Then events closer to home claimed his attention again.

He made a last effort against the Protestant movement. The Schmalkaldic League had been formed by German princes and free cities for the common defense of the reformed faith and to secure their political independence of the Holy Roman Empire. Charles was successful in causing defections among the members and then made war on the league. He defeated Frederick of Saxony and took Philip of Hesse prisoner. After this victory he called the Diet of Augsburg. On the political side he forced the incorporation of the Netherlands into the hereditary Hapsburg possessions. Apropos of the religious question he imposed the Augsburg Interim, a compromise confession of faith, to which he wanted the Protestants to subscribe.

In an attempt to enforce it he resorted to the use of Spanish troops. This so inflamed the Protestants in Germany that they sought the aid of France. Maurice of Saxony, supported by France, attacked Charles and very nearly succeeded in taking him prisoner at Innsbruck. For a while the Emperor was a fugitive. Charles was finally forced to conclude the Treaty of Passau in 1552, guaranteeing freedom of religion to the Lutherans. As his conscience would not allow him to subscribe to this, he left Germany, never to return, and empowered his brother Ferdinand to sign the treaty for him.

Disillusioned and world-weary, Charles V decided to give up his enormous power and possessions. He divided his vast realms between his son, who was to become Philip II of Spain, and his brother, later the Emperor Ferdinand. He gave Milan and Naples to Philip, then the Netherlands, next Spain and Sicily. He transferred the Holy Roman Empire to Ferdinand, adding it to the hereditary Hapsburg domain in Austria. Then the aging Emperor renounced the world, and withdrew to the monastery at Yuste in Spain. There, consoled by his Catholic faith, he prepared himself for eternity.

Charles V lives in history as a very great monarch who, despite his indomitable will, tenacity of purpose, and sense of duty, was unable to cope with the force of events that no man could have stayed: the Reformation and the birth of nationalism.

BENVENUTO CELLINI

[1500–1571]

BENVENUTO CELLINI wrote his own life story in such style that anyone curious about him need only go to the pages of his autobiography. There have been surmises that some of the things he relates are not too trustworthy, and we know he stretched the truth more than once, but later scholarship is inclined to hold that he usually stated the facts, though with all the dramatic zest and lusty bravado of his own personality.

Cellini lived in the final century of the Italian Renaissance, the hundred years of brilliance and glory mingled with political misfortune and disaster which the Italians call the Cinquecento. During his boyhood in Florence, Leonardo da Vinci, Michelangelo, and Raphael might have been seen among the passersby on the street. The Cinquecento saw the pinnacle of the Renaissance and then the beginning of the decline.

Cellini's father wanted him to become a musician, but as a young boy he discovered an art he preferred—the art of the jeweler. His bent being obvious, he was apprenticed to Antonio di Sandro, under whose tutelage he learned how to shape gold and silver, to enamel and anneal, to set gems and turn out the exquisite sculptures of the goldsmith's art.

Soon another side of his character showed itself. Florence was always famous for riots, and the many apprentices attached to the guilds formed a never-failing element of turbulence. Among them Benvenuto distinguished himself by a zest for brawling. In his biography he pictures himself as one of the notable roisterers of a roistering age, the hero of many a fracas and violent encounter. When only sixteen he disturbed the peace so violently that the authorities banished him to Siena.

Completing his apprenticeship as a goldsmith he left Siena and began to wander through Italy. He spent some time in Bologna and Pisa, making a reputation for fine artistic work, and then continued on to Rome where he could hope for commissions from the prelates of the Renaissance Church. He was not disappointed. A cardinal came to him for a silver casket. The Bishop of Salamanca commissioned a pair of ornate candlesticks. Cellini was already turning out masterpieces. From this period dates his medallion of "Leda and the Swan," which in time found its way to Vienna, a prized possession of the imperial Hapsburgs.

The Pope was Clement VII, a Medici pontiff, a great patron of the arts according to the tradition of his family. The hospitality of the papal court was offered to the great artists of the time, Cellini among them. He worked, won applause, roistered, and generally had a good time for himself. During this stay in Rome, moreover, he added to his achievements an exploit in war.

The papal reign of Clement VII, brilliant and unfortunate, sank to a nadir of disaster in the sack of Rome. It was the era of wars between the French King Francis I and the Emperor Charles V, sovereign of Spain, the lands of the New World, Austria, the Netherlands, and the Germanic Empire. The Pope was unlucky enough to side with France, and an imperial army campaigning against the French in Italy marched to capture Rome. The Reformation was rampant in Germany, and Charles V, though opposed to Luther, had come to an arrangement with the reformers, as a result of which there were many Lutherans in the army that besieged Rome. They stormed the city, forced the Pope to take refuge in the formidable fortress of Castel Sant' Angelo, and ravaged the city with unbridled violence and looting.

Benvenuto Cellini played a part in the futile defense of Rome, helping to guard the walls. In the storming of the city the Constable of Bourbon was killed, ending a notable and flamboyant career, and in his autobiography Benvenuto Cellini states that it was he who from the wall fired the shot that felled the enemy commander. He says he also killed Philibert, Prince of Orange. Never underestimating his own exploits, he pictured himself as a good deal of the hero in the events of the sack of Rome.

With Rome occupied, Cellini went to Mantua where he produced a seal picturing the Assumption of the Blessed Virgin. Then back to Florence. He opened a shop, attracted patrons, and wrought art works so superb as to extort praise from Michelangelo—among them a medal of "Hercules and the Nemean Lion."

Politics and war soon forced Cellini out of his native city again. He sided with Clement VII when the Pope sent troops to enforce the Medici claim to rule Florence. The papal forces won, but Cellini had aroused so much hostility among the Florentine republicans that he found it expedient to leave.

The master jeweler returned to Rome, became involved in a family vendetta, committed murder, and fled to Naples. Again he began to wander, for he was by temperament a vagrant, and the fame of his genius as a goldsmith won him a ready welcome from the eminent and powerful wherever he went in that glittering time of the Renaissance. His travels took him to France, where he was received at the court of Francis I. He had a flattering welcome from that brilliant, art-loving monarch, but stayed there briefly, resumed his journeys, and presently was back in Rome.

This stay in the Eternal City was memorable for the fact that Benvenuto Cellini soon found himself in a dungeon cell. He had embroiled himself with the law more than once in a fashion that might well have caused him to see the inside of a prison, but when that misfortune came about it seems to have been caused by malign intrigue and false accusation. Nor was it a charge of violence or manslaughter, but one of embezzlement.

He was accused of having committed robbery during the sack of Rome ten years before, the charge being that the artist had misappropriated a quantity of gold from the papal mint and had taken jewels from the papal tiara. All this Cellini denied, but the charge was pressed, and he was embittered because the Pope failed to support him. He was imprisoned in Castel Sant' Angelo, and remained in jail for seven months, during which time his wrath knew no limit.

Released, he returned to France, where again he was received as an honored guest by King Francis I, who gave him an apartment in the château of Fontainebleau, and paid him 700 gold crowns a year. Benvenuto Cellini lived in high style, working constantly and turning out some of his most famous masterpieces. Probably the most famous is the exquisite saltcellar, beautifully worked with the sculptured figures of Venus and Neptune. This saltcellar is now a treasure of the Vienna museum.

During this period in France, Cellini turned ambitiously to the higher forms of sculpture. Unfortunately most of his work in this medium has disappeared. We can judge the magnitude of the loss from what remains—especially from his "Perseus Holding the Head of Medusa," a masterpiece of bronze now in Florence.

Benvenuto Cellini's residence at the court of France was a prominent event in the trend characteristic of the time, the extension of the Italian Renaissance to other countries of Europe. Francis I, surrounded by scholars and artists, was a prime example of a series of sovereigns who fostered the importation of the new culture that had arisen in Italy. He granted his patronage to Leonardo da Vinci, though the career in France of that universal genius was a good deal of a disappointment. Benvenuto Cellini, a lesser artist, had a brighter success, produced some of his finest things for Francis I, and stands as a figure and symbol of the spread far and wide of the artists and the art of the Italian Renaissance.

In time, though, some seven years, he took his departure from France, ending a memorable story in typical style. He incurred the enmity of one of the great ladies of the court, the Duchess of Etampes, one story telling of romantic motives and jealousy which persuaded the Duchess to stir court intrigues against the artist.

Benvenuto Cellini returned to his native Florence, where he embarked on a new labor. He wrote his autobiography, feeling that so great a man owed his story to the world. His narrative is vividly alive with his own swashbuckling spirit, his gift for self-applause, his fiery loves and hates, his bellicose hostility toward enemies, his boasts of how right he was in his many quarrels. It is an ingenuous disclosure of a riotous and sumptuous personality in a career of sublime art and roisterous adventures, written in such high style as to make the autobiography a classic of Italian literature and one of the masterpieces of picaresque storytelling.

Perhaps the most astounding thing about the life of Benvenuto Cellini is that he survived for seventy-one years, and died in his bed.

CATHERINE DE' MEDICI

[1519–1589]

SCHOLARS still try to reckon the responsibility of Catherine de' Medici for the Massacre of St. Bartholomew. In what degree was she guilty of that historic crime? That question dominates our interest in the character and career of one of the most influential women in the annals of the nations.

A great-granddaughter of Lorenzo the Magnificent, she passed her youth in the splendor of Florence that was Lorenzo's greatest achievement. The Medici were clinging to power as the leading Florentine family, their enemies were trying to dislodge them, and as a result young Catherine de' Medici heard all around her the turmoil of contending factions. Personally in danger, the child was sent to Rome for safety, then lived for some years in a convent. The dangers of that period left their mark on her character. She became shrewd, reserved, watchful, suspicious of the motives of others.

Being a Medici, related to the Popes Leo X and Clement VII, Catherine naturally had many suitors, among them the King of Scotland, the Duke of Mantua, and the Duke of Milan. But Clement VII arranged for her to marry Henry, Duke of Orléans, the second son of Francis I, King of France.

Few weddings have exceeded in grandeur the ceremony solemnized in the cathedral of Marseilles in 1533. The Pope himself journeyed with Catherine to the French city on the Mediterranean, where he gave the nuptial blessing and said High Mass in the cathedral. His wedding gift to the bride consisted of seven magnificent pearls, destined to have a long history. In later years Catherine presented them to her daughter-in-law, Mary Stuart, Queen of France and Scotland. When Elizabeth had Mary put to death, the pearls became part of the Crown Jewels of England. In 1901 they were worn by Edward VII in the imperial crown made for his coronation and since were worn by George V, George VI, and Elizabeth II.

Catherine's position at the French court was a difficult one. The King, her father-in-law, was about the only friend she had. Her dull husband resented her intelligence and charm. Among the nobles at the court there was hostility toward the "Italian woman." The animosity grew when her husband's elder brother, Francis the Dauphin, died. This made Henry heir to the throne and Catherine the future Queen, and the jealous courtiers began to spread baseless rumors that the Dauphin had been poisoned by Catherine. Fortunately for her the King knew the truth.

Soon Catherine's young husband fell in love with Diane de Poitiers, a widow of thirty-seven. From the day Henry of Orléans met her he ignored his wife, and allowed his mistress to insult her openly. Francis I was outraged by his son's behavior, but the situation was one which Catherine had to bear for more than twenty years, till the day of her husband's death.

For nine years she had no children, and her husband, advised by Diane de Poitiers, wanted to divorce her. But again Francis I took Catherine's side. Then, at length, Catherine bore her husband a son, and after that she had other children. Three of her four sons—Francis, Charles, and Henry—succeeded one another on the throne of France.

In 1547, Francis I died and Henry of Orléans became King Henry II. His accession to the throne gave Diane de Poitiers all that she had ever hoped for, and till the day of his death she was all-powerful. This was a bitter predicament for the daughter of the proud Medici. But Catherine was not crushed. She even exercised authority in Paris when her husband was away fighting the Spaniards, and behaved so well as to gain a popularity with the French that she had never enjoyed before.

A great moment for Catherine was the marriage of her eldest son, Francis, to Mary Stuart, Queen of Scotland. The next year, however, brought tragedy when King Henry was killed accidently during a jousting match. Her son being too young to rule France, Catherine assumed the burden as Queen Mother. One of the first things she did was to command Diane de Poitiers to leave the court.

The young King Francis II died only eighteen months later. His widow returned to her own kingdom to play out the unhappy destiny of Mary Queen of Scots. Catherine's second son became King Charles IX. He was only ten years old, and she became supreme as the Queen-Regent of France. She was now approaching forty.

The situation she faced was one of the most bedeviling that ever perplexed a monarch. The problem was religious and political. The Reformation had made much progress in France, and religious war had been raging for some years between Catholics and Protestants. Catherine was no bigot. She had even shown some interest in the Reformed doctrines, but the Huguenot party, headed by powerful and ambitious nobles, was a danger to the throne. Next to Catherine's remaining sons the heir to the crown was young Henry of Navarre, reared a Protestant. He, in time, actually ascended the throne as Henry IV. The danger was equally great on the Catholic side, where the leadership lay with the Guise family, powerful and ambitious and capable of dominating the state. The Duc François de Guise was assassinated by a Huguenot, and his son Henri de Guise thirsted bitterly for revenge.

In the middle between dangerous forces, Catherine played the only game she knew, the game of her Medici forebears, the intrigues of power politics, balancing one side against the other. Protecting the interest of her son, the boy King, she found the religious struggle an incessant peril, and sought to compose the conflict, essaying the role of peacemaker. But the religious and political passions were beyond her power to quiet, and she could only seek to prevent either side from seizing control. Such was the state of affairs that led to the ferocious event which gives Catherine de' Medici her chief place in history, the Massacre of St. Bartholomew.

Catherine arranged a marriage of her daughter Marguerite to the Protestant Henry of Navarre, designing to keep the crown attached to her own family. She invited Admiral Coligny, the eminent leader of the Huguenots, to attend. He came, and quickly gained the favor of the young King, urging him to make war on Spain, the great Catholic power. The Queen-Regent disliked the influence of Coligny with her son, and sought to check him.

Protestant nobles trooped into Paris for the wedding and the celebration. The capital being strongly Catholic, an explosive situation developed. The catholic leader, the Duc de Guise, savagely determined to avenge the assassination of his father and planned to murder the Protestant leader, Admiral Coligny. What transpired in secret councils is a matter of doubt. The responsibility of Catherine de' Medici for what occurred is in dispute, but one version is that the Duc de Guise persuaded her that the Huguenots, under Coligny, were plotting a seizure of power, and that this could be thwarted only by striking first.

The wedding festivities were still proceeding on the night of August 23, St. Bartholomew's Day, when partisans of the Duc de Guise burst in on Coligny and murdered him. This was followed by a general massacre of Huguenots. Mobs were organized and Protestants were cut down throughout the city and indeed throughout France.

The Protestants blamed Catherine de' Medici for the massacre, which they said could not have taken place without her consent. The Catholics were equally anxious to show that the Queen Mother and the King were both on their side. So both Protestants and Catholics attributed responsibility to her.

Her son, Charles IX, was depressed by the horror of the night of St. Bartholomew, and sank into feebleness and lethargy, dying two years later. He was succeeded by his brother Henry, Catherine's third son. As Henry III's reign went on, it became clear that he would never have any children, a fact that created a grave political crisis since the next heir to the throne was the Huguenot Henry of Navarre.

The War of the Three Henrys erupted—King Henry III against Henri de Guise and Henry of Navarre, the latter two against one another. The Queen Mother Catherine went traveling, on her last long journey in the cause of peace, and en route heard of the execution of her daughter-in-law of long ago, Mary Queen of Scots. She felt deeply grieved and depressed. But her old fire remained, and she counseled her son throughout her last months with the same intelligence she had always shown.

Catherine de' Medici did not live to see the end of the War of the Three Henrys. But by working for her family and for the Crown of France she had made a final solution possible. When Henry of Navarre became a Catholic, there was no longer any reason for France to fear the pretensions of the House of Guise. Henry of Navarre mounted the throne as Henry IV, and a new era opened.

IVAN THE TERRIBLE

[*1530–1584*]

WHEN Ivan IV of Russia was twelve years old, he suddenly
ordered the most powerful member of the Russian nobility
to be seized, murdered, and thrown to the royal hounds. It was remarkable that a boy of that age should act so effectively, and so
cruelly, but he was only behaving in a way that Russia and Europe
would judge characteristic when they came to know him as a mature
man. Ability and cruelty joined together to bring this Muscovite
sovereign the nickname that has identified him ever since his own
time: Ivan the Terrible.

He is one of the most enigmatic and contradictory figures in history. His iron will was served by a brilliant mind. He read widely,
never backed away from new ideas, and tried to keep himself informed about what was happening in the rest of the world. He anticipated the ideas of Peter the Great for the expansion of his realm,
although he lacked the means to carry them out. No one ever worked
harder for the good of Russia, or strove more indefatigably to promote
the interests of the middle classes against the great nobles, the boyars.

These qualities were accompanied by innate brutality and vicious
manners. Human life meant nothing to him and he delighted in causing suffering. Ridden by an ungovernable temper, he was forever
being carried away by insane spasms of fury. He killed his eldest and
dearly beloved son in a fit of rage. By turn he was boisterous, glorious,
infamous, and repentant, and for forty years he ruled Russia with
statesmanlike ability and a rod of iron.

When he was three years old, his father, Basil III, died after ap-
pointing his mother and two of the great boyars to act as regents. His
mother was mysteriously poisoned, and the boy grew up in a vicious
and degrading atmosphere, ill-treated by the families of his regents,

who vied with one another for power and fought continuously among themselves. The conspiracies, intrigues, and murders that surrounded his early years, the insults offered him even though he was heir to the throne, made a deep impression on his mind, and he never overcame his dislike for the boyars as a class.

The great Shuisky family lorded it over Moscow when young Ivan asserted himself to the astonishment of everyone. Planning his move carefully, he had Andrei Shuisky arrested and executed. Only twelve, Ivan could not take over the government. But he won respect, and served notice of what was to come.

For the next five years he indulged his adolescent passions, urged on by the members of his court. Then, when he was seventeen, he tired of the dissipated life he was leading. He decided to get married, choosing Anastasia Romanov, of an obscure family of the nobility. This was the beginning of greatness for the Romanovs, who would become rulers of Russia and reign right down to the Bolshevik Revolution.

Ivan also announced his intention of being crowned Tsar of all the Russias. The title of Tsar, derived from Caesar via the Eastern Roman Empire, had not been used before owing to the jealousy of the other Russian grand dukes and princes. But Ivan was determined that his supremacy as Prince of Muscovy should be recognized by the boyars and that the ruler of Russia should be the equal of the monarchs of western Europe. He was crowned, and he was married. He loved Anastasia, and while she was with him he spent the sanest and best period of his life.

He surrounded himself with able and honest men. He summoned the first representative assembly ever to meet in Russia. He promised good government, and kept his promise.

Russia had only recently emerged from the long nightmare of Tartar domination that had followed the conquest of the land in the time of Genghis Khan, nearly three centuries before. Ivan's grandfather, Ivan Khalita, had won from the Tartars the independence of the principality of Moscow, the nucleus of modern Russia. To the east, on the Volga, lay the Tartar states of Kazan and Astrakhan. Accepting the advice of Sylvester, a monk who had become one of his chief advisers, the Tsar struck at the ancient foe. He led an army against the stronghold of Kazan, and took it by assault, a critical victory of

Christian Russia over the forces of Asia. Four years later Ivan marched downstream and conquered Astrakhan at the mouth of the Volga. These victories broke the Tartar power.

Ivan was not so successful in the Crimea or on the Baltic, but he foreshadowed the policy of Russia for centuries thereafter, the drive to the sea west and south.

This constructive phase of Ivan's reign was marked by the arrival of the first English ship ever to make the voyage to Russia. Captain Richard Chancellor, sailing a merchantman belonging to the newly formed English Muscovy Company, reached Archangel on the White Sea in 1555. Ivan was delighted, for he wanted more bonds with the West, and gave trading concessions to the English.

The death of the Tsarina Anastasia in childbirth was a tragedy for Ivan and for Russia. The moderating influence removed, he began an orgy of lust and violence, going through seven wives, whom he got rid of by divorce or execution. To his sixth wife, Ivan was married for only one day. After their wedding he decided that she was not virtuous, and the next morning he had her put in a closed carriage drawn by wild horses which were whipped into the Volga, where she was drowned.

He grew unreasonably suspicious of his best advisers. His son Demetrius died, and the blow unsettled him. In 1562, Ivan fell seriously ill. As he lay, to all appearances dying, the boyars started to quarrel among themselves as to which of them should be regent. Memories of his own boyhood surged through his mind, memories of the disgusting behavior of the boyars when he was too young to challenge them. On his sickbed he saw intimations of the same thing starting all over again. Contrary to all expectations Ivan recovered from his illness, and thereafter seems to have lived mostly for revenge upon the boyars.

As usual, he planned carefully, for his opponents were still powerful. In 1564 he left Moscow with his family. Early the following year he declared that he would abdicate. The people, whom he had defended against the boyars, were alarmed. They sent emissaries to beg him to remain as Tsar. He agreed, but on his own terms—which were that he should set up a state within the state. He divided the lands of his kingdom into two parts, one for the boyars to govern as they pleased, the other his own private domain. So was formed the

WILLIAM PITT

GEORGE WASHINGTON

"oprichina" of Ivan the Terrible. He drove out the boyars and ruled through his own henchmen, including his dreaded military police. He used terror as a political instrument and a private amusement. His fury fell upon all who irritated him, including members of his family, and he prescribed torture for prisoners before sending them to the block. When the Metropolitan of Moscow condemned the oprichina, Ivan had him strangled. The historic city of Novgorod resisted, whereupon Ivan doomed it to slaughter and destruction at the hands of his ferocious army. Eventually the terror became so insane that it turned against itself, with the terrible Tsar executing his executioners.

Ironically Ivan the Terrible was very religious. He asked the Church to pray for his victims. He presented one monastery with a thousand rubles for Masses for the souls of the dead. How many were the dead in this instance? Ivan gives the precise number—3,470.

During this period Ivan the Terrible lost a war for the possession of the Baltic coast line. However, this reverse was more than offset by success in another direction. The great drive of the Russians across Asia began, the march that was to take them to the Pacific. Under Ivan the Terrible, western Siberia was conquered by the Cossack hetman Yermak in 1581.

The following year the Tsar had some sharp words with his eldest son, fell into a characteristic rage, and struck him on the head with a walking stick. The son died of the blow. The father never forgave himself. He retired from Moscow to a little town near by where he lived in a palace with only his closest henchmen about him. His conduct became increasingly erratic, alternating between monastic piety and frenzied brutality. Weeks of strictest devotion, during which the Tsar was scourged for his sins, were followed by weeks of the wildest debauchery, during which persons suspected of disloyalty were tortured and put to death.

Two years of this broke Ivan the Terrible. He was overtaken by death at the age of fifty-three. On his deathbed he appointed Boris Godunov and Nikita Romanov to be regents during the minority of his son Theodore—the one to have a career of dramatic violence as the usurper Tsar, the other to be the link to the dynasty of the Romanovs.

QUEEN ELIZABETH

[*1533–1603*]

Wʜᴇɴ the Spanish Armada was sighted off England on July 19, 1588, Queen Elizabeth I was fifty-five years old, but still a strikingly handsome woman. Her main forces were assembled at Tilbury and to them she went, like a second Boadicea, armed for defense against the would-be invaders. Mounted on a noble charger, a marshal's baton in her hand, a cuirass of polished steel laced over her magnificent apparel, and followed by a page bearing her white plumed helmet, she rode bareheaded through the ranks of her soldiers and spoke to them as warrior and as queen:

"Let tyrants fear! I have always so behaved myself that, under God, I have placed my chiefest strength and safeguard in the loyal hearts and good-will of my subjects. And therefore I am come among you at this time, not for my recreation or sport but being resolved in the midst and heat of the battle, to live or die amongst you all, to lay down for my God, my Kingdom and my People, my honor and my blood, even in the dust. I know I have but the body of a weak and feeble woman, but I have the heart of a king, and of a king of England too. I think foul scorn that Parma or Spain or any Prince of Europe should dare to invade the borders of my realm. To which, rather than any dishonor should grow by me, I myself will take up arms. I myself will be your general, judge and rewarder of every one of your virtues in the field; not doubting that by your obedience to my commands, your concord in the camp and your valor in the field, we shall shortly have a famous victory over those enemies of my God, of my Kingdom and of my People."

In the sea fight that followed the sailors of England made good their Queen's boast. Drake, Hawkins, and Frobisher, under the command of Lord Howard of Effingham, caught the Armada at the entrance to the Channel. The massive Spanish galleons were no match for the agile craft of the English sea dogs. The number of ships was about equal on both sides, but the English carried more and better guns, greater firepower. They harried the enemy through the Channel, picking them off one by one, and then came the final attack that broke the Armada and sent its surviving remnants scurrying for safety north around Scotland in a desperate effort to get back to Spain. It was the greatest of English naval victories, the most famous event of Elizabeth's reign.

Queen Elizabeth I was the only surviving child of Henry VIII by his second wife Anne Boleyn. Many, who did not recognize the King's divorce from Catherine of Aragon, deemed Elizabeth illegitimate. She grew up with the knowledge of how her Bluebeard father had sent her mother to the scaffold. She was fourteen when Henry VIII died, and during the brief reign of her brother, Edward VI, she led a quiet life, studying under the scholars Ascham and Castiglione.

They taught the classical subjects of Renaissance education, and she was an apt pupil with a quick intelligence and retentive memory. She learned grammar, rhetoric, and the Italian style of penmanship—the "fine Italian hand." Music became her passion. But what struck most observers about Elizabeth's education was her command of languages. She learned Greek, mastered Latin as easily as English, and in later years could converse in their own tongues with ambassadors from France and Italy.

When her elder sister Mary came to the throne, Elizabeth, a Protestant, watched the fate of Mary's attempt to restore the old faith in England. The attempt ended in failure. Mary's Catholic policy, her mistakes and her misfortunes, made her unpopular, and her enemies called her "Bloody Mary."

The accession of Elizabeth after Mary's death caused a complete change. Elizabeth claimed to be both English and Protestant. Her policy in matters theological was in harmony with the public mood of England at the time, one of moderation and expediency. She loved ritual and cared little for religion. She understood the political significance of religion, its value in promoting patriotic fervor and domestic contentment. She hated Romanism and Calvinism; she looked upon Anglicanism as a sure guarantee of state unity.

Although she never married, she always had men around her. Of all her admirers and favorites, the brave and chivalrous, the generous and impulsive Earl of Essex was probably the one the Queen cared most for, although that did not save him from the scaffold. She was attracted to Sir Walter Raleigh, who laid down his blue mantle in the mud for her to tread upon, by his gallantry and literary talent; to Arundel by his lavish gifts, for he seemed always to choose the thing she wanted; to Sir William Pickering by his handsome face and graceful carriage; to Christopher Hatton by his exquisite skill at dancing, for which she made him Chancellor; to the Earl of Oxford by his brilliance; to Thomas Heneage by his pleasing wit, for which she appointed him King of the Bean at a celebration of Twelfth Night; to Leicester by his magnificence and political boldness. Leicester, influential statesman and military commander during the early part of her reign, was the most important of her favorites. The culminating instrument of her statecraft was the spiderlike elderly Burleigh, unloved for his personality but highly regarded for his consummate ability as minister and diplomat.

Her hand was sought in marriage by many royal suitors; but these offers, whether inspired by her representatives or not, were merely used to further her foreign policy. Before she came to the throne, she had refused the Duke of Savoy. No sooner was her sister Mary dead than the widower, Philip of Spain, offered his hand which was promptly refused. Marriage to Charles IX of France was suggested, but that came to nothing. Then the Archduke Charles, the younger son of the Holy Roman Emperor Ferdinand, joined the ranks of her suitors, and enabled her to conduct fruitful negotiations with Germany. The Duke of Anjou came next, and long and equally useful diplomatic exchanges with France took place. Elizabeth would have none of them.

Why did she attract men to her court and listen to offers of marriage when she had no intention of taking a husband? The historians have debated about this, but it was common knowledge in her own time that she was debarred from marriage by a physical defect. Apparently she tried to cover the defect with a display of femininity. We know that she resented the birth of a son to Mary Queen of Scots, saying despondently that she herself was only "barren stock."

The worst blot on her reign was the execution of this beautiful and unhappy cousin, Mary of Scotland. Many stage plays have been written about these two women who were rival queens enmeshed in the problems of church and state. In the eyes of Catholics, who did not recognize the divorce of Henry VIII from Catherine of Aragon, the Protestant Elizabeth was illegitimate and the Catholic Mary Stuart was the rightful Queen of England. Mary, fleeing her Protestant Scottish subjects, took refuge in her cousin's realm, and Elizabeth was faced with a terrible dilemma. She could not restore Mary to her Scottish throne. She dared not let her go to France, for Mary had once reigned there as Queen and could count on unlimited support against Elizabeth. She kept her a prisoner in England, where Mary inevitably became a center of Catholic conspiracy. After long years, and perhaps against her true will, Elizabeth signed the death warrant that her ministers had prepared and her Parliament approved. Real or not, she showed frantic sorrow when news of Mary's execution was brought to her.

The most romantic story about Elizabeth I recounts how the dying Countess of Nottingham asked the Queen to come to her. The Countess had a confession to make before she could die in peace. On Elizabeth's arrival, the Countess produced a ring which she said the Earl of Essex, after being sentenced to death for conspiracy and sedition, had sent to her with the earnest request that she should deliver it to the Queen. The ring, he said, was a token by which he implored the Queen's mercy. The Countess of Nottingham, a relative but no friend of Essex, had withheld the ring, for which she now entreated the Queen's forgiveness.

At sight of the ring Elizabeth at once recognized it as one she had given to her unhappy favorite with the promise that, if he ever sent to her that gage of her affection, she would allow him to justify himself in her presence for any crime of which he might be accused. Essex had sought to avail himself of the Queen's pledge, but had been thwarted by the bad faith of the Countess of Nottingham. Transported by rage and grief on learning this, Queen Elizabeth seized the dying Countess in her bed, shook her violently, and shouted, "God may forgive you, madam, but I never shall!"

Returning to her palace the Queen gave way to melancholy and despair, refusing food and medical attention. Three days before her death she left her bed and placed herself on cushions piled on the floor; she lost the power of speech, and sleepless, her eyes fixed, her finger pressed upon her lips, she died of a broken heart, after a long life of power and prosperity and glory.

Queen Elizabeth set England on the path to greatness. Her sailors—Drake, Hawkins, Frobisher—boldly ignored the Spanish claim to ownership of America. They plundered the treasure fleets of Spain. Drake sailed around the world. Frobisher sought for the Northwest Passage to India. Raleigh dreamed of an English colonial empire of the future. Chancellor connected England with the Russia of Ivan the Terrible by his voyages to Archangel. Soon Englishmen would be found everywhere around the globe—fighting, conquering, colonizing, trading.

But the most illustrious thing the reign produced was its school of writers. Never has there been a more splendid galaxy of poets and playwrights. Think of Christopher Marlowe and *Dr. Faustus*, of Ben Jonson and *Volpone*, of Thomas Kyd and *The Spanish Tragedy!* Think of William Shakespeare, the greatest genius of modern literature, the crowning glory of Elizabethan England!

MARY QUEEN OF SCOTS

[1542–1587]

THE name of Mary Queen of Scots is inseparable from that of Elizabeth of England. In history the two women are bracketed together in a contrast of drama and terror. Mary Stuart, beautiful, brilliant, imprisoned, full of the faults and follies and the superb qualities of dignity and loyalty that belong especially to a woman. Elizabeth, the Virgin Queen, at her worst, an aging shrew and coquette, false, vain, and unlovely, but sagacious, political, and redoubtable, so that she ranks as one of the greatest of sovereigns.

The relations of the two women were enmeshed in the relations of their countries. The stronger England inevitably sought to dominate Scotland, the weaker nation on the same island. The names of Wallace, Bruce, Douglas told of age-long Scottish resistance. Traditionally the Scots allied themselves with England's great continental enemy, France, and the story of Mary Stuart combines royal themes of Scotland, England, France.

Mary was the daughter of King James V of Scotland. Betrothed to the Dauphin of France when she was only six, she was sent to Paris to become familiar with the duties and ceremonials of French royalty. The King of France at the time was Henry II; the Queen, Catherine de' Medici. They had four children, and with them Mary was educated. To remind her of home she had with her four Scottish playmates, the Four Marys, daughters of noble Scottish families.

Even as a child she was distinguished. In the glittering scenes of the court Mary Stuart contrasted with the frail neurotic children of Henry II and Catherine de' Medici. She was healthy, vibrant, intelligent. She was petted by Henry II, by Queen Catherine, and by the King's mistress Diane de Poitiers. The Dauphin, her future husband, followed always at her heels.

Mary's marriage took place in 1558 at Notre Dame in Paris. Seven cardinals and eighteen archbishops and bishops all in full vestments waited as the King of France and the Duke of Lorraine led the young Queen of Scotland to the altar. She was not yet sixteen years old, but already a very beautiful young woman.

In the year following her marriage, Henry II was killed in a tournament, and she became Queen of France. Mary at seventeen dominated her fifteen-year-old husband. She was in actuality the ruling sovereign of France. Power was sweet to her.

Meanwhile back in Scotland turmoil reigned. The Reformation was sweeping through the country. Mary's mother, the Regent of Scotland, died, whereupon the Reformation party seized control. Mary watched from Paris in sorrow as the enemies of her religion went from strength to strength in her native land.

Then her husband died. She lost the title of Queen of France as his brother Charles IX mounted the throne. Mary wanted to remain in France, but her counselors insisted that her real future lay in Scotland, where she still held the title of Queen. She arrived home to find herself caught up in a perpetual crisis because of her Catholic faith.

She found an arch-enemy in John Knox, who headed the extremists among the reformers. They had historic encounters, in which he confronted her with the harsh preachings of a religious zealot. In the conflict between the beautiful young Queen and the dour anathematizing religionist, her bearing was as proud as his own. John Knox went from their first interview denouncing her "proud mind, crafty wit and indurate heart against God and his truth."

Politically Mary was in a strong position, for if Elizabeth died childless she would become Queen of England. She named a Privy Council, to which she was clever enough to appoint a majority of Protestant Lords. But the tasks to which she set herself were virtually impossible; reconverting Scotland to Catholicism and gaining recognition of her right to the succession of the throne of England. Elizabeth had something to say about that, although there was no doubt that Mary was legally the next heir.

A second marriage for the young Queen of Scotland was an international question. Mary followed the advice of her Italian secretary, David Rizzio, who proposed that she espouse her cousin Lord Henry Darnley. Rizzio pointed out that there were two advantages which would serve both phases of Mary's policy, the religious question and the English succession. Darnley was a prominent Catholic, and was next to Mary in the line of the English royal inheritance.

But Darnley soon showed himself to be cowardly, false, and foolish. He demanded royal authority equal to his wife's. Mary refused. In this she was advised by Rizzio, whom she now had made Chancellor. Darnley, infuriated with Rizzio, hitherto his friend, went over to the enemies of the royal favorite. He led a band of conspirators that burst into Mary's private apartment one night, found Rizzio supping with her, and stabbed him to death.

With her enemies raging around her, Mary did not panic. She persuaded her husband to leave his accomplices and escape with her. Aided by the Earl of Bothwell and his soldiers, the royal couple reached Dunbar Castle. There she regrouped her forces, demanded and received the allegiance of her subjects, and returned to Edinburgh in triumph.

Three months after that her son was born at Edinburgh Castle. The news caused Elizabeth to utter that despairing cry, "The Queen of Scots is lighter of a fair son, and I am but a barren stock." This son would live to become James VI of Scotland and James I of England.

Events now shaped up for the most disastrous occurrence of Mary's career—the murder of Darnley. There is no doubt that Bothwell formed the plot, and it is probable that she knew something about it. The murderers tried to blow Darnley up with a charge of gunpowder, and then, when he fled in time to escape the blast, strangled him. At his trial Bothwell was acquitted because no witnesses would appear against him.

The murder of Darnley had turned opinion bitterly against her, but this Mary could not realize. She was utterly infatuated with Bothwell, and plunged ahead. He had been married already, but was now divorced from his wife, which set the stage for the culmination. The Queen married Bothwell. At his insistence, the ceremony was performed by a Reformed cleric who had once been the Catholic Bishop of Orkney. The killing of the Queen's husband and her marriage to his murderer shocked all classes. The Protestant zealots, headed by John Knox, assailed her with unmeasured fury.

Revolt broke out. Bothwell retired to Dunbar. Mary was taken to

Edinburgh and held under house arrest. New misfortune came in the form of a silver casket. The story is that one of Bothwell's retainers was arrested carrying the casket to his master at Dunbar. In it were found letters sent by Mary to Bothwell before Darnley's murder which proved her to have been an accessory before the crime. The authenticity of these letters has been challenged, but their effect was decisive. Mary abdicated, tried to recover her throne by force, was defeated, and fled to England to beg asylum and aid from Queen Elizabeth.

The arrival of the Queen of Scotland in England placed Elizabeth in a most difficult position. If she allowed her to leave England, Mary would become the center of Catholic plots, the adherents of the old religion regarding Mary as the rightful Queen of England. If she allowed her to remain, and accorded her royal hospitality, Mary would be equally awkward as a guest at Elizabeth's court—the more so as Mary was the legal successor to the crown upon the death of Elizabeth. A way out was found in the charge against Mary for the murder of Darnley. A court decided that nothing had been proved, but Elizabeth still presumed Mary's guilt and had her confined.

For nineteen years Mary Queen of Scots remained a prisoner in England. As time went by and it became more and more obvious that the Virgin Queen would leave no heir of her own, Mary assumed a greater importance as the legal successor to the crown—Protestant England faced with the prospect of having a Catholic sovereign.

The royal prisoner became the focus of one plot after another. The culmination of the tragedy of Mary Queen of Scots came with the Babington Plot. A Catholic gentleman, Anthony Babington, and others, bound themselves to kill Elizabeth and release Mary. Elizabeth's ministers discovered the conspiracy. Babington and his accomplices were seized and put to death. Evidence was obtained that Mary was cognizant of the plot, and it was decided to put her on trial.

She was removed to Fotheringhay castle in Northumberlandshire. A royal commission was sent to try her. She denied their authority to do so, although she consented to answer their interrogations. She denied on oath the charge of abetting the plan to murder Elizabeth. But sentence of death was passed upon her by the Star Chamber in London. Parliament gave its approval.

Elizabeth hesitated to sign the death warrant. Mary was a queen, her cousin, her guest. She denied her guilt in the most solemn fashion. At last, after long wavering, Elizabeth signed the warrant, and sent it to the Lord Chancellor to receive the Great Seal. The next day she tried to recall it, but it was already on its way to Fotheringhay, where it was executed.

When her doom was announced to her, Mary bore herself with dignity. She said she was willing to die for her religion, and again denied any knowledge of the plot against Elizabeth. She took leave of her attendants, and distributed her possessions among them.

At eight o'clock on the morning of February 8, 1587, Mary Stuart, Queen of Scots, in a robe of black satin was led to the place of execution. Her little dog followed, hidden in her skirts. Her request that a Catholic priest accompany her had been denied. The Dean of Peterborough prayed in English, but she lifted up her voice in Latin against his. Her attendants removed her black robe and she appeared arrayed in a splendid dress of crimson velvet. She laid her head upon the block. Clasping her crucifix, she cried out in Latin, "I commend myself, Lord, into thy hands." The axe fell. And so, in the forty-fifth year of her age and the nineteenth of her captivity in England, died Mary Queen of Scots.

AKBAR

[1542–1605]

I<small>T MUST</small> indeed have been a strange and wonderful sight when, early in 1601, seven merchants of the City of London, wearing English court dress, appeared before the Great Mogul in Delhi. They came to present letters from Queen Elizabeth professing her friendship and informing him that she had granted them a charter to trade with his Empire of India, in peace and for their mutual profit.

Akbar received the English embassy seated upon the Peacock Throne, which was ascended by silver steps and stood upon feet of gold set with jewels, its back adorned with two peacock tails from which shone diamonds, rubies, and precious stones in dazzling profusion. Surrounded by a galaxy of Indian princes, whose turbans were studded and rich costumes sparkled with gems scarcely less splendid than those of their ruler, he welcomed the Virgin Queen's envoys and granted them full freedom to trade peacefully throughout his vast dominions and to enter his ports at will. They withdrew, overwhelmed by the wealth and magnificence of a court which far exceeded anything at that time existing in Europe.

Akbar's dynasty originated in central Asia. His grandfather had come down through the Khyber Pass, overthrown the Hindus, and established a strong system of Mohammedan rule. Akbar's father was a weakling, but he had a veteran soldier, Bairan Khan, to fight his battles. Akbar inherited both the throne and the soldier.

Advised by Bairan Khan, the young sovereign dismissed the learned scholars whom his father had appointed to educate him. Sports took the place of manuscripts. Akbar became a perfect horseman, played wonderful polo, and could control the most ferocious elephants. He was trained to face death without flinching, and killed tigers from the backs of elephants and on foot. Nor was he squeamish about shedding blood. When Akbar was fourteen, Bairan Khan invited him to prove himself a good Moslem and a slayer of the infidel: with one stroke of his scimitar he cut off the head of a Hindu prisoner.

The first five years of Akbar's reign were marked by wars for the consolidation of his realm. His troops captured Agra and pacified the Punjab; Ajmer was taken without a battle, and the Afghans driven out of Lucknow. Just before he was eighteen Akbar had a disagreement with Bairan Khan. The old warrior wanted to enforce, in what was rapidly becoming a highly luxurious and refined court, the same rigid discipline that he maintained in the army. Akbar ordered him to go on a pilgrimage to Mecca. On his way Bairan Khan was killed. Akbar ruled alone.

The young Mogul set out to widen the borders of his domain, and he never stopped till by ruthless war he had made himself master of virtually all Hindustan. By the time he was twenty-five the Rajput stronghold of Chitor had fallen to him. Before he was twenty-eight he had obtained possession of Oudh and Gwalior. When he was thirty he marched in person into Gujarat, received the submission of the last of the independent sultans of Ahmedabad, and added that province to his domains. During this time his generals were busy driving the Afghans out of Bengal and reuniting the lower Ganges to Hindustan proper. Not content with these conquests he annexed Orissa to Bengal, and took Kabul, Kashmir, Sind, and Kandahar. He conquered Berar from the Mohammedan kings of the Deccan.

All of these territories had to be integrated into a single system. Akbar ordered a survey and a census throughout his realm. He established a uniform system of weights and measures. He constructed roads and instituted a police force for both cities and country districts. Theology was a special concern of his. He made a careful study of all religions and established freedom of worship, decreeing that his subjects might frequent their temples as they saw fit. His officials were appointed without discrimination of race or creed. Although an agnostic himself in his prime, he evolved a faith of his own in his later years.

In youth given to overindulgence in the luxuries of the table, he became sober and abstemious with maturity, but never surrendered the use of opium. He had his lighter moments. To the ninth day of every month, he gave the title "day of diversion," and caused a sort of royal fair to be held, attended by the ladies of his harem and the wives of his dignitaries, going himself in disguise to hear the gossip and have his share of gay adventure. He remained an ardent devotee of polo, liking the game so much that he had polo balls painted with phosphorus so as to be able to play at night.

In his later years Akbar sought mostly the companionship of wise men and poets. A disbeliever in revealed religion, yet he would stand morning, noon, and night for a few brief moments in silent prayer. He had a great veneration for light and believed it to be an emanation of the one and only living God. "There is no God but God, and Akbar is his Caliph" was the assertion he frequently made when he was visited by priests of whatsoever faith: Brahmin, Buddhist, Parsee, Jew, or Roman Catholic. On one occasion a Jesuit missionary brought him a finely painted and ornamented image of the Virgin Mary. He gazed on it in admiration and declared that she appeared indeed the Queen of Heaven seated on her throne. With hopes of his conversion, the priest began to discuss Islam, when Akbar gravely proposed, as a means of deciding between the assertions of Christians and Mohammedans, that a famous mullah should leap into a furnace with a Koran in his hand to be followed by the Jesuit bearing a Bible. The ordeal was declined.

Akbar was a mystic who had one moment of spiritual exaltation. It happened, oddly enough, while he was out hunting. He and his companions were busily killing beasts of every kind, when suddenly he called a halt, moved by a feeling for the sanctity of life. Thereafter he was a changed man.

Pondering more and more over his mystical experience, convinced that none of the religions around him was true, he decided to become his own authority. He promulgated an Infallibility Decree which said that his opinion was to be accepted whenever there was a dispute between creeds. Already Emperor, he appointed himself a kind of Pope.

In his old age Akbar became estranged from his sons who were faithful Mohammedans and could not tolerate their father's religious liberalism. One rumor had it that he was poisoned by them, another that he tried to get rid of an obnoxious rajah by poison, only to drink the deadly potion himself by mistake. The fact is that we have no reason to doubt that the Mogul Emperor died a natural death.

Mullahs came to his deathbed in an effort to reconvert him to Islam; he chased them away. Akbar breathed his last without the benefit of prayers from any church. No great crowds followed his simple funeral. His sons and courtiers keenly felt his apostasy from the faith of the Prophet, and discarded the trappings of mourning on the morrow of his departure from the world. But they were happy to have the majestic imperial power he bequeathed to them.

SIR FRANCIS DRAKE

[1545?–1596]

F RANCIS DRAKE was the first Englishman to circumnavigate the globe. He accomplished his momentous voyage around the world in two years and ten months, starting from Plymouth, England, on December 13, 1577, and returning to the same port on September 26, 1580. He then took his ship, the "Golden Hind," to Deptford for repairs. Queen Elizabeth went on board and, as he knelt before her, she took the sword of Howard of Effingham, the Lord High Admiral of England, and striking Drake upon the shoulder said, "Arise, Sir Francis."

Never was knighthood conferred with less regard for political consequences, for Drake had preyed upon Spanish shipping for years and the Virgin Queen was giving official recognition to the chief aggressor against the King of Spain. Before leaving Drake's vessel the Queen ordered that it be preserved forever. It decayed and had to be broken up in the reign of Charles II, who had various pieces of furniture made from its timbers, among them a chair which he presented to Oxford University.

When Francis Drake was fourteen, his father apprenticed him to the master of a small bark. In this the boy sailed along the coast and occasionally crossed to France. He was a quick strong lad who loved the sea, and soon knew every shoal and reef along the coast. When he was eighteen, his employer died and, having no family, left his boat to young Drake, who promptly sold it and got a job as purser on a ship trading with Spain. The next year he sailed as second in command on a voyage to Guinea.

Sir John Hawkins, one of the foremost seafaring men of his time and a rich merchant of Plymouth, was a distant kin of Drake's mother. He had much to do with Drake's upbringing and education, and was now planning a voyage of adventure. Francis Drake went to call upon him. The upshot was that Sir John gave his young kinsman command of a merchantman in his flotilla.

Sir John Hawkins had a regular privateering commission from Queen Elizabeth which gave him the right to arm his merchantmen. On this expedition he made first for the coast of Africa to take a cargo of slaves, and then sailed for the Spanish Main to exchange them for gold and jewels. Sailing up the coast of Mexico they met with a violent storm and had to put in to Vera Cruz for repairs. A battle started, and it was with difficulty that Hawkins and Drake fought their way out. The incident confirmed both in their hatred of Spain.

Back home and determined on a career of his own, Drake obtained a regular privateering commission from Queen Elizabeth. He captured several Spanish ships and accumulated enough plunder to fit out a big expedition. This was to prove one of the most astounding raids in naval history.

Drake crossed the Atlantic, and entered a hideaway he had selected on the Spanish Main. From this point he set out with forty men and tried to capture the town of Nombre de Dios, where the Spaniards stored the gold brought across the Isthmus of Panama by mule train. This first attempt failed, as did a raid on the Isthmus of Panama to capture a large shipment of gold. But Drake got far enough to see a sight no other Englishman had ever beheld, the glistening waters of the Pacific. There and then he resolved that he would sail an English ship upon those waters.

His second attempt to capture Nombre de Dios was successful. Three mule trains laden with gold were seized when he took the town with a force of sixty Englishmen and less than a hundred natives. Quickly embarking with his booty, Drake eluded the Spanish warships at Cartagena and sailed back to Plymouth.

Drake wanted to continue his private war against Spain, but had to wait because of a decrease in international tension. He served for a while in Ireland, disliked it, and returned to the sea when Queen Elizabeth dropped the idea of conciliating Philip II. This time Drake had a very bold project. He would imitate Magellan and sail around the world. The plan appealed to the Queen's imagination. She helped finance the expedition.

Drake sailed for Africa, skirted the Cape Verde Islands, and crossed the Atlantic to Brazil. He entered the port of St. Julian, where sixty years previously Magellan had paused to make his ships ready to negotiate the treacherous straits into the Pacific.

Like his great Portuguese predecessor, Drake had to put down a mutiny. Continuing south, he entered the Straits of Magellan, emerging into the Pacific sixteen days later. But a great storm carried his ships back to the mouth of the straits. Drake's became separated from the others, and these turned back and sailed home to England. Drake continued alone in his own ship, which he renamed the "Golden Hind," under which name it gained immortality in the annals of the sea.

Then another storm blew Drake to the south, and there he discovered open water. Until then navigators had believed that South America was connected with a great southern continent, separated only by the Straits of Magellan. When the storm subsided, Drake sailed up the coasts of Chili and Peru, seizing Spanish ships till his men were satiated with plunder.

Off Nicaragua he made a capture of greater value than all his treasures. He pursued a Spanish galleon to the east and on board her found two China sea pilots and a complete set of secret charts for Spanish trade in the Pacific—priceless for the continuance of his voyage. He then sailed up the coast of what is now the United States and Canada. Determined to circumnavigate the globe, he returned south and entered the harbor of what apparently was present-day San Francisco, where with the help of friendly Indians he spent a month resting and preparing for the voyage across the Pacific.

On July 25, Drake set sail for the Moluccas with only the crudest instruments. After sixty-eight days without sight of land, he hit the Carolines, and went on to the Philippines and Indonesia. From there he set his compass for the Cape of Good Hope, from which it was a simple matter to sail up the African coast and back to Plymouth. He went to Deptford, the port where Queen Elizabeth came aboard and knighted him.

Soon he was at sea again and plundering the Spaniards. His most flamboyant achievement was his entering of the harbor of Cadiz, where he burned more than ten thousand tons of shipping, a feat he always referred to as "singeing the beard of the Spanish King." His exploit delayed the sailing of the Spanish Armada for a whole year.

When the Armada finally arrived, Drake was playing a game of bowls, and refused to interrupt the game, saying there was time to finish it and to beat the Spaniards too. At the critical moment he was aboard his ship, ready to fight a critical battle. The rest of the English sea dogs were ready too.

Drake fought a running battle all the way up to Calais, where the Armada came to anchor. He set eight of his own vessels on fire and let the wind drift them in among the Armada. In panic the Spaniards cut their cables and the utmost confusion reigned. Not a single enemy ship had been set on fire, but they had run into each other, others had run aground, and when daylight broke the Spanish formation had been entirely disrupted and the English were after them. All day the battle raged off Gravelines.

During the night a storm came up which finally dispersed the Armada. In the tempest Spanish vessels sailed north to pass around the tip of Scotland, and many were wrecked on the coasts of Scotland and Ireland. Spaniards who ran out of water landed in western Ireland, and many were killed. Of the 135 ships that had made up the Armada only about sixty returned to Spanish waters. England was safe from invasion.

Sir Francis Drake, needless to say, was not through fighting the Spaniards and he died a fitting death six years later—at sea, on board his flagship, prowling the Spanish Main.

SIR WALTER RALEIGH

[1552?–1618]

Whenn Sir Walter Raleigh set out on the series of adventures which led to the colonization of Virginia, named by him for the "Virgin Queen," Elizabeth I, he stood at the height of her favor. Tall and handsome, caressing of manner and quick of wit, he had first attracted the Queen's attention by stripping from his shoulders a handsome plush mantle and spreading it on the ground before her that she might cross a muddy spot without "defiling her feet." Then one day when he saw that the Queen's eyes were upon him, he went to a window and with his diamond ring scratched on the pane of glass, "Fain would I climb, but that I fear to fall!" Elizabeth went to see what he had written and beneath it wrote, "If thy heart fail, then do not climb at all."

He became one of the Queen's most intimate favorites. Elizabeth never gave him any great office of state, but she showered lands and wealth upon him. Few men better exemplified the energy, diversity, and splendor of her reign than this charming poet, brave soldier, and accomplished courtier.

Sir Walter Raleigh appeared at a time when the two great movements, the Renaissance and the Reformation, culminated in England. Literature, philosophy, and the arts had been transformed by startling new ideas spreading out from Italy. Religion had moved into a fresh epoch with the revolt of Martin Luther. Above all in the story of Walter Raleigh, Columbus had discovered the New World and opened it to European colonization.

Raleigh rose to favor with his Queen when he commanded a regiment during the war in Ireland. Elizabeth was so pleased that she made him Captain of the Queen's Guards. He spent what money he had on fine clothes and was soon one of the most gaily bedecked

courtiers who flocked around the Virgin Queen. Then came the incident of the cloak and the full favor of Elizabeth, who rewarded
him a thousandfold for his quick-witted gallantry.

Appointed Lord Lieutenant of Cornwall and Vice-Admiral of
England, with the right to engage in privateering, Raleigh plunged
into those ventures in American colonization which are his chief
claim to fame. He dispatched an expedition to Virginia under his
cousin, Sir Richard Grenville, who, on the return voyage, got into a
fight with twenty-four Spanish ships and captured three. Raleigh
sent another expedition to America in 1587 under Captain John
White. It was made up of 150 persons, including seventeen women.
One of these was White's daughter, the mother of Virginia Dare,
the first child of English parents born in what is today the United
States. This colonization failed. The colony vanished. But the trail
was blazed for future successes by others. To settle Virginia, named
by Raleigh, was his great idea.

Then, early in 1588, came the Spanish Armada. Commander
Howard of Effingham, ably seconded by his lieutenants, Francis
Drake, Martin Frobisher, and Walter Raleigh, led the royal navy to
the attack, to victory. Raleigh shared in the booty to the extent of
four thousand pounds and a heavy gold chain from the Queen.

Despite all the favors he had received, Sir Walter Raleigh was
never satisfied, and the Queen got a little tired of his greed. One day
she remarked, "When will you cease to be a beggar, Raleigh?" But
she smiled on him when he replied, "When you, madam, cease to be
a benefactress." But there were rivals for Elizabeth's favor, especially
the Earl of Essex. Raleigh and Essex hated each other, and oddly
each fell from royal favor by marrying against the Queen's wishes.
Raleigh even spent some time in the Tower of London for his
boldness.

But he was too able and too winning to be left unemployed. His
next assignment was to explore the coast and rivers of Guiana. He
sailed up the Orinoco for three hundred miles, and on his return to
England wrote a vivid account, mixed with a great deal of romance,
his *Discovery of Guiana,* which not only pleased the Queen but was
so popular that it was translated into many languages.

Raleigh played a part in the expedition to Cadiz which looted that
Spanish seaport. The Queen restored him to his old footing at court.

He was there when Essex made a desperate attempt to raise a rebellion in London, failed, and was condemned to death. Captain of the Guard Sir Walter Raleigh presided at the execution of his rival.

The death of Queen Elizabeth two years later ruined Raleigh when he seemed at the height of his fortunes. James I disliked him, suspected him of treason, and had him imprisoned again in the Tower. After one of the most unfair trials on record, marked by the brutal prosecution conducted by Sir Edward Coke, Sir Walter was sentenced to death, but the sentence was commuted and he remained a prisoner.

For thirteen years Sir Walter Raleigh lived in the Tower. His existence was not unpleasant and he both conducted scientific experiments and worked at a history of the world. But he wanted his freedom. Playing upon the King's cupidity, he promised to bring back much gold if he were allowed to lead another expedition to Guiana. The bait worked. At sixty-five, Raleigh was a free man—free to go exploring in South America, on pain of returning with golden treasure.

As the expedition sailed, Raleigh knew that King James had promised Spain to have him executed should he attack Spanish settlements or commit piracy against Spanish ships. Unfortunately Raleigh was stricken with fever, and the man to whom he gave command of the Orinoco expedition burned a Spanish town in retaliation for an ambush that killed some of his men. To crown Raleigh's misfortunes, no gold was found. He had failed.

He returned to England knowing what would happen. James had him arrested and ordered the death sentence to be carried out. Raleigh met his end like a brave man. As he mounted the scaffold he felt the executioner's axe and said, "This is sharp medicine, but it is a sure cure for all disease." Then he laid his head upon the block and told the executioner, "Strike, man, strike! What dost thou fear?"

GALILEO

[1564–1642]

THE year 1564 was a notable one in world history, although no
one knew it at the time. It was the year Shakespeare was born—
possibly the greatest of writers. It was the year Galileo was born—
possibly the greatest of scientists. We know too little about Shakespeare. But we know a great deal about Galileo Galilei.

His father opposed the career for which he was fated, and forbade
him to study mathematics. Not that the elder Galilei was blind to
the attractions of mathematical science—quite the reverse. He was a
good musician, a member of the group of amateurs who in Florence
invented the opera, and he had some ability at mathematics. But he
was poor. He could not see his son making a living outside the pro-
fessions. Hence it was that Galileo, his schooling completed, was sent
to the University of Pisa to study medicine.

He was a seventeen-year-old medical student at Pisa when
promptly there occurred one of the famous episodes of science.
Archimedes in the bathtub, Newton watching the apple fall—these
are companion pieces to Galileo and the pendulum. He was in the
cathedral one day, the beautiful duomo of Pisa. He was devoutly
religious, but his devotional thoughts were distracted. His eye fell
on the chandelier hanging above the altar—it was swinging. A gust
of wind from an open door had set it in motion, and the resplendent
chandelier oscillated slowly back and forth. Since the beginning of
mankind people had seen things swing back and forth, but nobody
had ever observed, or at least noted down, what the seventeen-year-
old medical student now saw.

Into his mind, always vividly perceptive and responsive, came the
realization that the cathedral chandelier took the same time for each
swing. After being set in motion by the wind, its oscillations slowed

down—but, fast or slow, each swing took the same amount of time. Galileo checked this with his pulse. He understood—each swing of the chandelier was slower, but at the same time each was shorter and covered less distance. The decrease in speed was exactly compensated for by the decrease in distance.

Galileo had discovered the fundamental law of the isochronism of the pendulum. He had made a basic discovery in physics before he had ever studied physics. He had timed the cathedral chandelier with his own pulse beats, and now thought of applying the pendulum as an instrument for timing the pulse. Moreover, he foresaw the application of the pendulum to clocks, though the actual construction of a pendulum clock was not achieved until later by Huygens. All of which was a clue to Galileo's essential genius—a profound understanding of theoretical implications, accompanied by a keen awareness of the practical side.

The parental plan for the son to have a medical career was badly damaged by the pendulum episode, and then was completely ruined by another accident. One day at the University of Pisa the student of medicine chanced to overhear a lesson in geometry. His interest was inflamed. He begged his father to allow him to study mathematics. The alarmed parent refused but the youth implored so insistently that he won a reluctant consent.

Young Galileo was permitted to have tutoring in mathematics. Whereupon it was soon evident that he had become so absorbed in mathematical studies that medicine had gone out of his mind. The chagrined father had the tutor dismissed, but it was too late. Galileo had learned enough to go on by himself. He mastered everything in Euclid and all the mathematics then available, after which he set himself to apply his theoretical knowledge to the study of nature.

He never completed his term as a student at Pisa. Family finances, so much the worry of the father, declined so far that the means were lacking to keep him there. He received, in any case, little credit at the university, where study consisted of memorizing Aristotle. Any tendency to doubt accepted theory was frowned upon, and from the first Galileo refused to accept any scientific fact on mere authority.

Returning to Florence, he gave all his time to researches in physics. He lectured before the Florentine Academy, and invented a hydrostatic balance. When he was twenty-four, he published a treatise on

GOETHE

MOZART

the center of gravity in solids. This was at the behest of his first patron, a nobleman eminent in science and a great influence. All his life thereafter Galileo had a succession of eminent patrons, nobles, ecclesiastics, princes, and popes. This was a dominating factor in the pageant and drama of his career.

He returned to the University of Pisa, this time as a lecturer in mathematics. There he enacted another great scene in the history of science, one of the most famous and dramatic of experiments. Characteristically it was a dramatic refutation of an age-old idea, one taken for granted for centuries. It was, at the same time, a spectacular demonstration of a basic fact in physics—the truth about falling bodies.

From Aristotle had been derived the notion that a heavier body falls faster than a body of lesser weight, gravitation pulling the heavier body more strongly than the lighter body and therefore with greater speed. This seemed more or less a matter of common sense, and was in line with Aristotle's basic theory of gravitation—the idea that things seek their natural places, the natural place of anything heavy being down, a heavier object seeking its natural place more strongly than a lighter object and therefore with greater speed.

It is untrue that Aristotle's theory had never been questioned. During the later Middle Ages there were scholars at the University of Paris who sought for a non-Aristotelian explanation of falling bodies. The real point is that they all failed. Aristotle held sway until Galileo came along.

Galileo had a flair for doing things in the grand manner. At the ancient city of Pisa there was an edifice theatrically adapted for the purpose of the experiment, the renowned Leaning Tower. A straight tower would not have served so well for the dropping weights, for they might have bounced off the walls. But at the side toward which the Leaning Tower leaned there was ample open space from the top to the ground below. A great crowd of university professors and students was assembled to behold. Galileo, at the top of the Leaning Tower, dropped two weights simultaneously, one of ten pounds, the other one pound. Both hit the ground at the same instant. This was a shocker—Aristotle was wrong. Save for such interference as the resistence of air, all bodies, no matter what their weight, fell at equal speed.

Galileo worked out the mathematics of falling bodies, the rate of fall. He found that the speed varies with the square of the time, which gives our familiar schoolbook formula—16 feet the first second, with an addition of 32 feet for every second thereafter. From this principle he worked out the basic mathematics of projectiles, and determined that the trajectory of a projectile is a parabola.

He experimented with inclined planes, and found that, if a ball rolls down a slope and then up a slope in a continuous path, the distance it rolls down one will be the same distance it rolls up the other —except for some small discrepancy due to friction or air resistance. If a ball, after rolling down a slope, continues on a level plane, it will simply keep going—and will only stop finally because of friction and air resistance.

Aristotle taught that the normal condition of a body was to be stationary, at rest, without motion. That was in accord with ordinary observation and common sense. On this earth moving things come to rest, sooner or later, their movement diminishing until they are motionless. We know now that this is because of factors that intervene to check motion—resistance of the air, friction, gravitation. Before the importance of these factors was realized, however, it was natural to think that all moving bodies anywhere would come to a stop sooner or later, unless there was some force to put them into motion and a continued application of force to keep them in motion.

This false hypothesis, held for many a long century, made any advance in the science of dynamics impossible, and dynamics could only come into its own when the true theory of inertia was established. Galileo performed the task.

He enunciated the basic law of motion—that a body will remain at rest until acted upon by some force, but a body in motion will remain in motion, at the same rate of speed and in a straight line, until acted upon by some force. Hence the Galilean theory of inertia—the tendency of a body either to remain at rest or to continue in motion at the same speed and in the same direction. Thus inertia is equal to the force it takes to set a body in motion or to alter its rate or direction of motion.

This immediately answered one major problem of astronomy. According to the Copernican theory, planets moved around the sun, and satellites moved around planets. But what caused them to move?

Why didn't they slow down and stop, according to the inertia theory of Aristotle? Copernicus, astronomer and mathematician, had reckoned only with the movements of the heavenly bodies and had reasoned on purely mathematical grounds. His thought had been limited to geometry, to the mathematics of celestial motion. He had not considered the dynamics of the matter—why the planets revolving around the sun, and the moon revolving around the earth, did not slow down and come to a stop. That was left for Galileo. According to his hypothesis, a body in motion will stay in motion, unless there is something to check it. So, naturally, the planets out in open space, with nothing to check them, keep moving right along, eternally.

But that left something else to be explained. His theory of motion held that a body tends to move in a straight line, while the planets and the moon, going around and around, move in more or less circular orbits. This discrepancy Galileo never explained, though in his mind seems to have hovered the idea of gravitation, some dim intuition of the theory later set forth by Newton, whose theory of universal gravitation completed the classic theoretical basis of the Copernican system.

Galileo's results were revolutionary, and so was the method by which he achieved them. He was the first great experimenter, a research scientist in the most modern sense. His approach to the study of nature had been foreshadowed by the miraculous Leonardo da Vinci, who had kept his brooding thoughts to the secrecy of his notebooks and whose fabulous scientific intuitions were not to be published until centuries afterward. Other experimenters had preceded Galileo, the alchemists and the iatrochemists and sundry bold innovators in physics, like Gilbert, physician to Queen Elizabeth I.

In Galileo's own day, Sir Francis Bacon was developing his own experimental philosophy, though he himself put nothing into practice by way of actual research. Bacon's experimental philosophy was extreme, holding as it did that the proper method of scientific advance was endlessly compounded experiment and little else. Bacon seems to have thought that all one had to do was to perform enough experiments, and the truths of nature would disclose themselves more or less automatically.

Galileo's method was different, far more modern. He too advocated experiment on all points, and practiced what he preached in prolonged arduous research, but he constantly gave experiment a mathematical treatment. He held that the proper method of physics was to interpret experiment mathematically. The stupendous success of physical science during subsequent centuries has been based on a constant interweaving of experiment with theory, and in Galileo's mind theory was essentially mathematical. This makes him the methodological starting point of modern physics, which always tends to be mathematical physics.

He had still another great gift, which served him both well and badly, a gift of words. He knew how to express his thoughts in superlative fashion, with great clearness and vigor, also with rough force and sarcasm. Impetuous and effective in controversy, he cut his antagonists with satire and mockery, the scorn of the clear fact against the foggy supposition. With his formidable powers of disputation, he plunged willingly into bellicose argument, and had a long life of it. He enjoyed the support of friends and patrons among the great, but his endless controversies established enmities as important as his friendships.

The opposition to Galileo began with his experiments at the University of Pisa, opposition so vehement that he was compelled to give up his post as lecturer in mathematics. Other professors, teaching Aristotelian physics, could only regard him as an enemy subverting their profession and livelihood. He went to the University of Padua as professor of mathematics. At Padua he remained for eighteen years, teaching, experimenting, theorizing. These years were his happiest, until new discoveries threw him into the maelstrom.

His work at Padua consisted of the development of his theories of dynamics, miscellaneous researches along various lines, and the invention of scientific devices. One of his first was the thermometer. It was a crude affair that was based on the principle that heat causes various substances to expand, and therefore the amount of expansion can be used to measure the degree of heat. Galileo at first employed water, and then found that alcohol was better. Later mercury was recognized as the best for general purposes, and so we have the mercury thermometer of today.

In 1610, when Galileo was forty-six, he came upon an idea that was to lead to the spectacular drama of his life. In Padua he picked up a rumor from distant Holland. Some traveler told him that a Dutch lens maker had found a way to make distant objects appear to be nearer by the use of lenses. The Dutch optician had hit upon what amounted to the principle of the telescope.

Lenses for magnification were known in the Middle Ages. Roger Bacon, that medieval marvel of science in the thirteenth century, describes a magnifying glass, a primitive lens used to enlarge writing, a reading glass. A portrait dating back to the middle of the fourteenth century shows a cardinal with two lenses mounted with a handle, like a lorgnette—the beginning of spectacles. With the development of printing and the multiplication of books, spectacles assumed their present place in life. Lens makers multiplied, and it was inevitable that sooner or later somebody would hit on the fact that if you look through two lenses of a certain kind, these being held a certain distance apart, you could magnify distant objects and appear to bring them closer. The first one to do this, as far as we know, was the Dutch lens maker Jan Lippershey.

Galileo worked out the optical theory, and made a telescope by mounting his lenses in a tube. With this things were brought nearer, a distant church steeple, the mountains—and the moon. Crude as his telescope was, he could distinguish the mountains and valleys of the queen of the night.

His invention became known as "the magic glass." It was copied and turned to practical uses, for instance by the Venetians, who could spy approaching ships two hours before they became visible to the naked eye. But for Galileo the key thing was scientific investigation. He did research, made calculations, and ended by constructing a telescope that had a magnification of thirty diameters. Then he studied the night sky.

New celestial phenomena became instantly visible. Having seen the mountains and valleys of the moon Galileo continued with a series of startling observations—sunspots, the rings of Saturn, the phases of Venus, the moons of Jupiter, vast numbers of new stars hitherto unseen, the character of the Milky Way as a sheen of innumerable faint stars. Two of these discoveries were of especial revolutionary import —sunspots and the moons of Jupiter.

In Aristotle's philosophy the sun figured as perfection, its face pure and unblemished. But Galileo through his telescope saw blotches on the disc of the sun. Today sunspots are a commonplace, but in those times they were a startling refutation of Aristotle and his theory of solar perfection. The moons of Jupiter, more revolutionary still, led to the climax of the drama of Galileo. The moons of Jupiter were visible proof of the truth of the Copernican theory.

All along Galileo had been inclined to hold the Copernican view that the earth and other planets moved around the sun, not the sun around the earth. Copernicus had given his theory to the world more than fifty years before, but the newfangled doctrine had made but little progress. It presented theoretical difficulties, and was not backed up by sufficient observed fact. Galileo himself, when he had discovered his basic laws of motion, had provided the theory of dynamics necessary for the Copernican system, but he had refrained from advocating the new doctrine. It would appear that he held back mostly for fear of ridicule. Probably Galileo felt there was simply not enough factual evidence to justify championing the Copernican theory merely to be laughed at. That is—until he saw the moons of Jupiter.

According to heliocentric doctrine, the planets move around the sun, and the moon around the earth, our own planet. Studying Jupiter through his telescope, Galileo saw new tiny stars near that bright planet. Observing them night after night, he saw them change position in such fashion that there was no doubt: they were revolving around Jupiter, moons of Jupiter. So there, before his own eyes, was the Copernican theory in action. There was no doubt about it now, and Galileo came forth with the advocacy and the evidence that established once and for all the dizzy revolution in man's concept of the cosmos.

In 1611, the year after he first turned the telescope on the sky, Galileo took his magic glass to the papal court in Rome. There he was received with enthusiasm by the highest prelates, which encouraged him to declare himself fully and formally on the Copernican theory. However, the notion of the earth's moving around the sun had points of religious difficulty, and this was a time of religious wars and fierce intolerance. Galileo defended Copernicus in a powerful book. He immediately came under attack. This was inevitable. The orthodox professors, whose astronomical teachings were upset by the heliocentric doctrine, rose in wrath, and the religious point was brought up. Had not Joshua commanded the sun to stand still?

Galileo did not back down. He argued that the Bible itself gave confirmation of the heliocentric view, and sought to interpret scriptural passages in a Copernican light. This drew a warning from Rome, unofficial advice to stick to physical science and avoid theological speculation. Later, theologians in Rome proclaimed that the heliocentric theory was heretical, and the Pope enjoined Galileo to discontinue teaching the forbidden doctrine. He promised to obey, and for some years remained quietly in Florence, continuing his telescopic observations.

In 1623 occurred an event that seemed to Galileo the height of good fortune. It was a papal election, and the prelate who became Urban VIII was a scholar and an intimate friend of Galileo's. As Cardinal he had disapproved of the theological order outlawing the Copernican theory and forbidding Galileo to propound it. Now he was head of the Church. Whereupon Galileo promptly published another defense of Copernicus, and had it printed in Rome with a dedication to the new Pope. The book was acclaimed by the ecclesiastical authorities as well as by scientists.

With this encouragement, he returned to Florence, and embarked on the writing of his most famous work, *The Dialogue of the Two Systems of the World.* In this the Copernican view was shown to be true, the old Ptolemaic system false. For its publication, papal permission was procured, the Pope merely requiring that the Copernican theory be presented as a hypothesis rather than as incontrovertible truth.

The book displayed all Galileo's gift for dialectic argument, brilliant disputation, scathing retort. The book won universal applause from the progressive thought in Europe, but aroused equal anger among the opponents of the Copernican theory. The hostile outcry could seem of only little import to Galileo—for had he not the support of the Roman pontiff?

What went awry has been a subject of endless discussion. Apparently the Pope was led to believe that he was ridiculed in the book, that some Ptolemaic arguments with which he had furnished Galileo were presented in an absurd light. Moreover pressures from the academic world and from the theologians may have persuaded the papal mind. In any case, there was a change, and Galileo's friend and onetime disciple supported action by Vatican authorities who charged Galileo with violation of his previous pledge not to uphold the Copernican theory. Thus it was that Galileo was summoned before the Inquisition in Rome.

He was treated with consideration, but was found guilty, and promised leniency if he would recant. Galileo, at sixty-nine, was too old and tired to fight back. He placed his hand on the Gospels and recited a formula, cursing and repudiating the heliocentric theory of a moving earth. Legend has made much of what he is supposed to have said as he turned away: *"E pur si muove"* ("And yet it does move").

The punishment inflicted on Galileo for heresy was mild. Condemned to imprisonment, he was allowed to reside in the palace of a friend, the Archbishop of Siena. Later he was permitted to return to Florence and live in the seclusion of his villa. He continued scientific researches, writing and digesting his early experiments in dynamics and studying the sky through his telescope.

His last five years were spent in blindness. Vision failed those eyes which had been the first to gaze through a telescope at the sky. Still he continued his intellectual labors. He maintained a great scientific correspondence with the savants of Europe, pouring forth new thoughts on the experiments he had made and on the celestial sights he had seen through his telescope. He suggested the use of a pendulum for the mechanism of clocks—the pendulum which harked back to the day when, in his seventeenth year, he had watched the chandelier swinging back and forth in the cathedral of Pisa. He was dictating scientific matter to two disciples—one of whom was Torricelli, inventor of the barometer—when he was seized with the fever that carried him off in his seventy-eighth year.

CAPTAIN JOHN SMITH

[1580–1631]

CAPTAIN JOHN SMITH was the most colorful of the English adventurers who visited America during the early colonial era. Brave and capable, endowed with the gift of command, he descended often enough to the level of the braggart and the brawler. When he recounted his exploits in word or print, he never let the truth interfere with a good story. Yet the plain facts would have been startling enough, and John Smith deserves a place among the fathers of America.

His early life, as he described it, was full of romantic escapades and hairbreadth escapes. Beginning as an apprentice in London he ran away to sea, after which he turned up in France serving as a soldier under King Henry IV—the celebrated Henry of Navarre. After helping Henry IV win the throne of France, John Smith, according to his own testimony, sailed for Rome from Marseilles aboard a pilgrim ship. The pious pilgrims, discovering that he was a heretic, threw him overboard, and he only survived because a passing ship picked him up and landed him in Egypt. He managed to get passage to Italy, helped his shipmates capture a Venetian galley, saw Rome, then went on to fight the Turks in Hungary and Transylvania. Captured by the Turks he became a slave. He escaped by killing his master, dressing in his clothes, and riding away on his horse. So, after more adventures, John Smith arrived back in England in 1605.

He now plunged into the business of colonizing the New World. Already known as Captain John Smith, he found a place with the expedition that founded Jamestown. Captain Newport's flagship, the "Susan Constant," carried a sealed box to be opened only after land was reached. When the expedition arrived at what is now Hampton Roads the seals were broken, and the box was found to contain a document setting forth regulations for the new colony and naming a board of seven to govern it. Among the seven names was that of Captain John Smith.

Unfortunately Captain John Smith was then in irons, in the brig, charged with "faultfinding and fomenting dissension." Finding his name on the list of governors, Captain Newport had Smith released, but decided to watch him closely. Once on land Captain John Smith proved a tower of strength. When the small band of colonists was attacked by Indians, he not only beat off the attack but settled the Indians' grievances and made friends with them. Jamestown was built within a month, or rather a small fort and a few shacks were erected where Jamestown now stands. After Captain Newport sailed back to England, Smith's ability soon put him in control of the colony. Most of those who had joined the expedition had done so in the hope of finding gold. Their food supplies soon ran out and in a country teeming with game and fish the colonists were going hungry.

Captain John Smith organized food-seeking expeditions into the interior. He penetrated more than a hundred miles inland, explored and mapped the coast line of Virginia and the James River, and engaged in trade with the Indians. It was on one of these expeditions that the most romantic episode in Smith's life occurred—presuming that the story is true.

During a trading expedition, some of the colonists began a fight with the red men, who killed three of them and carried Captain John Smith away as a prisoner. Brought before Chief Powhatan, the captive was condemned to death. Here, in Smith's own words, is what happened: "Having feasted him after their best barbarous manner, a long consultation was held after which two great stones were brought before Powhatan and as many as could lay hands on Smith dragged him to them and thereon laid his head. And being ready with their clubs to beat out his brains, Pocahontas, the king's dearest daughter, when no entreaty could prevail, got his head into her arms and laid her own upon his to save him from death. Whereat Powhatan was contented Smith should live."

At the time of this incident, Pocahontas was only thirteen years old. She later married John Rolfe, who took her to England where the Indian princess created a great sensation. She was presented to the King and Queen, but died of pneumonia in London in 1617.

Back at Jamestown, Captain John Smith labored to save the colony. He managed it by enforcing a policy of "no work, no food," and brought the colonists "through ordeals of peril, hardship and starvation" by his will power and resourcefulness. Under his guidance Jamestown turned the corner toward a prosperous future. The great history of the English in America had begun.

In 1614, Captain John Smith sailed for New England, of which he wrote a description and "first made the resources of the region favorably known to the English public." He was responsible for giving New England its name. He wanted to join the Pilgrims aboard the "Mayflower," but his flamboyant past was too much for the devout Puritan conscience to overlook. Thus he lost his chance for what might have been the crowning event of his career. Imagine the rowdy Captain John Smith swaggering around Plymouth! Instead he remained in London, living placidly for the rest of his life.

RICHELIEU

[1585–1642]

T HE figure Cardinal Richelieu cut is one of the most familiar in
history: tall, thin with an emaciated face, mustache, and small
beard, tight lips and cold piercing eyes. He was racked with illness all
his life, but had a formidably commanding presence that could make
the proudest noble defer. In the dramatic red robe of a Roman cardinal he stands in the picture gallery of history as the personification
of the strength of human will.

As a younger son he was destined for the Church, and became an
ordained priest at the age of twenty-one. Almost immediately, due
to the influence of his father, he received the bishopric of Luçon, to
accept which he needed a papal dispensation because he was under
the canonical age usually demanded of bishops.

Richelieu's election to the States-General of 1614 (the last popular assembly convened in France before the Revolution) started him
along the road to political power. The States-General accomplished
little, but it lasted long enough for the Bishop of Luçon to catch the
attention of Marie de' Medici, mother of young King Louis XIII. He
soon appeared at court as her adviser, only to fall from power when
Louis XIII, now sixteen, suddenly rebelled against the power of his
mother and the men around her.

For five years Richelieu suffered through political exile at Luçon.
During this period he made up his mind that France would have to
have a strong central government, for virtual civil war raged between
the partisans of Marie de' Medici and the partisans of Louis XIII.
At the end mother and son were reconciled to some degree. The
Queen Mother at once summoned the Bishop of Luçon back to court.
Largely through her support he was named a cardinal of the Catholic
Church, and rose in the administration of the kingdom to become

chief minister to the King in 1624. For the next eighteen years France and Cardinal Richelieu would be almost synonymous terms.

The policy of Richelieu, like that of any other national policy, had two facets—domestic and foreign. He began with the nobles, whose anarchy was illustrated amply in the story of his own rise to power. These magnates, in their castles, had established themselves as autonomous rulers of their own provinces; they had military forces of their own and were thus able to wage war against the King. Against this anarchic power Richelieu struck, reforming the system of provincial government and diminishing the authority of the territorial lords. He issued an order for the destruction of all castles save such as were needed by the nation for defense from foreign enemies. Edict after edict was issued, prefaced by the formula of royal absolution, "Such is Our pleasure." The nobles banded in wrathful opposition, but resistance was ruthlessly crushed by military force.

Richelieu also brought to a culmination the problem of the Huguenots. This Cardinal of the Roman Church was no bigot. His view of the Protestants in France was coldly political. In ending the religious wars, Henry IV, through the Edict of Nantes, had granted to the Huguenots full religious toleration and the possession of various strongholds, the chief of which was the sea fortress of La Rochelle. It was this semi-independent possession that ran counter to the policy of Richelieu. The Huguenots, like the great nobles, were able to play an autonomous role, and were, in Richelieu's view, a state within a state. He demanded a modification of the political privileges of the Huguenots, and this brought on war.

The principal event was the siege of La Rochelle. The position was powerful, the defense stubborn. England sought to aid the defenders, but the intervention by English warships was halfhearted and ineffectual. Richelieu's inflexibility was illustrated by his military strategy. He had a mole thrown with vast labor across the entrance of the harbor, a sea wall that prevented the entrance of English warships, and La Rochelle was starved into surrender. The Huguenots subdued completely, the statesmanship of Richelieu was shown by his moderation. He abolished the political autonomy of the Huguenots, but reaffirmed the Edict of Nantes, granting them full religious freedom.

Richelieu now seemed supreme but immediately encountered a

crisis of intrigue that nearly brought about his downfall. This was
the Day of Dupes.

The Queen Mother, Marie de' Medici, had turned against her
former protégé because he acted too independently. She urged her
son to get rid of his chief minister. At the climactic moment Louis
XIII seemed about to agree with her. They were in the Queen Mother's private apartments when Richelieu, in violation of all court etiquette, entered. Marie de' Medici was furious, and demanded that
the King choose between his minister and his mother. Louis XIII
dismissed Richelieu, who left uncertain of his fate. The nobles of
the court were convinced that the Cardinal had fallen. They were
the dupes on the Day of Dupes. That evening the King took counsel
with two grave advisers, friends of Richelieu, and before the Day of
Dupes was over Louis XIII received the Cardinal and assured him
of his continued support.

During these vicissitudes in domestic affairs Richelieu was pursuing a foreign policy which emphasized Germany. Religious strife in
Germany had culminated in an imperial effort to subdue the Protestant princes and bring about the supremacy and unified power of
the Hapsburg sovereign. It was Richelieu's aim to check this, and to
continue the religious division and promote the enfeeblement of Germany. A cardinal of the Roman Church, who had crushed the political power of the Protestants in France, he went to the aid of the
Protestants in Germany.

He gave subsidies to Gustavus Adolphus of Sweden for his victorious invasion of Germany to support the Protestants. When, after the
death in battle of the great Swedish warrior, the imperial cause was
on the rise again, Richelieu intervened more actively in behalf of the
Protestants and sent an army to help them. He died before the conclusion of the Peace of Westphalia, which sealed the success of his
policy—rights granted to the Protestant princes which kept Germany
divided until the time of Bismarck more than two centuries later.

Richelieu's health was always poor. His final illness was of short
duration. On December 1, 1642, at the zenith of his power, he realized his end was near. He sent for the curé of St. Eustache who
administered extreme unction and gave him the viaticum. "Do you
forgive your enemies?" asked the priest. "I have never had any save
those of France" was the instant reply.

Historians accept that answer. Cardinal Richelieu—the Terrible Cardinal, as his enemies called him—could be harsh, unyielding, and unmerciful, but only when he thought the good of the state was at stake. Otherwise he showed courtesy and aplomb to all who knew him. He patronized art and science. He founded the French Academy.

OLIVER CROMWELL

[1599–1658]

THERE's a legend which supposes that Oliver Cromwell, as a small boy, had played in childish games with the young prince who was destined to become Charles I. The time would come when Cromwell would send that sovereign to the headsman's block. Another story is that on the night after the execution of Charles, Cromwell gazed upon the face of the victim and murmured, "Cruel necessity." Thus does history place a dramatic focus on the personalities of the grim Puritan soldier and the unfortunate King.

The anecdotes follow from one undoubted truth. Cromwell came from a powerful and important family, so that at an early age he was accustomed to dealing with magnates of the realm. He himself showed no particular ability until the rebellion against the King erupted. Before that his mature existence was that of a country squire among many others. The most significant thing about him was his conversion to the Puritanism he would champion later on.

Committed to the Puritan cause, he made his house a refuge for persecuted preachers, trying to aid them within the law and enable them to get along financially. His piety was intense. He gave to the poor from his own pocket, and exhorted his farm hands to religion. An example of his attitude was his refusal to accept a knighthood, which was offered to him, and he was fined ten pounds for this implied rebuke to the King and the Established Church.

During these years, events in England were leading toward civil war between King and Parliament. In the Tudor period, under such monarchs as Henry VIII and Elizabeth I, the government of England had been a virtual despotism, with the authority of Parliament little more than nominal, although the Tudors gave heed to parliamentary forms. Then, under the Stuarts, Parliament had begun to assert itself increasingly during the reign of James I and in revolutionary fashion against Charles I. That monarch, lofty of spirit though politically obtuse, entertained a grandiose idea of the privileges and duties of the Crown and the divine rights of kings, while Parliament countered with pretensions of its own.

The political cleavage had its counterpart in bitter religious divisions. King and Royalists supported the Anglican Church, which ecclesiastical establishment stood for national religious unity under its own hierarchy. The parliamentary faction was identified largely with the Puritans, who represented extreme Protestantism within the Anglican fold, and were intensely hostile toward the prelates of the Established Church and their adherence to traditions of medieval ecclesiasticism. Allied with the Puritans against King and Church, though sometimes at odds with them, were the Presbyterians of Scotland, a country that had been joined with England through the accession of the Scottish King to the English throne. The mixed political and religious character of the conflict was exemplified, with tragic circumstance, in the trial and execution of the royal minister, the Earl of Stafford, and of Archbishop Laud, both sent to their doom by Parliament.

This was the Long Parliament, so called for the time it lasted, which was summoned after Charles I had ruled for eleven years with no Parliament at all. The new House of Commons was in a defiant mood, and one of its members was Oliver Cromwell, representing the town of Cambridge.

In the Long Parliament, Cromwell became immediately an influential figure. No orator, he played no showy part, but his strength and resolution made people listen to the counsel he gave, and he was active and effective in the work of committees. Soon he was a power in the political quarrel, the complexities of which were dominated by questions of taxation, the power of the purse, and in the religious conflict over the supremacy of the Established Church. Cromwell joined vociferously in the Puritan demand for religious liberty, but was equally with the Puritans in interpreting freedom of conscience in terms of their own dominance and intolerance.

Events drifted to civil war, which became inevitable when Parliament presented demands claiming supreme power virtually, a program which Charles I could not accept. The King left London, and with the Royalists prepared for war. So did Parliament, and Cromwell's parliamentary activity now concerned military measures. He assumed a prominent role in army affairs and, when war broke out, took an active part, though hitherto there had been little in his career to suggest military knowledge or ability. Oliver Cromwell has a foremost place in the list of civilians who, with little experience in the art of war, have revealed themselves suddenly as able commanders.

The Puritan squire went off to his own countryside and recruited a troop of horsemen. His role was to be that of cavalry commander, though his first company numbered only sixty. The civil war began with successes for the Royalists, but Cromwell's mounted troop distinguished itself for steadiness and discipline. He went home again, and recruited larger forces, until he had under his command a formidable cavalry unit. His power was in the discipline he imposed upon his soldiers, stern tactical training compounded with religious zeal. He said he wanted "such men as have the fear of God before them."

In an early encounter, they charged and defeated twice their number. At the Battle of Marston Moor, they smashed through on one wing, then wheeled around to save the day after the infantry had been routed by the Royalists. At Marston Moor, Cromwell's mounted Puritans were given their historic name. The King's cavalry was led by the dashing cavalier Prince Rupert, whose name flashes in history for gallantry and daring. Cromwell's Puritan horsemen prevailed over feats of chivalry, and Prince Rupert called them—Ironsides.

Again at Naseby the decision came when, as the parliamentary infantry was falling back, Cromwell's Ironsides won a cavalry victory, and then fell upon the enemy infantry. The cause of Charles I was lost.

The triumph of Parliament followed a military reorganization destined to have effects that Parliament never expected. The New Model Army, re-formed, trained, and disciplined along lines set forth by Cromwell, had a Puritanical morale and fanatical zeal that made it, not only one of the most efficient of war machines, but also a formidable instrument of political power. The New Model Army became the actual source of authority in England, and in it Cromwell was the dominant figure.

Defeated in the civil war, Charles I fled and took refuge with the

Scots, the native countrymen of the royal house of Stuart. The Scots were in the picture with the accent on religion, pressing the cause of their own national Presbyterian Church, founded by John Knox along the lines of Calvinism. The struggle between the Puritans and the Established Church was complicated by a quarrel between the Puritans and the Scottish Presbyterians, with complexities—theological, political, and military—of which the unfortunate Charles I was the chief victim. He was in the hands of a Presbyterian army, which sought to impose its own terms upon him, and compel him to accept a Presbyterian system of polity. Having gone to them as their guest, he was actually their captive, but even in his distress the King sought proudly to maintain the royal prerogatives of the House of Stuart. There were dickerings and negotiations, until finally the Scots came to an agreement with Parliament in London. Their army had not been paid, and large arrears were due. Parliament gave them the money, in return for which they handed over Charles I. Hence the bitter jibe that has come down through history—that the Scots sold their King.

Parliament, with the King in its power, sought to curb, not only the royal prerogative, but also its own military forces. Overshadowed by the New Model Army and its officers, Parliament proposed terms to the King whereby its authority would be supreme and the soldiery would be disbanded. But the New Model Army, with large arrears in pay, refused to be disbanded, and openly set itself up as a political power. Cromwell at first tried to fulfill his duty to Parliament, then joined the soldiers, who marched on London, coerced Parliament, and seized the King.

Cromwell was assigned to deal with Charles I, and made proposals for a reduction of the political authority of the Crown and an abolition of the King's control in religious matters. But Charles tried to take advantage of the quarrel between the army and Parliament, and dickered with Parliament. At this point Cromwell was moderate, seeking no overturn of the throne and holding a limited monarchy to be the best. The negotiations grew more intricate when Charles sought to play with a third party, the Scottish Presbyterians. He signed a treaty with the Scots. This caused both Cromwell and Parliament to break off negotiations with the King, and civil war broke out anew.

The Scots were in arms, and there were risings of Royalists in England. Once again Cromwell, at the head of the New Model Army, showed himself to be the greatest commander of the day. He put down the insurrection in England and marched into Scotland. There was a welter of campaigning and fighting, but the victory was Cromwell's.

This was followed by the doom of Charles I. The army demanded that he be tried and punished. Parliament was reluctant to take extreme measures against the sovereign, and the army replied with a military coup—a file of soldiers, commanded by Colonel Pride, invaded the Commons and drove out the members opposed to a trial of the King. The expelled members were a majority, and the minority left to do the army's bidding is known to history contemptuously as the Rump Parliament.

The proceedings that followed could be justified on no legal grounds. The Rump was a parliamentary farce, a council of military officers the real power. Cromwell was the dominant figure, and he was responsible for the trial and execution of Charles I. A tribunal was named for a trial, and the King was condemned and beheaded. Cromwell seems to have felt that this was compelled by harsh circumstance, as is illustrated by the story of how he gazed at the face of the executed victim and murmured, "Cruel necessity."

The Commonwealth was established. With the Rump Parliament a nonentity, the supreme authority was placed in the hands of a council named for life, though the real power lay in the New Model Army, commanded by Cromwell. Religious tolerance was granted to all except prelatists and papists, the old Anglican Church and the Roman Catholics. In this Cromwell followed the notions the Puritans held of religious tolerance, but he did show a breadth of mind by granting freedom to Quakers and Jews.

There was revolt in Ireland, where the Irish Catholics supported the royal cause, having little to expect from the Puritans except bitter persecution. Cromwell invaded the unhappy island, and the character of the warfare he waged was illustrated by the storming of Drogheda, where, at his command, the defenders were massacred and no mercy shown to Catholic priests. Cromwell carried fire and sword through Ireland in a similar way, with savage slaughters and ferocious religious persecution. He imposed on Ireland what is called the "Cromwellian Settlement," which reduced the Irish people to the depths of their age-long oppression; and, ever since, the name of Cromwell has been hated in Ireland.

Cromwell, returning from victories in Scotland, resumed his place as a member of Parliament, the Rump. He was voted a large pension and given a palace, Hampton Court. For a year and a half his career remained static; he was Captain General of the Army and an M.P. But proceedings in Parliament were less and less to his liking or that of the New Model Army. There were disagreements on religious matters and foreign policy, and a crisis was reached when the Rump schemed to perpetuate the status of its members by keeping them in a new Parliament that was to be summoned. Cromwell and the army objected, and took action. A file of soldiers marched into the legislative hall and drove out the Rump. Parliament, in its successful struggle against the monarchy, had created an instrument that had become its own master, a far stronger and more arbitrary master than the King had ever been.

Cromwell now assumed supreme power. There was some suggestion in the army that he be made King, the throne being so obviously a part of British political tradition. But Cromwell demurred, and accepted sovereign authority under the name of "Protector." Thus installed, he was the despotic ruler of England until his death five years later.

The other phase of Cromwell's career as Lord Protector was his foreign policy. A Puritan fanatic, he saw international relations in terms of religion, a continuance of the wars of religion. He was blind to the changes of the times, whereby the religious conflicts of the past were turning into commercial struggles. Hence he overlooked the imperial rivalry of Holland, preferring to fight Spain, which was already a declining power.

Long before the Lord Protector died, the English people were disgusted with dictatorship. When he was gone they declared joyfully for a return of the monarchy. Charles II came home, the Restoration began. The remains of Cromwell were disinterred and hanged ignominiously from the gallows. Since then historians have quarreled about his character and achievements, continuing extremes of love and hate that pursued Oliver Cromwell during his lifetime.

CHARLES II

[1630–1685]

No KING of England ever looked less of an Englishman than Charles II, dubbed the "Merry Monarch." His mother was Henrietta Maria, daughter of Henry IV of France and Marie de' Medici. His father, a Stuart son of Scottish James I and Anne of Denmark, was the ill-fated Charles I who died on the scaffold at the order of Oliver Cromwell. Of all these royal strains, the Italian prevailed, for no sign of Scottish or Danish blood was to be found in the appearance of Charles II, whose looks, bearing, and instincts stamped him as a descendant of Lorenzo the Magnificent, the great Renaissance Florentine.

The childhood of Charles II was peaceful enough until the Great Rebellion broke out. The quarrel between King Charles I and Parliament went on to an armed clash, and the young prince, barely out of his teens, fought in his father's cause. Cromwell's victory spelled death for Charles I, exile on the Continent for Charles II. Everyone in England wondered whether the monarchy would ever be restored.

As long as Cromwell lived, Charles II would have to fight his way back to London. Supported by the Scots, Charles invaded England and was defeated at Worcester, where he led his troops with great courage. Then followed a wonderful series of adventures in which Charles's cleverness and valor became famous. Once, at Boscobel, he took refuge in the branches of a great oak where he could look down on Cromwell's soldiers searching for him. It is now known as the "Royal Oak." Another time he rode for a day behind a lady of quality, disguised as her groom, humble Will Jackson. Everywhere he saw posters offering a reward of a thousand pounds for "the Discovery and Apprehending of Charles Stuart and Other Traytors, his Adherents and Abettors." Finally he escaped to France.

He lived a royal exile, making shift as well as he could, until after Cromwell's death. Then his chance came. Cromwell's son Richard was unable to fill the office of Protector, in which his father had ruled England. After less than a year, he abdicated and retired. George Monck, who had been one of Charles I's generals and who had later attached himself to Cromwell, saw that to avoid chaos it was necessary to restore the royal Stuarts to the throne. He marched into London and declared for a free Parliament. The people were tired of the dictatorship established by Cromwell, and went wild with joy. The bells of the churches pealed out the glad tidings. The gutters ran with wine and ale. Bonfires were lit on every hill. A new House of Commons was elected, and it invited Charles II to return to England, sending him a chest with 50,000 pounds in gold pieces. He landed at Dover on May 26, 1660, proceeded to London, and entered the royal residence at Whitehall on his thirtieth birthday.

The court was re-established with its old etiquette. His Majesty dined in state, served by noblemen, while ladies and gentlemen watched from the gallery. After dinner there was dancing. The women in flowing garments that billowed out, arms and bosoms bare, were less splendidly attired than the men in curled wigs, silks and laces, and velvet mantles trimmed with costly fur.

Charles was at the height of his popularity. The people loved him for his good nature, his urbanity, wit, and generosity. They were not disturbed by his many mistresses for it was a licentious time. The one who resented his behavior was the Queen, Catherine of Braganza, although she became resigned to it in time. Of all his mistresses, one still seems captivating after three centuries—Nell Gwynne, "pretty, witty Nell."

In 1662, Charles, in an attempt to secure toleration for religious minorities, issued a Declaration of Indulgence. This roused the strongly Anglican Parliament to pass the penal laws against non-Anglicans. After that, England never knew complete freedom of religion until the nineteenth century.

Two frightful disasters struck London during the reign of Charles II. First the plague—an epidemic that ran like wildfire through the overcrowded, unsanitary city. Close to a hundred thousand people died of the pestilence. A year later came the second calamity. The fire of London swept through about four fifths of the city, leaving a great heap of ashes in its path. Thousands of homeless were forced to camp out in the open fields surrounding the destruction.

However, the fire was a blessing in disguise. London was rebuilt. Wide streets lined with brick and stone took the place of narrow lanes with wooden houses. Sir Christopher Wren and other architects built beautiful churches, public buildings, and private homes, many of which are still in existence today. Wren produced the masterpiece of his career in the new St. Paul's, the splendid cathedral now known as "the parish church of the British Empire."

Charles was anxious to have a strong monarchy independent of Parliament, which meant that he had to have money from some other source. This was a main reason for his alliance with Louis XIV of France. By the secret Treaty of Dover, Charles was to keep England from joining the enemies of France, and in return was to receive over a hundred thousand pounds from the French treasury.

All through his reign Charles was suspected of being secretly a member of the Church of Rome. This suspicion was enhanced by the fact that his wife and his brother, the Duke of York (later, James II), were both devout Catholics. Charles certainly tried to help the Catholics. His moderation toward the Dissenters was part of a general plan to help those, including the Catholics, who suffered from the legislation in favor of the Church of England. He himself was no persecutor, and he reacted against persecution whenever he could.

In August of 1678 began the most atrocious persecution of his whole reign—the Popish Plot. Titus Oates, an unmitigated liar who was undoubtedly mentally unstable, swore that he knew about a Catholic conspiracy to seize the government, and his irresponsible accusations caused a panic, an anti-Catholic frenzy among the population. Many Catholics were tried and executed before reason could assert itself. Then Titus Oates was exposed and punished.

During the reign of Charles II there was great material and intellectual progress. Charles was too pleasure loving to concentrate deeply on public affairs, but he was remarkably intelligent and curious about new ideas. He dabbled in chemistry, and maintained a splendid laboratory which he permitted natural philosophers to use. He liked to pose problems for the scientists to solve. A group of these savants came together in an official body, and the King granted them a charter in 1662. This was the origin of the illustrious Royal Society.

LORD NELSON

ANDREW JACKSON

Charles enjoyed the theater and encouraged literature generally. He was a generous patron of poets and writers. English letters have enjoyed few periods when genius had freer play. Dryden, Congreve, Wycherley, Rochester, Otway, Pepys, Suckling, Oldham, Marvell, and a host of others gave to English the wit and sparkle that Molière and La Fontaine during the same period gave to French.

Politically Charles's reign was marked by a steady encroachment by Parliament on the rights and prerogatives of the Crown. The party names of Whig and Tory came into use. From the point of view of civil liberties the greatest achievement of the Restoration was the passage of the Habeas Corpus Act. By its provisions every prisoner was guaranteed the right to be tried within a given time of his arrest, and once released from a charge no person could be rearrested or tried again for the same offense.

In 1685, after reigning for twenty-five years, the Merry Monarch died very suddenly. On a Sunday he felt unwell, and the following day suffered a stroke of apoplexy. His brother James (heir to the throne since Charles had no legitimate children) brought him a priest in secret and he received extreme unction. The last words of Charles II were typical: "Don't let poor Nelly starve." His favorite mistress, "pretty, witty Nell Gwynne," was in his thoughts to the end.

LOUIS XIV

[*1638–1715*]

S ELDOM has the birth of a baby meant so much for a nation as the entrance into the world of the infant who would become Louis XIV. Louis XIII and his wife, Anne of Austria, had been childless for more than twenty years. It looked as though they would never produce an heir to the throne, and this raised the threat of civil strife and anarchy in France.

The threat was averted when Anne of Austria gave birth to a boy. Cannons boomed and church bells pealed in celebration, and the people sighed with relief. The popular feeling was illustrated by the nickname given promptly to the new heir to the crown, Louis Dieudonné, Louis the Gift of God.

The boyhood of Louis XIV was eventful and disturbed. Cardinal Richelieu died in 1642, after governing France for eighteen years, and Louis XIII died soon afterward. The new King was still a child, and his mother became regent. Another ecclesiastical statesman moved into Richelieu's place—Cardinal Mazarin. But Mazarin had little of Richelieu's ability, and France soon plunged into a civil war called the Fronde. It was a rising of lawyers and nobles bent on unseating Mazarin, who however weathered the storm with the support of Anne of Austria, and finally died knowing he was handing over a unified kingdom to the young King. It was 1661. The Age of Louis XIV was about to begin.

When his ministers asked him to whom they should submit their reports now that Mazarin was gone, Louis replied, "To me." The administration was to remain thus for over fifty years. The King served as his own prime minister to the end. The famous statement attributed to him, *"L'état c'est moi"* ("I am the state"), represented accurately his view. He regarded kingship as a trade, and worked hard at his trade.

Yet this diligent sovereign led a licentious life for years. As a youth he was infatuated with a young niece of Cardinal Mazarin's, Marie Mancini, and wanted to marry her. But reasons of state were too powerful for even a young king. Both the Cardinal and the Queen Mother were opposed, and insisted that Louis make a marriage of state. Hence Louis XIV was wedded to Maria Theresa, daughter of the King of Spain. It was strictly a marriage of convenience. The King neglected his wife for twenty years, and her place was taken by a succession of mistresses.

The first was Louise de la Vallière, young, blonde, blue-eyed, beautiful. She was devoted to Louis, and when she was superseded she retired to a convent and became a nun. The most notorious of the numerous bevy of King's mistresses was Mme. de Montespan, a woman of bold intelligence and ambition, who reigned over the palace for years, and wielded a proud influence. There were sinister stories about her—that she dabbled in black magic, and participated in sinister rites of sorcery. Montespan was the chief scandal of the reign of Louis XIV.

Finally came Mme. de Maintenon, who presents a very different picture. She was a governess in the royal family, intelligent, but plain of looks, austere in manner, and devoutly religious. The relationship between Louis and Mme. de Maintenon signalized the change that came over the King in about his fortieth year. After a youth of notorious licentiousness, he turned to religion and became intensely devout. In this he found pious Mme. de Maintenon an apt companion. After the death of the Queen, he married her morganatically, and they spent their life together with the propriety of a bourgeois husband and wife.

To help him run the state, Louis XIV gathered a circle of able administrators, diplomats, and soldiers. Of these the most important was Jean Baptiste Colbert, who headed the Department of Finance. Colbert became one of the greatest administrators in French history. He took over not only the finances but most of the business of internal affairs, besides building up the navy and assisting in the founding and developing of colonies overseas. One of his greatest triumphs was the canal of Languedoc, which completed the waterways between the Atlantic and the Mediterranean and became a pattern for the type of French engineering that later produced the Suez Canal.

Like most of the economic theorists of his time, Colbert was a mercantilist—that is, he thought that a nation must be self-sufficient in order to be strong, that it should try to conserve its wealth by exporting as much as it could and importing as little as possible. Through this exaggerated protectionism, Colbert strengthened France internally, but it involved ruinous tariffs on foreign goods, and led to a struggle for trade and ultimately to war.

Louis was not averse to going to war. He desired the glory of military conquest, and built military power with the aid of some of the ablest men the French army has ever produced. At the head of the military was the Marquis de Louvois, a great organizer, who reformed the service, and devised many features that became permanent in European armies. He raised the status of the infantry in battle by giving it the bayonet on the musket, which took the place of the pike. When the King decreed that no one should receive a commission in the aristocratic cavalry until he had served a term with the foot, the French infantry became the finest in Europe. Among the associates of Louvois was Sebastien de Vauban, possibly the finest military engineer in history. Vauban's particular genius lay in dealing with strong points—either attacking them in war or fortifying them during peace. He developed a new type of systematic approach in attacking a position, and the use of shells and ricochet fire in reducing it.

With the best army in Europe at his disposal, Louis XIV embarked on an aggressive policy that lasted almost until his death. The time was propitious, since Spain was falling into decay, Germany was disunited, and Austria was facing the menace of a Turkish invasion. England was virtually a tributary of France. Charles II, and James II after him, received subsidies from Louis in order to make themselves independent of their own Parliament, which held the purse strings.

Louis's first great war was fought against Holland. It was largely a trade war, which Colbert wanted. But the Dutch, under the leadership of William of Orange, broke their dikes and flooded their land rather than yield. After six years of war, Holland was still unconquered, and Louis concluded the Treaty of Nimwegen.

Louis's aggressive intentions caused the neighbors of France to form the League of Augsburg, which included Austria, Spain, and

Holland. England joined later, when the Revolution of 1688 drove James II from the throne and made William of Orange king. William remained the great antagonist of Louis XIV, and was all the more formidable as King of England.

The War of the League of Augsburg broke out in 1688 and continued until 1697. The fighting swayed back and forth with neither side able to conquer the other. The war ended in the Treaty of Ryswick.

Meanwhile the King of France had outraged European Protestants by his religious policy. He revoked the Edict of Nantes, which had guaranteed religious liberty to French Huguenots. By this act Louis caused a mass emigration of one of the most enterprising elements of the French population, and also strengthened the determination of the Protestant nations of Europe.

In 1701 the War of the Spanish Succession broke out, lasted until 1713, and included the great campaigns of Marlborough and Prince Eugene of Savoy. Louis XIV sustained a series of defeats, which immortalized the military genius of Marlborough, and would have led to the capitulation of France if the allies had not demanded such harsh terms. The French roused themselves to a last-ditch national effort, and staved off disaster.

When the war had dragged on for twelve years and there was still a French army in the field, the allies agreed to make peace. By the Treaty of Utrecht, Louis lost many of his conquests but won the major point for which he had been fighting: his grandson retained the crown of Spain. This became a permanent settlement, for the Spanish royal family, including those in exile today, have been Bourbons ever since.

This last of the wars of Louis XIV left France exhausted, and most of the elements which later caused the French Revolution had already become prominent. The worst of the evils was the maladministration of finances. Under the pressure of war Colbert's great reforms had lapsed. Taxation was ruinous and unjust. The nobles had lost their power but not their privileges. They still paid less taxes than the common people, and could compel the latter to work periodically on their great estates.

Nevertheless the age of Louis XIV is rightly remembered as the classical age of French culture. His court was the most dazzling in

Europe, and neighboring countries imitated it as far as they were able. Through the magnificent palace at Versailles passed famous men of genius. Molière wrote comedies, and Racine tragedies for the court. Bossuet preached sublime funeral orations before the King, and wrote one of the earliest of scientific histories. The spectacle of the court was embalmed in the memoirs of Saint-Simon and the letters of Madame de Sévigné.

Manners and morals were portrayed in the fables of La Fontaine and in the book of characters by La Bruyère. Philosophy was represented by Malebranche, called the French Plato, and by Pascal, who invented the calculating machine and who foresaw many of the problems of religion and science which are agitating the Atomic Age. In painting France had Poussin, frequently regarded as the finest of French artists, and in architecture Mansard worked on the palace of Versailles and invented the type of roofing which bears his name.

Later generations tend to forget the disasters of the latter part of the reign of Louis XIV so that the glories stand out. He remains the Sun King, the Grand Monarque of European history.

LA SALLE

[1643–1687]

ROBERT CAVELIER was one of the great explorers of all time. If the name means nothing to you, you undoubtedly will recognize Robert Cavelier under the name he assumed and by which he lives in history—La Salle. Robert Cavelier studied to be a Jesuit, abandoned a clerical vocation for that of pioneer in the New World, went to Canada, and there became René de la Salle from the title of an estate owned by his family.

He arrived in Montreal just as New France, founded by Champlain, was rising to its zenith under the powerful and able Count Frontenac. La Salle promptly fell in love with the wilderness. He learned Indian dialects. He sounded out the natives about the territory to the west beyond the Great Lakes. He made the penetration of that territory his lifework.

After various minor excursions into the wilderness, he started out in 1669 with a well-equipped party to explore the lands south of Lake Ontario and Lake Erie. The following year he made another trip and appears to have gone through Lake Erie and up the Detroit River into Lake Huron and then Lake Michigan and to have landed on the southern shore.

His ability and popularity with the Indians made La Salle a favorite with Count Frontenac, who planned to build a fort and trading post on the shores of Lake Ontario. La Salle was sent to negotiate with the Iroquois and other Indian tribes and was so successful that the Governor himself was able to visit the site. Even the most hostile of the chiefs had been won over by La Salle's friendly overtures. The new Fort Frontenac was established in 1673, on the site of what is now Kingston, Ontario, and La Salle was made its commander. So high did he stand in the Governor's opinion that twice he was dispatched to France to defend Frontenac's policy in New France, and did so with complete success.

His last return to Quebec was triumphal. He brought ample funds, merchandise for trading, supplies to build boats for lake and river exploration, a number of artisans, and a right-hand man, Henri de Tonti. Tonti became his close friend and most loyal lieutenant. The following year a new fort at the outlet of the Niagara River was completed, and a forty-five-ton bark, well rigged and furnished, was launched. With great difficulty they got her past the rapids into Lake Erie, and the "Griffin" became the first ship ever to sail on the Great Lakes. La Salle traded with the Huron and Ottawa Indians, and found that a party of men he had sent on ahead into the Illinois country had turned back in the belief that his vessel would never get through the lakes.

La Salle finally arrived at Green Bay on Lake Michigan, where he met with a sincere welcome from the chief of the Pottawattomie tribe, with whom he traded. Here he loaded the "Griffin" with a cargo of furs and sent her back to pick up supplies and additional men from France. The ship also carried letters and maps which he asked Frontenac to send on to France. The next day La Salle started out again and led the few men he had kept with him up the shores of Lake Michigan and on to the Illinois River. From there he sent the famous missionary, Father Hennepin, and two men with Indian porters southward to explore the upper reaches of the Mississippi.

The previous November, La Salle had detached two of his men to try to locate the "Griffin," of which nothing had been heard since she left Green Bay. Anxious as to her fate, he now set off on foot to return to Fort Frontenac. He caught up with his two agents, who informed him that the supplies for his expedition were in storage awaiting his ship to come to fetch them. It was obvious now that the "Griffin" had been lost with all on board.

La Salle returned to Montreal and with the assistance of the Governor and his brother raised more money, loaded his supplies on canoes, and started back for the wilderness. On this journey he heard rumors that some of his men had revolted and that his advance post was abandoned. The rumors proved true.

Once again La Salle turned east to Fort Frontenac and Montreal. A fresh expedition was organized, new supplies and tools were obtained, and a larger band of Frenchmen, with a number of Indians, started out under the leadership of La Salle, Henri de Tonti, and the Jesuit Father Membré. Having reached the Illinois, they followed the river south to its junction with the Mississippi, which they reached on February 6, 1682. Father Membré blessed the "Father of Waters," and La Salle named it the Colbert, after the great minister of Louis XIV.

For more than two thousand miles they followed the mighty stream down to its delta, the first white men ever to sail the length of the Mississippi. They reached the Gulf of Mexico on April 9. In the name of the King of France, La Salle took possession of "all the sundry lands drained by the Colbert"—in other words, the Mississippi Valley. He drew up a notarial deed to that effect, witnessed by Henri de Tonti and Father Membré, and upon the banks of the Mississippi planted the golden standard of France, calling the new territory Louisiana. The lower reaches of the river had been discovered by De Soto in 1541; Marquette and Joliet had reached its banks somewhere in the neighborhood of La Crosse in 1673; but to La Salle belongs the glory of having explored the Mississippi from the Illinois to the sea.

His return journey upstream was uneventful. On his arrival in Montreal, La Salle met with anything but the reception he deserved. Frontenac had been recalled to France, and the new Governor deprived La Salle of all authority and sent out men of his own to take over along the Mississippi.

La Salle sailed for France immediately. He was received by Louis XIV, who appointed him Governor of all the lands lying between Lake Michigan and the Gulf of Mexico. He was now just forty and is described as a singularly handsome man, tall, hearty, and robust, with dark hair, a large nose, a strong jaw, and a fine mustache. His presence was commanding, and he was entirely at ease among the glittering courtiers who surrounded the most powerful monarch in Europe.

Most careful preparations were made for the success of La Salle's new venture. Henri de Tonti, who had accompanied him to France, was sent back with instructions to the Governor of New France to respect the territory of Louisiana of which La Salle had been appointed Governor. La Salle himself started out for the Gulf of Mexico in the summer of 1684, with a fleet of four ships and more than four hundred men, intending to plant a colony on the shores of what is now Lake Pontchartrain, near New Orleans. From the start he met nothing but trouble. His naval commander refused to take orders from him while at sea; on approaching the Gulf of Mexico, his main supply vessel was captured by the Spaniards off Florida. The three remaining vessels put in to some West Indian island, where La Salle was stricken with fever. When he finally recovered, La Salle sailed for his final destination with two remaining ships and about 180 men.

Without an experienced navigator, he made for the coast too far west. He mistook what is now Matagorda Bay, in Texas, for one of the mouths of the Mississippi, and disembarked his colonists there. When he discovered his mistake, he made two unsuccessful attempts to find the place where he had planted the flag of France; but instead of following the coast toward the east, he appears to have struck out overland. Gradually the plight of his followers became desperate. At last, when their number was reduced to forty-five, La Salle, taking with him the seventeen strongest, started north to obtain badly needed supplies from Canada. Under circumstances which have never been fully explained, the great explorer was shot and killed by some of the men in his party. He was forty-four years old. His friend, Henri de Tonti, carried on his work, and later French explorers made his dream a reality, asserting the claim of France to the Mississippi Valley, with New Orleans as a new metropolis, events which culminated in the Louisiana Purchase.

MARLBOROUGH

[1650–1722]

IN THE early years of the eighteenth century John Churchill, first Duke of Marlborough, rose to supreme military reputation. Voltaire wrote of him with truth that "he never besieged a fortress which he did not take, nor fought a battle which he did not win." After the Battle of Blenheim, Parliament, as a reward for his services, transferred to him the manor of Woodstock. It voted him a quarter of a million pounds of public money—an enormous sum in those days—to build Blenheim Palace, one of the most stately of the many great houses of England.

During the reign of Queen Anne, Marlborough may almost be said to have governed the country. His wife, Sarah, had obtained complete ascendancy over the sovereign. His daughter was married to the son of Godolphin, the minister who directed England's foreign policy. He was given the Garter, the highest honor the Crown bestowed, and he was made Captain-General of all English troops at home and abroad.

He won all this because he was greatly gifted, and because he had no scruples about the way he used his gifts. His rise began when his sister Arabella entered the service of the Duchess of York, and became the mistress of the Duke of York, brother of King Charles II, who was later to ascend the throne as James II. Arabella Churchill bore the Duke two sons and two daughters before she was twenty. Her influence in her brother's behalf was all-powerful. He became a page to the Duke. She obtained for him a commission in the King's own regiment of Foot Guards, now the Grenadier Guards.

Arabella is also credited with bringing her brother and his future wife, Sarah Jennings, together. Sarah was the favorite companion of Anne, daughter of the Duke of York, who was later to become Queen

Anne. As a subaltern in the Guards, young Churchill served Charles II, at whose court he attracted the attention of the Duchess of Cleveland. She made him a present of five thousand pounds, which he at once invested in an annuity. He was then barely eighteen. He rose to be a colonel and in December 1682 was created a Scottish peer, with the title of Churchill of Eyemouth.

He was now on the verge of his great career, and notice must be taken of a reverse side to the picture of his glory. For England he gave all, sparing nothing that could bring her greatness, but his loyalty to England was not expressed in loyalty to his sovereigns. Nor did his sense of honor prevent him from misusing public funds to satisfy his greed for personal wealth and political power. Although he was virtually penniless when he entered the service of the Crown, his wife, who inherited his fortune and survived him for twenty-two years, left no less than three million pounds sterling when she died. A great general, generous in action, gentle in temper, a devoted husband and a pious Christian, he gained a reputation for being avaricious, unscrupulous, and perfidious. He was accused of taking bribes from army contractors and of robbing his soldiers of their pay. Undoubtedly his conduct was loose in such matters, although in this he was perhaps no worse than many other generals of his time.

The Duke of York succeeded to the throne as James II, and to Arabella's brother he gave an English peerage, making him Baron Churchill of Sandridge in Hertfordshire. James raised him likewise to the rank of major general. He served the King well as a military commander during civil strife, and was covered with honors. Despite this, Churchill was among those who made secret overtures to William of Orange in the scheme to dethrone James and make the Protestant William king. He was opposed to James's idea of making England Catholic, and played a double game. When the Dutch prince landed to make his bid for the crown, Churchill was promoted by James and sent against William with 5,000 men. Then the King learned that during the night his general had gone over to the enemy camp. James fled to France, and William of Orange ascended the throne. Churchill was rewarded richly. He became a privy councilor and the Earl of Marlborough.

However, William could never quite bring himself to trust Marlborough, who had so smoothly betrayed his former sovereign, and thought he could best be employed out of the kingdom. So the new King sent him to command English troops in the Netherlands, where the British were opposing the French, and the following year to Ireland, which had revolted in favor of James. There Marlborough gave immediate proof of his military ability, taking Cork and Kinsale without difficulty.

He returned to London, and was thrown into the Tower on charges of treason. It was shown that he had been in communication with the exiled James II and had even disclosed to his former master, whom he had betrayed, the intention of the English to attack Brest. But Marlborough managed to get the charges dropped. When he was implicated in another plot, William didn't even bother to have him arrested. Marlborough's ability was such that before the end of his reign William had restored him to favor and placed him in high military command.

This was nothing to the honors heaped on Marlborough when his wife Sarah, as Queen Anne's closest friend and Mistress of the Robes, virtually ruled the court. She had the Queen completely under her influence, and used her power unsparingly in behalf of her husband. The Marlborough faction virtually controlled the realm, with foreign affairs handled by Godolphin, whose son was married to the daughter of the Marlboroughs. But, most of all, Marlborough's military genius swept everything. The War of the Spanish Succession broke out. This was a sort of world struggle against the might of France and the ambitions of Louis XIV. Marlborough rose to his supreme opportunity.

He drove the French out of Spanish Guelders and forced Louis XIV to surrender Kaiserwerth on the Rhine, Venlo on the Meuse, and the fortress of Liége. After these victories he was raised from Earl to Duke of Marlborough and given five thousand pounds a year during the Queen's life. The war went on. Louis XIV launched an offensive against Austria, his assumption being that the English were unlikely to fight so far away from their bases. Marlborough guessed what was in the French King's mind, made a feint at Alsace, and then marched straight into Bavaria.

The two armies met on the banks of the Danube near the little village of Blenheim. Marlborough's allies, the Austrians, were commanded by one of the great veteran generals of the age, Prince Eugene of Savoy. Blenheim was one of the fiercest battles in history.

Three times Prince Eugene's troops were driven back. It was only after Marlborough himself led a great cavalry charge against the French center that the victory was won. The French broke and fled, leaving two hundred standards in the hands of the victors.

The victory of Blenheim brought Marlborough's popularity to its highest pitch. There was something so personal about his triumph, he having divined the French plan and having led the great charge that won the day. Addison, called upon to commemorate Marlborough's victory in verse, wrote "The Campaign, 1704"—comparing the English commander to "the angel" who passed over "pale Britannia" in the storm of war.

The armies of Louis XIV were soon re-formed and striking again. Although Marlborough was greatly hampered by strife and jealousy among the allies, he defeated French Marshal Villeroi in the battle of Ramillies. In quick succession Brussels, Antwerp, Ostend, Menin, and Dendermonde surrendered. Again in 1708, Marlborough defeated the French at Oudenarde.

The following year Marshal Villars took the field at the head of an army of more than 100,000 men, and Marlborough met him at Malplaquet, just south of Mons. Both the English and French have always claimed Malplaquet as a victory, but it was really a drawn battle. The French, it is true, finally retreated, but in perfect order; and the losses they inflicted on the allies were greater than their own. The French now were ready for peace, but the terms the allies sought to impose were so drastic that Louis XIV sent for Marshal Villars and begged him to make one last effort to save France. Villars won the Battle of Denain and France was able to negotiate the Peace of Utrecht.

In this final anticlimax Marlborough played little part. His position at court had been ruined by his wife's loss of favor. Queen Anne had revolted against her overbearing friend, the Duchess of Marlborough. Their love had turned to hate. Anne seemed to be animated by a fixed idea: to humiliate the Marlboroughs. There was a political change; their party was overthrown. Godolphin, the minister connected with the Marlboroughs by marriage, was the first to go. Then the Duchess of Marlborough was dismissed from her offices at court. The fall of Marlborough himself came at the end of 1711. Enough evidence of corrupt practices had been collected against him to enable his enemies to remove him from the command of the army. He went abroad.

Walpole restored him to command during the reign of George I, but Marlborough took little part in public business. When he died he left a legend of greatness that inspired many Englishmen in subsequent generations—pre-eminently the Churchill of our time, the mighty Prime Minister who outfought a more terrible foe than any the Duke of Marlborough ever faced.

PETER THE GREAT

[1672–1725]

THE Tsar who created modern Russia was a giant. Physically he stood six and a half feet of muscular brawn. His energies were stupendous, his statecraft of imperial scope. His feasts and orgies were gargantuan, his religion a vast belief that he was divinely destined. His ferocity and cruelty were monstrous, while his generosity and magnanimity could be equally great. His violence was appalling, his decisions summary and extreme. His enlightenment was of revolutionary brilliance, his darkness that of the somber Russian past. It is one of the dramatic themes of history that this rampaging giant, wielding the absolute authority of a Muscovite Tsar, should have taken it upon himself to modernize backward Russia by means of a domestic program of westernization and a foreign policy of European imperialism.

His father died when Peter was four. For over a decade the heir to the throne lived amid scenes of terror, as factions fought for supremacy in the Russian state. Peter and his mother were in frequent danger for their lives. The boy saw his uncle killed by the mob and his mother's adviser torn from his own grasp and hacked to pieces. It was supposed that the shock of such experiences disposed Peter to fits and paroxysms that afflicted him during the rest of his life.

In his teens he got away from the horror and bloodshed by frequenting the "German section" in Moscow, where lived specialists from various European countries, hired by the Russian government. Their houses were better, their dress was different, their way of life attractive to those who knew them and especially to Peter who went to their dances, drank with them, and even learned to smoke a pipe, a thing forbidden by Muscovite law. In this Western kind of society he developed a love for matters pertaining to the sea. His favorite pursuits were the building of boats and sailing, nautical amusements that he shared with his foreign friends.

In 1789 Peter assumed power as Tsar. He also married, but his wife was an old-fashioned, strait-laced Russian, full of the Muscovite prejudices he disliked, and he soon abandoned her for his boon companions of the "German section."

The new Tsar soon turned his mind to the enlargement of his realm. He realized that the White Sea, an arm of the Arctic Ocean, was too narrow and icebound an outlet for Russia, and for an alternative he looked south. The Turks held the shores of the Black Sea. Peter attacked their stronghold at Azov, suffered one defeat, then returned and took Azov. His fleet sailed in warm water for the first time.

Peter now decided to visit the West, traveling incognito. At an East Prussian foundry he studied how to cast cannon. In Holland, working in a shipyard, he gained practical experience about how to build better ships. He spent some time in England, where he bought charts and sextants and astrolabes, books and surgical instruments. He visited Paris.

The Tsar had to cut his trip short because of a rebellion in Moscow led by his reactionary nobles, the boyars. Peter hurried home, and took bloody reprisals. Hundreds of persons, leaders of the rebellion, participants, sympathizers, were sent to the gallows, the Tsar participating in public executions. He took the revolt as an occasion for crushing all opposition by terror. His journey through western Europe had more than ever convinced him that backward Russia must be westernized.

In characteristic fashion he decided to begin reform by outward and visible signs. On April 26, 1698, a most extraordinary scene was enacted. The chief boyars and leading men of Russia, heavily bearded in old Russian fashion, were gathered together, and the Tsar, armed with a pair of scissors purchased in Paris, cut off their beards with his own hand. The wearing of the ancient Russian costume was forbidden. Short jackets, knee breeches, and hose were to take its place. A revolution in fashion was Peter's way of emphasizing his program of reform, which extended wholesale into various phases of Russian life.

Two years later Peter started his great northern war. Here he faced a military genius in Charles XII of Sweden. But Peter of Russia was

determined to gain a foothold on the Baltic. He even shifted his capital west from Moscow to the Neva. He selected a site suitable for a
fine port although the surrounding marshlands made it exceedingly
unhealthy. Hosts of workers perished but the Tsar drove the construction of a new city with unrelenting energy, and St. Petersburg
was raised.

In the war the Swedes had the upper hand at first, and at the
Battle of Narva Peter suffered a humiliating defeat and lost most of
his artillery. But he never lost courage. Church bells were sent to
furnaces to make new guns. Nine years after the beginning of the
conflict, Charles XII was in the Ukraine, after a march through
Russia. Peter the Great moved against him, and won a decisive victory
at Poltava. This victory marks the beginning of Russian greatness in
modern history.

Peter's reforms completely changed the face of Russia. The Church
became state controlled. In the administration of the government,
the old Russian boyars gave up their places to foreigners, picked
without consideration of social rank or extraction. A former Portuguese sailor became chief of police of St. Petersburg; a Lithuanian
swineherd became President of the Supreme Court; a Polish Jew became Vice-Chancellor; Menshikov, Peter's most trusted assistant, had
begun life as a baker and was raised to be a prince. But he himself
was the Russian despot of old, crushing opposition with blood and
torture. Even his son, Alexis, was put to death with horrible cruelty
for scheming to restore the old order.

In international relations Peter won successes and suffered reverses. He was defeated by the Turks, who pushed him back from
the Black Sea. But he went from victory to victory in the north, beating the Poles and the Swedes, seizing Estonia and Livonia, Finland
and Karelia, and Ingermanland. Then it was that after a solemn service in the Troitsa Cathedral, the Tsar proceeded to the Senate and
was formally acclaimed as Father of the Fatherland, Peter the Great,
Emperor of all the Russias.

Every summer Peter, at his new capital of St. Petersburg, spent
what time he could at his favorite palace where, from the terrace
overlooking the Baltic, he could see the fortress of Kronstadt and
the masts of the ships. Nothing could keep him from sailing his beloved Baltic no matter what the weather. In the winter he would have

the ice on the Neva cut away in front of his palace so that he could have his daily exercise in a stout rowboat.

The sea which had been Peter's great joy was also the cause of his death. One dark and stormy November afternoon a boat carrying soldiers to Kronstadt ran aground and was being broken up by the waves. Peter, who had been inspecting a nearby arms factory, saw the disaster and went to the rescue. Although he had been in failing health for some time he jumped into a small rowboat and, on reaching the sandbank, stood waist deep in the icy water until all the men had been saved. He never recovered from the shock. Two months later he was dead.

Peter's qualities, like his faults, were all of a gigantic scale. He figuratively picked his great slumbering country up in his two hands and flung her bodily into European history. He lived and loved, fought and ruled, like the colossus he was. His nobility of sentiment, his broad statesmanlike vision, his ardent patriotism, his readiness to work for the good of his country, are to be contrasted with his blood-thirsty ferocity and the depths of cruelty to which he descended. He laid the foundations of Russian greatness, and in history he stands like the giant that he was.

JOHN WESLEY

[*1703–1791*]

DURING the first half of the eighteenth century, there was at Oxford a small pious group whose members were strict in religious observance and took the Anglican communion once a week. This drew a jeering remark from a fellow Oxonian, who mocked their devout regularity and called them "Methodists." The name stuck. The members of the Oxford group accepted it, and the leading spirit among them, John Wesley, applied it later to the great religious movement he instituted.

John Wesley kept a journal in cipher, which, when decoded at a later time, revealed vividly his spiritual progress. From his earliest years he was of a religious turn of mind. Raised as a member of the Church of England, he could not be satisfied even after he graduated from Oxford and became an Anglican clergyman. He went searching and seeking for an explanation of his spiritual troubles, and found the explanation in the realization of how many professing Christians paid little more than lip service to their faith, how few heeded the call to genuine repentance and a better life.

The great turn in his life, when he was thirty-one, came in the form of a visit to America. On board his ship were a number of German immigrants to the New World, members of the Moravian Church, an austere pious sect. John Wesley was impressed by the simple earnest Christianity of the Moravians. He felt that he did not have a faith as deep as theirs. In Georgia he continued to associate with them, and was affected more and more by the Moravian colonists in America, whose belief it was that they were following in the plain, unpretentious fervor of the primitive church. At this time his brother, Charles Wesley, beginning a career as a writer of hymns, translated some from the German, a sign of the influence of the Moravian brethren.

The Wesley brothers came under attack, charged with ecclesiastical innovations because they formed a small group which gathered every week for what John Wesley called "a free conversation, begun and ended with singing and prayer." Later in life he wrote, "I cannot but observe that these were the first rudiments of the Methodist Societies." Wesley never did think of himself as having broken with the Church of England; he considered himself as evangelizing within the Church. But the Church thought differently.

Returning home, he tried to stay within the Anglican fold even though he preached independently around England. It was one of Wesley's group, George Whitefield, who forced the break. The churches were closed to Whitefield, so he preached in the open, and attracted huge throngs. Wesley at first disliked defying the Anglican authorities; but Whitefield's method proved effective, and soon Wesley began field preaching too.

Now came what Wesley called "the third beginning of Methodism." The first he reckoned as having been the fraternity he had gathered at Oxford. The second, the meetings for devout talk, prayers, and hymns in America. In this third beginning of Methodism, he founded small bands of co-workers in London, groups that assembled together for a general meeting each week. There were dissensions, and Wesley withdrew with several score of his followers, who met weekly at a place called the Foundry. This was the nucleus of what now became the Methodist Revival. The year was 1739, which is regarded as the birth year of Methodism.

John Wesley was off on a career of immense activity, storming England with enthusiastic revivals, preaching to vast crowds, gathering disciples, organizing a great church. He had a genius for organization. He knew how to deal with men and direct their activities, how to create a system, how to take advantage of circumstances and make the correct move. His inner fervor was intense, his insight into religious problems illuminating, his preaching of a sort to arouse multitudes to conversion and repentance.

He encountered intense opposition from the Established Church, though he insisted that he was a member of the Anglican community. On doctrinal points, in general, he followed older ideas, though with innovations concentrating on conversion and repentance. The rules he issued for the admission of members prescribed "a desire to flee from the wrath to come." He instituted love feasts, and services in which testimony was given. In the Methodist Society lay preachers had a place in what was considered to be a revival of the simplicity of the primitive church of the Apostles, a concept that harked back to those Moravian brethren from whom John Wesley drew so much of his early inspiration. Actually it was a break away from the Anglican communion, and this was signalized by a decisive step which Wesley felt impelled to take.

Methodism was spreading widely in America. But the revolt of the Colonies in the American Revolution brought one serious religious problem. The ordination of American bishops by the Church of England was interrupted, and Wesley was faced with the problem of creating Methodist clergymen in America. He solved the problem boldly by himself ordaining ministers and instructing his assistants to do likewise. This was a definite rupture with the ecclesiastical system of the Anglican Church, and in contradiction to the doctrine of apostolic succession, which postulated an uninterrupted line of bishops descending from the Apostles. John Wesley expressed his disbelief in the succession of bishops down the centuries from the times of the Apostles, and held himself, on scriptural grounds, to be a bishop.

For the rest of his long life he preached, missioned, and proselytized throughout England. It has been estimated that he traveled a hundred thousand miles—most of them on horseback and over the atrocious dirt roads of the period. He lived to preach in the shade of trees that he himself had planted. And despite quarrels and secessions among his followers, he established one of the great religious denominations of the world. When John Wesley died, he knew that his work was not dying with him. It still survives, still influences humanity, still summons men and women to repentance, virtue, and charity —the Methodist Society.

BENJAMIN FRANKLIN

[*1706–1790*]

BENJAMIN FRANKLIN was the first man to show Europeans that America was developing a culture of her own. When he visited Paris at the height of his fame, the French lionized him as a rare combination of scientist, philosopher, educator, statesman, diplomatist, and author. French intellectuals accepted him as their peer.

Yet this prodigy of learning had no university background. A native of Boston, he left school at the age of ten to go to work in his father's business as a candle and soap maker. Two years later he became an apprentice in the printing shop of his brother James, where he toiled for long hours at the cumbersome printing press that was operated by hand. In his spare time he read voraciously every book he could lay his hands on. And he began to write little essays in imitation of those published by Addison and Steele in their urbane and witty *Spectator*.

But he did not get on well with his brother and seized the first opportunity to leave the printing shop. James published one of America's earliest newspapers, the *New England Courant,* in which appeared a series of articles highly distasteful to the Massachusetts Council. The publisher was arrested for "bringing authority into contempt" and sent to prison for a month. This did not chasten his spirit and for a repetition of his offense he was forbidden to publish his paper. The *Courant* continued to appear, however, in Benjamin's name. It was only an artifice with James, but the latter canceled his brother's apprenticeship to make it legal. Benjamin, aged seventeen, took advantage of the change to strike out on his own. He left Boston and went to New York, then continued on to Philadelphia, where he got himself a job as a printer with Samuel Keimer.

In Philadelphia, Benjamin Franklin soon made many friends. He impressed everybody with his quiet self-confidence and passion for work. They were struck by his knowledge of writers like Addison, Steele, Swift, Defoe, and Bunyan. They admired his skill at logic, something he developed from reading Locke's *Essay concerning Human Understanding*. He titillated them with magic squares, which he invented as a sideline to his interest in mathematics.

He took up languages, and taught himself first Latin and then the modern tongues derived from Latin—French, Italian, and Spanish. Sir William Keith, the Governor of Pennsylvania, heard about this industrious youth and offered him a great opportunity. Franklin was to go to England to buy equipment for his own printing business in Philadelphia, the Governor promising to lend him the money and give him the government printing.

Franklin arrived in London in December 1724, but waited in vain for the letters of credit the Governor had promised to send. Pinched for money, he got a job with a leading firm of London printers, remained with them for eighteen months, and returned to Philadelphia an accomplished craftsman. He rejoined Keimer as foreman, and the following year opened his own printery. His skill, his industry, his personal charm, all contributed to the success of this venture, and two years later he bought the *Pennsylvania Gazette* from Keimer and started his remarkable career as a journalist.

Franklin had many affairs with women, but he was discreet and we know little about them. His illegitimate son William was the result of one such liaison. At about the same time he married an old flame, Deborah Read, by whom he had two children.

From 1728 to 1748 Benjamin Franklin lived and worked in one house where, in addition to his printery, he opened a shop. He dealt in everything from coffee to slaves, from stationery to patent medicines. He was frugal and industrious. In his own words, "I drest plainly. I was seen at no place of idle diversion. I never went out a fishing or a shooting. A book indeed at times debauched me from my work, but that was seldom, snug and gave no scandal. To show that I was not above my business, I sometimes brought home the paper I purchased at the stores thru the streets in a wheelbarrow."

Franklin, who had been a heavily built youth, became quite portly in his early forties. He was about five feet ten with a very large head and heavy square hands. His hair was light brown, his eyes gray, his

SIMÓN BOLÍVAR

BYRON

gaze steady. His mouth was large and gave the impression that he was always smiling.

Poor Richard's Almanack brought him a reputation for wit and wisdom. He did not invent his epigrams, but he gave them sharper expression. Thus the old Scottish proverb, "Fat housekeepers make lean executors," appeared as, "A fat kitchen, a lean will."

Franklin had a hand in everything that was going on in Philadelphia. He started a club called the "Junto," which developed into the American Philosophical Society, and an academy that became the University of Pennsylvania. He organized a volunteer fire department. He founded the first free library in America, the forerunner of our many great public libraries. He was Philadelphia's leading citizen when he retired from business at the age of forty-two. His life was now to be that of public servant and scientist.

In 1736, Benjamin Franklin had been appointed clerk of the Pennsylvania Assembly, a post which he held to the end of his life. In 1737 he had been elected postmaster of Philadelphia and in 1754 became deputy postmaster for the Colonies.

Soon after his retirement from business, Franklin began his experiments with electricity. He proved the identity of atmospheric and ordinary electricity by his famous kite experiment in the midst of a raging thunder and lightning storm. This led him to suggest the protection of buildings against lightning by the erection of conductor rods.

Science remained a passion with him. He took up meteorology and tried to plot the weather pattern across America. He investigated the Gulf Stream, recording its temperature with a thermometer. He experimented with the spectrum to see how sunlight affected the various colors. Applying his science to the improvement of living conditions, he invented a new kind of stove.

His achievements won international recognition. He was elected a Fellow of the Royal Society in London, and received honorary degrees from Oxford and Edinburgh. These were granted in 1754 when he went to Britain as political representative of Pennsylvania.

In 1764 he was back in England to contest the right of the mother country to tax the colonies without representation. He made every effort to prevent the passage of the Stamp Act, and then fought to get it repealed. But his position as both an American patriot and a loyal subject of the King became more difficult to sustain.

During his eleven-year stay in England, Franklin twice visited France. Among his French friends were Mme. Helvetius, the comely wife of the great philosopher, Mme. Brillon, and the Countess de Houdetot. In his advanced age he became a favorite of the ladies of aristocratic circles in Paris. He had an enormous attraction for women, and made unsparing use of their influence in his political and diplomatic missions.

On his return to America in 1775, just after the death of his wife Deborah, Franklin at last saw that continued allegiance to the King was incompatible with his ideal of a self-governing commonwealth in America. Elected to the Continental Congress he took an active part in the deliberations which led to the Declaration of Independence. He served on the committee that approved Jefferson's draft after a few amendments, some of which were due to Franklin himself.

Then came his mission to France to obtain arms and ammunition, men and money, to help the American Revolution. This was the apogee of his success—decisive for the victory of the American Revolution. The crown of achievement was placed upon his efforts when, on September 3, 1783, Britain, in the treaty of peace, finally and formally recognized the independence of the United States of America. Franklin remained in Paris as the most popular American ambassador ever accredited to France.

Franklin was a delegate to the convention which drafted the Constitution of the United States. When disagreement rose between the states as to the method of representation, it was Franklin who suggested the famous compromise whereby in the Senate each state has equal representation, while in the Lower House representation is based upon population. The acceptance of this arrangement and the approval of the Constitution by Pennsylvania, which he was instrumental in obtaining, were his final achievements. He retired from public life in 1788 and died in Philadelphia two years later at the age of eighty-four. All America, and many nations of Europe, mourned his passing.

WILLIAM PITT

[1708–1778]

W ILLIAM PITT, Earl of Chatham, is the personification of British imperialism. Before him it seemed as though Britain might lose her major colonies to France. After him Britain stood alone as the world's foremost power around the globe. He was the architect of colonial rule in Canada and India, both of which members of the Commonwealth remain as monuments to his courage and sagacity.

Pitt, descended from an old aristocratic family, followed a career typical of the aristocracy. After Eton and Oxford, he studied on the Continent, joined the army, and then went into politics. Two particular actions made him a leader of the House of Commons. He joined in the opposition that overthrew Prime Minister Robert Walpole. And he criticized King George II for putting the interests of Hanover in Germany, where George ruled as Elector, before the interests of Great Britain. Walpole strove to keep Pitt in obscurity. George II did not want him in the Cabinet. But despite both he became Prime Minister.

One ministry suceeded another, with complex shifts of policy, domestic and foreign, during all of which William Pitt retained his seat in Parliament and found no lack of opportunity to exercise his powers of political attack. He assailed the weakening of the British armed forces, ridiculed the feebleness of Britain's diplomacy, and in one burst of invective aroused such anger that he was deprived of his post as paymaster. But now he was recognized as the first man in Parliament, the most gifted statesman in England, and had only to wait for his time to come. George II continued hostile, and Pitt's own dominant personality created a determination in lesser men to keep him out, but the time would come when they could not keep him out.

The Seven Years' War broke out and began badly for the British. In the American forests an army under General Braddock was annihilated by the French and Indians—an early spectacular incident in that phase of the Seven Years' War which American history calls the French and Indian War. The British sustained other reverses, and lost the Mediterranean island of Minorca. The struggle with France for India was touch and go. In England discontent soared against the ministry and belief grew that William Pitt was the man to head the government. Pitt himself did not disagree. He said, "I know that I can save the country, and that no one else can." The popular demand became irresistible, and despite the reluctance of George II, Pitt was called to office as Prime Minister. He was then forty-eight years old.

Pitt now had the direction of what was virtually a world war, an antecedent of the Napoleonic conflicts and the global fighting of the twentieth century. He was a driving force in the action of war, pressing plans, selecting competent generals and urging them on. Whipping up popular spirit at home, and giving inspired urgency to matters abroad, the spirit of William Pitt animated the British triumphs in India and America.

India was a family tradition—Pitt's father having been Governor of Madras and head of the East India Company—and now the decisive conflict was waged with France for possession of golden Hindustan and its wealth. Pitt, as Prime Minister, was fortunate in the emergence of a fabulous commander, Clive of India, whose dazzling successes broke the power of France and made India a British possession.

In America he had another great general, one of his own selection, Wolfe, the conqueror of Canada, who defeated Montcalm on the Plains of Abraham. British armies established a supremacy in America that resulted in the acquisition of Canada and of the widespread French possessions in the Mississippi Valley, the lands between the Allegheny Mountains and the great river. As token of the part the Prime Minister played in all this we have the name of the metropolis in western Pennsylvania, Pittsburgh.

Pitt was out as Prime Minister before the war ended. A new king, George III, ascended the throne determined to take control into his own hands, and declared for peace. Pitt resigned. He attacked the treaty of peace on the score that Great Britain, in view of all the victories won, had not gained enough.

His career now took its final turn with the question of the American

Colonies. The breaking of the power of France in America was followed by disputes between the settlers along the Atlantic seaboard
and the mother country. Pitt opposed the policy that alienated the
Americans, and assailed the imposition of navigation restrictions,
taxes that angered the colonists. This attitude in favor of the American cause was in keeping with his own role as empire builder. He
was staunch for the political rights of Britons, was opposed to acts
of oppression in England. Similarly he upheld the rights of the
colonists, deeming them to be British and entitled to British privileges. With that policy in mind, he became Prime Minister again.

It is possible that a full-fledged ministry of William Pitt might have
averted the American Revolutionary War, but by now he was in ill-
health. At fifty-eight his powers were enfeebled, his administration
comparatively ineffectual, and he held office for only two years. His
strength was waning to such a degree that he felt impelled to retire
to the ease of the House of Lords. Hitherto he had been the Great
Commoner, but now he accepted the title of the Earl of Chatham.

He took his place among the Lords, but sank into an ailment of
mind that kept him in seclusion for two years, until 1770, when he
again emerged with his old burning eloquence to assail the sub-
servience of Parliament to George III. In the final years of his life he
saw the American Revolutionary War, which broke away so vital a
segment of the empire he had done so much to create, and cried out
more and more bitterly against the policy that he was unable to avert.

He broke with his own party, when the Whigs decided that the
game was lost and American independence could not be averted, and
his bitterness was all the greater because the insurgent colonists had
joined forces with England's ancient enemy, France. As a liberal
statesman he vindicated the rights of Americans, but as an empire
builder he opposed their independence. In 1778, while the war in
America still continued, the Earl of Chatham made his dying speech
in the House of Lords—the William Pitt of old in a desperate protest
against the loss of so precious a part of the empire he had done so
much to win.

His last days would have been less tragic had he been able to look
forward to the political career of his son. The second William Pitt
also became Prime Minister, also led Britain in a titanic war—that
with Napoleon. And this William Pitt guided his country into the
path that led ultimately to victory.

FREDERICK THE GREAT

[1712–1786]

H E GREW up from a plump and pretty boy, with keen blue-gray eyes and curly hair, into a rather stout youth with an aversion to women which endured all his life. As he became older he lost weight and in young manhood was described as "handsome with a well knit frame, but below average height." He was always vigorous and active. As an old man, he was hard and lean. When he laughed his whole face lit up. Although most attentive to his dress in his youth, he became careless with advancing age and except on parade or at court functions usually wore an old blue uniform liberally sprinkled with snuff. This was the Old Fritz, beloved by the Berliners.

As a child and when in his teens Frederick was disgracefully treated by his father. Frederick William I of Prussia was a martinet to the point of parody. He gave his kingdom an excellent and frugal administration and a powerful well-disciplined army, but his very solid merits were obscured by the extravagances of his passion for soldiering. History has laughed at his giant Potsdam Guards, for which he recruited gargantuan specimens of tall humanity from all over Europe. Corporal punishment was about the only form of discipline that Frederick William knew. It was the discipline he used on his son, and he emphasized it in the Prussian army. He gave each sergeant a stout cane with which to punish his soldiers.

Young Frederick, however, loved poetry and music, and learned Latin in secret against his father's orders. The King considered the boy frivolous and effeminate, and was so incensed as to denounce him even in public. The father showed his hatred so clearly that when he was seventeen Crown Prince Frederick decided to run away.

He was prompted to this also by the fact that there were plans for his sister Wilhelmina, who sympathized with him thoroughly, to marry the Prince of Wales, son of George II of England, and for Frederick himself to marry the English Princess Amelia. Frederick thought of the marriage as a means of evading his father's tyranny, and believed he could live happily in England.

In the course of a journey to southern Germany, Frederick planned an escape with his friend Lieutenant Katte and a Scottish officer named Keith. The secret leaked out and the trio were arrested and brought back to Berlin. Keith was expelled from Germany. Frederick was tried by court-martial, deprived of his rank as Crown Prince, and sentenced to solitary confinement in the fortress of Cüstrin. Lieutenant Katte was condemned to life imprisonment. When the decision of the court-martial was sent to the King, he changed Lieutenant Katte's penalty to that of death. Frederick, prisoner in the fortress, was compelled to watch as the sentence was carried out, the beheading of his friend. He was told that if he again incurred his father's displeasure he would meet the same fate. This had a sobering effect on him, and after a time he was released from solitary confinement and put to work at the fortress for twelve hours a day on army accounts. In this way he learned army organization and finance.

Outwardly he was reconciled with his father and submissive, but he had become cynical, skeptical, and self-centered. He became an atheist. He hated all things German, especially the language. He wrote and spoke French whenever he could and corresponded with Voltaire, for whom he had a great admiration. Then his father died and he became Frederick II, King of Prussia, inheriting a well-organized kingdom, a full treasury, and a strong army.

Frederick embarked on an aggressive policy. In four years of the confused events of the War of the Austrian Succession, he made himself the most powerful monarch in Europe. He had a standing army of 165,000 men, well supplied with arms and enormous quantities of ammunition, ready at any time to take the field. Then for the next ten years he devoted himself to improving the internal administration of Prussia. An early riser, he was up at five in summer, at six in winter. He devoted the whole morning to public affairs, followed by a parade of troops. The afternoon was devoted to literary work, receiving visitors, or playing upon the flute, at which he excelled.

He built a famous palace at Potsdam, Sans-Souci, and in high style played his part of the liberal autocrat. Frederick once remarked, "I think as Epictetus did: 'If evil be said of thee, and if it be true, correct thyself; if it be a lie, laugh at it!'" He stopped his carriage one day to see what was interesting a crowd and found it was a placard directed against himself. He made his coachman lower it, so that the people could read it more easily. He once observed, "My people and I have come to an agreement which satisfies us both: they say what they please, I do as I please."

One of his first acts on coming to the throne had been to invite Voltaire to visit him at Sans-Souci, but it was not until some years later that the great French writer accepted. Voltaire stayed two years at Frederick's court. Both were egoists and masters of invective, and it was not long before dissensions arose. Voltaire lost no opportunity to libel the Prussian King behind his back; but Frederick overlooked the fact since he found Voltaire witty and entertaining, and needed him as a mentor in the art of writing French verse. Later Voltaire wrote a satirical account of his sojourn at Sans-Souci.

The Seven Years' War broke out. If Frederick hated women, they certainly had no love for him. Mme. de Pompadour, who was the power behind the throne in France, the Empress Elizabeth in Russia, and his old enemy Maria Theresa in Austria were all bent on destroying the power of Prussia. They instigated a powerful coalition, including Sweden and Saxony, and were about to attack Frederick when he, sensing the danger, struck first. He was allied with England, which sea power engaged in a maritime and colonial war with France, won Canada and India, and brought the British Empire into full being. On land Prussia withstood the whole continent in arms during seven years of kaleidoscopic campaigns and battles.

Frederick won the Battle of Lobositz and then invaded Bohemia, defeating the Austrians at Prague. Beaten at Kolin and again by the French at Hastenbeck and by the Russians at Grossjagersdorff, Frederick came back with a smashing victory at Rossbach and another at Leuthen, which he capped by a victory over the Russians at Zorndorf. Then, with the Duke of Brunswick in command, the Prussians and British together won the Battle of Minden.

The Battle of Torgau reversed everything again. Frederick lost a third of the men he led to the attack. Prussia had used up all her reserves. The Prussian campaigns were financed by English money, and England now threatened to withdraw her subsidies. Things looked black indeed for Frederick.

Then, at the eleventh hour, the Tsarina Elizabeth died and her successor, Peter II, who admired Frederick, at once offered to make peace and even to place men at the disposal of the Prussian King. These terms were accepted with alacrity. The Treaty of St. Petersburg restored all of Pomerania to Prussia and 18,000 seasoned Russian veterans were made available to Frederick. Russia's withdrawal from the conflict was followed by that of Sweden. France had lost her colonies to England and wanted peace. Austria was weary of the struggle. The war dragged on for a few months more, and then the treaty of peace left Frederick to enjoy his gains, his military genius recognized by all the world. He now received the title of Frederick the Great.

He began by demobilizing his cavalry and sent the horses to work on the farms. He provided free seed for replanting. He released as many men as possible to work in the fields, retaining only a nucleus of trained veterans and noncommissioned officers to build up a new army from the youth of the nation. He drained marshes, reformed tariffs. During seven years of constant fighting he had managed to keep his finances in far better shape than any of the other belligerents. Thanks to the subsidies received from England he had not had to borrow, and taxes had not been increased. So he soon had his finances back to normal and was able to found the Bank of Berlin with a capital of eight million thaler. The codification of German law, begun under his direction, was a sound combination of Roman and natural law. He fostered schools, education, science, art.

Frederick the Great was fond of animals and often said that his dogs were more faithful than any other of his friends. In his old age he had two large greyhounds as constant companions; they slept in his room and often on his bed. The chargers he rode in his many battles or for his pleasure in times of peace were never destroyed but turned out to grass and cared for until they died a natural death.

In 1772, Frederick the Great took part in the first partition of Poland, together with Maria Theresa and Catherine the Great of Russia. As his share he received East Prussia and a slice of Poland proper. Then in 1778, on the death of Maximilian of Bavaria, Frederick once more led a splendid Prussian army into the field to prevent Austria from acquiring Bavarian territory she coveted. Russia supplemented this by a contingent of 60,000 troops and the "war" ended without a battle the following year. Frederick was now to complete the remaining years of his long reign in peace.

One of his last achievements was the formation of a League of German Princes, which, although primarily designed as an additional check against Austria and dissolved after his death, undoubtedly showed the way to the Prussian-dominated German Empire that emerged eighty-five years later, after Prussia's victory over France in 1870.

Frederick the Great died at Sans-Souci of bronchopneumonia after being drenched by a rainstorm during a review of his troops. He left a durable nation, a powerful army, a full treasure—all inspired by his reputation as monarch and conqueror.

CLIVE

[1725–1774]

WHEN Robert Clive was seventeen his parents procured a "writership" with the East India Company for him and "shipped him off to make a fortune or die of a fever." They saw nothing better to do with him, for he was a difficult youth—moody, sensitive, and given to bouts of despair. India was almost the ruin of this pessimistic young Englishman, who hated the work and the climate and the inevitable debts caused by low pay. One day when a friend entered his room, Clive asked him to fire a pistol out the window, which the friend did. Clive sprang up, exclaiming, "Well, I am reserved for something. That pistol I have snapped twice at my own head."

His two suicide attempts failing, he did indeed go on to many great and glorious deeds. But after acquiring fame and fortune through heroism and statesmanship, after frequent narrow escapes from violent death, Lord Clive of Plassey died finally by his own hand.

When he arrived in India, English and French forces were fighting for the fabulous spoils of Hindustan. In 1746 the French commander, Dupleix, captured Madras and Robert Clive was among the prisoners of war. Clive for the first time showed himself to be a man of courage and resourcefulness, escaping by night disguised as a Mohammedan, joining the British army although he never had had any military training. He was now caught up in the game of war, diplomacy, and international rivalry—with India as the prize.

The great empire of the Moguls was in confusion, with leaders striving for power, provinces striving for independence, and Britain and France competing for control through puppet princelings. At Arcot the French candidate, Chunda Sahib, held sway. Clive volunteered to attack Arcot. The city had 100,000 inhabitants, while Clive was allowed only 200 British soldiers supported by 300 native sepoys. Shrewdly judging the mentality of the defenders, he began his assault during a raging thunderstorm. The garrison, superstitious about an enemy who defied the forces of nature, abandoned their posts, allowing Clive to march into Arcot with hardly a shot fired.

Chunda Sahib, who was in the field fighting the British at the time, rushed his army back to his capital. Then followed the famous siege of Arcot, when Clive held out against a besieging army of 10,000 led by French officers. For almost two months Chunda Sahib threw everything he had against Arcot, including elephants with iron plates covering their foreheads, living battering rams that would have crashed through the gates if they had not been maddened by the bullets of the defenders. The elephants turned and trampled the besiegers, Clive rationed his food and water in order to avoid being starved out, and he had the pleasure of seeing Chunda Sahib lift the siege and retreat.

Clive gave the throne of Arcot to the British candidate, Mohammed Ali, who bestowed upon him the title of Sabut Jung ("daring in war"). It was a title Clive used afterward on his personal seal. William Pitt referred to him in the House of Commons as a "heaven-sent general." The East India Company voted him a sword of honor. He was granted time off to visit England.

He arrived home with a brand-new wife. How he got married is another of the romantic stories about Clive. An acquaintance in India showed him a picture of his sister, and Clive was so struck by the beauty of the image that he swore then and there that he would marry the lady—which he did not long after he was introduced to her.

Clive received an enthusiastic welcome in England, and then returned to Hindustan as Governor of Fort St. David. The scene of action had shifted north to Bengal. The nabobs of Bengal had always been friendly to the British, but trouble broke out when the finance minister of Bengal fled and asked the European intruders for protection. The Governor of Calcutta refused to give him up, whereupon the Nabob, Suraj-ud-Dowlah, seized the fort of Calcutta, plundered it, and shut up 146 British captives, including several women, in a prison chamber only twenty feet square. This was the infamous Black Hole of Calcutta, from which after a night of stifling tropical weather only 23 survivors emerged the next day. The rest had been either suffocated or trampled to death.

Clive marched to wreak vengeance. With 600 British soldiers, 800 sepoys, and seven field guns he attacked and routed a force of 34,000 Bengalese supported by 40 pieces of cannon and 50 elephants. Suraj-ud-Dowlah hastened to sign a treaty dictated by Clive.

But the Nabob of Bengal intrigued with the French, and Clive decided to get rid of him with the help of two conspirators, a soldier named Mir Jaffar, and a merchant named Omichund. During the negotiations Clive did one of the things that helped to tarnish his reputation. When everything was ready, Omichund tried blackmail by threatening to disclose the conspiracy to the Nabob unless he was paid off. Clive met this danger by drawing up a fictitious agreement containing the financial clause Omichund wanted. Clive's admiral refused to be a party to this deception, whereupon Clive coolly had his name forged. The fictitious agreement satisfied Omichund, who only discovered how he had been outmaneuvered when Clive produced the true agreement in which the blackmail was not mentioned. Clive always defended his action as the deception of a criminal, but he was strongly denounced in the House of Commons for it.

With his conspiracy all set, Clive declared war on Suraj-ud-Dowlah. The key point in the conspiracy was the promise of Mir Jaffar to defect to the British at the critical moment. But would the Nabob's commander keep his word? There was some doubt as the two armies jockeyed for position near Plassey, the obvious battlefield. Should Mir Jaffar break his promise, the British would find themselves in an impossible situation, outnumbered by at least twenty to one. The Nabob had over 50,000 foot soldiers, 18,000 cavalrymen, many elephants, and 53 pieces of artillery. Clive had 1,100 British and 2,100 native troops with nine guns.

Clive thought at first it would be folly to attack without being sure of Mir Jaffar. He withdrew into a clump of trees, thought out the problem, and returned to tell his officers that he had changed his mind. He ordered them to be prepared to advance to Plassey the next day.

The sun rose bright on the morning of June 22, 1757, over the plain of Plassey. Clive crossed the Hooghly and during the day established his little force in the grove of trees along its bank. Headquarters were set up in a hunting lodge. Before dark his men were all drawn up within a mile of the Nabob's sprawling camp. All night long the sound of drums and cymbals kept Clive awake. At sunrise the plain seemed alive with enemy infantry and cavalry as the Nabob's army swarmed to the attack. The British guns opened up. The 39th Regiment, which still bears on its banners the words "Plassey" and "*Primus in Indus*," advanced and poured rifle fire into the advancing horde.

Mir Meden, one of the Nabob's two chief captains, was hit and mortally wounded. Mir Jaffar, who had faltered in his secret agreement with Clive, was sent for and bidden to avenge Mir Meden's death. He now carried out his treacherous compact. He advised immediate retreat. The fatal order was issued. Utter confusion ensued and the greater part of the Nabob's forces fled, only Jaffar's division remaining with grounded arms to await the arrival of the English.

Clive lost twenty-two killed and fifty wounded in a battle that gave him, besides immense spoils of war, the paramount authority over Bengal, a province larger and more populous than his native country. He installed Mir Jaffar as Nabob, and shortly afterward heard that Suraj-ud-Dowlah had been murdered for the gold and jewels he carried with him in his flight from Plassey.

The public ceremonial was followed by a private division of the spoils. Clive was moderate in the amount of money he took from a treasury containing gold, silver, and jewels piled to the ceiling. He procured a revenue of a hundred thousand pounds a year for the East India Company and a million and a half to cover the company's losses at Calcutta and to meet the military costs of the expedition. Twenty-four thousand pounds were distributed among the troops. Clive personally took one hundred and sixty thousand pounds. Moreover he accepted from Mir Jaffar as a personal gift a *jaghire*, or estate for the support of a military contingent, worth thirty thousand pounds a year.

The Battle of Plassey had given India to Britain. The French saw their prestige among the potentates of Hindustan disappear. They were forced back to minor holdings on the coast. The British raj was being formed, and would last for almost two centuries.

In 1760 Clive left for England, where he was hailed as a national hero, given an Irish peerage as Baron Clive of Plassey, and elected to the House of Commons.

Returning to India, Clive proceeded to place the East India Company, or rather Britain itself, in control of the Great Mogul at Delhi. Clive thus made the British virtual rulers of India, doing in Delhi what he had already done in Madras and Bengal. He founded the British Empire in India, which was to be formally taken over for the Crown by Disraeli a hundred-odd years later.

For the last time Clive returned to England in 1767. His health was undermined, and he had made many enemies. It was not long before General John Burgoyne, later to figure in the American Revolution, sought to have the House of Commons impeach Clive, but Burgoyne was no more successful then than ten years later when he surrendered at Saratoga. The House found that "Robert, Lord Clive did render great and meritorious service to his country."

Clive himself was furious and bitterly complained about the way he was interrogated. His old despondency returned. The use of opium aggravated the disturbed state of his mind, without giving him much relief from his physical ills. On November 22, 1774, Lord Clive was found on the floor dead, victim of a self-inflicted wound. His third suicide attempt had been successful.

CAPTAIN COOK

[*1728–1779*]

Today a magnificent monument stands on the shore of Kealake-kua Bay in Hawaii. It represents Captain James Cook, who put much of the Pacific on the map for the first time, and then perished at the hands of the natives of Kealakekua.

From his earliest years James Cook wanted to be a sailor. He began as an apprentice on a barge carrying coal from Newcastle to London. In winter, when the colliers were laid up, he studied assiduously, poring over books on navigation and seamanship, mastering the sea routes of the world as they were then known. One fact quickly struck his eye as he scrutinized the maps—how little of the vast Pacific had been charted.

Graduating from his barge to sailing ships, he served as seaman, mate, and officer on voyages to Iceland, Norway, Sweden, and other ports of call. Finally he enlisted in the Royal Navy, where he was posted to Canada during the Seven Years' War (or the French and Indian War, as it was known on this side of the Atlantic).

The French had removed all buoys and landmarks from the St. Lawrence, making navigation of the narrows almost impossible. So Cook, who was known to be good at taking soundings, was sent ahead in a small and heavily armed boat to guide the way as the British moved upstream. He managed to get nearly two hundred ships through in safety, and without his help the siege of Quebec could not have been undertaken. He participated in other actions, and made a series of charts for navigation, these of a highly competent sort.

Cook's charts of the St. Lawrence proved remarkably accurate and were published by the Admiralty. He had been highly commended by his officers, who had forwarded a recommendation that he be given further work of this kind. Sir Hugh Palliser, under whose command he had seen much service, was made Governor of Newfound-land. At his request Cook was appointed "marine surveyor" of the coasts of Labrador and Newfoundland, a post he held for five years.

During this period he observed an eclipse of the sun and made it possible to calculate for the first time the exact longitude of the New-foundland coast; he also brought out sailing instructions which showed him to be a highly competent navigator. Cook's work in Newfoundland completed, to the entire satisfaction of the Admiralty, he was given six months' leave on full pay.

At the expiration of his leave Cook received a commission as lieu-tenant in the Royal Navy, the first instance of any enlisted man's being so promoted. He was placed in command of the "Endeavour" and sent on an astronomical expedition celebrated in the history of science. This was a voyage undertaken at the urging of the Royal Society, to observe the transit of Venus (the passage of that planet between the earth and the sun) from Tahiti, where climatic condi-tions were ideal for the purpose. He was accompanied by Sir Joseph Banks and a number of scientists.

The "Endeavour" was slow and hard to handle, but she was safe and tough. Cook left England, and after touching Rio de Janeiro and Tierra del Fuego, reached Tahiti in plenty of time to get everything ready to observe the transit of Venus. The natives proved friendly, the weather ideal, and Sir Joseph Banks and his fellow-scientists made some highly successful observations. This British expedition to Tahiti to observe a transit of Venus was in many ways remarkably like one made almost two centuries later—the 1958 American expedition to Danger Island (named by Captain Cook, incidentally) to observe an eclipse of the sun by rocket astronomy.

Cook had been ordered, on leaving Tahiti, to explore the South Pacific, which he did till he came upon the east coast of New Zealand, hitherto unexplored. He discovered the strait between the north and south islands. He sailed around both islands and charted the coast line. He then proceeded in the direction of Tasmania, which had been discovered by the Dutch explorer Tasman and was thought to be a peninsula. He reached Australia at a point he named Botany Bay because of the strange and interesting plants the scientists found there.

After running aground on the Great Barrier Reef and floating off the "Endeavour" by a combination of luck, superhuman effort, and throwing things overboard, Cook recorded that the tides were higher at night than in the daytime. Then he rounded the northern tip of Australia, sailing between Australia and New Guinea. He next made for Batavia, a Dutch colony in Java, which was the first civilized place he had seen since Rio. Up to this time Cook had not lost a man because of sickness, although two scientists who had gone ashore at Tierra del Fuego had been frozen to death. But during three months in Batavia many of his men became ill with fever, probably some form of malaria, and forty of them died before his ship reached home by way of the Cape of Good Hope.

The Royal Society, greatly impressed by his reports on New Zealand and Australia, was anxious that a thorough exploration of the islands of the Pacific be made. Cook was persuaded to be commander, and set to work on plans for a second expedition. Suggesting that for greater safety two vessels be sent out, he was given the "Resolution" and the "Adventure." Taking two vessels did not prove too successful in practice. They became separated in fog, but met again at an agreed rendezvous in New Zealand. A second time they became separated in a storm; and when Cook arrived at the meeting place he found signs of conflict and possibly shipwreck and could only understand that something tragic had happened. Not until he reached home did he learn that the men of the "Adventure" had fallen afoul of the natives and that many of them had been killed and eaten. The captain had managed to get back, arriving a year before Cook.

During the voyage, Cook made explorations below latitude 71 degrees, venturing into ice fields which no man had ever sailed before and where very few have sailed since. He did not reach the South Polar continent. Turning north, when he found no land, he proceeded to Easter Island, then across to Tahiti for supplies and water, and on to the New Hebrides which he was the first to explore. Then, steering south to search for more islands between the New Hebrides and New Zealand, he discovered New Caledonia and the Norfolk Islands. He returned home after visits to St. Helena, Ascension, and the Azores. He had covered 20,000 leagues, had been more than a thousand days at sea, and had lost only one man of the 118 who had sailed with him.

Commander Cook had conquered scurvy, a disease that for centuries had been the bane of navigators everywhere. His success in dealing with this scourge was due to a program of rigid cleanliness on board ship, and the procurement of plenty of fresh water and as much fresh foodstuffs as he could get, especially fruits and vegetables. He highly recommended sauerkraut and lime juice, both of which were made compulsory in the British navy from then on.

For his discoveries Captain Cook was elected a member of the Royal Society which awarded him the Copley gold medal, one of the world's highest awards for achievement in science. His *Voyage towards the South Pole and round the World* was deemed so important that the first edition was issued before the maps, charts, views, and portraits included in the final edition were ready.

Having charted the South Pacific, Cook's next task was to do the same for the North Pacific. It was his last task, for he never returned from his third voyage.

He traversed the Pacific, making many new discoveries, until he reached Hawaii. These islands had been first visited by the Spaniards in 1555. Cook rediscovered them in 1778, and renamed them the Sandwich Islands for his friend the Earl of Sandwich, then head of the Admiralty—the very one who had cuts of roast beef placed between slices of bread so that he could eat without rising from the gaming table, thereby inventing the sandwich.

From Hawaii, Captain Cook made for the western coast of America, sailing north to the Aleutian Islands, already discovered by the Russians, and passing through Bering Strait, proving that the two continents were separated by a narrow strip of water. Then back to the Sandwich Islands for a rest.

Cook went ashore with a party of marines after one of his boats had been stolen. A scuffle began. Captain Cook ordered his party, vastly outnumbered, back to their boats. He himself was the last to retire, and as he neared the water's edge he was struck from behind and set upon with spears and stones by the natives, who finally held him under water to drown. They then disappeared into the jungle, carrying his body with them.

GEORGE WASHINGTON

[1732–1799]

L EGEND MAKERS, headed by Parson Weems, have embellished the childhood of George Washington with myths. The best known of these legends is, of course, the one about the cherry tree, which young George cut down and about which he refused to lie—"I cannot tell a lie, I did it with my little hatchet." The tale of how George threw a silver dollar across the Potomac ignores the fact that the American dollar, along with the American Republic, did not come into existence until long afterward.

But the legend makers had a good subject to work with. Washington is a monumental figure in American history. He is rightly called "the father of his country." President Eisenhower once referred to him as the greatest man ever produced by the English-speaking race.

Washington belonged to one of Virginia's aristocratic families. He grew up on the family estate at Mount Vernon. His early desire was to go to sea on the ships trading in tobacco, but his mother vetoed the plan in favor of a career in surveying. He was still in his teens when he got the job of surveying the extensive Fairfax lands on the other side of the Blue Ridge Mountains. He did his work so well that it brought him an appointment as public surveyor.

He was a young man when he inherited the Washington plantation at Mount Vernon. The leaders of Virginia recognized his ability, and he joined the staff of Governor Dinwiddie with the rank of major. It was a hopeful time for rising officers. The British and the French were beginning their struggle for the Ohio Valley.

Washington's first military campaign was not a success. Sent by Governor Dinwiddie to retake a fort on the present site of Pittsburgh, the Virginian attacked a French advance party without warning, and killed the commander along with nine of his men. Washington had to retreat when the main body of the French came up, whereupon they besieged him in a stockade called Fort Necessity, forced his surrender, and made him promise that for another year no British strong point would be established in the area. Washington also had to admit his responsibility for killing the French commander, although he later denied the French report that he had confessed to "assassinating" the Frenchman.

Washington's adventure in the wilderness was a beginning for the widespread conflict known as the Seven Years' War (in America, the French and Indian War).

General Braddock arrived from England with two picked regiments. Washington joined his staff with the rank of colonel. Then followed the ill-fated march into the wilderness, where Braddock was ambushed and killed, with Washington salvaging what he could from the retreat. British Prime Minister William Pitt sent a new expedition. Washington joined this one too. He had the satisfaction of marching into the ruins of Fort Duquesne, now Pittsburgh—an easy enough task since the real battle took place in Canada, where General Wolfe overthrew New France.

From 1759 to 1774, for fifteen carefree years, Washington's life at Mount Vernon was one of tranquil happiness. His own inheritance was ample, and his marriage to Martha Custis made him one of the wealthiest men in the colonies. His diaries abound in references to his pure-bred Arabian horses, blooded hunters, English hounds, his dinners and receptions, his famous wines. George Washington, in his thirties, might have seemed destined for the life of a prominent and honored Virginia squire dedicated to the care and cultivation of his ample acres. But a new turn of history was at hand to project him into immortality.

The Colonies were quarreling with the mother country. Washington wanted to exhaust every peaceful remedy first, but he preferred war to submission to England's demands. He was on his way to Philadelphia as a delegate to the Second Continental Congress when word of the fighting at Lexington and Concord reached him. Shortly after his arrival in Philadelphia he was named commander of the Continental Army.

The history of the Revolutionary War is dominated by the personality of George Washington, but his fame does not rest on brilliant genius as a military strategist. He lost too many battles to rank with the masters of warfare, while he was not even present when the Continentals won the key victory of the war, the victory over Burgoyne at Saratoga. Washington's greatness lay in holding together his bedraggled forces and urging them on to victory. His finest moment came at Valley Forge, for it was a miracle that he was able to keep his army in existence during the terrible winter of 1778. After Valley Forge he had unbounded faith in his men, and they trusted him to see them through to freedom.

His superb gifts of character won the admiration and reverence of the young French aristocrat Lafayette, who was so influential in bringing France to the aid of the Americans, and Lafayette's lifelong homage was typical of the reputation of Washington that spread through Europe, where he was hailed as a hero of liberty and lofty champion of republican freedom.

Victory achieved, he spent the winter of 1781–82 with the Congress in Philadelphia, and rejoined his command at Newburgh on the Hudson in April of 1782. His fame was such that it was suggested he found an American monarchy and accept the crown. All such notions Washington firmly and summarily rejected. On December 4, 1783, at Fraunce's Tavern in New York, he parted with his closest officers in an affecting scene.

When the Constitutional Convention met in Philadelphia on May 13, 1787, Washington, leader of the Virginia delegation, was chosen to preside. After that he strongly urged the states to ratify the Constitution, which they did.

There could be only one choice in the first presidential election. Washington received a unanimous vote. Notified of his election as first President of the United States, George Washington left Mount Vernon for New York, then the site of the federal government.

He took into his cabinet Thomas Jefferson as Secretary of State and Alexander Hamilton as Secretary of the Treasury. The two were leaders of political extremes. Jefferson thought the first thing to be done was to protect the democratic rights of the people. Hamilton was just as convinced that the primary need was a strong central government to hold the states together and organize the new nation. Washington kept both men in his cabinet, although his own leaning was more toward Hamilton's ideas than Jefferson's.

Jefferson finally left the cabinet because he could not approve of the government's attitude toward the French Revolution. Washington took Hamilton's view that, despite what France had done for America in the winning of freedom, the United States should disregard the treaty made with the French King now overthrown by the terrorists.

Washington served two terms and refused a third, retiring after a great farewell address in which he urged national unity and warned against entangling alliances with European powers. He returned to Mount Vernon and resumed plantation life. He and Martha Washington entertained some of the greatest figures of the time, including Lafayette who returned for a visit with his old commander.

When Washington died, British warships and regiments of Napoleon paid him honor. In the United States he was mourned and eulogized in the words of Henry Lee—"first in war, first in peace and first in the hearts of his countrymen."

JOHN PAUL JONES

[*1747–1792*]

OHN PAUL JONES is the most famous example of the American immigrant who serves his adopted country with devoted loyalty in war against the land of his birth. He, who came from Great Britain, wrote his name into history as the sea hero of the American Revolution. But he was not English. He was a Scot.

He did not actually belong to the multitude of Joneses who had come out of Wales and spread over Britain. Originally he was simply John Paul, the son of a landscape gardener who dwelt on the Solway Firth. From his mother, a MacDuff, he inherited the blood of the Highlands.

By his early teens young John Paul had become an expert boatman and fisherman on the Solway Firth. One day a shipowner saw him maneuver his fishing smack against a high wind, and gave him a job as apprentice on a brig bound for the West Indies and Virginia.

To Virginia an elder brother, William Paul, had already gone, and had become the manager of the estate of a prominent planter, William Jones. There John Paul visited William, who stood high in the favor of the employer. This favor was now extended to the younger brother, and the wealthy planter offered to adopt the lad. But John Paul preferred to follow the sea.

For the next few years he had the usual career of life before the mast. Then on one voyage yellow fever killed his captain and most of the ship's crew. John Paul took command, landed the ship at its port, and claimed salvage. He was awarded 10 per cent of the value of the vessel and its cargo. John Paul was now well to do.

On a subsequent voyage as captain, he was accused by British authorities in the West Indies of killing one of his seamen. It is not clear whether he surrendered to the British authorities at Tobago, was

DISRAELI

ROBERT E. LEE

tried and acquitted; or whether he escaped from the island and went to Virginia. In any case, the episode figures in the British attitude toward him—their opinion in later years that he was little better than a pirate. It likewise plays a part in his own subsequent enmity for the English and his decision to become an American.

The decision was the easier because the Virginia planter William Jones had died and left his estate to William Paul—with a reversion to John Paul if he adopted the name of Jones. When William died, John Paul, now in Virginia, assumed the name of John Paul Jones, and inherited an estate of three thousand acres, with twenty horses, eighty head of cattle, sundry sheep and swine, and thirty slaves.

He was now twenty-eight, a rollicking sailor turned Virginia plantation owner. By virtue of his land holdings John Paul Jones attended the Virginia House of Burgesses, where he applauded the speeches of Thomas Jefferson and Patrick Henry.

The outbreak of the Revolution, the shots fired at Lexington and Concord, found him in New York. On his way home he stopped off in Philadelphia and offered his services to the Second Continental Congress, which asked his advice on the formation of an American navy.

He received fighting commands aboard the "Providence" and the "Alfred," sank many enemy vessels and brought others in as prizes, and in five weeks bagged seven British ships, including a large transport with supplies and reinforcements for General Burgoyne. After that he raided the fisheries along the coast of Nova Scotia. The following year, on June 14, 1777, Congress gave him command of the "Ranger," one of the most powerful ships in the American navy. As it happened, this appointment of John Paul Jones was the second half of a twofold resolution, the first clause of which decreed the adoption of the American flag.

"Resolved, that the Flag of the Thirteen United States of America be thirteen stripes, alternate red and white, and that the union be thirteen stars on a blue field.

"Resolved, that Captain John Paul Jones be appointed to command the ship 'Ranger.'"

Of the double resolution he said, "That flag and I are twins, born in the same hour from the same womb of destiny. We cannot be parted in life or in death. So long as we can float we shall float together. If we must sink we shall go down as one."

He took the "Ranger" to France, his mission being to deliver to Benjamin Franklin and the American commissioners the news of Burgoyne's surrender. Operating out of Brest, he raided ports on the Irish Sea, including Whitehaven, his former home base, and distinguished himself greatly when the "Ranger" captured the more powerful H.M.S. "Drake" and took that warship back to France as a prize of war. The "Ranger" was sent to Brest for repairs in 1779, and John Paul Jones took command of the "Bonhomme Richard," in which he was to win immortality.

The vessel was a refitted French craft obtained through Benjamin Franklin and renamed after the character in Franklin's famous publication, *Poor Richard's Almanack*. John Paul Jones sailed the "Bonhomme Richard" into British waters, and encountered a fleet of merchantmen convoyed by two warships. The larger of the two was the "Serapis," which John Paul Jones selected for himself. As the "Bonhomme Richard," with forty-two guns, approached the fifty-gun "Serapis," she was raked by broadside after broadside. Of the 140 officers and men on the main gun deck more than eighty fell during the cannonade. But the "Bonhomme Richard" succeeded in closing with the "Serapis" and threw grappling irons aboard. English Captain Parsons, looking at his badly battered enemy, called for surrender, and John Paul Jones gave his historic reply, "We have not yet begun to fight!" Hand-to-hand battle raged until a young American midshipman, laying out on a yardarm, managed to throw a live grenade into the ammunition supply of the "Serapis." The explosion blasted the British vessel, and put an end to the battle. Captain Parsons struck his flag.

John Paul Jones took the "Serapis" as a prize, but the "Bonhomme Richard" was so badly shot up that she sank, John Paul Jones himself giving this account:

"No one was now left aboard the 'Bonhomme Richard' but our dead. To them I gave the good old ship for their coffin and in her they found a sublime burial. She rolled heavily in the long swell, settled slowly by the head and sank peacefully in forty fathoms of water. Our torn and tattered flag had been left flying when we abandoned the ship. As she plunged down at the last, her taffrail momentarily rose in the air, so the very last vestige mortal eye ever saw of the 'Bonhomme Richard' was the defiant waving of her un-conquered and unstricken flag."

France went wild over the exploit and Louis XVI presented the American captain with a sword of honor. But John Paul Jones was less successful when he tried to collect pay for his men. He was re-ferred from one place to another in a typical exhibition of buck pass-ing. His health began to give way. With the exception of a brief cruise in the "Ariel," his active participation in the war was ended.

In Paris and at Versailles, John Paul Jones became a favorite figure. The English spread the report that he was a savage pirate, and the French were not a little surprised to meet a most courteous, graceful gentleman of slight build and delicate features, faultlessly attired, exquisitely polite, and speaking their language fluently.

Returning to the United States in 1781, John Paul Jones super-vised the construction of what was to be the largest vessel in the United States Navy, the "America," of seventy-four guns. He should have commanded her, but the ship was given to the French instead. When the Revolutionary War ended, he went back to Paris as "an agent of the Treasury to collect the money due to the United States for the many prizes he had taken."

In 1788, Catherine the Great of Russia asked him to accept an appointment as rear admiral in the Russian navy. He was to serve in a war between Russia and Turkey. Eager for action, he hurried to St. Petersburg—only to find an enemy in Potemkin, the all-powerful minister. Potemkin turned the Empress against the American sailor by reviving the old accusations of piracy and murder. Catherine dis-missed John Paul Jones despite her promise of an admiralship for him. Disgusted and disappointed, he returned to Paris.

There he lived through three years of the French Revolution, three years of illness and neglect. In 1792, George Washington, now Presi-dent, gave him a commission to go to Algiers, to deal with Barbary pirates who were preying upon American shipping in the Mediterra-nean. John Paul Jones did not have the satisfaction of receiving this commission. He died just before it reached Paris. He was buried in the Protestant cemetery; a distinguished French clergyman pro-nounced the funeral oration, speaking of him as "one of the first champions of American liberty, one of the first harbingers of the liberty of the world."

In 1905, President Theodore Roosevelt instructed the American ambassador in Paris to have a diligent search made for the grave of the great naval commander. The Protestant cemetery had long been closed and forgotten, but with assistance from the French authorities the grave was finally located. The remains were brought back to the United States in 1913 under escort by a fleet of American warships. Reburied in the crypt of the beautiful chapel at Annapolis, John Paul Jones received belated recognition of his immense services to his adopted land.

GOETHE

[1749–1832]

JOHANN WOLFGANG VON GOETHE, the greatest figure in German literature, was much more than a writer. He may be called the Leonardo da Vinci of his age, for he reflected European thought in almost all of its manifestations. He engaged in politics, experimented with scientific theories, helped develop the novel in its classical form, wrote exquisite lyrical poetry comparable to that of Burns, and rivaled Shakespeare as a dramatist. He touched philosophy, classical studies, history, art criticism, linguistics.

Born into the eighteenth century, the century of Classicism, he did as much as anyone to overthrow the old mentality and push Europe into Romanticism. His father wanted him to be a lawyer, and he studied law at Leipzig for a while, but abandoned his classes to write, carouse, and make love.

His dissipations at Leipzig impaired his health, and after a severe illness he returned home to Frankfort. His father was bitterly disappointed. His mother and sister set about nursing him back to health. A woman friend, who dabbled in mystical theology and science, cured Goethe with some mysterious drug. This set him to brooding on religious and occult matters, and he dabbled in alchemy. An end result of this was seen later in his greatest work, *Faust*, with its love of medieval alchemy.

When he had recovered completely his father sent him to the University of Strasbourg to continue his study of law. There he was deeply impressed by the medieval architecture of the city, the prevalence of the Gothic style of old. He met Herder, the great art critic of the time, who explained to him the significance of the Gothic. This was an important influence for Goethe, turning him from the elegant

grace of the French style and inspiring him with the somber gran-
deurs of the pre-Renaissance style.

Goethe received his licentiate in law, and returned home to Frankfort to practice the legal profession. He alternated law with writing,
and now turned out the work that began his reputation.

His play, *Goetz von Berlichingen*, reflected his Gothic enthusiasms.
The subject was strong, violent, Germanic, a tale of a soldier of the
years gone by. The treatment was broad and free, along Shakespear-
ean lines, as against the trim refinement of the French classical drama.
Goetz von Berlichingen was a landmark in the development of the
Romantic school which in Germany took the form of the *Sturm und
Drang* (Storm and Stress) movement.

Goethe followed it with a novel that swept Europe with Romanticism from Poland to Scotland. This was *The Sorrows of Werther*, a
tale of unrequited love, based on a real episode in the novelist's life.
The suicide of the hero, Werther, is said to have caused many suicides
among the millions who read the story. Its powerful impact may be
judged from how early it appeared in the development of European
literature—1774, fifteen years before the French Revolution.

During this time Goethe poured out a stream of writing as the
premier author of the Storm and Stress school. He wrote lyric poetry.
He started his first labors on *Faust*, though long years were to elapse
before he produced any of it for publication. He had begun to think
of the subject at Strasbourg amid Gothic architecture and under the
influence of Herder. Now he undertook to write it, then put it aside.
But it is clear that *Faust* begins with the Romanticism of his Storm
and Stress.

In 1775, Goethe was invited to the court of the young Duke of
Saxe-Weimar. At Weimar the poet spent the rest of his life. He was
consulted on affairs of state, given a part in the administration of the
principality, made a privy councilor. He worked hard. He was responsible for the theater and the mines, public works and irrigation,
plans for the new ducal castle and the University of Jena, and even
for the army.

In 1786 he set out for Italy, on a journey that brought a transformation of his thought. Goethe had often dreamed of visiting the ancient land, and now the result was a new trend, a new period. In
Rome his interest focused on classical antiquity. He had little con-

cern for the medieval glories of the Eternal City, for the ecclesiastical aspects or even for the beauties of the Renaissance. He saw chiefly the antique art of Greece and Rome, so imposing in the mighty ruins and the museums filled with remnants of the past. He became a Classicist. Chief German protagonist of Gothic Romanticism, he entered a new phase mirroring the harmony, balance, and serenity of Hellenic culture.

Back in Weimar, Goethe, who had long been interested in science, now threw himself into scientific research. His interest in poetry flagged, as he studied and experimented in various branches, especially optics and biology. He conducted valuable investigation into the nature of light and color, opposing Newton's theories of optics. His biological work marked an important step forward in morphology and the metamorphosis of plants. He made useful observations in anatomy, and foreshadowed later evolutionary ideas.

He continued to work and write amidst the upheaval of the French Revolution and the Napoleonic Wars. He deprecated the revolutionary excesses, although he was happy to see the end of aristocratic abuses. Napoleon he regarded as a liberator. The two titans of war and literature met and were very impressed with one another. Napoleon told Goethe he had read *Werther* seven times.

Meanwhile Goethe's attention was being drawn ever more powerfully to the theme of Faust. Partly this was due to his friend Schiller, another master poet of German literature, who urged him to keep at a work so much in harmony with his genius.

Goethe produced his masterpiece in two parts. It is on the first part, with its concentrated lyricism, passion, intelligence, and philosophical meaning that his fame rests. *Faust* is the end product of sixty years of meditation by one of the most sublime of human spirits, and reflects the range of experience from early youth to old age. Nothing comparable to this can be found in the whole realm of art.

Goethe began it in the time of his Gothic Romanticism, and continued it through his Classical period. The colossal work mirrors the transitions of his own thought—Gretchen for the Romantic, Helen of Troy for the Classic. In the second part the poet moves from the pathos of human drama into a world of philosophical symbolism. Goethe's *Faust* was instantly recognized as a masterpiece. To our popular lore it added the figures of Faust and Mephistopheles. Wagner and Berlioz wrote symphonic music on the theme. Gounod used it for one of the most popular of operas.

When Goethe died, all Europe knew it had lost the peer of Homer, Dante, and Shakespeare.

MARIE ANTOINETTE

[1755–1793]

DAVID, one of the greatest of French artists, made a sketch of Marie Antoinette as she was being taken to the guillotine. Seated on a chair in the tumbrel, the Queen of France is shown in profile. Her hair, once so elaborately curled, is cut short and hangs straight under a cotton cap. Her face is cold and set, her eyes are sunken, her nose is prominent, her lower jaw reaching forward grimly. The cords in her neck stand out. Although she was not yet thirty-eight, in the sketch she is old and worn by suffering. Once the most fashionable woman in France, the Queen went to her death with calm courage, but she had paid for her sins, whatever they were, and the payment was stamped on her face.

Marie Antoinette was the ninth child of the Empress Maria Theresa of Austria and her consort, the Holy Roman Emperor Francis I. She was reared austerely by her imperial mother, who destined her for an alliance with France, had her educated to that end, and then married her to the Dauphin of France, the grandson of Louis XV, before she was fifteen. Perhaps no young bride in history has faced a more difficult situation than that which confronted Marie Antoinette upon her arrival at the French court. Her marriage was the pledge of a Franco-Austrian alliance, yet within a year of her arrival Mme. du Barry, in whose hands Louis XV was as wax, succeeded in jeopardizing the Austrian alliance. The King's mistress took a violent dislike to Marie Antoinette and always referred to her as "the Austrian woman."

More important, however, the royal bridegroom showed little interest in the bride. He had never had anything to do with women and was interested only in hunting and in his two hobbies: laying bricks and making locks. Marie Antoinette was a beautiful girl, slender and graceful, with tiny hands and feet, blonde hair, sparkling blue eyes, an oval face, and a most charming manner. She was a good musician, had a sweet voice, and danced to perfection. She spoke several languages and her French was without even a trace of accent. She was extremely gay and fond of amusement, and did her best to make her husband love her. The trouble with him was physical, but an operation left him capable of reciprocating her affection.

During the seven years of her married life before the King's operation and her own motherhood, the young Queen felt the public disfavor that led her to eventual doom. She gained a reputation for frivolity. She was impatient of the stilted etiquette of the court of Versailles and craved amusement. The King's brother, the Comte d'Artois, had surrounded himself with a young and gay circle of friends, and to these Marie Antoinette was quickly attracted. She went with them incognito to the opera and to masked balls in Paris.

After the accession of Louis XVI, Queen Marie Antoinette rapidly eliminated all elderly women from official positions at court and surrounded herself with pleasure-loving youth. Her passion for luxury and her prodigality were unrestrained. Her husband denied her nothing, never questioned why she should throw millions away in carefree abandon.

Louis XVI wanted to reduce the expenses of his coronation, but the Queen insisted on the most extravagant outlay. The whole court moved to Rheims, in a long procession of gilded coaches. No jewels were too splendid, no adornment too expensive, no liveries too sumptuous, and that at a time when the people of France were overtaxed and many of them on the verge of starvation.

Neither Marie Antoinette nor her husband took the slightest interest in public affairs. The King's diary, consisting of hundreds of carefully scrawled pages, is inane from beginning to end. When he thinks nothing of importance is happening, he writes, *"rien."* This word "nothing" he applies to some of the most critical events leading up to the French Revolution.

His indifference to public affairs was equaled only by Marie Antoinette's ignorance, a complete and total ignorance of the conditions in which the people of France lived. Her interest in public affairs was limited to obtaining places and pensions for her favorites, their families and their friends. She also sought to further the interests of her native Austria.

Marie Antoinette took to playing cards for high stakes—once she sat at the gaming table for thirty-six hours at a stretch—and to creating new fashions in clothes. She set the styles and had new colors named after her.

When she became a mother Marie Antoinette began to live a quieter life. Within the park of Versailles, laid out by Louis XIV, were two smaller palaces, the Trianons. The smaller, or Petit Trianon, became the favorite residence of Marie Antoinette, who had it surrounded by rustic villas and an English garden. There she and the ladies of her court led a mimic peasant life.

During all this idyllic existence, Marie Antoinette never suspected the rumblings of the Revolution, the storm clouds that were gathering fast. Then came the affair of the diamond necklace. This was bought by the Cardinal de Rohan for 1,600,000 livres, he having been led to believe the Queen wanted it. He gave it to a woman whom he took for the Queen. He failed to pay the jewelers, and they complained to Marie Antoinette, who was astonished. She had the Cardinal arrested, and a scandalous trial ensued. It turned out that he had been duped by a woman who had carried on a correspondence with him in the Queen's name and afterward had impersonated her at a midnight meeting in the gardens of Versailles.

The scandal aroused fierce hostility toward Marie Antoinette in spite of her innocence. Her spendthrift ways were contrasted with the bankruptcy of the nation. She was nicknamed "Mme. Deficit." Her own extravagance and the slanders of her many enemies made her an object of public loathing. Confined to her small aristocratic world, she never realized what was going on.

Then came 1789, the meeting of the States General, and the beginning of the French Revolution. It all left Marie Antoinette unconcerned. When the revolutionary women marched the twelve miles from the great market of Paris to Versailles to shout their imprecations at her, she could not understand why all these horrid people had come to her home to annoy her.

Lafayette, the hero of the American Revolution, who was now a national leader, tried to help the royal family. He arranged for the Flemish regiment to come to the protection of the King. At the

Queen's suggestion an elaborate banquet was given to celebrate the occasion. This frivolity was like dropping a match into a powder keg. The people of Paris stormed Versailles and carried off the King and Queen. They were lodged in the Tuileries in Paris.

Humiliated, Marie Antoinette made a fatal move. She persuaded the King to try to escape from France. Aided by loyal subjects, they rode out of Paris in disguise, only to be overtaken and seized by revolutionary troops at Varenne. They were taken back to Paris and imprisoned in the Tuileries.

The entire fury of the Revolution was turned against the royal couple, whose fate was sealed when the allied powers opposing the Revolution threatened to hold the French people responsible should anything happen to the King and Queen. The reply of the revolutionaries was to throw Louis and Marie Antoinette into jail, preparatory to sending them to the guillotine.

Louis died first. Those loyal to Marie Antoinette redoubled their efforts to save her. Everything failed—everything except her nerve. She faced her accusers like a queen, her frivolity gone, leaving a courageous dignity to take its place.

From the court that condemned her to death on a charge of treason, she went back to her cell and spent the night in prayer and in writing her *Testament*. When the jailers came for her, Marie Antoinette calmly took her seat in the tumbrel and was driven to her death amidst the imprecations of the people of Paris.

MOZART

[*1756–1791*]

WOLFGANG AMADEUS MOZART stands as a classic of the child prodigy. More than any other of the great in the arts, he was the consummate example of the precocious infant, the *Wunderkind*. Born at Salzburg in 1756, his musical education began at the age of three—some say four. His teacher was his father, a musician of eminence, Kapellmeister to the Archbishop of Salzburg. Soon the child was composing little minuets, noted down by his father and preserved by his elder sister Nannerl, herself a precocious youngster in music. The child wonder made his debut before he was six, playing on the harpsichord in a double appearance with Nannerl. This was at Munich, and was reckoned as the boy Mozart's official debut, although actually he had been a performer at the University of Salzburg four months earlier, when he was five and a half.

Mozart's father was a worthy musician and a devout parent, but he worked his *Wunderkind* to the limit of profit and renown. Beginning with the Munich debut, when the boy was not yet six, the father took the two children on a tour—Linz, Vienna, Pressburg. This was as nothing compared with the professional journeyings that began when Mozart was seven and lasted for three years. The tour included cities in Austria, Germany, Switzerland, France, Belgium, Holland, and England, with concerts in the theaters, mansions, and princely courts.

In Vienna the Austrian Emperor Francis I sat beside the boy Mozart at the harpsichord and called him his "little magician." In the imperial palace the child slipped on the polished floor and fell. The Archduchess Marie Antoinette, later the ill-fated Queen of France, picked him up. The little Mozart said, "You are very kind. When I grow up I will marry you."

At Frankfort the child musician was heard by Goethe, then in his own boyhood. Later in life Goethe wrote to Eckermann, "I was only fourteen years old, but I see as if I still were there, the little man with his child's sword and his curly hair. . . . A phenomenon like that of Mozart remains an inexplicable thing."

In Paris the first musical compositions of Mozart were published, four sonatas for piano and violin—he was then seven. In London he composed his first symphony and a motet in English, inspired by a visit to the British Museum.

Returning home at ten, Mozart wrote an oratorio when he was eleven, and the next year was commissioned by the Austrian Emperor to compose his first opera. This was not produced until the next year. However, a smaller operatic work was performed at the home of the famous Dr. Mesmer—that astonishing physician who, with his mesmerism, was an innovator in science, as well as a mystical dreamer and something of a charlatan. When he was twelve, Mozart conducted his *Solemn Mass* at the Vienna court in the presence of the Emperor of Austria. Back home at Salzburg the opera not produced at Vienna was performed by order of the Archbishop, and Mozart was appointed concert master at the archiepiscopal court. He was now a recognized composer of established reputation in music—at the age of thirteen.

At thirteen his days as an infant prodigy were considered to be over, and it was as a full-fledged musician competing with other musicians that he set out on his next journey. Papa Mozart took him on a trip to Italy—"the golden land of music." In Italy it was another triumphal tour from city to city. The boy musician's exploits were prodigious, almost incredible, a legend and a wonder in the history of music.

At Mantua the program scheduled his performance to be as follows: He was to play "a Symphony of his own composition; a Clavichord-concerto, which will be handed to him, and which he will immediately play at sight; a Sonata handed to him in like manner, which he will provide with variations, and afterwards repeat in another key; an Aria, the words for which will be handed to him, and which he will immediately set to music and sing himself, accompanying himself on the clavichord; a Sonata for clavichord on a subject given to him by the leader of the violins; a Strict Fugue on a theme to be selected, which he will improvise on the clavichord; a trio, in which he will execute a violin-part *all' improviso;* and finally, the latest Symphony composed by himself."

In Rome occurred the incident most often repeated to illustrate the astounding musical gifts of the boy genius. In the Sistine Chapel during Holy Week they sang the *Miserere* of Allegri, which treasured composition was performed only in the Sistine Chapel, forbidden elsewhere, the score carefully guarded, only one copy, no other permitted to be made. Mozart heard the elaborate work of ecclesiastical polyphony, went home, and wrote it out. From memory he prepared a full score of the *Miserere* of Allegri, and made only one mistake—which he corrected upon hearing the work again the next day, Good Friday.

The honors heaped on him in Italy were immense. The Pope bestowed on the boy the Order of the Golden Spur—"the same as Gluck's," proud Papa Mozart wrote home. At Bologna he was elected a member of the Accademia Filarmonica. At Milan he composed and produced a three-act opera, which had twenty consecutive performances amid tumults of applause—"*Evviva il Maestro! Evviva il Maestrino!*" The little maestro was commissioned to write an opera for a forthcoming carnival in Milan, and the Empress Maria Theresa of Austria bade him compose a dramatic serenata for the marriage of the Archduke Ferdinand.

The *Serenata* for the Empress was composed first. The fifteen-year-old boy made a trip home, then back in Milan set to work. There was a delay in the delivery of the libretto to him, which left him with only the briefest of time. He wrote the *Serenata* in two weeks, which was all the more remarkable because "he had a violinist overhead, an oboe-player underneath, and a pianoforte-teacher next door, all hard at work the whole day long." In Milan the prominent composer Hasse, who had been commissioned to write an opera for the Archduke's marriage, was hard at work on it. He and young Mozart became friends. Hasse said, "This boy will cause us all to be forgotten."

But soon Mozart was afflicted with the curse of his life—poverty. The Archbishop of Salzburg, his protector and patron, died. The new Archbishop was of another sort, and Mozart found little favor with him. He remained at Salzburg in the archiepiscopal service for a

year and a half, until things became so disagreeable that he left and
went traveling for a while, but presently was back in the service of
the Archbishop again. He composed his *Mass in F Minor,* a model
of church music, and symphonies and string quartets that showed
the way to the later and greater Mozart development. But his position
at the archiepiscopal court grew worse. He had to endure indignities,
was forced to eat at the servants' table. This led to a final acri-
monious break, and Mozart left Salzburg for Vienna. His employment by the Archbishop having been his only source of steady
income, he was left to financial insecurity, uncertain earnings,
poverty.

Yet Mozart was hailed increasingly as the phenomenal genius of
his time. Haydn, venerable and immensely successful dean of music,
was a devoted friend, and held Mozart's talent to be the finest ever
bestowed on any composer. Other musicians were not so compli-
mentary. They conspired to keep this youthful intruder from competing with them. Salieri, the fashionable opera composer of Vienna,
wanted the field to himself, and his opposition hampered Mozart.

Now a strange romantic figure enters the story—Lorenzo da Ponte,
son of an Italian Jew, protégé of an Italian cardinal, boasting a
Viennese reputation, and destined to end his days in New York. Da
Ponte became interested in Mozart's music and formed a partnership
with him, the first result of which was *The Marriage of Figaro.* Produced with great success in Vienna in 1786, *The Marriage of Figaro*
retains to this day its magic as a masterpiece of lyric comedy.

Da Ponte then prepared the libretto for *Don Giovanni,* and Mozart
wrote his greatest dramatic music. There are many who put *Don
Giovanni* at the very summit of musical dramatic art, and few will
deny it a place among the very greatest. The rapidity and ease with
which Mozart composed is illustrated by a familiar story. The night
before the première, in Prague, the overture to *Don Giovanni* had
not yet been written. Mozart hurried it out during the night, while
his wife kept him awake by giving him coffee and telling him stories,
as he wrote page after page of the music. The overture, like the
rest of the opera, remains one of the sublime treasures of European
civilization.

With inexhaustible fertility Mozart continued to turn out compositions of the highest order—symphonies, quartets, rondos, dances,

songs. Also operas like *Così fan Tutte* and *The Magic Flute,* both of which still belong to the international repertoire.

All the while this stupendous genius was fighting a losing battle against money troubles. He had an official post at the Viennese court, but it amounted to little more than a high-sounding title with a small stipend attached. The worry affected his health. He was weak and ailing when his last commission came to him in a way dramatic enough for an opera scene.

A mysterious stranger appeared at Mozart's home, and, laying down a sum of money in advance, ordered a requiem. This individual, with a manner and air strange and occult, insisted on secrecy, the composition of the requiem to be disclosed to no one.

Mozart set to work. The mysterious stranger put in another appearance, demanding that the composition be hastened and paying another sum of money in advance. Mozart was deeply impressed by the cryptic visitor. His illness becoming worse, he suffered from illusions.

He seems to have had typhoid. Most of all, his fantasies turned to the anonymous patron who had ordered the requiem. He began to believe it a supernatural sign, a command to write his own death music. Haunted, he plunged into the composition of one of his greatest works. The *Requiem* marked a new advance in musical style, and placed Mozart on one of the great heights of music.

He knew he was dying as he worked to complete his *Requiem.* The scene on his last day is a classic page of tragedy. Around Mozart's sickbed a group was gathered, his wife, his sister-in-law Sophie, and his principal pupil, Süssmayr. From his manuscript pages they sang the *Requiem,* most of which had been completed. With Mozart himself singing one part, they performed the composition, until they reached the first bar of the "Lacrymosa," when the dying composer burst into a violent fit of weeping. That night, holding the manuscript of the *Requiem* in his hands, he turned to his wife and said, "Did I not tell you I was writing this for myself?" At midnight he died, as he approached his thirty-sixth birthday.

His funeral played out the tragedy with pity and violence. So impoverished was the supreme genius of the age that he was buried in a pauper's grave. While the funeral procession was on its way, a violent thunderstorm broke, the heavens fairly exploding and pouring down a deluge of rain. The tempest drove the mourners away, and as a result nobody ever knew where Mozart was buried.

The mysterious stranger who had ordered the *Requiem* returned, only to find that the composer was dead. In time the secret was disclosed. There was a Viennese nobleman whose habit it was to have musical compositions written, paying for them and passing them off as his own. Wanting a Mozart composition to grace his musical reputation, he had sent a servant to make the secret arrangements.

Mozart left some six hundred compositions, 23 operas, 20 masses, 49 symphonies, 60 other orchestral works, 17 piano sonatas, 29 piano concertos, 6 violin concertos, 45 violin sonatas, 50 other pieces of chamber music, 40 songs—all this during so brief a life, he having begun to compose at five, and dying at thirty-five.

ALEXANDER HAMILTON

[1757–1804]

Through the life of Alexander Hamilton runs the theme of the irregular circumstances of his birth. Crusty old John Adams, his irascible political enemy, put it brutally, calling Hamilton "the bastard brat of a Scottish peddler." The remark was only half true. Hamilton's parents had, indeed, never been married. But his father, no mere peddler, was actually the black sheep of an aristocratic family of Scotland.

Alexander Hamilton began life on the West Indian island of Nevis. The irregular union of his mother and father created no special problem for the family, morals in the West Indies being at that time extremely lax. But the elder Hamilton disappeared, and the mother of his children died soon afterward. Two boys were left to be raised by relatives.

Alexander's remarkable ability showed itself in his earliest years. At fourteen he was put to work in the office of a trader, and two years later had learned enough to take charge of the firm. He might have gone on to become a commercial magnate except for an accident that brought to light his great gifts of thought and expression. An earthquake struck the islands. Alexander Hamilton, who saw the havoc and terror created by the cataclysm, wrote an account of it for a newspaper. Prominent people were impressed. They decided to see that this able young man was properly educated. And so he received financial backing to go to New York and study at King's College, now Columbia University.

Hamilton's college career showed him a good student avid for classical learning, but affairs were stirring of a sort to distract the fiery youth from books. The American Revolution was in the making. The focus was Boston, but there was abundant agitation and disturbance in New York. Students were prominent in patriotic sedition, and Hamilton threw himself into the American cause.

Young Hamilton had visions of military glory, a trait that never deserted him. The angry Colonists were forming armed units to enforce their demands, and Hamilton joined one of these. He studied military matters, particularly artillery, and presently was in command of a company with cannon.

The news was coming of battles around Boston, the fights at Lexington, Concord, Bunker Hill. The Virginian, George Washington, took command of the Continental forces. From England an army came to occupy New York and put down insurrection there. This led to the Battles of Long Island, Harlem Heights, White Plains. Hamilton's artillery company participated in the fighting, and distinguished itself in what turned out to be heavy defeats. On Manhattan Island they narrowly escaped capture, which good fortune they owed partly to timely action by another young officer about Hamilton's age. His name was Aaron Burr, who appears thus early in the Hamilton story.

The young soldier from the West Indies accompanied Washington's army in its retreat to Pennsylvania. He attracted favorable notice, and presently was given a post of dazzling importance for a mere youth. Hamilton became the aide to the commander. Washington, overburdened with heavy responsibility, needed assistants to deal with military correspondence, write out orders, handle detail. Hamilton was a first-rate penman and a writer of clear fluent prose, and understood military matters. He served as Washington's aide through most of the Revolutionary War.

But in time there came a break between the General and his young aide. Hamilton began to resent Washington's peremptory ways and occasional grumpy humors, and felt he was getting nowhere. He broke with Washington on a mere petty matter of flaring tempers, after he had kept the General waiting one day. He quit his post as aide, and procured an artillery command in active warfare. This took Hamilton to the siege of Yorktown. There, in the storming of redoubts, he finally found the opportunity he craved. Leading a detachment to the attack, he distinguished himself with gallantry on the field of battle.

The war was about over now, and Hamilton went on to the business of carving out a career in peacetime. He had married recently, his bride being a daughter of Philip Schuyler, one of the foremost magnates of New York State. The Schuylers were old-time Dutch patroons, with great lands near Albany and in the Mohawk Valley, and they were proud to be connected with the aristocratic Hamiltons, the precise nature of which connection never was explained to them. Alexander Hamilton did not prejudice his marriage by mentioning his illegitimacy.

He now studied law, was called to the bar, and then went into politics. His profound intelligence divined the need for a new system of government for the states, the old Articles of Confederation being obviously incapable of holding the country together. He became enthusiastic about a new constitution, which he defended in print before going to the Constitutional Convention as a member from New York.

However, Hamilton had little faith in the constitution that was being formulated under his eyes in Philadelphia. He thought it much too democratic, leaving too much power to the states. In a great speech he set forth his own proposal for a constitution based on the model of the British monarchy, with a president for life who would amount virtually to a king. This was so far from the mood of the convention that Hamilton thought it not worthwhile to attend many of its sessions.

But, when the Constitution was presented to the states for ratification, he threw himself into the fight with all his energy. He simply thought the document an advance over the present intolerable state of affairs. Again he took to letter writing and to pamphleteering, and was responsible chiefly for the *Federalist Papers,* which argued the cause of the new Constitution in such style as to place them among the world's masterpieces of political exposition. In the *Federalist Papers* he collaborated with John Jay and James Madison.

The Constitution was adopted, and Washington became the first President. He called into his cabinet the one-time military aide with whom he had quarreled but with whom he was on good terms again. Hamilton, in the controversy over the Constitution, had displayed his financial knowledge in such fashion that he was Washington's natural choice for Secretary of the Treasury.

As Secretary of the Treasury, his financial policy required that the government pay off its obligations, the debts incurred by the Continental Congress during the war and afterward. Secondly he called for the new federal government to assume debts contracted by the individual states, and pay these off in good money. The two measures, funding and assumption, were the keystones of his policy as Secretary of the Treasury. He pushed both through in spite of violent opposition by those who held that most of the benefit would go to speculators and the wealthy.

Hamilton sponsored the chartering of a National Bank modeled on the Bank of England. His view was that the capitalists interested in the bank would have a vested interest in a strong central government, and would support it. Again he was condemned for favoring the rich.

In all this the Secretary of the Treasury could only come into violent collision with Thomas Jefferson, who was in Washington's Cabinet as Secretary of State. Jefferson had an agrarian vision of an America of small independent farmers, which he considered the only type of society capable of maintaining liberty. He was hostile to the mercantile and industrial classes, the moneyed interests, and city populations. He was the arch-champion of states' rights, and held that a strong central government would lead to tyranny.

The quarrel between the factions was exacerbated by foreign policy. The French Revolution was raging with its murderous excesses, and the terrorists in Paris got into war with Great Britain. The United States had a treaty of alliance with France, left over from the Revolutionary War, and the question was: Should the young republic join France against Great Britain? Hamilton recoiled from the horrors of the Terror, and more than ever looked with favor on Britain. Jefferson, who had been Ambassador to France, applauded the overthrow of the ancient aristocratic regime and the triumph of democracy.

The feud in Washington's Cabinet was bitter, each faction lampooning the other. Jefferson's partisans brought charges of corruption against Hamilton in Congress, but he was able to refute these. Jefferson resigned from the cabinet, later to continue political agitation as a private citizen.

All this brought about the formation of political parties and the beginning of the American two-party system. The Federalists, with Hamilton as their leader, had the predominance for the time being. Their party was destined to extinction, but would have its successors down to the Republican party of today. Jefferson lined up agrarian interests with the workingmen of northern cities, and founded the Democratic party, which at first called itself "Republican."

Hamilton resigned from the cabinet, and returned to law practice in New York. His political influence remained great, especially after John Adams, a Hamiltonian Federalist, entered the White House. But Hamilton's power in the party was too much for President Adams to tolerate, and the two men eventually drifted into political enmity.

With the Federalists divided, Adams was defeated in the election of 1800. The peculiarities of the electoral vote system were such that Thomas Jefferson, instead of being elected, was tied with Aaron Burr. The contest was thrown to Congress for decision, and there seemed a good possibility that, with the aid of Federalist votes, Burr might become President.

This would have been the bitterest blow of all for Hamilton. Hostile as he was to Jefferson, he preferred the arch-apostle of democracy to Aaron Burr. He did what he could to prevent Federalists in Congress from supporting Burr, and had the dubious satisfaction of seeing Jefferson become President.

During his term as Vice-President, Aaron Burr returned to New York and made alliances with the Federalists. He ran for Governor with Federalist backing. Hamilton could not stand aside while the leadership of his party passed to his enemy. He wrote scathing attacks on Burr, picturing him as a ruthless opportunist. Burr lost the election and challenged Hamilton to a duel.

History's most famous duel was fought across the Hudson, on the heights of Weehawken, with all formality. To this day there is dispute over what really occurred. Before he went to the fatal meeting, Hamilton stated that he would not fire at Burr. Yet, at the first exchange, there were two shots. One supposition is that Hamilton pulled the trigger in a convulsive movement when he was hit. It was said that he fired into the air and the bullet cut the twig of a tree. However, there is an eyewitness statement that Hamilton aimed at Burr, and missed. But Aaron Burr did not miss. His first shot struck Hamilton, and inflicted a fatal wound.

Public feeling revolted against the whole concept of dueling. Burr, who thought he had acted correctly on the field of honor, was reviled, his public career ruined. He went on to dubious adventures in the

West, and was tried for treason. Hamilton gained popularity by his tragic end, and as time went on his renown rose higher as the greatest Secretary of the Treasury, one who had fought mightily to establish the new Republic on a sound foundation.

ABRAHAM LINCOLN

RICHARD WAGNER

NELSON

[1758–1805]

"ENGLAND Expects Every Man To Do His Duty" was the signal made from Nelson's flagship "Victory" in the early morning of October 21, 1805, when the greatest of English admirals caught sight of French Admiral Villeneuve's fleet of thirty-three vessels attempting to escape from the harbor of Cadiz. Nelson had only twenty-seven ships, but his plan of action had been carefully prepared. He divided his fleet into two squadrons. Fifteen ships under Admiral Collingwood were to cut off Villeneuve's rear. With the remaining twelve, Nelson would prevent the main body from giving aid or running away. Two hours after Nelson made his immortal signal, Collingwood had cut off fifteen enemy ships, and Nelson sailed down the French van toward the center in search of a gap to break through. He found it astern of the "Bucentaure," Villeneuve's flagship, which was twelfth in the line of eighteen. As he cut through, Nelson raked the "Bucentaure" and the "Redoutable," which was next. He was in full uniform, wearing all his decorations, when, as he walked the quarterdeck with his flag captain, Thomas Hardy, he was struck by a sharpshooter's bullet, fired from the crow's-nest of the "Redoutable." The bullet shattered his spine. He was carried below in great agony, but had the satisfaction before he died of knowing that his victory was complete. More than 60 per cent of the enemy had struck their colors. His last words were, "Thank God, I have done my duty."

Horatio Nelson came up the hard way. He was the sixth of eight children born to a hard-pressed rector of Norfolk. His mother dying when he was ten, young Horatio had to make his way in the world, and his father decided on the sea. The boy entered the Royal Navy. By the age of fourteen he was already an accomplished seaman.

He sailed with an expedition that attempted to find a Northwest

Passage through the polar ice. He made the long voyage out to the East Indies and back. He served against American privateers during the Revolutionary War. He commanded British naval forces in an attack on the Spanish base of Port San Juan—a complete fiasco because yellow fever struck down his men. He himself contracted the dread disease, and his health remained precarious for the rest of his life.

By now he was a top figure in the Royal Navy. Also a man with a decided weakness for the ladies. It is said that his virulent anti-French animosity began during a visit to Paris when a pretty young Parisienne snubbed him. Once while ashore at Portsmouth, Nelson had a horse run away while he was sharing the carriage with a feminine companion. One of his amorous adventures ended in his marriage to a widow, but he stayed with her only five months. His habit of falling in love with attractive women who came his way was too strong to allow him to settle down to wedded bliss.

The French Revolution broke out, and presently the Prime Minister, William Pitt, flung aside his peace policy and war was on with Republican France. Two days before hostilities were declared, Nelson received command of the 64-gun "Agamemnon" which formed part of Lord Hood's Mediterranean fleet.

From the day he took command of the "Agamemnon," on February 5, 1794, to his death on October 21, 1805, for nine and a half years, Nelson was continually on active service except for the short period of the Peace of Amiens (1802–3). The victories he won, the wounds he received—he lost his right eye and his right arm—his courage, his wonderful seamanship, his famous love affair with Lady Hamilton, made him a legend in his lifetime.

Under Admiral Hood's orders Nelson took part in the occupation of Toulon, and was sent to Naples to fetch troops to garrison the captured French seaport. There he met Emma, the wife of Sir William Hamilton, the British minister in Naples. Meanwhile the French had driven the British from Toulon in an operation that first brought into prominence a young artillery officer named Napoleon Bonaparte. Nelson was sent to Corsica, where he captured Bastia and Calvi. Landing at the latter place he was hit in the eye by a stone thrown up from a parapet struck by a cannon ball. The wound healed without any disfigurement, but he lost the sight of the eye. He was then sent to bring off the garrison and stores left on the island of Elba and successfully accomplished this risky mission in the frigate "Minerva," rejoining Sir John Jervis on the eve of the Battle of Cape St. Vincent.

This famous battle was fought on February 14, 1797, between a Spanish fleet of twenty-seven sail of the line and fifteen smaller English ships under Sir John Jervis. Nelson was in command of the "Captain," a 74-gun ship. During the engagement Nelson saw his opportunity and, without waiting for orders, threw his ship across the bows of the Spaniards. Jervis saw and approved the maneuver and ordered the other ships to follow Nelson's example. The "Captain" attacked the enemy flagship, the huge "Santissima Trinidad" of 130 guns. After heavy firing the Spanish vessel was believed to have struck its colors. Nelson then boarded and took the "San José" of 112 guns and the "San Nicolas" of 80 guns. Whereupon the enemy flagship rehoisted its colors and ran away before a prize crew could be put on board, and Nelson was cheated of that prize. The naval victory off Cape St. Vincent, due almost entirely to Nelson's initiative, made England mistress of the seas. Jervis was created Earl St. Vincent, and Nelson was made a rear admiral and given the Order of the Bath. A picture showing Nelson receiving the swords of the Spanish officers on board the "San José" did much to build him up as a popular hero.

Nelson was then sent to capture Santa Cruz de Tenerife, one of the rashest orders ever issued by the Admiralty. No troops were available for this operation, and the strongly fortified town was to be taken solely by boats from the ships. Nelson attacked with the most reckless daring on the night of July 24, but the garrison was on the alert and the English were forced to withdraw with heavy loss of life after Nelson had been shot through the elbow. He was taken on board the "Theseus," where a hurried amputation of his right arm was clumsily performed, and he had to be invalided home.

After months of suffering, in London and Bath, he rejoined the fleet at Gibraltar with his flag on the "Vanguard," a 74-gun ship of the line. He was sent into the Mediterranean in command of three battleships and five frigates, ordered to keep an eye on the French fleet at Toulon. A storm dismasted his flagship and his five frigates became separated and returned to Gibraltar. He refitted his ship off Sardinia and returned to Toulon, to find that the French fleet had left that port. Actually Napoleon had sailed on his famous Egyptian adventure. Joined by Troubridge with ten sail of the line, but deprived of his fast frigates, the eyes of the fleet, Nelson started on a hunt of the French all up and down the Mediterranean. Since he was not yet forty, he knew that if he failed to find the enemy fleet, Lord St. Vincent would be blamed for having chosen the youngest admiral for the important Mediterranean command.

Napoleon was winning land battles in Egypt when Nelson found the French warships in Aboukir Bay, fifteen miles east of Alexandria. The British admiral's warships cut into the French line and then ran between the French and the shoals offshore. Only one English vessel went aground. The entire French fleet was accounted for, except two battleships and two frigates which were destroyed in subsequent actions. The Battle of the Nile was the most complete victory in naval history. It enabled England to retake Malta and Minorca, and restored her power and prestige in the Mediterranean. Nelson was given a peerage and was acclaimed as the most distinguished officer in the Royal Navy.

From Egypt, Nelson set sail for Naples where things at once began to happen. The Neapolitans revolted against their government, and Nelson had to evacuate the King and Queen of Naples to Sicily. This he did with the help of Lady Hamilton, with whom he was conducting the famous love affair. The liaison quickly became so notorious as to bring from Lord Keith an order for Nelson to sail, on the ground that "Lady Hamilton has commanded the English navy long enough." Nelson refused to leave Naples. After that he disobeyed a command to take his ships to Minorca. He knew at the time that no hostile fleet lay in the vicinity of Minorca, but even so it seems surprising that he received from the Admiralty nothing worse than a reprimand. He did serve in an invasion of Corsica and then he was given leave to go home. Traveling with Sir William and Lady Hamilton, he landed in England in November 1800.

On January 1, 1801, Lord Nelson was gazetted a vice-admiral and sent as second in command to Sir Hyde Parker who had orders to break up the neutrality of the Scandinavian powers. By the time they reached Copenhagen, Nelson had persuaded his chief to allow him to attack the Danish capital with half the fleet. The Battle of Copenhagen illustrated Nelson's extraordinary ability in hitting the weak spot in the enemy's defenses. It was famous, likewise, for the story of how Nelson put his telescope to his blind eye when his attention was called to a signal from Parker ordering him to withdraw. To obey would have been disastrous. Parker was recalled and Nelson left in command.

Soon after, he returned home and was created a viscount. Then he went to live with Sir William and Lady Hamilton at Merton, whence Nelson's wife withdrew to live with his father. The unfortunate Sir William Hamilton had not the will power to save his own reputation. He stayed on with his wife and her paramour, a cuckolded husband and the butt of countless jokes.

Only Nelson's going to sea broke up this ridiculous situation. In the spring of 1805 the French evaded him and after failing to find them in the Mediterranean he rightly guessed that they must have gone to the West Indies, whither he followed in search of them. The chase led him back from the Caribbean Sea to Cadiz where he found the enemy fleet commanded by Villeneuve. Leaving Admiral Collingwood to blockade the French in Cadiz, he returned to Lady Hamilton at Merton for a brief visit and then set out again "to give Villeneuve a drubbing." This he did at Trafalgar, where he fell gloriously in the hour of final victory.

ANDREW JACKSON

[1767–1845]

LATE in July of 1776 a tall, red-haired lad of nine stood facing a
gathering of North Carolina neighbors. In his hand he had a
document, which he read to them. "When in the course of human
events . . ." The Declaration of Independence, adopted earlier in the
month at Philadelphia, had come to the frontier settlement at Wax-
haw. The boy chosen to read it to the citizens was a bright pupil at
the local school. He was destined to become the seventh President
of the United States.

He was a lively, pugnacious lad of the backwoods who early
developed a sulphurous vocabulary. This, we are told, dismayed a
neighboring boy who became a famous preacher. Years later the
eminent divine refused to vote for presidential candidate Andrew
Jackson "because he swore so fearful."

Young Andy Jackson also had a stubborn streak. He was only fourteen, but already a soldier in the patriot army opposing the British
in North Carolina, when the enemy captured him and his brother.
The stripling prisoner of war was ordered to polish an officer's boots,
refused, and received a saber cut on his hand, the scar of which he
retained all his life.

With her two sons captives of the enemy, Andrew Jackson's mother
took horse and rode to the headquarters of Lord Rawdon, the British
commander, to plead for them. Lord Rawdon was so impressed by
the courage of the mother and the youth of the prisoners of war, sixteen and fourteen, that he released them.

Andrew and one of his cousins had contracted smallpox, to which
the latter succumbed. Elizabeth Jackson, nursing the boys, fell victim
to the malady. She died with this advice from a frontier mother to

her sons, "Never tell a lie . . . nor take what is not your own . . . nor sue . . . nor slander. Settle the cases yourself." This last item of maternal counsel was one that Andrew Jackson in later life would have much reason to recall.

The following year he received a legacy and set up for himself as a licensed appraiser of horses. In the style of youth on the frontier, he fancied himself "a sportsman and a judge of horseflesh." But his luck was bad or his business skill insufficient, and in a year he lost most of his legacy.

With what was left he went to Salisbury, resolved upon another profession than horses. He studied law. His education was meager, his legal learning never great, but he was admitted to the bar, and entered practice before he was twenty-one. He was now a frontier lawyer, a stalwart young six-footer, with red hair and blue eyes, admired by the women and respected by the men for his hard riding and straight shooting.

Those were days when the West was beckoning, the land beyond the mountains. What is now Tennessee was then a part of North Carolina, and Carolinians saw opportunity in the West when they could find none at home. Andrew Jackson was one of these. Presently the young enterprising lawyer obtained the post of Prosecuting Attorney in the Western District.

This was how Andrew Jackson emigrated to the new territory which was destined to expand so rapidly and to become the sovereign state of Tennessee. He established himself at Nashville, which had just been founded, and his fortunes flourished with the rise of the West.

He acquired a reputation as a lawyer and wealth as a real estate speculator. Prices were going up rapidly, and a man who bought land in the morning and sold at night was likely to make a profit.

At Nashville, Andrew Jackson lived with a family by the name of Donelson. Their daughter Rachel was married to one of the Kentucky Robards, a prominent and influential family. Mrs. Robards met Andrew Jackson, and the story is told in a court record, part of the legal proceedings that surrounded the case: "Rachel Robards did elope from her husband Lewis . . . with another man." That other man was Andrew Jackson.

He and Rachel went to Natchez, where they were married. Jackson was under the impression that Rachel had been divorced from Robards, but the latter invoked technicalities of the law to deny the divorce, making Jackson's union with Rachel null and void, giving rise to the report that they were living together in adultery. Finally, after more legal maneuvers, they had a second marriage ceremony, which put matters right in the eyes of the law. But the complications and the attending gossip left a long and bitter aftermath for Andrew Jackson and his wife.

He was rising, meanwhile, in the profession of the law and in Tennessee politics. He sat as a member of the convention that wrote the state constitution, when Tennessee was admitted into the union. He won election to the House of Representatives and then to the Senate, where he served two years before resigning.

His career in Washington had been undistinguished. He was remembered by his colleagues on Capitol Hill as an uncouth frontier lawyer who hardly fitted into the society of Virginia and Massachusetts aristocrats who dominated the federal scene.

For the next six years, Andrew Jackson was a member of the Supreme Court of Tennessee. His popularity caused him to be elected a major general of the state militia. Governor John Sevier opposed Jackson on the ground that he had rendered no great service "except taking a trip to Natchez with another man's wife." Jackson challenged the Governor to a duel, which was declined. Jackson branded the Governor as "a base coward and a poltroon." Eventually they met, but no blood was spilled—nothing more than heated words.

Jackson made a reputation as a duelist. He had abundant cause for taking offense at the ugly talk that persisted about his marriage. He fought with Charles Dickinson after a rancorous quarrel, killed his man, and received a wound, the effects of which he felt for the rest of his life. He was wounded again in a tavern shooting match at Nashville with Thomas Hart Burton and his brother.

When the War of 1812 against Great Britain broke out, Jackson commanded the Tennessee forces in a campaign against the Creek Indians. He was a leader of immense energy, swift decision, and iron will, and his victories against the Creeks drew national attention. He was made a major general in the United States Army, seized the Spanish Peninsula, which the British were using as a base, and was given the command at New Orleans. He won the Battle of New Orleans by posting his frontier riflemen behind a barricade of cotton bales and cutting down the disciplined ranks of the enemy as they tried to storm his position.

The battle was fought after peace had actually been signed in Europe, but it was the only spectacular success won by an American army in the war. Andrew Jackson was a national hero.

He received command of the campaign against the Seminole Indians along the border of Spanish Florida. He followed the Indians into Spanish territory and seized Pensacola, a violation of international law. In Florida he hanged two British subjects on a charge of inciting the Indians to hostilities. This was an international outrage, and angered the government in Washington. In the Cabinet, Jackson was defended by Secretary of State John Quincy Adams, and the controversy ended with the purchase of Florida from Spain. Jackson was appointed the first governor of the Florida territory.

In 1824, again a senator, he ran for the Presidency of the United States. He received more electoral votes than anyone else, but not an outright majority, which threw the contest into Congress. There a coalition of the supporters of two other chief candidates, Henry Clay and John Quincy Adams, brought about the selection of Adams as President. There was talk of a bargain, for Adams promptly made Clay his Secretary of State. Jackson, with savage bitterness, felt that he had been cheated out of the election.

In the campaign of 1828, Jackson, representing the rude democracy of the frontier, opposed John Quincy Adams. The partisans of both sides hurled unmeasured abuse. In Nashville Mrs. Rachel Jackson, attending a dinner in her husband's honor, emerged from semiretirement. She was a sensitive religious woman and in ill-health, who hitherto had been unaware of the mud slinging. Now she chanced to hear a slurring reference to the marriage complications of long ago, the talk of adultery, her first intimation of campaign scurrility which pictured her as a loose woman. She went home, suffered a heart attack, and died.

Jackson raged at his opponents, and it was an embittered man who heard the election result—a sweeping victory for him. In his two terms as President much of his conduct, with his burning indignation at what he thought to be wrong, is to be traced to the circumstances surrounding the death of his wife.

Jackson's first administration began with a wholesale dismissal of officeholders, who were supplanted by Jackson partisans. This procedure has perhaps been exaggerated, but it is regarded as the beginning of the spoils system—political office as a reward for political service.

Then soon the administration was shaken by the Peggy Eaton affair, one of the most curious episodes in American history. The President's choice for Secretary of War was John Eaton, who precipitated a storm by marrying Peggy O'Neil, daughter of a Washington tavern keeper. Peggy had a reputation with which gossip made sport, and the wives of the other cabinet members refused to accept her.

Jackson's own attitude is to be explained in large measure by the part that slanderous talk had played in his own marriage and the death of his wife. He brought a niece to Washington to act as his hostess in the White House. She snubbed Peggy, the new Mrs. Eaton, and the President sent her back to Tennessee. His conduct toward his Cabinet was of a similar order. The behavior of the wives toward Peggy caused an upheaval, disruption and cabinet resignations. Jackson, later on, sent Eaton as American minister to Spain, and in Madrid Peggy was as much of a success as she had failed to be in Washington.

The one cabinet member who retained the President's friendship was Martin Van Buren, Secretary of State, a smooth and able politician from New York. He had no wife. His courtesies to Peggy Eaton won Jackson's undying regard, and did no little to advance Van Buren to the Presidency. He became Jackson's successor.

In 1832, Jackson was re-elected easily over Henry Clay. His second administration brought to the front the two great issues of national policy that distinguished his tenure as President. These were nullification and the bank.

Congress passed a tariff bill protecting northern manufacturers against foreign competition. South Carolina, led by John C. Calhoun, invoked states' rights against the federal government and threatened to nullify the new law. President Jackson at once announced that he would send federal troops into South Carolina to enforce obedience to the tariff. Only a compromise worded out in Congress prevented civil war. South Carolina withdrew nullification, and Jackson did not have to use the army.

The quarrel over the Bank of the United States was noisy. Jackson believed the bank to be an instrument of aristocracy and a deadly menace to freedom. The statesman from the frontier made himself a symbol of the cause of the people against the money power. The working people in the industrial North rallied to him, and he strengthened greatly the alliance forced by Jefferson between southern agriculture and northern labor against northern big business. That has continued to this day, with Jefferson and Jackson as the patron saints of the Democratic party.

The financial policies of the administration are accused of having caused the Panic of 1837, but that occurred as Jackson retired from office, and the blame fell on his successor, Van Buren. Jackson returned to his home near Nashville, and retained a lively interest in national politics until the defeat of his successor and his party in the Whig triumph of 1840. He died in 1845, lonely and embittered, at the age of seventy-eight.

NAPOLEON

[1769–1821]

B ENEATH the gilded dome of the Invalides in Paris is Napoleon's tomb, a huge monolith of red granite, placed in an open circular crypt twenty feet deep and thirty-six feet in diameter. Every day for more than a century, hundreds of people have come to look down in awe upon the sarcophagus that shields the mortal remains of one of the greatest men in history. At one time master of all Europe, by the sheer force of his military genius, he was cursed as a despot, blessed as the embodiment of order and progress. He gave France laws and institutions which still endure, crowned by the Code Napoleon. His memory remains vast and imposing.

By blood he was not a Frenchman, for he was born in Ajaccio, Corsica, the year after Genoa ceded Corsica to France. But he grew up to look upon France as his native land, the place where he would make his career. His father sent him first to a military academy at Brienne and then on to the Ecole Militaire in Paris.

In 1789, just prior to the fall of the Bastille, Napoleon passed his final examinations as an artillery officer. The entry in his *livret militaire* read, "Corsican, studious, aloof, most audacious. Will go far, if circumstances favor him."

His first real opportunity came in 1793 at the siege of Toulon. This vital seaport had revolted against the revolutionary Convention and harbored a British squadron which had taken possession of its defenses. After setting up his batteries in positions commanding the roadstead, Napoleon drove off the British vessels and enabled General Dugommier to recapture the port in December 1793.

During the Reign of Terror, Napoleon was away inspecting fortifications, but did not entirely escape suspicion after the fall of Robespierre, with whose brother he was on friendly terms. He was ordered to the command of an infantry brigade in La Vendée, to suppress the royalist and Catholic uprising there. Napoleon, detesting the ferocious civil strife, refused on the ground that he was an artillery-man, and was struck off the active list by the Minister of War.

Deprived of all rank and pay, he now went through a period of dire poverty. He had to sell his watch, then his books. He went to live in a little room hardly better than a garret.

Suddenly opportunity burst upon him. A royalist uprising, caused by inflation of the currency and the high cost of food, flared in Paris. Napoleon was given a post with the Republican forces. He seized the artillery the insurgents had hoped to use, and mowed them down in the streets. The Republic was saved, and the people of Paris acclaimed their twenty-six-year-old savior.

In March of 1796 Napoleon married Josephine de Beauharnais, a Creole widow much older than himself. He was infatuated with Josephine, and their union lasted until it collided with affairs of state.

Napoleon now received command of the campaign in Italy. His army did not exceed thirty thousand men, many of them veterans of the Revolution. Their uniforms were in tatters; they were without rations or even shoes on their feet, without artillery, without cavalry; and they had lost faith in their officers. These men Napoleon soon bent to his will. He galvanized his starved and sullen army into a fighting force. His orders of the day are famous in military annals.

Hilaire Belloc has called Napoleon's Italian campaign "Lightning in the Hills." Striking the Italians with hammer blows, he forced them to capitulate. Wheeling on the Austrians he beat them in a series of battles, and befuddled them by the rapidity with which he marched his troops from one place to another. He entered Milan triumphantly. He forced Austria to the Peace of Campo Formio. From his battle flags flew the emblems of his victories—Arcole, Rivoli, Montenotte, the bridge at Lodi. No one has ever been more completely the man of the hour than was Napoleon Bonaparte on his return to Paris.

But the politicians, fearing his popularity, assigned him to a command in Egypt. They wanted to get him out of France. So to Egypt he went, took Cairo and won the Battle of the Pyramids. In three weeks, by a campaign of breathtaking audacity, he subdued Egypt. He marched into Syria, only to be stopped before the British fort at Acre. His position in the East had become insecure because of Nelson's great victory over the French fleet at Abukir. He decided to return to France, where the affairs of war and politics were going badly.

The youthful conqueror dazzled the politicians. Soon he was chosen First Consul, with full powers to deal with the enemies of the Republic at home and abroad.

He struck at the Austrians, who had retaken much of Italy. He crossed the Alps, and covered himself with glory at Marengo. French General Moreau won the Battle of Hohenlinden, Austria capitulated and recognized all French conquests. Russia withdrew from the alliance against France. England was left alone. In a bid for peace he knew was essential, Napoleon offered terms, and the Treaty of Amiens was signed, with mutual concession on both sides.

Napoleon was now both powerful and ambitious. There were plots against his life, whereupon he seized a young royalist leader, the Duc d'Enghien, in the duchy of Baden, neutral territory, and had him court-martialed and shot. It was a crime about which Napoleon suffered a bad conscience for the rest of his life. But he was determined to make himself Emperor of France. He held a plebiscite and was elected by a tremendous majority of the French people.

Napoleon brought Pope Pius VII to Paris to preside over the coronation, which took place in Notre Dame on December 2, 1804. At the last moment, without a word to anybody, Napoleon changed the ritual. When the Pope lifted up the crown, he seized it from the pontiff's hands and placed it upon his own head. Josephine, graceful and beautiful as ever, was crowned Empress.

From among his victorious generals and the great men he had gathered around him, Napoleon built up a new nobility, a nobility of achievement. He was now able to carry through three things that were very near to his heart: a concordat with the Vatican; the institution of the Legion of Honor; and the creation of an entirely new and uniform system of law, the Code Napoleon. The Empire satisfied the French love of glory. It pleased the left and it pleased the right. Revolutionists saw a final break with monarchy, and monarchists saw the re-establishment of the hereditary monarchial system. Prosperity followed upon the heels of order. Napoleon impressed his personality and his taste on architecture, furniture, even women's fashions. The Empire style was well proportioned, powerful, and ornate.

The truce with England lasted less than a year. When war broke out again Napoleon gathered his forces at Boulogne for an invasion thrust across the Channel. But the French fleet failed to carry out its mission to keep the British fleet occupied. So the Emperor decided to hit his continental enemies instead. He made a lightning thrust into Germany, and won the battle of Ulm, forcing an Austrian army to surrender. Forty-eight hours later Nelson destroyed the French fleet at Trafalgar. England ruled the waves. All hope of invasion was lost. As he could not subdue England, Napoleon set out to make himself the undisputed master of the Continent.

The land campaign in which he engaged was his most brilliant. The Battle of Austerlitz was his masterpiece. Here, facing a superior force of Austrians and Russians he maneuvered them into concentrating on the wings, then burst through their weakened center, and rolled up their line. They retreated in disorder, leaving in the hands of the victor more than thirty thousand prisoners, forty-five standards, one hundred and fifty pieces of cannon. Well might Prime Minister William Pitt say, when he heard the news of Austerlitz, that the map of Europe would not be needed for ten years.

The subjugation of Europe continued with a series of dazzling Napoleonic victories. The Prussian army made famous by Frederick the Great was destroyed at Jena in 1806. In the following years other lightning blows fell upon the Russians at Eylau and Friedland and the peace of Tilsit was concluded with the Tsar. A continental blockade was declared against England.

Portugal was still open to trade with England and so Napoleon sent Marshal Junot to subdue the tiny monarchy. Spain was giving trouble too and Napoleon drove out the Spanish Bourbon kings. He had made Joseph Bonaparte, his brother, King of Naples. Now he moved Joseph and made him King of Spain. But the people of Spain refused to accept Joseph, and war began in the Iberian Peninsula. A British army landed to support the Spaniards. The Peninsular War followed. The Austrians, rising against the French, were defeated at Wagram, after which Napoleon captured Vienna.

The year of Wagram, 1809, the Emperor of France divorced his Empress. Josephine had not given him an heir, and he was afraid that his Empire would crumble after his death. He forced the aged Emperor of Austria to give him the hand of Princess Marie Louise.

The marriage took place in 1810. The next year a son and heir was born. The Napoleonic dynasty seemed secure.

The international situation, on the other hand, was deteriorating, especially in Spain which would not surrender and waged a fierce guerrilla war against the French invaders. Wellington was on his career of victories in the Peninsular Campaign. In spite of his Spanish dilemma, Napoleon chose this moment for what was to prove the worst of his blunders. Knowing that the Tsar had violated the continental blockade, he decided to invade Russia.

The die was cast on June 24, 1812, when Napoleon at the head of the Grande Armée—640,000 men, 60,000 horses, and 1,250 pieces of cannon—crossed the river Neman at Kovno, in Poland. The river was the border, with Russian-held territory to the east. He staked everything on rapid victory before winter set in. But the Tsar Alexander would not face him in the pitched battle he wanted. The Russians harassed the French advance on the flanks, cutting off stragglers, attacking outposts. They scorched the earth as they fell back. They left rear guards that forced Napoleon to fight ferociously to win at Smolensk and Borodino. Their strategy was to wear him down.

He entered Moscow on September 16. The population had been evacuated, all stores removed. Then, with the French in occupation of the city, flames appeared on all sides, and for five days the fire raged, burning down four out of every five houses. The Kremlin was saved by its walls, a few churches by their massive stone construction. The burning of Moscow marked the turning point in the Napoleonic epic. The Grande Armée could advance no further, not into the vast spaces of Russia. The Tsar refused to negotiate. On October 19 the order to retreat was given. Harried by the Russians, who cut off supplies and destroyed everything, and with the terrible Russian winter coming, the great host melted. When Smolensk was reached, Napoleon's army had been reduced to 60,000 men. The thermometer fell to near zero. At the fearful passage of the Berezina, 24,000 were lost. Leaving Murat in command of his snowbound starving troops with orders to make for Vilna where the French had large supplies, Napoleon hurried back to Paris.

The retreat from Moscow was the beginning of the end. Napoleon took the field again with a new army, campaigned in central Europe, and suffered his first great defeat when the combined forces of Russia,

Prussia, and Austria beat him at Leipzig in the Battle of the Nations. He abdicated on April 11, 1814. The allies chose the Mediterranean island of Elba as his place of exile.

On March 1, 1815, Napoleon at the head of a few hundred men left Elba and landed near Cannes on the French Riviera. France was disgusted with the restoration of the monarchy, and the memory of the glories of the Empire evoked passionate emotions. Near Grenoble, Napoleon met the first troops sent against him, and advanced alone to meet them: "Is there a man among you who would slay his Emperor?" A great shout of *"Vive l'Empereur!"* answered him. Marshal Ney, sent to capture him, joined him at Auxerre. On March 20 he made his triumphal entry into Paris. In less than three weeks he had reconquered France. Not a shot was fired, not a drop of blood shed to re-establish the Empire.

Napoleon knew that a decisive battle would have to be fought, for Britain and Prussia were moving to meet him. Working heroically in the few weeks available to him, he raised an army and advanced into the Low Countries. The issue would be decided on the field near the Belgian town of Waterloo. Wellington was ready with his British troops, Blücher with his Prussians. Napoleon's strategy was to deal with Wellington himself while Marshal Grouchy kept the Prussians from intervening. The strategy might have worked except that Grouchy lost contact with Blücher, and wandered around in the woods while Blücher came up to Waterloo.

Napoleon had 72,000 men left when he clashed with Wellington who had 67,000. But before the close of the battle, Wellington was joined by Blücher's 50,000 Prussians. Had they not come up, had Grouchy carried out his assignment, the result might have been different. The last great charge of Napoleon's old guard won them immortal fame. But Waterloo was lost.

For the second time Napoleon abdicated. For a second time he went into exile. The British, taking no chances on another escape, imprisoned him on the island of St. Helena, far away in the South Atlantic. There the former Emperor of France lived among a faithful entourage of his devoted followers until his death in 1821.

Nineteen years later the mortal remains of Napoleon Bonaparte were taken back to France, and with national ceremony were placed in the tomb under the golden dome of the Invalides.

WELLINGTON

[1769–1852]

THE Iron Duke lives in history as the very figure of the cold reserved British soldier. There is something stiff, even stuffy, about him, especially when he is posed against his mighty antagonist, Napoleon—the mercurial brilliance of whose genius makes Wellington seem like a monument of sober-sided ability, rigid will power, and unimaginative character.

He was born plain Arthur Wellesley. As a younger son he went into the army; as a born soldier he stayed. He saw service in Belgium against the armies of the French Revolution; and then in India where he fought the Mahrattas, who had risen against the British. One critical battle smashed the Mahratta forces and made a reputation for Arthur Wellesley. He returned to London to be knighted. His services would soon be needed again. The war with Napoleon was on.

One day Sir Arthur Wellesley paid a visit to the Colonial Office, and was shown into a waiting room where he saw a one-eyed sailor whom he immediately recognized as Lord Nelson—the victor of the Battle of the Nile. Admiral Lord Nelson, finding himself with a major general he did not know, talked at length—"in a style," Sir Arthur said later, "so vain and so silly, as to surprise and almost disgust me." Then the boastful sea hero asked someone who the major general was. He was told, and knew of Wellesley's reputation in India. "When he came back," Sir Arthur related, "he was an altogether different man—he talked like an officer and statesman. . . . I don't know that I ever had a conversation that interested me more." A few weeks later, Nelson put a final end to Napoleon's plan for invading England. He won his greatest victory at Trafalgar, and lost his life. There was some intention of putting Sir Arthur Wellesley at the head of a British force on the Continent to participate in land operations against Napoleon, but such notions vanished with that most brilliant of Napoleonic victories—Austerlitz. Instead Sir Arthur took a seat in the London Parliament.

But he was still a soldier waiting for further military orders. His big chance came when the London government decided to send an expedition to help the Spaniards in their resistance to the French. In a classical campaign of maneuver, Wellesley beat the French and drove them back to the Pyrenees. He drove into France, defeated Marshal Soult, and was prepared to turn north for Paris when he learned that Napoleon had gone down at the Battle of the Nations, overwhelmed by Austrians, Prussians, and Russians. The Emperor of the French abdicated. The British general returned home to be named a duke for winning the Peninsular Campaign. He chose the title of Duke of Wellington.

With the return of Napoleon from Elba the Great Powers found that they would have to fight him once again. The British landed a powerful army in Belgium. Naturally it was under the command of the Duke of Wellington. He was joined by Britain's closest continental ally, Prussia, whose contingent was led by General Blücher. Napoleon drove into Belgium to meet his enemies, and the strategy of the campaign came to a focus on the plain near a Belgian town called Waterloo.

Napoleon's plan was to defeat Blücher and Wellington separately. First he drove back the Prussians and detailed Marshal Grouchy to keep them from regrouping and returning to the battlefield. After that, the Emperor swung around for a frontal assault on the British. Two things are memorable about this assault—the courage with which the French delivered it, and the courage with which the British met it. Napoleon thought he had won the battle. Afterward Wellington said that Waterloo had been "a close thing." But fortune had deserted Napoleon. Marshal Grouchy lost contact with the Prussians, and blundered around in the woods while Blücher doubled back to Waterloo, arriving just in time to hit the French with a decisive flank attack. The victory for the allies was complete. Napoleon fell, abdicated, was captured, and ended his days on St. Helena. He left to the languages of the world the word Waterloo, meaning a defeat so absolute that no recovery is possible.

After Waterloo, Wellington returned to London, hailed as the Iron Duke, idol of the British people. He was given a seat in the Cabinet, and named Commander-in-Chief of the Army. In 1828 he became Prime Minister. No politician, he could not handle most of the pressing political problems of the time. He did succeed with Catholic emancipation in Ireland, something he considered necessary and which he put through over intense opposition. But he remained hostile to reform in Britain. A change had to be made in the old system, whereby so much of the membership of Parliament was controlled by a few aristocratic families. Wellington, as Prime Minister, resisted, and this led to the fall of his Cabinet. He continued his opposition to the Reform Bill, until finally he himself realized it was hopeless.

His reactionary stand brought to a head his unpopularity, which had long been increasing. There were demonstrations against the Iron Duke on the anniversary of Waterloo, and precautions were taken to prevent his house from being attacked by mobs.

As the years went by his popularity gradually returned. At eighty, he retired from public life altogether, and was a favorite national figure once again. The storms of the Reform Bill were forgotten, and the Iron Duke stood as the very symbol of Great Britain. He died in 1852, and was interred in St. Paul's Cathedral, under the dome. His funeral was the greatest military display that London had ever seen.

SIMÓN BOLÍVAR

[1783–1830]

THE Liberator of South America was, like George Washington, an aristocrat who could have made a career in the service of the mother country. Simón Bolívar counted among his ancestors men who had reached high rank among the officials of Spain. His immediate family belonged to the oldest and wealthiest in Venezuela. Yet, in imitation of Washington, he turned his back on the good life he might have had in order to strike a blow for freedom.

Born just before the French Revolution, Bolívar grew up amid reports of the new liberties sweeping over Europe. This was something he could understand, for he was himself not addicted to the observation of rules and regulations laid down for him. He was as a boy restless, imperative, audacious, willful, and very charming. He wasn't interested in learning out of books and never acquired anything but a smattering of the sciences, an elementary knowledge of mathematics, grammar, geography, history, literature.

He grew up without any religious convictions and when he went to Europe shared in the agnosticism so prevalent in society after the Napoleonic Wars. He read Voltaire and Rousseau, as did the radicals of his generation. He met Talleyrand, von Humboldt, and Mme. de Staël, and considered himself a nineteenth-century liberal. While on a walking tour of Rome, he paused with his tutor amidst the relics of the ancient Republic and vowed solemnly to free his country from Spain.

Bolívar visited the United States in 1809, and this strengthened his conviction that a republican form of government was the best. Returning to Venezuela he joined a secret group of revolutionary patriots, whose first attempts at insurrection were easily put down. Bolívar raised a force of volunteers, won several battles against the

Spanish army, and even managed to take Caracas. But in the end he
was beaten and had to flee for his life. The same disaster overtook his
next attempt at raising a revolution.

From all this he learned one lesson that many rebels have had to
learn. He could not defeat disciplined troops with raw levies and
volunteers. He needed professional soldiers. He set about forming a
"foreign legion" of British and Irish veterans of European wars.

With this "foreign legion" he struck first in Colombia. Sailing up
the Orinoco River to the town of Angostura, now Ciudad Bolívar, he
landed his troops and began one of the most extraordinary exploits
in military history. From tropical plains he crossed the frozen Andes,
and then was confronted by a royalist army of five thousand. He
gathered what local reinforcements and arms he could, boldly attacked, and utterly defeated the main Spanish force. This blow broke
the grip of Spain on Nueva Granada.

Here Bolívar was first acclaimed as "El Libertador." Men and
money were placed at his disposal by the grateful Colombians,
whereupon he returned over the same hard Andean route to the
revolutionary capital which the Venezuelan insurgents had been able
to set up at Angostura. The revolutionary fever began to run through
South America like an epidemic. Rebels attacked Spanish troops in
Venezuela, Quito (Ecuador), and Peru. Everywhere Bolívar inspired
the movement, and was elected the first President of both Colombia
and Bolivia. Farther south victory did not come so quickly. Fighting
went on for fifteen years, from 1810 until 1825, before Spain realized
that most of the New World was lost to her for good.

Bolívar always advocated one great confederation in which all
Latin American countries could join, and at his instigation the first
Pan-American Congress was held at Panama in 1826. He failed in his
attempt to establish a South American commonwealth, but his ideas
of democracy were clearly stated in the constitution of Bolivia, written by Bolívar himself. It provided for a President to be elected for
life, a hereditary Senate on the lines of the British House of Lords,
and an elected Congress. The President had wide powers but could
deprive no citizen of his life, liberty, or property. Civil liberties were
safeguarded, slavery abolished, freedom of worship and of the press
guaranteed.

Despite his prestige and his labor, Bolívar was unable to hold together the great Republic of Colombia he had created. After fourteen years as supreme Chief of State and President of Colombia, he tendered his resignation and it was accepted by the Congress at his own request. Venezuela separated itself from the confederation and resumed its separate existence. The union of South America into a single confederation foundered on local jealousies. Democratic government itself was in jeopardy when Bolívar went back to private life.

His last years were embittered by this failure. He died still hoping for a better future for his continent, and secure in the knowledge that the bad old days of Spanish rule would never return. He had done more than any other man to bring about the change. He was El Libertador—*The* Liberator.

BYRON

[1788–1824]

THE great-uncle of George Gordon, Lord Byron, was known as "the Evil Lord." In his youth he had killed his cousin in a duel, been tried by the House of Lords and found guilty of homicide. In his later years he lived alone at Newstead Abbey, an eccentric recluse, always armed with pistols. The poet's grandfather, younger brother of "the Evil Lord," had been a distinguished admiral, known as "Foul Weather Jack" for the number of storms at sea and the scrapes on land that he had successfully ridden out. The poet's father, "Mad Jack," a handsome young libertine in the Grenadier Guards, devoted himself to gambling, women, and the dissipation of the fortunes of his two wives.

"The Evil Lord," "Foul Weather Jack," "Mad Jack"—fate could not have chosen more appropriate relatives for the man in whom the passion, violence, and despair of Romanticism would become incarnate.

Byron remembered his father only as a very handsome man adored by everybody, a romantic figure. His mother he disliked. In her moments of temper she stormed at him and called him "a lame brat," a cruel reference to the paralysis of the tendons from which he suffered, and which left him with a noticeable limp. He was acutely sensitive about this deformity. It affected his whole outlook on life.

As a young nobleman, he was sent to Harrow to be educated. He boxed, rode, swam, and played cricket in spite of his limp. Reading voraciously, especially in English literature, he began to write poetry.

When Lord Byron went up to Trinity College, Cambridge, he was seventeen, very shy and very conscious of his lameness. He had an allowance of five hundred pounds a year, which he spent with furious abandon, being determined to hold his own among the hard-drinking

BISMARCK

QUEEN VICTORIA

and gambling students of a gentleman's college. A madcap, during one visit to London he fell in with a prize fighter and an Italian fencer, both of whom he brought back to college with him along with a dancing bear. He kept the bear in his rooms, saying that a dog would have been against the college regulations.

When he was nineteen, *Hours of Idleness* appeared. It was immature and showed little promise. The *Edinburgh Review* attacked it savagely. At Cambridge he took his degree with a double first, a very high honor meaning that he passed both of his set examinations *cum laude*.

He came into his inheritance and paid off the three thousand pounds of debts he had accumulated at Cambridge. He took his seat in the House of Lords, proud and aloof in the midst of the dignified aristocrats who ruled Britain. At Newstead he kept a chained bear at the entrance, and pistols by his bedside. He and his friends got their entertainment by shooting, fencing, reading, talking, and drinking wine from a skull after dinner. Byron wrote *English Bards and Scotch Reviewers,* a virulent reply to the attack of the *Edinburgh Review*. A brilliant satire, it fastened the attention of the world of letters upon the author.

In July 1809 he set out with half a dozen servants to visit the Mediterranean. Landing at Lisbon and undeterred by war raging in Spain, he rode seventy miles a day to Seville, then to Cadiz and Gibraltar. Going by sea to the Adriatic, they landed in Albania which then formed part of the Ottoman Empire. From Albania the poet went into Greece, to Athens and Marathon. A tour of Asia Minor followed, during which Lord Byron swam the Hellespont—the Dardanelles—as Leander in the ancient legend had done for so many nights to meet his beloved Hero. It was no mean feat, and Byron, sensitive of his lameness, was proud of it. To his stay in Athens we owe that lovely lyric:

> Maid of Athens ere we part
> Give oh give me back my heart.

Returning home, Byron resumed his seat in the House of Lords and created a sensation with his maiden speech. He opposed a bill to make it a capital offense for workers to destroy stocking-frame machines. Byron described in short, telling sentences the sufferings of the workers "liable to conviction of the capital crime of poverty," and ended by assuring their lordships that "Never, in the most oppressed provinces of Turkey, did I behold such squalid wretchedness as I have in the heart of a Christian country." It was a brilliant and courageous speech, and gained him the ear of the Whig party.

The first two cantos of *Childe Harold* were published on March 10, 1812. Within a week Byron was famous. Before the year was out five editions had been sold. The people craved for a poet who could breathe into his songs the fierce and passionate spirit of the Napoleonic age.

He followed this success with *The Waltz, The Giaour, The Bride of Abydos, The Corsair,* and *Lara.* They made him not only a popular idol but the poet of all rebels, of all in Europe who strove for personal freedom and political liberty.

Byron moved like a conqueror through the high society in which his birth entitled him to a place. He was handsome, vigorous, intelligent, a brilliant conversationalist—and at the same time as haughty with men as a lord should be, as tender with women as a gentleman should be. Even his limp created interest. The list of his liaisons began to lengthen—Lady Oxford, Lady Wedderburn, and, above all, Lady Caroline Lamb, who threatened to commit suicide when he left her.

As might have been foreseen, Byron's marriage was a fiasco. His wife, Annabella Milbanke, proved to be, in his description, "a little encumbered with virtue." He himself was not cut out for domesticity. Shortly after the birth of their daughter, Byron's wife left him. Her father's lawyers started separation proceedings, and the affair terminated with Byron's exile from England.

The story, endlessly debated, connects Lord Byron with his half-sister, with accusations of incest. Society turned against him. In the House of Lords he was snubbed. England became an impossible place for him, and he left, never to return, followed, as Macaulay said, by "a howl of contumely across the sea."

He adopted a vagabond life, visiting the Low Countries, Germany, Switzerland, Italy. In Geneva he met Shelley, with whom he visited Chillon, inspiration of the *Prisoner of Chillon.* In Venice he watched the carnival and wrote:

So we'll go no more a roving
So late into the night.

He read Goethe's *Faust,* and then turned out *Manfred,* a poem in the despairing, defiant mood of Romanticism.

Byron's Byronic pilgrimage was possible because he did not have to worry about making a living. He had his family fortune, besides which his poetry was selling very well despite his reputation. He could live wherever he wanted (as long as it wasn't England), write as he pleased, support his mistresses in sumptuous fashion. To this period we owe some of his finest work, including that masterpiece of comic satire, *Don Juan.*

At the end of 1818 he was at Ravenna with Teresa, the wife of the Cavaliere Guiccioli. This, the most notorious of his love affairs, proved to be a last mad fling for him. He could not ignore the revolutionary ideas sweeping through Europe. Not only did he write manifestoes in favor of freedom for Italy, but he even joined the Carbonari, the secret society of Italian patriots conspiring to throw off Austrian rule.

Next Greece drew his attention—the land of classical beauty, the origin of Western civilization. The Greek rebellion against the Turks fired the blood of Byron the Romantic. He went to Greece, landed at Missolonghi, declared his solidarity with the revolution, caught a fever, and died before he could see action. He was just thirty-six.

His death contributed to his legend. He influenced not only Romantic literature but the whole of Romanticism—its art, its philosophy, its attitude toward life, even its posturing. No man was ever more Byronic than Byron.

BRIGHAM YOUNG

[*1801–1877*]

O N JULY 24, 1847, a file of horsemen wound its way slowly to the
crest of Utah's mountains and gazed down into the valley of
the Great Salt Lake. The leader of the group rode out in front, sur-
veyed the terrain for a moment, and then said, "This is the place."

With these four simple words Utah began its existence as a settled
community. The newcomers were Mormons. Their leader was Brigham Young.

He came from the East, from Vermont. Always religious, he frequented many different sects until he happened to read the *Book of
Mormon* by Joseph Smith. Brigham Young became convinced that
Smith was a true prophet, and moved to Ohio to be with him. Smith
named Young one of the Twelve Apostles, the governing council of
the Mormons. The new faith flourished in Ohio. Conversions were
numerous.

Their neighbors disliked the Mormons, who were accused of
fanaticism and vice. Smith led his followers to Missouri to escape
persecution. But the old charges were revived, and the Governor
warned them to leave. This time they went to Nauvoo, Illinois. Again
the community throve. Again it was persecuted.

Mormon polygamy was the main cause of hostility. Joseph Smith
advocated plural marriages, and even those of his followers who disliked the idea (Brigham Young was one) obeyed the prophet. Violence broke out at Nauvoo. A lynch mob seized Smith and murdered
him.

Brigham Young now made his great decision. To the west was the
vast wilderness, far from the reach of persecutors. He wanted to get
away from American control. The country off toward the western
mountains then belonged to Mexico, which had a vague sway over

the great emptiness. There, thought Brigham Young, the Mormons could live in their own way without molestation.

On April 7, 1847, Brigham Young set out with a party of picked men to find a place of settlement for the Mormons in the West. They crossed the Great Plains, leaving guide posts for those who were to follow. His choice was influenced by studies of government publications, and talks with military men, explorers, and fur traders. When he came to the valley of Salt Lake, he stopped, sat on his horse, and gazed at one of the most impressive sights in America. He said, "This is the place." It was indeed an ideal site for an isolated community. There were few obvious attractions for those who sought wealth. Only arduous labor could wrest riches from the spectacular desolation.

Arduous labor was what the Mormons were prepared to give. Ground was broken with the plow on the very day of their arrival. Brigham Young planned the future city, wide streets with houses set back, a sewage system—city planning advanced in its day. Adobe houses were set up as the land was bare of timber. By the next year, 1848, Salt Lake City had several thousand Mormons, and every year others arrived, including many from England. During the first ten years no less than 17,000 converts came from overseas.

In Salt Lake polygamy was made public. This was all right until the Mexican War, when Utah became an American territory. President Fillmore appointed Brigham Young the first Governor of Utah. But Washington did not look favorably on the Mormon institution of plural marriages. There was tension and violence, capped by the Mountain Meadow Massacre, when a band of Mormons ambushed and killed some Gentiles (as non-Mormons were known) who were passing through en route to the West Coast.

Soldiers were sent to occupy Utah. They accomplished little because of Brigham Young's opposition. Then the Civil War diverted the nation's attention.

When the Civil War ended, the Mormons had to face the United States government once again. Throughout the country clergymen, women's societies, and editors kept up a campaign against polygamy. As the isolation of the Mormons lessened, and the nation learned more about them, public hostility increased. In 1871, President Grant in a message to Congress urged that polygamy be abolished. New laws were passed and upheld by the Supreme Court.

The Mormons sought to preserve their cherished institution. They felt the laws against polygamy were an infringement of religious freedom. In the end, the Mormons yielded to the inevitable, and in 1890 the church leadership issued a decree abolishing polygamy. It was just as well that the greatest Mormon did not live to see this decree. Brigham Young had died thirteen years before, leaving seventeen wives and forty-four children.

ALEXANDRE DUMAS

[1802–1870]

A LEXANDRE DUMAS was the product of two strangely different genealogical lines—the petty nobility of France on the one hand, and the slaves of San Domingo on the other. His paternal grandfather was Antoine Alexandre Davy, marquis de la Pailleterie, who, after a brilliant military career, went to the West Indies, bought a plantation on San Domingo, established himself as a colonial magnate among his Negro slaves, and by one of the women had a natural son. Her name was Marie Cessette Dumas. She died in 1772, and shortly afterward the Marquis and his son, Thomas Alexandre, returned to France.

In search of a livelihood, the son followed in the parental footsteps: he joined the army. And to mark his complete independence he abandoned the family name for that of his mother, calling himself Alexandre Dumas. He rose rapidly through the ranks during the period of the French Revolution until he became a general—the celebrated Mulatto General of the French army. The most striking thing about him was his tremendous strength: the Mulatto General could raise four rifles simultaneously with no other grip on them than one finger stuck into each muzzle. He was the model for Porthos in *The Three Musketeers.*

His infant son he had baptized Alexandre Dumas; thus was the name of a West Indian slave bestowed on the individual who was to make it one of the most celebrated in French, and in European, literature.

His father was the first important influence on young Dumas. The second was politics. His childhood was passed during the great period of the rise and fall of the Napoleonic empire. Twice he saw the Emperor himself. The second occasion was during the retreat from

Waterloo, a scene which Dumas later described in his *Conscience de l'Innocent*.

Intended for the law, young Alexandre Dumas found literature more to his liking. He studied German and Italian, read Shakespeare, Goethe, Schiller, Byron, Scott, began to frequent the theaters. For some years he experimented with his own writing, including some immature plays. Then he abandoned the law, and went up to Paris in search of fame and fortune.

One of the first things he did in the metropolis was to fall in love with Marie Catherine Lebay, by whom he had a son in 1824. The child was to become hardly less famous than his father, after whom he was named: this second Dumas is known to us as Alexandre Dumas *fils*.

Alexandre Dumas *père* was busily writing. Intoxicated by the theater, he produced a series of dramas in the Romantic vein, full of passion and violence, and managed to have some of them staged. Dumas's *Henry III and His Court* actually appeared before Victor Hugo's revolutionary *Hernani*.

In his second period Dumas turned from the theater to the novel. He formed a collaboration with Auguste Maguet, who did an immense amount of hack writing for him. The association with Maguet led to the great series of novels on which Dumas's fame now rests.

One day Dumas picked up a volume on one of the second-hand book stalls along the Seine—the *Mémoires de M. d'Artagnan*. He bought it for a few sous and took it home to read. From this chance purchase sprang the most stupendous set of "cloak and dagger" novels ever written. *The Three Musketeers*, telling of the thrilling adventures of d'Artagnan and the three immortal musketeers—the huge Porthos, the wily Aramis, and the inscrutable Athos—appeared in 1844. A sequel, *Twenty Years After*, was published within a year. One by one, the other books of the prodigious series appeared, completing the cycle derived from an old volume picked up at a second-hand book shop.

The manuscripts of his tremendous literary output still exist in Dumas's own handwriting, a monument to his untiring industry and fantastic imagination. He, however, employed a number of highly talented men to collect material and do research work for him, the best known being Auguste Maguet. The general method in this collaboration was for Dumas to propound an idea, the scheme for a story; the other writers would fill in the background of incidents and descriptive passages; finally Dumas would take over again, rewriting the entire work by hand, editing it, and making additions as he went along. The wholesale system of collaboration devised by Alexandre Dumas explains, but in no way detracts, from his amazing fertility, inexhaustible imagination, and dramatic power of dialogue that bring his characters into such sharp focus that they seem to step from his pages like living folk.

He loved the occult and the picaresque, a trait that may have been a heritage from Marie Cessette Dumas, to whom he owed a great deal more than his name. He had in him very much of the Count of Monte Cristo, that enigmatic personage of enormous and secret wealth who, working through mysterious channels, was able to call to his aid bankers of Paris and fishermen of Marseilles and bandits of Rome. In a sense, Monte Cristo was the true Dumas, the Romantic ideal into which the novelist put more of himself than he did into any other of the thousands of characters that sprang from his teeming imagination. For anyone who wants to know about Alexandre Dumas there is no better introduction than *The Count of Monte Cristo*.

The period climaxed by *Monte Cristo* and *The Three Musketeers* was the high tide of Dumas's career. The incredible rapidity with which masterpieces poured from his pen caused him to be called "a force of nature"; it seemed as if the source of his inspiration would never dry up, as if he would go on forever turning out romances bearing the inimitable stamp of his genius. A familiar story about this "force of nature" tells us that when the news of his death arrived in Paris many people refused to believe it.

But even in the days of his greatest success Dumas was laying up trouble for himself. The third and last period of his life was one of gigantic toil to meet an ever increasing extravagance of life (accentuated by the parasites and hangers-on who swarmed around him) and to carry the burden of financial obligations that mounted as he got rid of one mistress after another, built himself a splendid mansion on a great estate (he called it "the château of Monte Cristo"), and founded the Théâtre Historique for the production of his own plays.

His political agitation brought down great difficulties on his head.

For one thing, he was forced to neglect the Théâtre Historique, which ultimately went under, leaving him with a mass of debts to pay. But secondly his inveterate sympathies with popular rebellion put him under suspicion when Napoleon III rose to power. In consequence, Dumas fled to Brussels for safety. After a couple of years in exile he returned to Paris, took to journalism, and edited a paper which he called after his two most celebrated novels: as a daily it was *Le Mousquetaire,* and when it was changed to a weekly it was known as *Monte Cristo.* It was in *Le Mousquetaire* that Dumas's memoirs first appeared.

In 1858 he began to travel widely in Europe. He visited Russia; and not being content to see the westernized aristocracy of St. Petersburg, he penetrated the vast land of the steppes as far as the Caucasus Mountains. Two years later he visited Sicily, where he joined Garibaldi just after the Italian revolutionary leader had conquered the island in the first great step toward the unification of Italy under the House of Savoy.

Dumas returned to France for good in 1867. By now he was an old man beset with creditors and harassed by the many women of his past. He lived first with his daughter, Mme. Petel, and then his son, Alexandre Dumas *fils,* came to the rescue. The son greatly disapproved of his father's manner of living. A typical Parisian cartoon of the period shows Dumas *fils* as a grown man and Dumas *père* as an infant, with the caption, "Here is a child who gives anxiety . . . to his son."

In 1869, Alexandre Dumas *père* was moved to his son's house at Puys, near Dieppe, and there he died on December 5, 1870. His funeral was simple and sparsely attended: Frenchmen had other things to think about in December of 1870, for the Franco-Prussian War was raging, and the troops of Bismarck were already invading France.

Alexandre Dumas *fils* was himself a man of letters in his own right. He began his literary career only three years after his father had published *Monte Cristo,* the earliest product of his pen being a volume of poetry. Then came his first novel, *La Dame aux camélias;* in 1849 he turned the novel into a play, and this has remained his chief claim to a permanent place in French literature. The part of the heroine has ever since been a favorite role with practically every great actress; and sopranos began to feel the same way after Verdi turned the story into his great opera, *La Traviata*.

Father and son, their names are linked together in literature, and yet they offered as dramatic a contrast as anything in the stories they wrote. If Dumas *père* was the mysterious, powerful, wealthy Count of Monte Cristo, Dumas *fils* was the faithful, ill-starred, and tragic lover, Alfred Germont, of *La Dame aux camélias*.

VICTOR HUGO

[1802–1885]

T HE object of modern art," wrote Victor Hugo, "is not beauty but life." That sentence became a basic text of the Romantic Movement. It also epitomized the career of Hugo himself, for he was caught up in the momentous events of his time—a poet who spoke trenchantly of war, politics, government, diplomacy. Today we remember him as the author of *Les Misérables* and *The Hunchback of Notre Dame*. We also remember him as the impassioned patriot who hated Napoleon, and castigated Napoleon III.

His father became a general during the Napoleonic era. He accompanied Joseph Bonaparte, Napoleon's elder brother, to Naples and Spain where Joseph enjoyed the somewhat flimsy title of King. Young Victor Hugo, aged five, always retained a vivid impression of crossing the Alps on sleighs over the winter snow.

The downfall of Napoleon brought misfortune to the Hugo family, whose main source of income had been cut off. Victor Hugo's education was sporadic, but intense. Preparatory school, followed by studies at the Polytechnique, gave him no profound formal erudition, but he was a tremendous reader of books, especially the classic literature of France and the new Romantic style that was coming into vogue. His great talent was revealed early. Living in Bohemian poverty, he wrote poems, a tragedy, a melodrama, a comic opera, a novel, and contributed articles to a magazine. One poem of his won a provincial prize. Young Victor Hugo, in his teens, revealed himself as a juvenile prodigy.

His ambition was set. He was determined to retrieve his fortunes by writing, and with his pen recover the splendors he had known as a boy in Spain, when he was the son of a notable close to a throne. He knew the track to take, the proper method of winning quick success. The youth had genius in poetry, and a knack in the practical business of getting ahead. Politics would help.

After the fall of Napoleon, a Bourbon King, Louis XVIII, was on the throne. Victor Hugo, at the age of twenty, published his first volume of poems, and most of the verses were strongly Royalist in character. The King granted a pension to the young poet, who went on to spectacular success as a royalist. He was made a Chevalier of the Legion of Honor.

During this time he married. There were Romantic overtones to this event—Romantic in both the psychological and literary meanings of the word. Hugo's elder brother, Eugène, was also in love with Adèle Foucher; her wedding to his brother drove him out of his mind, and he was sent to an institution for the insane. It was like something from a novel by Victor Hugo.

Shortly afterward the poet made a violent break with the court. He had recently attended the coronation of the new King, Charles IX, and had written some flattering verses to His Majesty, but this he followed speedily with a poem that signalized his new departure. Victor Hugo despised the tawdry pretensions of this monarch, and said so in print, even going so far as to compare him unfavorably with Napoleon.

Rebellion in art went hand in hand with rebellion in politics. The preface to his drama *Cromwell* stunned the literary world. It was a fiery manifesto of the Romantic Movement. Victor Hugo, with scathing ridicule, assailed the rules of the past. He called for the shattering of the standard dramatic forms, the restraint, the effort for elegance, and trumpeted a war cry for the freer expression of Romanticism.

His dramatic masterpiece in the new style was *Hernani,* set in Spain which he had known as a youth. For his hero the author depicted a noble Spanish brigand of the accepted Romantic type. All the rules of classical French drama were broken, the classical unities defied. The play proved to be an epoch maker, showing the way to a whole series of practitioners of Romanticism, like Alexandre Dumas and George Sand. The traditionalists protested, but they could not sweep back the literary tide.

For Hugo this was a period of glory. He published his first vastly successful novel, *The Hunchback of Notre Dame,* with a setting typical of the Romantic period, the hunchback bell ringer, the somber gifted cleric caught in the toils of the gypsy girl Esmeralda, all set amid the Gothic spires and gargoyles of the great cathedral in Paris.

Victor Hugo's dramas have not lasted as well as his novels. Today the world at large knows his plays chiefly as operas, although the author quarreled violently with musical settings of his works by Verdi. Out of *Hernani* the Italian composer made an opera, *Ernani*, which became a favorite everywhere, and is still given. *Le Roi s'amuse* became Verdi's opera *Rigoletto*, the popularity of which has never dimmed.

Meanwhile Victor Hugo the poet was working busily. His verse won him the final crown of recognition in 1841, when he was elected to the French Academy. He luxuriated in the glory of an Academician and, surrounded by a group of admirers, played the agreeable part of the giant of French letters.

He became a member of the House of Peers, and then ran for President of France after the collapse of the monarchy in 1848. When the votes were counted, Victor Hugo's name was last. The winner, overwhelmingly, was Louis Napoleon, nephew of the great Napoleon, swept in by a tide of resurgent Bonapartism. Louis Napoleon staged a coup d'état, seized complete control, and called an election on the question of re-establishing the Empire. He won, and became Napoleon III.

Victor Hugo's reaction to all of this was characteristic. He made public harangues and agitated on the streets, urging resistance and calling upon the soldiers to revolt. All he got for his efforts was exile. To escape arrest he disguised himself as a workman, and fled to Belgium.

This began another period in the variegated life of Victor Hugo, eighteen years of exile. These he spent in the Channel Islands, just off the coast of France, but under the British flag. For three years he lived on Jersey, then on nearby Guernsey, where he procured a house and waited. He was a refugee during the entire reign of Napoleon III, set himself up as a political martyr, and returned to literature.

He vented his spite against Napoleon III in the scathing satire of a book *Napoleon the Little*, and in a collection of bitter verses. More important were his nonpolitical writings. During his exile, he produced some of his most perfect poetry, work that reaffirmed in summary style his position as the greatest French poet of the nineteenth century.

He wrote *Les Misérables,* a huge work ringing with pity, protest against injustice, sympathy for the poor and outcast. With its great scope, fevered emotion, and copious melodrama, *Les Misérables* became the chief vehicle of Victor Hugo's world-wide popularity as a novelist. The scenes of the Channel Islands, their rugged coasts and seafaring people, provided him with material for another successful novel, *The Toilers of the Sea.*

In 1870, with France defeated by Prussia and Napoleon III made a prisoner and then exiled, Victor Hugo returned to France. He was now sixty-eight. As a long-time political martyr, he was hailed by the new Republic and made a member of the National Assembly. But the Commune broke out, ferocious revolutionary activity in Paris. In the disturbances Victor Hugo left again, this time for Belgium.

His second exile was brief, and his return to France brought him new honors from the moderate republic now established. He became a member of the Senate, where he made a great speech on public education. He turned his house into a rendezvous for the world of literature and learning. A performance of *Hernani* was given to commemorate the fiftieth anniversary of the première of that battle piece in the Romantic Movement, and public ovations acclaimed France's greatest master of literature.

His death was mourned as a national catastrophe, his funeral solemnized with the utmost pomp. He wished to be interred in the coffin of a pauper, and was—in melodramatic contrast to the funeral splendor. In death as in life, Victor Hugo remained the great Romantic.

DISRAELI

[*1804–1881*]

I**N NOVEMBER** of 1875 news reached Lord Derby, then Disraeli's
Foreign Secretary, that the Khedive of Egypt was anxious to sell
his Suez Canal shares for four million pounds ($20,000,000). As soon
as he heard of it, the Prime Minister realized the importance of secur-
ing a controlling interest in the gateway to India. The French government, anxious to obtain England's support against Bismarck, persuaded a group of French bankers not to take up an option they held.
The British cabinet approved the purchase, but Parliament was not
in session and it was impossible to obtain from the Treasury so large
a sum for which the budget provided no credit.

Without hesitation Disraeli sent his secretary, Montague Corry,
to borrow the money from Rothschild. The great banker, who was
just finishing lunch, received the Prime Minister's envoy at table:
"Mr. Disraeli, sir, needs four million pounds tomorrow morning."
"What security?" he asked. "The British government." "You shall have
them."

By this masterly initiative, without waiting for parliamentary sanction, Disraeli caused Britain to make a sensational re-entry into
European affairs. Under Gladstone she had held aloof. Bismarck
thought himself the arbiter of the Continent. Now, with Britain
throwing her support to France because of Suez, the balance of power
had changed. Of the many services Disraeli rendered to his country
and his Queen, this was one of the greatest.

Benjamin Disraeli was the most colorful and romantic of all British
Prime Ministers. He came of a family of Spanish Jews who had been
expelled from Spain at the time of Ferdinand and Isabella. They went
to Italy, remained until the eighteenth century, and then migrated to

Britain. This background never ceased to move Disraeli with interest and pride.

His father, Isaac Disraeli, was a scholar of note, the author of *Curiosities of Literature* and other works. Isaac left the synagogue and had his family baptized into the Church of England, a move that allowed young Benjamin to think of a political career.

Before he was twenty he had become a young dandy, dressed in the extreme of fashion, and gambled on the stock exchange with poor success, so that he started life under a heavy load of debt. He turned to literature and published *Vivian Grey,* an exaggerated account of some of his own experiences and an audacious satire on society. He traveled widely from Spain to Palestine, continued to write novels in the Romantic, Byronic tradition, and began to harbor political ambitions.

His first attempts to win a seat in the House of Commons were unsuccessful. But he wrote so much and so well about the political needs of Britain, taking always the Conservative side, that he became known as the most eloquent spokesman the party had. Wellington and Peel became interested in his career. Backing from politicians so powerful could not be denied. Disraeli entered the House of Commons with the first Parliament to be elected after Queen Victoria's accession.

True to his character, Disraeli delivered his maiden speech on an Irish issue, calculated to make trouble. His rather too pompous oratory was soon interrupted by laughter and cries from the Irish benches. Again and again he tried to make himself heard, facing his tormentors with head raised and eyes flashing, until at last he gave up the unequal struggle. Raising his arms and his voice until it dominated the tumult, he cried, "I will now resume my seat, sir, but the day will come when the House will listen to me."

This apparent failure really helped the new member. The next time he rose to speak, the House felt that he had not had a fair chance and listened to him with attention. He lowered the key of his oratory and sat down amidst continued applause. In three weeks he had won over the House; he was plucky, he spoke well, he seemed to know what he was talking about. He drew great satisfaction from the knowledge that his friends were watching him with admiration, his opponents with apprehension.

At first Disraeli supported Sir Robert Peel's Conservative administration, then turned against him by supporting economic reforms in
favor of the working class. Peel fell, to be followed by a kaleidoscopic
shifting of parties and governments. Disraeli achieved cabinet rank.
Chancellor of the Exchequer under Lord Derby, he was largely responsible for the great Reform Bill which made parliamentary elec-
tions truly democratic.

In 1868, Lord Derby retired on account of ill-health. By now there
was only one possible choice of successor. The Queen sent for the
Chancellor of the Exchequer, and Benjamin Disraeli realized the ambition of his life by entering No. 10 Downing Street as Prime Minister
of Great Britain.

He said at the time, "I have climbed to the top of the greasy pole."
The figure of speech was apt. His control of the country through his
party was not strong enough to keep him in power once his titanic
struggle with Gladstone began, and the two exchanged places within
a year, the election going against Disraeli. Five years later they exchanged places again. Disraeli overthrew the Gladstone government
with a powerful speech in which he described his opponents as "a row
of extinct volcanoes." He became Prime Minister for the second time.

He was now a man of seventy, but his vigor continued and he took
his old place as the favored statesman of the Queen. Their relations
became much closer. By his purchase of shares in the Suez Canal, by
his triumphant success at the Congress of Berlin when he secured
Cyprus and brought back "peace with honour" from his conversations
with Bismarck, and above all by forcing a reluctant Parliament to
confer upon his sovereign the title of Empress of India, he won not
only Victoria's admiration but also her affection. She used to send him
primroses regularly, and they became the emblem of the Conservative party, a symbol perpetuated to this day by the Primrose League
of Britain.

Disraeli was now an old and tired man. The Queen insisted that
he move to the House of Lords where his labors would be less strenu-
ous. He became the Earl of Beaconsfield, Viscount Hughenden of
Hughenden. He himself was not averse to titles, but he seems to have
accepted this one mainly to please his wife.

Disraeli charmed the House of Lords. The House of Commons felt
his departure keenly. One observer remarked, "It is now like a game

of chess without the queen, a miserable struggle of pawns"—a judgment unfair to Gladstone's immense ability, but adequately reflecting the truth that no one could match Disraeli's flair for ringing
oratory and grand gestures.

The Earl of Beaconsfield watched international affairs with much
concern, especially the Afghan War which broke out after a British
mission to Kabul had been massacred. Though no man was ever more
of an imperialist than Disraeli, he thought that British aims could be
achieved by better diplomacy and less violence. His political influence, however, was gone. Gladstone was riding high. Disraeli retired
to Hughenden to write, and produced his last novel, *Endymion*.

In 1881 he came down to London, where he caught a heavy chill.
Anxiously Queen Victoria followed the illness of her old friend. So
did the nation. When he succumbed, his old political adversary offered the final tribute, Gladstone suggesting that Disraeli be buried
in Westminster Abbey; but Disraeli's executors decided to follow his
own wishes, and his final resting place is the little churchyard at
Hughenden. Over it stands a monument, of which the inscription
reads:

To the Dear and Honoured Memory of Benjamin, Earl of Beaconsfield,
This Memorial is Erected by His Grateful Sovereign and Friend Victoria
R.I. "Kings Love Him That Speaketh Right."

ROBERT E. LEE

[*1807–1870*]

I N THE American southern states Robert E. Lee is venerated,
idolized, almost deified. This is in accord with historic logic. The
Confederate commander in the Civil War represented in the highest
degree the traditional merits of the South and its time of glory. The
plantation aristocracy, along with many ill qualities, had the virtues
of chivalry, loyalty, the amenities of culture and family, and a high
gift of public service, and in Lee's personality these were summarized.
It is part of the American drama that the Old South, resisting its
downfall, had for its military commander a very symbol of its best
qualities.

Robert E. Lee of Virginia went through West Point without a single
demerit. The Mexican War gave him his chance. He was named chief
engineer in the army commanded by General Scott, which landed
at Vera Cruz and marched on Mexico City. There was fierce fighting
at Chapultepec. A chief engineer might not seem a likely candidate
for glory in hand-to-hand battle, but Lee led an infantry detachment
against the Mexican fortress and was severely wounded. During the
campaign he was cited three times for gallantry in action, was promoted to major, and returned home a military figure of distinction.
In 1852 he was named Superintendent of West Point.

In 1859 he was in Virginia when the news came of John Brown's
raid, that most famous of events leading to the Civil War. Colonel
Robert E. Lee was summoned to take the command of a party of
United States Army soldiers and put down the attempted insurrection. He turned over his prisoners to the civil authorities, and John
Brown was tried and hanged. Less than a year later Abraham Lincoln
was elected President. The southern states seceded from the Union.

President Lincoln, upon taking office, looked about for a commander of military operations, in case there should be war. The aged General Winfield Scott recommended Colonel Robert E. Lee. So Lee was Lincoln's man, and that is one of the ironies of history—Lincoln seeking the service of the soldier who was to inflict such bitter defeats on Lincoln's armies. We have Lee's answer in his own words: "I declined the offer—stating as candidly and as courteously as I could although I was opposed to secession and deprecated war, I could take no part of the invasion of the Southern States. . . . I concluded that I ought no longer to retain the position I held in the United States Army, and on the second morning thereafter I forwarded my resignation to General Scott."

He returned to Virginia where a state convention was enacting an ordinance that proclaimed secession from the Union and joined Virginia with the other southern states in the Confederate States of America. The Governor of Virginia summoned Lee to Richmond, and offered him the command of the military forces of the state. Lee accepted.

In the spring of 1862 the Northern commander, General George B. McClellan, was pressing with a campaign to capture Richmond. The North having the command of the sea, his program was to land a large army on the coast opposite Richmond, the Norfolk area, and march against the Confederate capital via the peninsula formed by the York and James Rivers. Simultaneously there was to be a push, overland, from Washington, the two Federal forces to meet in front of the Confederate capital.

The Confederate commander in Virginia was General Joseph E. Johnson, who proposed a strategy of allowing McClellan to advance to the outskirts of Richmond and fight a defensive battle there. Lee thought this too timid, and recommended that the invading army be fought all the way along the peninsula. Jefferson Davis accepted this plan.

At the same time, Lee proposed measures to check the march of Northern troops from Washington and block the second phase of the Federal offensive. For this he resorted to the officer who was to figure so largely in Lee's own career as his greatest lieutenant, General Thomas J. Jackson. For the part he played in the victory of Bull Run, Jackson had won the epithet of "Stonewall," and now, counseled by Lee, he set off on one of his most brilliant campaigns. The strategy was to strike through the Shenandoah Valley, a line of march that would threaten Washington, alarm the Federal commanders for the safety of the capital, and persuade them to draw off troops intended for the drive to join up with McClellan in front of Richmond. Jackson, in a dazzling campaign, won a series of battles in the Shenandoah Valley. Washington was thrown into a fright, forces were sent hastily to oppose Jackson, and McClellan was left without the support he expected.

His army was now approaching Richmond, and in the fighting the Confederate commander, Joseph E. Johnson, was wounded and had to be replaced. Robert E. Lee was named to succeed him. Now began a series of battles in which by skillful maneuvering Lee thrust back one wing of the Federal army and forced McClellan to make a general retreat.

The Peninsular Campaign was followed by spectacular operations against the Federal army in front of Washington, in the course of which the daring maneuvers of Stonewall Jackson brought on the second Battle of Bull Run. Lee won a complete victory over Northern General Pope, and then marched into Maryland, invading the Northern territory. Once again Lee faced McClellan, and the result was the drawn battle of Antietam, after which the Southerners turned back into Virginia.

The theater of action shifted to the Rappahannock River, a stream flowing east along the line between Washington and Richmond. Lee's army lay entrenched on bluffs along the south bank of the stream, while the Federal Army of the Potomac faced him on the other side. The Northern commander, now General Burnside, resolved on a frontal assault, and in the Battle of Fredericksburg masses of Northern troops pushed across the Rappahannock, and swarmed up the slopes against Confederate earthworks on the ridge. It was a murderous blunder, a disastrous defeat that brought another change in Northern commanders, General Joseph Hooker taking charge for a new offensive against Lee in the spring.

The result was Lee's masterpiece—the Battle of Chancellorsville, Napoleonic in conception and execution. Hooker had an advantage of two to one in numbers. His strategy was to pin down Lee's front, and then hit him from the rear with a flanking force. Lee and Jackson held a battlefield consultation during which they agreed on one of the boldest counterstrokes in the history of war.

The decision was to hold the front line on the heights of the river bank with a minimum of soldiers, a mere ten thousand, and depend upon fortifications to check a frontal drive by the Federals. Lee, who had begun as an engineering officer, was a master of the art of using entrenchments to neutralize superior enemy forces. The main body of the Confederates, under Jackson, was to oppose the encircling movement, not by checking it, but by outflanking the flanking forces.

Stonewall Jackson made one of those tremendous marches for which he was famous. With woods concealing the movement of his columns, he threw his troops around and behind the Federals who had crossed the Rappahannock and were driving to get to the rear of Lee's army. In fact, Hooker had a clear way. Jackson was not facing the Northern flanking forces at all, but was marching around them. But this the Federal commander never suspected, until Jackson fell upon the rear of the army of encirclement. The great masses of troops that had crossed the Rappahannock to threaten Lee with a trap were themselves trapped, cut to pieces, captured, or driven in rout, and the fame of Robert E. Lee shone high over the American Civil War.

Yet, in his moment of highest success, he sustained his greatest loss. By a sad mischance of war, Stonewall Jackson was killed. On a scouting party at night, he was shot down by his own soldiers and fatally wounded. This remarkable officer was second only to Lee himself in importance for the Confederate cause. The loss of Jackson offset the victory at Chancellorsville.

Lee now struck into Federal territory again, invading Pennsylvania. The result was the Battle of Gettysburg, which he lost when a Confederate assault to drive through the center of the Union lines failed. Pickett's charge was broken. It has been said again and again that Lee would have won at Gettysburg if his chief lieutenant had been, not Longstreet, but Stonewall Jackson. As it was, Gettysburg marked the turning point of the Civil War. The South could not conquer the North. The end was in sight.

President Lincoln's nomination of Ulysses S. Grant to the supreme Northern command marked the beginning of inexorable defeat for Robert E. Lee. Grant was no scintillating genius of strategy, but he had an accurate and stubborn grasp of the fact that with enormously superior manpower he could wear Lee down by sheer weight of numbers. Beginning with the late spring of 1864, the huge armies commanded by Grant pressed forward toward Richmond. Lee, on the defensive, fought brilliant battles, winning striking successes and inflicting costly losses; but, relentlessly, he was forced back. He inflicted heavy defeats on Grant at Spotsylvania and Cold Harbor, but was always on the defensive, and finally stood siege at Petersburg, outside of Richmond. Here he gave a great example of his skill with defensive entrenchments, but Grant's army was too large and determined.

Meanwhile the fighting in the West was sealing the final outcome of the war. From Tennessee, Sherman drove into Georgia and captured Atlanta. This was followed by Sherman's march to the sea, and the Confederacy was cut to fragments. Lee, as a last hope, abandoned the defense of Richmond and tried to march south to join the Confederate army opposing Sherman, but his depleted and starving army was trapped, and surrender was the only alternative that faced the great Southern commander. He met Grant at Appomattox in a scene memorable alike for Grant's generosity in victory and Lee's dignity in defeat.

Today we ask: What was the hope of Robert E. Lee in the Civil War? Did he think the South could win? He did have, it seems, the hope that the Federal government might be persuaded to make peace, and this was the object of his two invasions of Northern territory. But, for the most part, he realized that he was fighting a lost cause. Shortly before the surrender at Appomattox, he told one of his officers, John Pendleton, "I have never believed that we could, against the gigantic combination for our subjugation, make good in the long run our independence unless foreign powers should, directly or indirectly, assist us. But such considerations made no difference with me. We had, I was satisfied, sacred principles to maintain and rights to defend, for which we were in duty bound to do our best even if we perished in the endeavour."

He reacted to defeat in a spirit that was his heritage, the spirit of the gentleman and the soldier. He accepted the presidency of Washington College at Lexington, Virginia, a post that he held until his death five years later. His tomb is in the chapel of the college, which today bears the proud name of Washington and Lee.

SUN YAT-SEN

MAHATMA GANDHI

GARIBALDI

[*1807–1882*]

ON THE Mediterranean Riviera a fifteen-year-old boy stole a sailboat and set forth to seek his fortune on the broad blue sea. He was soon picked up by the authorities, who sent him home. His conduct seemed the more reprehensible in that his parents intended him for a religious career, the life of a monk—a plan most incongruous in the case of a lad destined to become one of the most famous of all the blood-and-thunder adventurers of the nineteenth century.

The theft of the sailboat for a one-boy voyage came to a quick end, but the father of the runaway saw the point. He forgave the escapade, and got his son a berth as a cabin boy aboard a steamship trading with South America. Thereafter, for ten years, the sea was the home of Giuseppe Garibaldi. By his twenty-fifth birthday he was the captain of a freighter plying between European ports and the Rio de la Plata.

He might have pursued the career of a seafaring man, sailing across oceans and piling up wealth as a competent trader, but Italy in his day was aflame. During his voyages the young ship's captain came into contact with the revolutionary movement that was sweeping the ancient peninsula, the rise of national feeling, the cry for independence.

Italy was divided between native despotisms and foreign domination. Sicily and southern Italy were governed by a corrupt, backward regime of Bourbon Kings. Rome and the Papal States were under the dominion of the Popes, with an ecclesiastical rule illiberal and out of date. Most of northern Italy was under the heel of Austria. The only Italian territory of any promise was Piedmont, ruled by the House of Savoy.

Unrest had spread far and wide. A secret society, the Carbonari, plotted to free Italy, as did a nationalist movement led by Mazzini, who won the support of liberals throughout Europe. Garibaldi, the ship's captain trading with South America, adhered to the cause, and made it his lifelong aspiration.

His first attempt failed—an insurrection at Genoa, betrayed, crushed—leaving Garibaldi to fly for his life. He went to Brazil. Rebellion was now in his blood, and he joined a group of insurrectos, from whose leaders he received letters of marque to operate as a privateer. A bold sea rover, he preyed on the shipping of the Brazilian government, after which he distinguished himself as a guerrilla fighter on land. Later he fought for the independence of Uruguay, commanding forces in battle and scoring signal victories. His fame rose; he became known as one of the ablest guerrilla leaders of his time.

In South America he formed a legion of Italians serving insurrectionary causes. Their uniform, South American style, was distinguished by a red shirt. This was the beginning of the army of the Red Shirts that Garibaldi was later to lead in the winning of Italian freedom.

One day he was aboard his ship in a Brazilian harbor, gazing idly through his telescope. As he peered through the glass, scanning the shore, his attention was attracted by the figure of a girl standing before a house on a hill. After studying her for a while, he went ashore, proceeded to the house, made the girl's acquaintance, courted her impetuously, and within forty-eight hours she sailed away with him as his wife.

In South America, Garibaldi and his Red Shirts had their eyes on events in Italy. Eighteen forty-eight was a year of insurrection for many parts of the Continent. Italy saw widespread revolt against Austria. Piedmont now was taking the lead in the national cause, and Garibaldi sent an offer of his services to King Charles Albert. Then, without waiting for a reply, he sailed to Italy with a band of his Red Shirts. By the time they arrived, the fortunes of war had turned against the Piedmontese, who were being defeated by the Austrians. Garibaldi's Red Shirt legion was able to win some success, though in a futile effort. His fame was such that three thousand Italian patriots joined his force, and he was now a major factor in the struggle for Italian liberation.

He turned his attention to Rome. The Papal States were seething with revolt. Pope Pius IX had begun as a liberal pontiff, only to grow alarmed at the violence of revolutionary events and to turn back to reaction. Rebellion broke out under the guidance of Mazzini, and a Roman republic was set up.

Garibaldi and his Red Shirts hastened to the Eternal City, where the revolutionary leaders entrusted him with a military command. France supported the Papacy, and a French army advanced to suppress the Roman republic. Garibaldi, with his guerrilla fighters and numbers of untrained civilians, had to face regular troops. He won sharp victories, but organized military force won out in the end. Rome fell. The Roman republic was a short-lived dream.

Garibaldi, with a force of four thousand, carried out a famous retreat. Columns of enemies, French, Austrian, Neapolitan, converged to intercept him, but he made an amazing march of desperate fighting and swift maneuver. His wife was with him, campaigning clad in a red shirt, her hair cut short. During the bitter ordeal of the retreat she succumbed and died in his arms. Sick with grief, Garibaldi led his retreating troops northward, and they were able to make their way across the plains of Lombardy to safety in Switzerland.

Garibaldi, a political fugitive, crossed the Atlantic to the United States, where he landed in New York. Famous as a revolutionary leader, he worked as a candle maker on Staten Island, employed in a small candle factory. This continued for about a year, after which he went to sea again and soon was a prosperous trader once more.

He returned to Italy, purchased the tiny island of Caprera, and settled down to farming. Thereafter Caprera was to be his home, his place of seclusion during intervals between the performance of new exploits and the winning of new renown. He lived in retirement for five years, during which time events were building up to a new effort for Italian unity and freedom.

The kingdom of Piedmont was now dominated by a statesman of the first magnitude, Cavour, who became the great practical architect of his country's freedom. Working with subtle diplomacy, he lined up international co-operation to bring about the expulsion of the Austrians from northern Italy. He made a deal with the French Emperor, Napoleon III, who fancied himself for liberal ideas and war-like adventures. This brought about a conflict between France and Piedmont on one side and Austria on the other. Garibaldi responded to the call, and was placed in command of Alpine troops. The army of France decided the issue, defeating the Austrians in Lombardy at the Battles of Magenta and Solferino.

The war ended with a disputed peace treaty. The agreement between Cavour and Napoleon III had provided that the Austrians should be expelled from both Lombardy and the Venetian province, but only the first half of that was gained. Lombardy was acquired by Piedmont, but Venice was left in the possession of Austria. The price that Cavour had agreed to pay was the cession of Nice and Savoy to France. The price was paid. Nice, a thoroughly Italian city, was Garibaldi's birthplace, and he never forgave Cavour for handing it over to France. Thereafter the two great leaders of the Italian cause were enemies.

Garibaldi returned to Caprera, and there, at his island home, he planned the liberation of Sicily and Naples from the corrupt despotism of the Bourbon Kings. He mustered a force of about a thousand Red Shirts for an invasion of Sicily. It was a pitifully small expedition to conquer a populous kingdom defended by a large army, but in due time Garibaldi and his Red Shirts landed on the Sicilian coast, under the protection, not official but understood, of two British warships. The landing was accomplished without loss, and Garibaldi told his Red Shirts, "Here we make Italy or die."

He advanced against the Sicilian capital, Palermo, and won the city by a ruse. In the dimness of evening, the Neapolitan forces in Palermo saw a column march away into the interior, and thought it was the Red Shirt invaders in flight. Actually the column consisted of camp followers and local civilians whom Garibaldi had enlisted for the trick. The garrison of Palermo hastened out in pursuit. That gave Garibaldi his chance, and he entered Palermo. The next day 20,000 soldiers, disaffected patriots who hated the Bourbons, surrendered to the 1,000 Red Shirts.

The victory brought volunteers flocking to the standard of Garibaldi, who captured Messina and from that city crossed the narrow strait to the Italian peninsula. The landing, under the friendly survey of British warships, encountered little opposition.

The Red Shirts struck out for Naples, volunteers flocking to them. Garibaldi's forces increased to some 20,000 and he took Naples. But he still had to contend with the main army of the Neapolitan King, which was concentrated to the north. The decisive victory was won on the river Volturno. The Neapolitan King fled, and possession of the kingdom of Naples and Sicily was taken by King Victor Emmanuel of Piedmont, who with his army came to the scene. Garibaldi saluted him with these words: "I hail the first King of Italy!" The liberator and the monarch made their entry together into Naples.

But there was quick disillusion. Officialdom frowned on the guerrilla leader. The generals in authority decreed that the Red Shirts should be disbanded. Garibaldi, feeling himself a victim of ingratitude, returned to Caprera and an embittered solitude. He was offered military rank in the United States, where the Civil War had broken out. President Lincoln, through Secretary of State Seward, wanted him to serve as a major general in the United States Army. Garibaldi preferred to bide his time in Italy, waiting for another chance to strike at the oppressors of his native land.

It came in 1866 with war between Prussia and Austria. Shrewd diplomacy ranged Italy on the Prussian side in an alliance intended to wrench Venice from Austria. The conflict was short, with Bismarck's Prussians winning an easy victory. In Italy matters were equally decisive. Garibaldi played a prominent part in the campaigns that gave Venice to Italy. But the politicians called a halt when he would have pushed into Trentino.

He fought subsequent battles in a bid to seize Rome. He never succeeded in this, but had the consolation of living to see Rome become the capital of Italy after the withdrawal of French troops at the time of the Franco-Prussian War.

EDGAR ALLAN POE

[1809–1849]

THE melancholies of Edgar Allan Poe began with his birth. His mother was an English actress, his father an American actor, in the days when theatrical life tended to be somewhat raffish and disreputable. They eked out a hard living for a few years together, and then the actor disappeared under circumstances that have never been explained. He left his wife to care for two young sons, of whom one, Edgar, was the future poet, aged one.

The sorrows through which his mother suffered haunted Edgar from the time he became old enough to think about them. The family had always been so poor that the playbills of the time show her performing on stage only three weeks after his birth. With her husband gone, the entire burden now fell upon her—and she was a victim of tuberculosis. Moreover, another child was on the way, and there was much whispering about the paternity of the daughter born to her. Her son always felt sensitive about the rumors, which he tried to scotch by insisting that his parents were together almost until the end, dying "within a few weeks of each other."

Left with two children to support (one son had been adopted by his grandfather) Mrs. Poe played engagements wherever she could get them, which took her soon to Richmond. There she got along well enough for a short while, but her stage appearances became fewer, and she lay dying, keeping her two children with her.

She occupied an attic room above a dressmaking shop patronized by women of wealthy Richmond families, and these took a compassionate interest in the unhappy actress and her small boy and girl. Two of these ladies, Mrs. John Allan and Mrs. William MacKenzie, wives of Scottish merchants in Richmond, visited the stricken actress often, pitying her and attracted by the two children, who are described as of singular beauty. They saw Mrs. Poe fade and die, and carried away the little boy and infant girl. Mrs. Allan took Edgar, Mrs. MacKenzie Rosalie, and thereafter brought them up as their own children.

In the tragic life of Edgar Allan Poe a factor of the first importance is his long-troubled relations with his foster father, whose name he incorporated into his own. As he grew older there arose an inevitable conflict. This was partly because of Mrs. Allan's overweening love for her foster son, which Poe returned with frantic intensity. All his life he was to be dependent on the mothering fondness of women. In his boyhood he became attached to the mother of a school companion, a beautiful stately woman, whose early death threw him into uncontrollable grief. She, apparently, was the original of "Helen," of whom Poe's verses sing with such lyric beauty.

In time, it would seem, John Allan's philanderings and illegitimate children came to the knowledge of his wife, creating a family situation in which Edgar, at sixteen, could only rally emotionally to the side of his beloved foster mother. The possibilities of quarrel and resentment can be easily imagined, with John Allan regretting that he ever took the orphan into his house. This conflict seems to have played its part in Poe's going to the University of Virginia, John Allan being glad enough to have him away.

With Poe's university career, which lasted for one term, began the interminable series of disasters which were to befall him throughout life. In his studies he did well, brilliantly in languages and literature, but his story now brings forward the word—drink. He began the indulgence in alcohol which was again and again to wreck his hopes.

Now too begins the lifelong story of financial harassment. John Allan, while paying Edgar's way at the University of Virginia, was niggardly with expenses. By now he had inherited his uncle's large fortune, but was still parsimonious, and the amounts of money he sent to his foster son were insufficient for Poe to keep up appearances among his fellow-students. He was placed in a humiliating position, and he was desperately proud.

However, there were ways out. The merchants at the college town of Charlottesville advanced ready credit to the students, as sons of affluent families, and Poe, rated as the adopted son of a wealthy man, had no trouble in gaining credit. He ran up bills.

Moreover, he gambled, as was the custom among his fellow-students, sprigs of the plantation aristocracy. Poe had no money for it, but the very way his guardian stinted him was an incentive—by gambling he might win what he needed. He lacked luck or skill or both, and ran up gambling debts.

Returning home for the Christmas holidays, eighteen-year-old Edgar ran into a storm. John Allan had learned about the drinking, debts, and gambling, and the bills were coming in. His Scottish prudence outraged, he heaped furious reproaches on the youth. Poe had the support of his foster mother and her sister, his "Aunt Sally," who sought to excuse him and mollify the wrath of the outraged merchant. As a businessman, John Allan finally recognized his liability for the bills run up with the tradesmen at Charlottesville, but he absolutely refused to pay the gambling debts. For Poe they were debts of honor, and he could not think of going back to the university until they were paid.

In the background of all this was a determination to be a poet. Poe had been writing verses. In college he had begun to compose "Tamerlane," and was now thinking of the publication of a book of verses. For John Allan the notion of Edgar's becoming a poet seemed a monstrosity. His idea was that his foster son should embark on a professional career, for which the youth had no taste whatever.

Both nursed angry bitterness, which culminated in a wrathful scene during which John Allan flung the taunt that was now his habitual accusation—ingratitude. Poe left the house, saying he would not return. He went to a Richmond inn, but, having nothing, humbled himself to write and ask John Allan to send him his belongings and a little money. There was no reply. Relief came from his foster mother, who begged him to return. Instead he went to Boston, perhaps choosing it because it was his birthplace.

He stayed in Boston for two years, living in penury and want. But he did contrive to have a book of verse published, his first, a tribute to his pertinacity as a poet. He struck up a friendship with a young printer who had a job printing shop, and persuaded him to turn out a thin booklet, *Tamerlane and Other Poems,* a work which revealed a precocious gift for versification, and the themes that were to run through the poet's subsequent work, dark melancholy and a preoccupation with the thought of death.

His next move hints at an inability to make a living—he joined the army. Poe was now twenty, and seems to have selected a soldier's life for little more than the board and lodging. Enlisting in the artillery, he was assigned to a battery ordered to Charleston, where he was soon serving at Fort Moultrie. He was the company clerk, with ample leisure for writing verse.

The South Carolina surroundings could only stir the romantic imagination of the young poet. The islands were a legendary haunt of the pirates of old, the semitropical thickets an appropriate setting for strange adventure. The company clerk went on long rambles amidst scenes which, with a characteristic finesse of detail, were to appear some years later in "The Gold Bug," a tale of mystery laid along that Carolina shore.

He had been transferred to Virginia when a message from John Allan summoned him home. Frances Allan was dying, and begging to see her foster son again. In a frenzy of grief Poe hastened to Richmond, but arrived too late.

In this time of mourning his relations with John Allan were better, and they discussed an idea Poe had in mind. He knew John Allan would never help him with his literary career. So the young soldier suggested West Point. He asked his foster father to use his influence to get him an appointment, and this John Allan was willing to do, preferring an officer for a family connection.

Poe's career at the Military Academy began promisingly enough. The routine bored him, but he did well in his studies, showing gifts in languages and shining at mathematics. Some money from home was needed, and John Allan was, as usual, stingy. The Scottish merchant became colder than ever when he remarried and began to have legitimate children, a development that removed from Poe even the hope of one day coming into the family fortune.

The poet's stay at West Point lasted for a year and four months, during which time he wrote verse and was able to bring about the publication of another volume. In a display not merely of pertinacity but also of resourcefulness, he showed his manuscripts to the superintendent of the Military Academy who approved of a plan whereby the cadets subscribed for copies, seventy-five cents each, thereby assuring an advance sale. With this guarantee, Poe wrote to a New York publisher who accepted the volume. Thus it was that *Poems by*

Edgar A. Poe appeared, including some of the best known, "Israfel,"
"To Helen," "Lenore."

By the time of publication Poe's stay at West Point had terminated.
He was expelled—by his own deliberate doing. He had taken to
drinking again, but his dismissal grew out of his realization that
military life was of no further use in his now hopeless relations with
John Allan. He violated rules and disobeyed orders, staying away
from parades and other academic duties, was tried by court-martial,
pleaded guilty, and was expelled. He was resolved to set out on a
literary career.

After a brief stop in New York he went on to Baltimore, where he
joined some relatives of his father's, and now became involved permanently in the strange family situation that was to distinguish the
remainder of his life. It was a pitiful household. At the head of it
was Poe's aunt, Mrs. Maria Poe Clemm. With Mrs. Clemm was her
daughter Virginia, then nine years old, who only four years later
became the child bride of Edgar Allan Poe. She inspired "Annabel
Lee."

In this Baltimore period first appears the dark mention of drugs,
Poe resorting to opium, laudanum. Still drinking, he sought refuge
in narcotic dreams as well. Soon his physical health and his sanity
alike were undermined.

Desperate poverty brought a turn in Poe's literary labors, an important and fruitful development. He started to write short stories,
entering a field in which he would become one of the greatest masters, author of "The Gold Bug" and "The Pit and the Pendulum" and
"The Murders in the Rue Morgue." With "The Purloined Letter" he
created a literary type with a great future—detective fiction. Poe's
C. Auguste Dupin is the forerunner of Sherlock Holmes, Philo Vance,
and Charlie Chan.

He enjoyed a measure of success as author, critic, and editor, but
ultimately failed because he could not give up either alcohol or drugs.
He traveled around with Virginia and her mother—to Richmond,
New York, Philadelphia. Struggling with poverty and depression,
he was crushed when his young wife contracted tuberculosis. His
wretched state is shown by the way he ruined one of the brightest
opportunities of his life.

A friend of his knew the son of President Tyler, and arranged for

Poe to go to Washington to see the son and the President. Poe set out for Washington in high hopes, then drank himself into a stupor, and was unable to go to the White House for his appointed interview with the President.

In agony, he returned to Virginia and Mrs. Clemm. The three somehow managed to get to New York. Edgar Allan Poe was famous. He continued to write and to be published. But he could not make a living from his work. Thus "The Raven" was an instant success, selling thousands of copies, but the poet received only a pittance in the way of royalties.

Virginia died in a cottage they occupied at Fordham. Poe passed the two years remaining to him in the shadows of madness, dreams, drugs, drinking, hallucinations. Then, just before the end, he pulled himself together by a superhuman effort. He went to Richmond to propose to a wealthy widow who had been the object of one of his early romances. A wedding was arranged, and it seemed as if Poe's years of poverty were over at last. He set out to break the good news to Mrs. Clemm, got as far as Baltimore, but never boarded the train for New York. What happened during several days is unknown. On October 3, 1849, Edgar Allan Poe was picked up in a gutter. He had gone on a drunken debauch, and was in a state of alcoholic collapse. He lingered for four days, in raving horrors of remorse and delirium, before death, mercifully, put an end to his tortured life.

ABRAHAM LINCOLN

[*1809–1865*]

O N A day in 1784 a frontier farmer was working in a Kentucky
field with his two boys when he was shot down by lurking
Indians. The elder boy ran to the cabin for a gun, and emerged to
see the younger lad being carried off by an Indian. He fired with
expert aim. The Indian fell, and his small captive scurried away. The
boy thus saved was Thomas Lincoln, later to become the father of
the emancipator president. So relates an early story in the lore of
Abraham Lincoln, who more than any other American is surrounded
by legend and anecdote.

He was born in the Kentucky backwoods, his father a shiftless
farmer. Young Abe had less than a year of schooling, but read avidly
what books he could lay his hands on—the Bible, *Aesop's Fables,
Robinson Crusoe, Pilgrim's Progress,* a *History of the United States.*
He practiced arithmetic on a wooden shovel, shaving off the figures
so as to write new ones. His thriftless father hired the boy out for
farm work at six dollars a month. A certain Mrs. Miller had him split
rails and paid him with cloth for a pair of trousers, four hundred rails
for every yard of brown jeans. Thus began Lincoln's lifelong nickname of the Rail Splitter.

In 1825, when Lincoln was seventeen, the family moved to Illinois
and settled on the banks of the Sangamon River. There they cleared
fields for a farm, young Abe doing his share of the work. He was
long and gangling but immensely strong, fond of idling but capable
of huge exertions. The move to Illinois was of dominant importance
in the Lincoln story. During the same period young Jefferson Davis,
the future President of the Southern Confederacy, was leaving the
border slave state of Kentucky for Mississippi in the Deep South of

plantation slavery. Lincoln, the future emancipator of the slaves, moved the other way, to the free state of Illinois.

His first contact with life beyond the log cabin came with the advent of one Denton Offutt into the neighborhood, a wandering trader who had a cargo of produce—hogs and corn—to be taken down the Mississippi to New Orleans. He hired nineteen-year-old Abe and two other boys for the job of boating down the river, paying them fifty cents a day each, with a bonus of sixty dollars for the three when the work was done. In New Orleans Lincoln first saw slavery on a mass scale. Twelve years later when he was thirty-one he made another trip to New Orleans. The stories differ about which trip it was that caused him to say about slavery, "If ever I get a chance to hit that thing, I'll hit it hard."

Offutt hired Lincoln to run his store, and it was in this capacity that Lincoln first got the name of Honest Abe. How he earned it is illustrated in the incident of a man who overpaid him four cents and was gone before he noticed it. Before he went to bed that night he walked several miles to repay the pennies. Another time he did the same thing to make up the deficiency, after having inadvertently used too small a weight in measuring out a pound of tea.

Offutt's store failed in less than a year, its owner drifting off into the unknown. The Black Hawk War of 1832 broke out, and Lincoln enlisted in the militia to fight the Indians. However, he did not see any fighting although he rose to the rank of captain in the Fourth Illinois Regiment.

Returning home with no military glory, Lincoln went into politics. An incident leading to this was an encounter with a gang of tough young fellows at New Salem who made it a practice to test the prowess of any newcomer. Their leader took Abe on for a wrestling match, and to the surprise of all was promptly overthrown. But Lincoln, far from trying to humiliate him, made friends with him and won over the whole gang. Thereby he acquired a staunch following ready to back him in politics.

His political career began in desultory fashion. He ran for the state legislature as a Whig and was defeated. Disappointed, he went into the grocery business, and failed. He became postmaster at New Salem, then a surveyor, during which time he began to study law. In 1834, Lincoln, again a candidate on the Whig ticket, was elected to the Illinois legislature. His election at the age of twenty-five appears to have been due to his great physical strength—an imposing asset on the frontier—his sense of humor, his tolerance, his reputation for honesty, and the purity of his life.

While he was a member of the legislature his romance with Ann Rutledge occurred. She was the daughter of the innkeeper. Lincoln fell madly enamored of her, but he was a timid suitor and delayed too long. Ann contracted a fever that killed her suddenly and tragically. Lincoln, crazed with grief, gave way to such deep melancholy that his friends feared he would take his life.

Recovering his equanimity (although he remained subject to bouts of melancholy for the rest of his life), he returned to politics and was re-elected twice again to the state legislature. He had been studying law, reading Blackstone, and admittance to the bar on the frontier was not too difficult. In 1837, Abraham Lincoln, at the age of twenty-eight, began practice, the custom of the time making it common enough for a political officeholder to work at the profession of attorney. During this time the state capital was transferred from Vandalia to Springfield. Lincoln played a large part in bringing about the change, for he was popular in Springfield, and there found a good field for his legal practice. Thus he entered upon his notable career as a frontier lawyer.

Lincoln was past thirty when he became engaged to marry in one of the most singular of romances. Mary Todd was a high-bred, brilliant, and witty young woman being courted by the proud and gifted Stephen A. Douglas, later to become a brilliant senator and Lincoln's political rival. Why Mary Todd preferred Lincoln to the accomplished Douglas is a mystery. Perhaps she foresaw future greatness for Honest Abe, or perhaps it was merely the inscrutable way of romance. The marriage was arranged for January 1, 1841, and what happened is clouded by doubt. When the guests assembled at the appointed hour, with Mary Todd in all her bridal finery, no Lincoln appeared. The next day his friends found him in such depths of morbid gloom that, as at the time of the death of Ann Rutledge, they were afraid he would kill himself. He was in one of his fits of utter black melancholy. His friend Joshua Speed hurried him off to his native Kentucky to recover.

Some time later Lincoln returned to Mary Todd, received her

forgiveness, and allowed a new date to be set for their marriage. This time it went off on schedule. The union proved to be a stormy one; Mary Todd Lincoln was given to neurotic outbursts, but her husband was capable of an almost superhuman patience with her just because he knew how hard it was to control his own psychological compulsions.

Now there developed a marked change in Lincoln. He abandoned his habit of rough sarcasm, and his frontier coarseness of speech gave way to intellectual lucidity and cadences of grandeur. He had made fun of backwoods revivals and hell-fire theology. After his marriage he ceased to ridicule the beliefs of other men. Later in life he wrote, "When any church will inscribe over its altar as its sole qualification for membership 'Thou shalt love the Lord thy God with all thy heart and with all thy soul and with all thy mind and thy neighbor as thyself' that church will I join with all my heart and with all my soul."

He served a term in Congress, after which he abandoned politics for a while and formed the historic law firm of Lincoln and Herndon. No scholar in jurisprudence, he left the legal technicalities to Herndon, and became a great trial lawyer. Riding the circuit from one court session to another, he became an outstanding figure in the rough-and-ready law proceedings, as the system of jurisprudence and justice developed in a frontier community. Abraham Lincoln, dealing with clients, and pleading before courts on the Illinois circuit, found the real basis of his historic personality, his humanity, understanding, justice, and honesty. He had always been poor. Now he became prosperous. But in rising to affluence he only increased his reputation for honesty. In one case his client was crooked and gave him a false account, which Lincoln presented to the court. During the trial he discovered the deception and immediately threw up the case.

This was during the early eighteen-fifties, and events were shaping up for a new great crisis in the national problem in which Abraham Lincoln was destined to achieve immortality—the problem of slavery. Thirty years before, in 1820, there had been a crisis. Vast new territory had been acquired through the Louisiana Purchase, and the question had been raised: Should the new western country have slavery? The quarrel had been settled by the Missouri Compromise, which had made Missouri a slave state but provided that all other territory north of the southern border of Missouri should be free. Now the Mexican War, with the resultant annexation by the United States of great lands extending to the Pacific Coast, had posed the question all over again: Should the new territories be slave or free?

Lincoln opposed the extension of slavery. At the same time he was a moderate who disliked the fanatical abolitionists, who raged with intemperate fury against the slave owners of the South and who were provoking the southern states to an equal anger. In 1854 the Kansas-Nebraska Act was passed in Washington, opening those territories to slavery and repealing the Missouri Compromise. In this the prime mover was Stephen A. Douglas, that same Douglas who had been Lincoln's rival for the hand of Mary Todd. Douglas had meanwhile risen to brilliant prominence in Congress, his small stature and large abilities winning for him the name of the Little Giant. A northerner, he supported the slave cause, thereby winning the support of the South for his ambition, which was the Presidency.

Lincoln now re-entered politics. Called upon to speak against the Kansas-Nebraska Act championed by Douglas, he made an address at Peoria which brought him into national prominence and began the great Lincoln-Douglas feud. The Peoria speech was Lincoln's first great pronouncement. It was reasoned, moderate, and statesmanlike. Opposing the extension of slavery, Lincoln argued that "new free states are places for poor people to go and better their condition." Instead of a hatred of slavery, the chief concern he expressed was for the poor among the free whites.

The success of the Peoria speech renewed Lincoln's ambitions. Hitherto he had been a member of the Whig party, a combination of factions united only in their opposition to the Democrats. On the slavery question the Whigs were hopelessly divided, and that issue now caused the disappearance of the party. The opposition to slavery rallied to form the Republican party, which Lincoln, after some hesitation, joined. In 1856 he was mentioned as a possible presidential candidate of the Republicans, and made a series of speeches that again drew country-wide attention to him. He had found his place in the political arena, that of an advocate and a statesman in a great national debate. He was becoming a foremost leader of the new Republican party.

The outstanding leader of the Democratic party was Stephen A.

Douglas, rising consistently in national eminence. In 1858, Douglas entered the Illinois race for the Senate, and the Republicans summoned Lincoln to oppose him.

Lincoln's acceptance speech was one of the greatest of his career, one of the greatest in political history. His opening paragraph set forth phrases destined to be momentous slogans.

"'A house divided against itself cannot stand.' I believe this government cannot endure permanently half slave and half free. I do not expect the Union to be dissolved—I do not expect the house to fall—but I do expect it will cease to be divided. Either the opponents of slavery will arrest the further spread of it, and place it where the public mind shall rest in the belief that it is in the course of ultimate extinction; or its advocates will push it forward, till it shall become alike lawful in all the States, old as well as new—North as well as South."

Douglas replied, and Lincoln challenged him to a series of debates. Douglas accepted, and one of the most memorable debates of all time was staged—the Little Giant versus the long lanky Rail Splitter. They met in seven platform encounters at various places in Illinois. Argument and counterargument were on a level of high statesmanship. Contending against the extension of slavery, Lincoln was able to exploit an inconsistency in the position of Douglas with such effect that the presidential chances of Douglas were ruined.

Douglas set forth a doctrine of "popular sovereignty"—the people of a territory to decide for themselves whether or not to have slavery. The inconsistency was that he also upheld the decision of the Supreme Court in the Dred Scott case, which held that it was illegal to exclude slavery in any way from a territory that was not yet a state. At Freeport, in the closing round of the debate, Lincoln asked Douglas whether the people of a territory could exclude slavery by their own legislation. Douglas's answer was—yes. Cornered by Lincoln's insistent questioning, he declared that, the Supreme Court notwithstanding, slavery should exist in a territory only by the decision of the local people. This appealed to the voters of Illinois, but it won for Douglas the enmity of the South, which vehemently supported the Supreme Court decision in the Dred Scott case.

The outcome was that Douglas won the Illinois election, and went to the United States Senate. But the Democratic party was split wide open, and two years later, when the Democratic National Convention nominated Douglas for the Presidency, the southerners walked out and nominated a candidate of their own.

Lincoln, after some indecision, sought the Republican nomination, and it was as a potential presidential candidate that he made his speech at Cooper Union in New York, not his finest speech but one of his best known. He tried to keep the Republican party clear of the recent attempt by John Brown to start a revolt of slaves in the South, and to set a reasoned and moderate party policy toward slavery. It was his political debut in the East, and established him as a prominent competitor for the nomination.

When the Republican National Convention met in Chicago, Lincoln was nominated on the third ballot. In the election he received only a minority vote—less than 2,000,000 of a total of 4,500,000 votes cast. But there were four candidates in the race, with the Democratic vote so badly split that Lincoln was elected President.

The personal aspects of Lincoln's presidency present a pattern familiar throughout his life—alternations of high vigor and melancholy depression, tranquil strength of purpose and harassed indecision. He was at a crest of his powers when he was elected, and had to wait through November till March before assuming office. During that interval the southern states, refusing to accept his election, seceded from the Union. Efforts were made for a compromise to avert war, and Lincoln was approached at Springfield. He was at a peak of resolution, stating that slavery must be excluded altogether from the territories but would not be interfered with in the South. The compromise efforts came to nothing, and the Civil War approached inevitably.

Then came a period of depression for Lincoln. Traveling to Washington to assume office he made futile statements belittling the crisis, though the Southern Confederacy had already been formed. Holding a provincial frontier view, he seems to have misjudged completely the gravity of danger, and only after a while in Washington did he attain a statesmanlike view of the issues of slavery and civil war. During the first eighteen months of his administration he gave strange displays of indecision. His inaugural address had a fine literary quality, but merely exhorted the southern states to return, and was followed by no action. When the South started the Civil War by firing upon Fort Sumter, on April 13 and 14, 1861, Lincoln sought refuge in the advice of his cabinet, as if unable to make up his mind. He accepted the Southern challenge, and called for volunteers, but allowed a handful of senators to interfere with the military operations which resulted in the defeat at Bull Run. Again and again he vacillated, appointed McClellan to command the army, lost faith in him and dismissed him. Generals were appointed for political reasons, and were bedeviled by White House interference in military action. Congress organized a committee, which harassed Lincoln, and meddled in strategies of war. All this contributed to the disgraceful defeats of Northern armies that marked the first phase of the Civil War, and Lincoln's period of depression was deepened in anguish by the death of his favorite son.

Suddenly, he rallied his powers. The change seems to have occurred during a trip to West Point and a conference with the veteran General Winfield Scott. Thereafter the President took matters into his own hands and emerged a new Lincoln, sure of himself, master of his soul and of his world.

On September 22, 1862, after the victory of the Union troops at Antietam, Lincoln issued his Emancipation Proclamation, declaring that after January 1, 1863, all slaves would be free in states then in rebellion. This was followed later by the Thirteenth Amendment to the Constitution, which he planned and urged, abolishing slavery forever. He rose to his greatest utterance in his Gettysburg Address, delivered on the first anniversary of the battle that turned the tide of the Civil War.

He was still the man of anecdotes and droll humor. When in one encounter of war the Southerners captured a number of horses and several Union generals, Lincoln said he could create new generals but the loss of the horses was serious; and there is endless quotation of his remark, when somebody commented on Grant's drinking, that he would like to know the brand of Grant's whiskey, so that he could send some of it to his other generals.

On April 9, 1865, General Robert E. Lee surrendered to General Grant at Appomattox, and five days later President Lincoln was assassinated by John Wilkes Booth, a fanatical secessionist. The historic crime was committed at Ford's Theater in Washington, where the President was attending a performance of *Our American Cousins*. As the fatal shot rang through the theater the President fell forward on the front of his box, unconscious and dying. The assassin leaped onto the stage, crying, *"Sic semper tyrannis."* He mounted his horse at the stage door and disappeared into the night, later to be cornered and killed.

Abraham Lincoln never regained consciousness. Because of his rugged physique he lingered until 7:25 in the morning of April 15, 1865. When he finally stopped breathing, his Secretary of State William Seward said, "Now he belongs to the ages." It was the most fitting tribute that could have been uttered, an intimation of the place the Great Emancipator would hold forever in the heart of the American Union that he saved.

RICHARD WAGNER

[1813–1883]

Opinions about Richard Wagner's personality fall into two schools of thought. One is that, aside from being a supreme musical genius, he was the most unworthy of human beings, a sort of monster, an egotist devoid of all humanity of feeling and decency of conduct. The other school holds that his genius excused everything and placed him above the morals of other men. This was Wagner's own opinion.

About Wagner's music there are also two schools of thought. The public often finds his operas too long and with too few of the melodious arias that make Verdi and Puccini so popular. But the critics tend to see the Wagnerian music drama as one of the stupendous achievements of art.

Early in life Wagner became intoxicated with music. He was much affected by Carl Maria von Weber, composer of the opera *Der Freischütz*, a work written in the new vein of European Romanticism. But, above all, young Richard Wagner loved the titan of music, Beethoven. Wagner was not, however, interested in music only. He read voraciously—Aeschylus, Shakespeare, Goethe. His operas show the influence of all three.

While at the University of Leipzig he began serious composition— overtures, operas, and his only symphony. This early work, hardly ever heard today, trained his critical faculties and convinced him that he had enough ability to succeed.

As Wagner's musical genius developed, so did the unpleasant side of his character. Not long out of the university, he was an expert at borrowing without repaying. He had a firmly ingrained opinion that because of his genius everyone around him owed him a living. He took the lordly attitude that he was doing a favor when he allowed his friends to help him.

In 1834 he was given the post of musical director with the Magdeburg opera troupe, and threw himself into his work, preparing and conducting operas. He threw himself likewise into the pursuit of Minna Planer, a young singer. He was ardent, she was coy. After two years they were married. It was during the wedding ceremony, according to his own account, that he suddenly realized that she was not the right one, not the proper companion for him in his life of art.

The next few years were full of trouble for Wagner. He could not get along with his wife. His opera *Das Liebesverbot* failed. He fled from Magdeburg to escape his creditors. On top of all this he contracted an irritating skin disease, erysipelas.

Then came the first of his memorable trips to Paris. He had a vague notion that he might get some of his compositions produced there, with the help of Scribe, the renowned playwright and librettist, and Meyerbeer, then at the height of his success as the lion of grand opera. He took with him the partly finished score of *Rienzi*. Wagner and Minna, bickering and quarreling, made part of the trip by sea, Paris via London. The voyage to London was beset by violent storms. Minna was terrified by the tempest. Wagner conceived the idea of writing an opera about the legendary storm-tossed "Flying Dutchman."

In Paris, Scribe did nothing for him, but Meyerbeer was helpful. At the height of his own fame, he so far aided the unknown young German as to persuade the Théâtre de la Renaissance to accept *Das Liebesverbot* for a performance. Wagner's hopes soared high, but bad luck intervened again. Before his opera could be produced, the theater failed. This was the more calamitous because he and Minna, optimistic of profits, had taken a fashionable expensive apartment, and now were faced with the problem of paying the rent. They tried the expedient of taking in boarders, but in the end Wagner made the acquaintance of the debtors' prison for a short time.

In Paris he met Liszt, lord of the piano at the height of his glory. Liszt gave Wagner encouragement, and lent him money, a thing he was to do repeatedly thereafter. In the generous and faithful Liszt, Wagner found his greatest friend. He completed the score of *Rienzi* and sent it to the King of Saxony. This time his persistent ill-fortune changed. He received word that *Rienzi* would be performed in Dresden. His hopes at fever heat, he turned again to his obsession— *The Flying Dutchman*. It was accepted by the Berlin Opera.

Rienzi, produced in 1842, made a success, as a result of which Wagner was given the position of conductor at the Royal Opera House in Dresden. The salary was 15,000 thaler—sumptuous, but the composer was now so deeply in debt to almost everybody that he continued to be in financial hot water. In Dresden he met the Schumanns, Robert and Clara, and renewed his acquaintance with Liszt. He also met Hans von Bülow, then a boy of sixteen, who was later to become the great conductor of Wagner's work.

The pattern of Wagner's musical life was now set. From his pen came a succession of masterpieces that stunned Europe and transformed the art of music—*Tannhäuser, Lohengrin, The Ring of the Nibelungen, Parsifal*. By the time of his death he stood alone as the greatest opera composer of his time.

With his major works Wagner plunged into new theories of musical art—a greater dramatic continuity, music drama, a freer harmonic structure, sensuous dissonance, rich and imposing orchestration, and the use of the leitmotif—the musical phrase to signify a dramatic idea. These elements, germinating in *Tannhäuser*, were to be developed in subsequent works to the full splendor of Wagnerian music drama.

Since Wagner was interested in almost every side of life, he inevitably became caught up in the politics, the revolutionary fervor, of his time. In 1848 he joined the Saxon uprising, and had to flee when it was put down. Borrowing money from Liszt, he sought sanctuary in Switzerland.

At Zurich his chief financial benefactor was Otto Wesendonck, with whose beautiful wife Wagner, as might have been expected, fell in love. This time there was no turmoil, save the romantic turmoil in the Wagnerian soul. This was so great that the composer now set to work on *Tristan and Isolde*. In that marvelous medieval romance of love and doom, he found an outlet for his infatuation. Herr Wesendonck gave Wagner and wife Minna a summer house on the Wesendonck estate free of rent. Living thus with Frau Wesendonck next door, Wagner stopped work on *The Ring* and wrote the libretto of *Tristan* in four weeks. This was followed by a memorable gathering. The Wagners were there and the Wesendoncks. So were Wagner's devout disciple, the conductor Hans von Bülow, and his wife Cosima, the daughter of Liszt. To the company Wagner read the libretto, the dramatic poem of *Tristan and Isolde*. At the time no one but Wagner and Frau Wesendonck realized the personal implications of the tragic story of the love of Tristan and his uncle's wife. However, there is an item of drama in the fact that Frau von Bülow, born Cosima Liszt, later on became Frau Wagner.

It appears that Cosima was determined to be the inspiration of the greatest genius she could find, and Richard Wagner was unquestionably that. While still married to von Bülow, she bore Wagner several children. Von Bülow, the betrayed friend, was personally embittered, but remained loyal to the music of Wagner. He finally divorced Cosima. Wagner was divorced from Minna and married Cosima.

Von Bülow even conducted the first performance of *Die Meistersinger*, humiliated though he was by the fact that Cosima, still his wife, was living with Wagner.

Wagner's final dream was the Bayreuth Festspielhaus. *The Ring*, produced as a whole, was in his mind too great and revolutionary for an ordinary opera house. He put his royalties into Bayreuth, everything he could borrow, and even a special fee of five thousand dollars he got from the Philadelphia Exposition for composing the "American Centennial March." Bayreuth proved a huge success when the four parts of *The Ring* were played on successive days, but still there was a deficit, a melancholy theme of Wagner's life, one that hounded him to the grave.

In 1882, Wagner was so ill he could hardly endure the strain of the Bayreuth Festival, signalized by the première of *Parsifal*. With Cosima he went to Venice, the city on the lagoons which he liked to visit. There he was joined by Liszt. He thought that a warm climate would help him to improve, but he continued to decline. Death carried him off at the age of seventy. His music is immortal. Every year crowds come to Bayreuth from all over the world to experience the incomparable art of Richard Wagner. On opera stages everywhere can be heard the lordly themes of *Lohengrin* and *Die Meistersinger* and *Tristan und Isolde*.

BISMARCK

[1815–1898]

B Y USING war as an instrument of national policy, Prince Otto
Eduard Leopold von Bismarck-Schönhausen welded a group
of jealous kingdoms and feudal principalities into a united nation
which for a brief spell became one of the world's great powers and
the dominant factor on the continent of Europe. Germany's Man of
Blood and Iron, Bismarck hammered together the political entity that
disturbed Europe in his own time, frightened the nations when his
successor, the Kaiser, replaced him, and terrified them under the
leadership of Adolf Hitler.

Bismarck came from the Prussian aristocracy. He was the complete
Junker, stiff, dictatorial, courageous, paternalistic toward the lower
classes of his country, arrogant toward non-Germanic peoples. He was
well educated, spoke several languages—and fought about twenty
duels while at the university.

Bismarck entered politics by accident. Widespread political agitation, a rise of liberalism that culminated in 1848, was flaring throughout Europe. In Prussia the democratic movement brought about the
summoning of a parliament, with an election of representatives. The
representative of Bismarck's district had already been chosen. He was
planning to settle down to the life of a Junker when he was suddenly
called upon to take the place of the appointed member, who had
fallen ill.

Bismarck went to Berlin, where he became a powerful figure among
the Conservatives. His speeches in support of the divine right of kings
and the maintenance of the patrimonial rights of the nobles in the
country districts attracted much attention. When revolutionary disturbances broke out in 1848, he urged the King to take vigorous
measures. Frederick William IV, however, granted a constitution un-

der which a new parliament was set up. To this Bismarck was elected
as a member of one of the two chambers. He continued his powerful
advocacy of the royal prerogative and aristocratic rights. He likewise
sounded a theme which echoed in the hearts of the people. He called
for German unification, the amalgamation of the scores of petty states
and principalities into a German nation under the leadership of
Prussia.

This now became his monumental labor. By means of powerful addresses and a strong political machine he swung the tide of public
opinion, and the liberal revolution of 1848 was succeeded in Germany
by a rally to the cause of national unification. Bismarck took care to
keep this in line with his desire for the dominance of Prussia. He went
abroad on visits to Russia and France, studying foreign opinion of
the program he championed. The matter of German unification, with
Prussian dominance, was of obvious concern to Germany's neighbors.
Austria had claims to Germanic leadership, and Russia and especially
France would have cause for alarm.

In September 1862, William I became King of Prussia after the
death of Frederick William IV. Bismarck was called to become head
of the Prussian cabinet and Minister of Foreign Affairs. He was now
in a position to carry out his ideas. This meant armed aggression. He
emphatically declared that Germany's problems could be solved only
by "blood and iron."

His first move was to form an alliance with Austria and launch a
joint attack in 1864 against Denmark, with the Scandinavian province of Schleswig-Holstein as the prize. It was an easy and inglorious
war. When it was over Bismarck turned to attack Austria after a
dispute over the disposition of Schleswig-Holstein. This war, the
Seven Weeks' War, ended in complete Prussian victory, enabling
Bismarck to proceed with the formation of the North German Confederation. Into this union he was able to bring the South German
states.

Next came the Franco-Prussian war of 1870. Bismarck believed that
the showy Second Empire of Napoleon III would have to be defeated
in battle for German unification to be complete. He was well aware,
however, that a wanton and unprovoked attack upon France might
bring England into the conflict, so he resorted to a trick to force
France into declaring war.

A question had arisen over the succession to the Spanish throne. Bismarck favored a Prussian prince, Leopold of Hohenzollern-Sigmaringen, while France naturally opposed this extension of Prussian power to Spain. Bismarck then withdrew his candidate. A short time later King William of Prussia was taking the waters at Ems. Benedetti, the French ambassador, had an interview with him there during which he suggested that the King forbid Prince Leopold ever to seek the Spanish throne again. He also suggested that the King express his regret at the incident to Napoleon III. The King refused anything in the nature of an apology.

William sent a telegram to Bismarck giving a full account of the interview, and ordered him to communicate it to the other powers and to make it public. Bismarck distorted the Ems telegram by making public only the fact that France had demanded an apology and that Prussia had refused. This blow at French prestige had exactly the effect Bismarck desired. Napoleon III declared war.

Bismarck had everything in readiness with the Prussian General Staff directing the finest army in the world. France was utterly defeated, Napoleon III taken prisoner, Paris captured. Alsace and Lorraine were torn from France and added to what was to be the German Empire. On January 18, 1871, King William of Prussia was crowned German Emperor in the Hall of Mirrors in the Palace of Versailles.

Now Bismarck faced the task of peacetime consolidation of the new Empire created through war. It was difficult indeed for the old Junker, saturated with feudal ideas and an agricultural complex, to adapt himself to an era of industrialism and foreign trade. His efforts to solve the great financial problems posed by the confederation of the German states, his conflict with the Roman Catholic Church, his difficulties with labor, and the spread of socialism resulted in alternate successes and failures. Nevertheless he remained a towering figure, the real ruler of Germany, the Iron Chancellor.

At the accession of Kaiser William II there was an immediate clash between Bismarck and the headstrong, inexperienced monarch. Naturally the statesman could not win. Bismarck was dismissed, and in a way that inspired one of the greatest cartoons ever published. In *Punch,* the London weekly, appeared a drawing showing Kaiser William II leaning over the rail of the German ship of state as Bismarck descended the ladder. "Dropping the Pilot" was the appropriate caption. Bismarck never forgave the Kaiser. Even at death he resented him, for he had inscribed on his tomb, "A True German Servant of the Emperor William I."

After his dismissal as Chancellor, Bismarck retired to an old ancestral estate near Hamburg. From time to time an article under his name would appear in the *Hamburger Nachrichten* sharply criticizing the policy of the Emperor and his new advisers. He was also busy with his political testament, *Gedanken und Erinnerungen*, the first two volumes of which were issued immediately after his death. The third volume was not allowed to see the light until after World War I. It dealt with the period of his dismissal and while William II was on the throne the imperial censorship would not permit its publication.

Bismarck did not live to see the collapse of the German Empire he had built. What he would have thought of the Kaiser's war policy we cannot say. But he surely would have despised Hitler as much as did that other great Junker, Marshal von Hindenburg.

QUEEN VICTORIA

[*1819–1901*]

QUEEN VICTORIA is the symbol of British greatness in the nineteenth century. In many ways she hardly seemed cast for the part. Her background in blood, training, and influence was mainly German. She did not sympathize completely with cabinet government as it worked through the House of Commons. And she epitomized cautious respectability while her people were raising the imperial standard, with drawn swords and naval displays, in some of the most romantic spots on earth.

Consider the German aspect. On her father's side Victoria was descended from the Hanoverians who had come from Germany to rule England. Her mother was Princess Victoria Maria Louisa of Saxe-Coburg-Gotha. When Victoria's father, the Duke of Kent, died, her mother turned for advice to the child's uncle, Leopold of Saxe-Coburg-Gotha. Little Victoria was given a German governess, Louise Lehzen, who molded her character. Becoming Queen at the age of seventeen, Victoria relied on a German adviser, Baron Stockmar. Finally, the crowning German influence—Victoria's marriage to Prince Albert of Saxe-Coburg-Gotha. No wonder Victoria's great-great-granddaughter, the present Queen Elizabeth, has mentioned her own Teutonic descent.

Victoria's independent attitude toward the House of Commons came out soon after her coronation. The Whig Prime Minister, Lord Melbourne, fell. The Leader of the Opposition, Sir Robert Peel, should have become Prime Minister. But he told the young Queen she would have to replace the Whig-appointed ladies of her household with his own appointees. She refused. Peel could not take office without the confidence of his sovereign. So Victoria adopted the entirely unconstitutional strategy of persuading Melbourne to stay on as her Prime Minister. During her reign she quarreled with several other leaders of the House of Commons, but fortunately she had Albert at her elbow to smooth over the difficulties.

Albert's hand can be felt throughout the first part of Victoria's reign. He was a man of great worth and ability, and after a while he gained an ascendancy over his wife. He acted as her private secretary, and in that way was able to steer her course through the perplexities of court life and government. Gradually officialdom and the public became aware of his sound merits and the value of the service he was giving to his adopted country.

Albert scored a memorable success with the great exhibition in London in 1851. It was the first world's fair, and Albert was responsible for it more than anyone. Many scoffed at the spectacular project when he broached it. There was a chorus of denunciation and ridicule, but he pressed the work to completion, and Queen Victoria herself opened the exhibition. The success was immense. London was thronged with visitors, who gazed in wonder at the glittering splendors of the Crystal Palace.

As the reign progressed, the British Empire rose to its greatest glory. There was the Crimean War, with its Charge of the Light Brigade and the heroic nursing of Florence Nightingale. To repay heroism in this war the Queen instituted the Victoria Cross, still Britain's highest decoration for valor in the field. There was the final conquest of India after the Sepoy Mutiny. Prime Minister Disraeli struck the imagination of the nation and the world when he had Queen Victoria crowned Empress of India. There was war in the Sudan, where Gordon lost and Kitchener won at Khartoum. Singapore was founded in Malaya. Disraeli bought for Britain a commanding share in the Suez Canal. At the end there was the Boer War, closing out the era of imperial expansion.

For the Queen herself there was just one real crisis during her long years on the throne. The death of Prince Albert, officially Prince Consort by her demand, marked a turning point in her life. She was forty-two, and the remaining forty years of her life may be considered one long period of mourning. She went into seclusion, and wore the black of a widow for the rest of her days. She devoted herself conscientiously to labors of government. That was what Albert would have wanted her to do. During the forty years, she appeared in state only nine times.

The decades rolled by, carrying great names with them—Melbourne, Peel, Palmerston, Russell, Disraeli, Gladstone. One of the world's mightiest literatures arose, Victorian literature—Dickens, Thackeray, Tennyson, Browning, Arnold. Over all presided the Widow at Windsor, to use Kipling's phrase. Never was so brilliant an era led by so dowdy a figure.

But Victoria's respectability became popular. The British people went Victorian, with all the virtues and evils the word implies. The terrible suffering of the working classes might have provoked rebellion anywhere else, but Victorians were not rebels, and the social problems of the time were worked out gradually through a succession of compromises.

In 1897, the Queen celebrated her Diamond Jubilee. She had been on the throne for sixty years, longer than any other British sovereign. The vast majority of her subjects had been born during her reign, and had never known any other monarch. Her Diamond Jubilee was an apotheosis of the British Empire, that globe-girdling domain on which the sun never set.

In 1900 her health began to fail. She suffered from rheumatism and eye trouble. The end came in 1901, within a few months of her eighty-second birthday. Her funeral lasted for two days, and all Britain mourned a great queen and matriarch. Five of her nine children survived her. Among her grandchildren were both King George V and Kaiser William II, cousins destined to be antagonists in World War I. It was fortunate for Queen Victoria that she did not live to see the day when the British people would apologize for the German blood of their reigning monarch, a heritage of which she herself was so proud.

FOCH

[1851–1929]

FERDINAND FOCH was born at Tarbes, France, into a devoutly religious family. His mother had been a childhood friend of Bernadette Soubirous, who in 1858 had a vision in the grotto at Lourdes, now a world-famous shrine. Her grandfather had fought with distinction in the Grand Army of Napoleon. Foch's father was a lawyer who had many clients among the ecclesiastical authorities.

It was generally assumed that young Ferdinand would enter the Church. However, his strongest suit was mathematics and it was decided to prepare him for the Ecole Polytechnique, the great institution, founded by Napoleon, which specializes in scientific and military subjects. With this in mind, the future Marshal of France entered a Jesuit school.

Foch's studies were interrupted by the Franco-Prussian War of 1870. Nineteen years old, he at once enlisted in an infantry regiment, but the war was over before he saw any actual fighting. He sat for his examination at Nancy which was still occupied by German troops, was admitted to the Polytechnique, and proved so brilliant a pupil that he was given a commission in an artillery regiment in 1873, having completed a three-year course in two years.

He served with his regiment at Fontainebleau, Tarbes, and Rennes, then spent a year at the war college, Ecole Supérieure de Guerre. He was next attached to the general staff and in 1894 was appointed professor at the great institution of military learning where he had recently been a pupil. His lectures created a sensation. Whether dealing with the principles of war or with the conduct of war, Foch was always breaking new ground and quickly became a pioneer of military doctrine.

On leaving the Ecole Supérieure de Guerre, Foch was appointed a staff colonel and given command of a regiment of artillery. Four years later he was transferred to a regiment of heavy artillery and then in 1905 made chief of staff of the 5th Army Corps. At the general maneuvers in 1905 and 1906, Foch so greatly distinguished himself that the French high command put pressure on the government to appoint him commander of the War College. At that time Clemenceau the anticleric was Premier of France and a leader in the fight to separate Church and State. He sent for Foch to tell him of the appointment. "I fear you don't know all my family connections," said Foch. "I have a brother who is a Jesuit." But Clemenceau told him his ability was too great to be passed over.

For four years Foch worked to create a picked corps of officers to lead the French armies should France go to war with Germany again. He succeeded so well that when the test came the staff work of the French was superior to that of the Germans, and to that of France's British, Italian, and American allies.

When war came, the Kaiser's army struck through Belgium. The French, on their part, drove into Alsace, but their offensive was stopped with heavy losses. Foch, who participated in the futile assault, withdrew his corps in good order, took up a strong position on the flank of Nancy, and threw his troops against enemy forces attacking to collaborate with the main German invasion. Joffre, the French commander, summoned Foch to headquarters and ordered him to stop a breach between French forces retreating before the enemy advance through Belgium. Foch quickly organized his troops and played a decisive part in the First Battle of the Marne. Then, before Paris, the French halted their retreat and turned to fight, and the full force of the German attack fell on the newly formed army counseled by Foch. His right wing was giving way when he quickly transferred his left wing to his center and launched a desperate attack which threw back the Germans. This was the occasion of his famous report that his right wing was shattered and that he was attacking.

Beaten at the Marne, the Germans started a race for the sea in the hope of seizing the Channel ports. Joffre gave Foch every available man and told him to check the enemy plan. In the German race to the sea, Belgian and British forces were hard pressed. Foch established close liaison with Belgian King Albert and British General

French, found needed reinforcements for both his allies, provided them with additional artillery, and finally won the Battle of Flanders.

The war bogged down into the brutal stalemate of trench warfare. Foch did a tour of inspection of French reserves, after which he was summoned to serve under Marshal Pétain, who had stopped the Germans at Verdun. Then, in the spring of 1918, the First World War came to its culminating crisis.

The Germans launched an all-out offensive, broke through the British Fifth Army, crossed the Somme, and were advancing upon Amiens, whence they expected to follow the Seine in a triumphal march upon Paris. The threat to the Western Front of the Allies was so grave that the necessity of a supreme command had become obvious to everybody. Hitherto there had been separate commands. Now the peril was so great that both the British and the Americans consented to put their forces under one supreme commander, who would be French. To Ferdinand Foch went the ultimate responsibility of his life—responsibility for driving the Allies to victory over the Kaiser's armies. He was raised to the rank of Marshal of France.

Almost immediately after Foch's appointment, the Germans broke through the French front and the Second Battle of the Marne followed. The Kaiser's legions were slowed and stopped. Foch immediately ordered a counterattack. He knew that the enemy had passed the peak of strength and that an implacable Allied advance would end the war.

The British in the north, the French in the center, and the Americans in the Meuse-Argonne went forward and never stopped their victorious onslaught until the enemy asked for an armistice. Foch was so sure of victory that he had begun drawing up the terms more than three weeks before. The Germans accepted, and on November 11, 1918, at 11 A.M. the First World War ended.

Foch was showered with world-wide acclaim. In company with Joffre, he led the victorious parade of the Allies through the Arc de Triomphe on July 14, 1919. He was made a British Field Marshal and a Grand Commander of the Order of the Bath. He visited New York and London, Brussels and Warsaw. Everywhere this small, elderly, wiry man was acclaimed. He looked more like a professor of mathematics than a dashing soldier. When he spoke it was in calm even tones, without gesture other than an occasional movement of his right forearm to emphasize a point.

Foch retired, living a quiet, religious, and almost ascetic life, attending Mass every morning in peace as he had done in war. When he died, his funeral was one of the most magnificent military spectacles ever seen. He lay in state beside the Unknown Soldier under the Arc de Triomphe, and was interred in the Invalides beside Napoleon.

SUN YAT-SEN

[1866–1925]

OUR time has been racked by revolutions, and it seems odd that in some ways the most impressive of the revolutionaries was the first—Sun Yat-sen, who rose to power in the breakup of the Chinese Empire long before Lenin and Hitler were heard of. He never resorted to persecution or terror, but his accomplishment was remarkable in its own way.

Sun Yat-sen did not look the part of the conspirator. Mild-mannered, preferring persuasion to force, he seemed a throwback to the mandarins of the past. He was, however, a westernized Chinese— a Christian by faith who studied in both Honolulu and Hong Kong, emerging with the degree of Doctor of Medicine. He became involved in politics only because of the terrible condition of his native land.

The ancient Dragon Throne of China was tottering. The Manchu dynasty, powerful for centuries, had fallen on evil days. Foreigners from the West had arrived with warships and soldiers, and were extorting privileges, territorial concessions, favorable trade agreements. China, helpless and divided, fell into anarchy. Local warlords ravaged the provinces. Civil war raged. Furiously the Chinese rose against the foreign exploiters in the Opium War and the Boxer Rebellion. The old sinister Dowager Empress of the Manchus ruled as of old while her empire was collapsing around her.

It was under these circumstances that Sun Yat-sen joined the Young China Society, a secret society bent on overthrowing the Manchu dynasty.

At first the members thought they might gain their ends peacefully. They signed a petition pointing out the need for reform if their country was to be saved from the foreign invaders, and suggesting in polite terms certain basic measures that might be undertaken at once

—for example, more popular representation in the government, and less corrupt administration. The petition reached the Dowager Empress, who ignored it. Even the moderate men of the Young China Society now realized that force would have to take the place of persuasion. They plotted an armed rising in Shanghai, smuggled in arms from England, and then discovered that agents of the Empress knew all about the plot. Some members of the society were arrested, others escaped, among them Sun Yat-sen.

He came to America with his head full of plans for another attempt. Realizing that undisciplined mobs could not meet the organized armies of the Peking government, he engaged an American soldier of fortune, Homer Lea, as a sort of chief-of-staff of the coming revolution. Lea, author and wanderer, prophet of the coming rise of Japan, later went to China and worked with the revolutionary regime of Sun Yat-sen. But before then another failure intervened. Sun Yat-sen returned to his homeland to lead a second insurrection, and for a second time the rising proved abortive. He barely escaped down the Canton River disguised as a boatman. He resumed his travels in the West.

London was the scene of an event in the life of Sun Yat-sen that sounds as if it came from the pages of *Fu Manchu*. He happened to be on his way to church one Sunday morning when a carriage drove up to the curb alongside him. A group of men jumped out, seized him, dragged him into the carriage, and sped off to the Chinese legation. There he was confined to one room, while plans were made to smuggle him out of Britain and back to China. But a British servant became aware of the prisoner, gave the alarm, and brought the London police into the picture. They threatened to keep a constant watch on the legation, and to free Sun Yat-sen the moment he was taken beyond privileged territory, whereupon the minions of the Dowager Empress gave in and released him.

Now more sure of himself, the great revolutionary began to formulate his guiding principles. These he set forth in a declaration involving three major parts: nationalism, democracy, socialism. Nationalism meant that China had to be freed from foreign domination and allowed to take her place among the nations of the world. Democracy meant that the Chinese people would be summoned to govern themselves once the old imperial power had been destroyed.

Socialism meant that feudal barons and semi-independent warlords would have to give up their privileged positions, and in particular their monopoly of land and wealth. The author of this declaration of principles always thought of socialism as necessarily bound up with democracy, but in the long run his adherence to the former ruined the latter.

Sun Yat-sen now founded the Kuomintang, the political party destined to eventual control of China. The Kuomintang was republican, and through its instrumentality Sun Yat-sen was able to turn anti-Manchu discontent in China into a demand for a republic. The Kuomintang made a rapid gain of adherents and influence in China, and its founder and head became the acknowledged leader of the revolutionary movement, which he directed from his exile.

The dam burst with the death of the Dowager Empress. Riots began, followed by sporadic attacks on the imperial army, and then insurrection erupted and spread far and wide throughout China. The Kuomintang took the lead, proclaimed a republic, and summoned its founder and head, Dr. Sun Yat-sen. He hurried back to China from London to direct the revolution. Homer Lea joined him, the military man fighting for the statesman.

The Manchus were removed easily enough. Forming a new political system was something else. Local warlords, generals of the old Empire, men of wealth, influence, and power—all these had to be conciliated. As a result Sun Yat-sen, architect of the republican revolution, never did become the unchallenged head of the Chinese Republic.

The years following the revolution were chaotic, with power split up territorially, and powerful men bidding against one another and against Sun Yat-sen. On several occasions he had to flee for his life. But he always came back, enjoyed moments of real power, and was supreme in Canton at the time of his death.

His real triumph was the formation of the political party that would eventually represent all China—the Kuomintang, which alone of the contending forces was capable of being more than a local, temporary, anarchic power. Wedded to Sun Yat-sen's principles of nationalism, democracy, and socialism, the Kuomintang did for a time establish the first two as working realities.

All the party needed was another leader, and he appeared in the person of Chiang Kai-shek. In 1926, Chiang began the drive of the Kuomintang forces which swept north from Canton and crushed the opposing warlords. Riding on a tide of victory, he made Sun Yat-sen's principle of nationalism a reality by assuming sovereignty over all China. Chiang did not forget his political and spiritual father. Monuments to Sun Yat-sen rose all over the Chinese nation.

Perhaps democracy would have followed if China had been left to work out her own destiny. But as the Western powers departed from Chinese soil, the Japanese moved in. Chiang Kai-shek had to turn from nation building to a struggle for the independence of his country. With little equipment and few supplies, he was compelled to fall back before the powerfully armed Japanese. Moving into the interior, he made his base at Nanking, and held out until the Second World War brought about the fall of the Japanese Empire and the Japanese evacuation of China.

Chiang Kai-shek went back to the task of implementing Sun Yat-sen's political philosophy. Ironically the failure of this attempt can be traced directly to that third principle, socialism. Before his death, the creator of the Kuomintang took the Chinese Communists into his party, for his socialism caused him to look with some favor on the Communism of Soviet Russia, a backward nation that had raised itself up as he was trying to raise backward China. Chiang Kai-shek inherited this policy, and worked with the Reds as long as he could. Then, finding that they were more concerned with their despotic ideology than in helping to build democracy, he was forced to turn on them and drive them out.

The Communists, however, had help from a powerful ally. Mao Tse-tung received Soviet supplies while he and his troops were hiding in the north. Their movement stayed alive. Then, with the end of World War II, Chiang Kai-shek had to try governing with their cooperation again, this at American insistence although he protested that a suicidal policy was being thrust upon him. The result was inevitable. The Communists rose under Mao Tse-tung, seized power, and drove Chiang into exile on Formosa.

For their showpiece, the Red regime selected Mme. Sun Yat-sen, widow of the patriot rebel who would have been horrified if he could have foreseen the Communist perversion of his principles of nationalism and socialism, and their betrayal of his principle of democracy.

MAHATMA GANDHI

[*1869–1948*]

Reformer? Saint? Unscrupulous politician? To the world at large Mohandas K. Gandhi was a reformer, a little man in a loincloth preaching civil disobedience. By his followers he was looked upon as a saint. To many of Britain's civil servants and military men he was something of a charlatan and unscrupulous politician, using his saintliness as a means of political bargaining. Whatever view history takes of him, to most of us in the twentieth century he was the living symbol of India.

The India he was born into was imperial India, the imposing British raj of which Kipling sang. Gandhi learned to admire the Westerners who ruled his land, especially their system of justice, and when he was nineteen he went to London to study law. He passed with high marks and was called to the bar by the Inner Temple. These years in London, living in cheap lodging houses, cooking his own vegetarian meals, avoiding rather than fighting the snubs of white and Brahmin alike, were also years of enlightenment. His strict Hinduism already abandoned, Gandhi studied not only law but Christianity and the literature of pacificism. From Christ, he said later, he learned nonviolence, from Tolstoi non-co-operation, from Thoreau civil disobedience.

When Gandhi returned home he began to practice law, and it was while handling one particular case that he turned to politics. The case took him to South Africa, where he found the many Hindu immigrants suffering from civil disabilities. They were treated largely as an inferior race. Gandhi at once took the lead in the fight for equality, developing the use of passive resistance as a political weapon, going to jail, ultimately forcing the authorities to remove some of the second-class citizen stigma from the Indians of South Africa.

Back in his native land, Gandhi apparently saw the complete picture for the first time. He was shocked by the squalor and misery, shocked by the degree to which the caste system was carried out, shocked by the degradation of the untouchables and by the misery of those who did menial work in towns and cities. As he saw it, his people, enslaved by antiquated traditions and superstitious beliefs, were being exploited by the British colonial system. However, his ideas developed gradually. During World War I, Gandhi supported the British in India and advocated the enlistment of all those who had no religious scruples against war. By 1918, however, when the reforms for which he was campaigning were still not an actuality, he began in earnest to organize the Satyagraha movement—literally, "insistence upon truth"—which he defined thus: "Satyagraha differs from passive resistance as the North Pole from the South. The latter has been conceived as a weapon for the weak and does not exclude the use of physical force or violence for the purpose of gaining one's end, whereas the former has been conceived as a weapon of the strongest and excludes the use of violence in any shape or form."

Satyagraha spread like wildfire across India. Gandhi established his famous non-co-operation, nonviolence campaign. He preached civil disobedience, revolt without anger, refusal to yield to laws imposed by an unjust authority. His campaign featured a boycott of government service, of the legislatures and all law courts; the surrender of all public offices; the withdrawal of children from all government schools. Along with this Gandhi pushed a program boycotting foreign goods, fighting the liquor and opium trade, and furthering Moslem-Hindu relations.

By now he was the leading figure in Indian politics and was revered by most of his followers as Mahatma, or Great-Souled One. To the British he was "the little brown man in a loincloth" who spun his spinning wheel, lived as an ascetic, and shook their Empire without firing a shot. They tried putting him in jail, which only made him a martyr and more of a hero than ever to the Indian masses.

Early in 1930, Gandhi announced that from then on he would refuse to pay government taxes imposed by the British. He singled out the salt tax as the object of a dramatic gesture. Leading a host of his followers, he walked deliberately through the countryside and down to the shore, and there set them to work extracting salt from sea water. This was Gandhi's famous salt march. For it he was thrown into jail again. But his nonviolent campaign could not be stopped. From his cell he was summoned to London to discuss the entire Indian situation. The conference accomplished nothing, but Gandhi heard himself cheered by large crowds in London and the provinces, and came to the conclusion that India should remain friends with Britain, if not with the British government.

Still fighting for his country's freedom, he launched another campaign of civil disobedience, and again found himself in prison. This time he made greater use of the hunger strike—the "fast unto death." As usual he placed the British in a dilemma. They could not afford to have him die on their hands and had to release him.

As World War II approached, Gandhi became more involved in party politics. Hating Nazism, he called on his followers to support Britain. At the same time he demanded that the British give independence to India, something London refused to agree to as long as the war was going on. Gandhi would not wait. With Pandit Nehru as his chief aide, he set out to break the Defense of India Act which prohibited speeches aimed at hindering the conduct of the war. Both men were jailed for urging the people to disregard the laws and courts, not to co-operate with the manufacture of munitions, not to enlist, and to withhold contributions of funds. Soon the prisons began to fill up with Gandhi's followers.

The rest of the war was a chaotic period for India. Gandhi, rejecting anything but immediate independence, was in and out of jail, fasting, politicking, preaching, defending Britain against Germany, denouncing British administration of the vast subcontinent. He was deadlocked with the Moslems, and even with some of his own followers, on the coming status of India.

The war won, the British Labour government announced that India would be set free with the Moslem state of Pakistan becoming independent in its own right. Gandhi disliked the idea of partition, but ultimately agreed to it as the best that could be had, saying, "Partition is bad. But whatever is past is past. We have only to look to the future." On August 15, 1947, India's independence became an actuality. Viscount Mountbatten, the new viceroy, saluted Gandhi as the "architect of India's freedom through nonviolence."

As for Gandhi himself, however, he hailed the moment of victory seated on a wooden cot in a Calcutta hut, scorning the celebration that marked the observance of independence throughout India. He announced that he would take up residence with the Hindu minority in the Pakistan sector.

The division of India was accompanied by riots and communal clashes which killed thousands and injured countless numbers. From his residence in Calcutta, Gandhi announced his first hunger strike in independent India, a strike, he said, which would end only when Calcutta "returned to sanity." The charm still worked. Assured that the rioting would cease, Gandhi, credited with restoring peace to the largest city in India, broke his fast. Moslems and Hindus by the thousands surrendered to him the guns, ammunition, and swords that had been used in the riots.

He went to New Delhi to renew his efforts there, for violence and communal strife had broken out more violently than ever along the Punjab border and in Delhi itself. Preaching peace, Gandhi urged all non-Moslems to accept their Moslem neighbors. A short time later, however, he told the Hindu Youth Organization that "if the Dominion of Pakistan persists in wrongdoing there is bound to be war between India and Pakistan." By this time Gandhi's birthday, October 2, had been declared a national holiday by the government of India. According to the Hindu custom of considering a child one year old at birth, Mohandas Gandhi was now seventy-nine. On January 12, 1948, striking for still greater unity among Hindu, Sikh, and Moslem, Gandhi started another fast. It lasted only five days—all it took for the Hindus and Moslems of Delhi to agree to live peaceably together.

On January 30, at 5:15 P.M., Gandhi, following his daily custom since his arrival at Birla House, home of G. D. Birla, millionaire industrialist, in Delhi, was making his way through the gardens to the pergola to deliver his prayer meeting message. He paused at the top of a short flight of brick steps. Someone addressed him. Removing his slender brown arms from about the shoulders of his two granddaughters—Manu, seventeen, and Ava, twenty—who were supporting him, Gandhi turned to give the Hindu salute—palms together and finger tips to the chin, as in a Christian attitude of prayer. The crowd, which had opened to form a path for his way to the pergola, drew aside and as it did so a youth stepped forward. Three feet from the beloved leader he paused. Suddenly three pistol shots rent the air. Gandhi seemed to lean forward, then crumpled to the ground. One bullet had struck him in the chest, two in the abdomen on the right side.

The crowd, too stunned to act, slowly came to life and began pushing the assassin, more in bewilderment than anger. There was no outcry, no excitement. Then a vice-consul attached to the American embassy who was attending the meeting for the first time, as most visitors did sooner or later, seized the man and shoved him toward several police guards. Immediately the crowd sprang into action. Feet and fists rained blows upon him as he was dragged, leaving a bloody trail, to the pergola where Gandhi was to have addressed the crowd.

Gandhi was carried by attendants back to the room where he had spent most of his waking and sleeping hours. Minutes later he died.

The next day his body was carried from his New Delhi residence to the burning ghats on the bank of the sacred Jumna River for the orthodox Hindu cremation service. There his ashes were scattered on the Jumna's waters, to mingle eventually with the Ganges at the temple city of Allahabad, where the two rivers meet. Mahatma Gandhi had already erected his most impressive monument—a free India freely choosing to become a member of the British Commonwealth of Nations.

WINSTON CHURCHILL

[*1874–*]

O N THE night of May 13, 1940, a new Prime Minister spoke to the British people. "I have nothing to offer but blood, toil, tears and sweat. You ask, what is our policy? I will say it is to wage war by sea, land and air, with all our might and with all the strength God can give us, to wage war against a monstrous tyranny never surpassed in the dark, lamentable catalogue of human crime. That is our policy!"

Thus Winston Churchill at the moment when France was collapsing under the blows of the Nazi armies, when the British soon would be driven from the Continent and forced to fight alone to save their island from invasion. In the darkest moment of World War II, Churchill flung defiance at Hitler, and vowed that Britain would fight on to victory.

Winston Churchill was born at Blenheim Palace, the son of Lord Randolph Churchill and Jennie Jerome, who came of a prominent American family. His paternal grandfather was the Duke of Marlborough, so he spent his childhood in the magnificent structure presented to his illustrious ancestor, the first Duke of Marlborough, as a reward for the victory at Blenheim. His education at home and at Harrow showed little distinction. He never went to a university, and only managed to get into Sandhurst, the British West Point, on his third try. He came out with a commission in the Queen's Own Hussars.

As a soldier he saw service in India along the northwest frontier, fighting invaders from beyond the Khyber Pass, and then in the Sudan, where he took part in Kitchener's famous victory at Omdurman. Leaving the army, Churchill became a journalist and was sent to cover the Boer War. Taken prisoner almost immediately after his arrival in South Africa, he eluded his guards, scaled a fence around the prison camp, and escaped on a freight train by hiding under some sacks of coal. He returned to Britain where he went into politics, writing *From London to Ladysmith via Pretoria* by way of diversion.

Churchill was never strictly speaking a party man. As a Conservative he opposed the Conservative plan for army reform. He joined the ranks of the free traders, then changed over to the Liberal party. He spoke with such authority on self-government for South Africa that a place was found for him in the Liberal government of Campbell-Bannerman. Churchill sponsored minimum wages in sweated industries, labor exchanges, old-age pensions. He had now become a first-class public speaker and gave valuable support to the Liberal cause.

Then came World War I. Churchill was in the Admiralty and had the Royal Navy ready to meet the Kaiser's U-boats. His most controversial decision of the war was to send an expedition to the Dardanelles. His opponents bitterly assailed him in the House of Commons after the British had been stopped by the Turks with terrific losses. Churchill strongly defended the campaign, claimed it would have succeeded had the attack been adequately supported in London, and then went off to take part in the trench warfare in France.

After the war he was in and out of politics as the parties alternated in forming governments. He happened to be Chancellor of the Exchequer during the general strike in 1926, which brought Britain to the brink of disaster. Churchill's persuasive eloquence did as much as anything else to end the strike. But the election of 1929 resulted in a victory for the Labour party, and for ten years Churchill was out of office. By no means idle, he wrote a splendid biography of his illustrious ancestor, *The Life of Marlborough.* He visited America, painting the Canadian Rockies, getting knocked down by a taxicab in New York, and lecturing throughout the United States. Back home, his pen continued busy, his private life uneventful.

He was watching international politics closely. Soon he began to warn about the rise of Hitler. Churchill's critics called him a scaremonger and denied him the right to address the British people by radio. The French, however, agreed with him.

Churchill seemed to be crying in the wilderness when he told the House of Commons that the Luftwaffe was growing stronger than the Royal Air Force. To make matters worse the British government, behind the back of France, connived at Hitler's rearming of Germany in violation of the Treaty of Versailles. Mussolini raided Abyssinia, defying the League of Nations. The Axis was growing more confident.

Then a constitutional crisis in England blanketed foreign affairs— the royal romance. Churchill, who had been a fatherly adviser to the Prince of Wales, did all he could to prevent the abdication of Edward VIII. Then the King bowed to the inevitable and announced his abdication over the air; he left with "the woman I love."

The Second World War was approaching. Neville Chamberlain came to power and signed the Munich Pact which he hoped would give "peace in our time." Hitler made sure of "war in our time" by invading Poland in September of 1939. Britain declared war, the cabinet was reorganized, and in obedience to public clamor Chamberlain made Churchill First Lord of the Admiralty. Days of dark defeat came. When Hitler invaded the Low Countries, Chamberlain resigned and Churchill became Prime Minister. No man in history has ever so completely embodied the stern resolve, the will to win, the lofty aspirations, the faith in victory that welded the British people into a single soul.

That Churchill's eloquence was a determining factor in victory no one can doubt. His words were like a lash: "We are at war, and we are going to make war, and persevere in making war, until the other side have had enough of it." Then his call to arms: "Let us to the task, to the battle, to the toil—each to our part, each to our station. Fill the armies, rule the air, pour out the munitions, strangle the U-boats, sweep the mines, plough the land, build the ships, guard the streets, succour the wounded, uplift the downcast and honor the brave."

After Dunkirk, when Britain stood in mortal peril, her great Prime Minister rallied his fellow-countrymen. "We shall not flag or fail. We shall go on to the end. We shall fight in France, we shall fight on the seas and oceans, we shall fight with growing confidence and growing strength in the air, we shall defend our Island whatever the cost may be. We shall fight on the beaches, we shall fight on the landing grounds, we shall fight in the fields and in the streets, we shall fight in the hills, we shall never surrender, and even if—which I do not for a moment believe—this Island or a large part of it were subjugated and starving, then our Empire beyond the seas, armed and guarded by the British fleet, would carry on the struggle, until, in God's good time, the New World with all its power and might, steps forth to the rescue and liberation of the Old."

For some time before he came to power, Winston Churchill had been in correspondence with President Roosevelt and in August 1941 they met at sea for a conference, the outcome of which was the Atlantic Charter. When, in December 1941, Japan attacked the United States at Pearl Harbor and war was declared by Germany, Italy, and their satellites, Churchill visited the United States, conferred at length with President Roosevelt and his advisers, and addressed a joint session of Congress, closing his speech with the words, "Still I avow by hope and faith, sure and inviolate, that in the days to come the British and American peoples will for their own safety and for the good of all walk together side by side in majesty, in justice and in peace."

He was accompanied by Mrs. Churchill on their visit and together they spent Christmas with President and Mrs. Roosevelt. Mrs. Churchill never left the Prime Minister's side, for the great strain was beginning to tell even on his robust health. She was with him at Casablanca when he conferred again with President Roosevelt and they decreed—unconditional surrender. She was with him when he visited Stalin in Moscow. She was with him at Teheran, at Yalta, and at Potsdam.

In September 1944 he met President Roosevelt for the last time. They conferred at Quebec, and agreed that the war was going well. Then, on April 12, 1945, President Roosevelt died suddenly at Warm Springs, Georgia. Churchill lost his good friend and his strongest ally in the struggle for peace.

The first British election after the war drove Churchill from power. The Socialists formed a government with Clement Attlee as Prime Minister. Churchill, bitterly disappointed, became Leader of the Opposition. Now he was warning the world about Communism. He came to America and in a great speech at Fulton, Missouri, coined the phrase "Iron Curtain"—behind which were held captive historic nations of eastern Europe.

The following election went to the Tories, and Churchill became Prime Minister again. But age was catching up with him, and in 1956 he retired, turning the office over to his right-hand man, Anthony Eden. Queen Elizabeth knighted the wartime hero, now become the Grand Old Man of Britain, Europe, and the free world—Sir Winston Churchill.